Ribbin', Jivin', and Playin' the Dozens

Ribbin', Jivin', and Playin' the Dozens

The Unrecognized Dilemma of Inner City Schools

Herbert L. Foster

Ballinger Publishing Company ● Cambridge, Mass.
A Subsidiary of J.B. Lippincott Company

Library of Congress Catalog Card Number: 74-7393

International Standard Book Number: 0-88410-150-9

Printed in the United States of America

Library of Congress Cataloging in Publication Data
Foster, Herbert L
    Ribbin', jivin', and playin' the dozens.
    1. Education, Urban—United States. 2. Negroes—Education. 3. School discipline. I. Title. II. Title: The unrecognized dilemma of inner-city schools.
LC5141.F67   371.9'672   74-7393

To my wife Anita
and my daughters Donna and Andrea
And to my parents

Contents

vii

Preface

Having completed this book, I am anxiously, in fact eagerly, anticipating the lay and professional reaction to it. I am looking forward to participating in the debate this book will stimulate and the changes in inner city schools that I hope will result.

It is also my hope that this book will inspire a new generation of ideas that will suggest pragmatic approaches to solving our inner city school problems, that will move us beyond well-meaning but ineffectual, if not damaging, rhetoric.

Acknowledgments

I am indebted to a number of people whose suggestions, advice and, in some cases, critical analysis of portions of the book, helped me. I am indebted to Professor Murray Levine and Sid MacArthur for continually being after me to complete the book. I am particularly indebted to three who labored over the manuscript, checking to make it readable: my brother Jerry, Robert L. Infantino, and my wife, Anita. And, of course, my daughters Donna and Andrea who supported my efforts to write by leaving me alone more than a father should be left alone. My thanks, too, to Jeanne Ferry who typed the manuscript.

Thanks also must go to my many friends from the New York City "600" schools who influenced me while I was there. Most particularly, though, to those who made suggestions or who helped me refresh my memory. Included are Jud Axelbank, Donald Brown, Coy L. Cox, Emory Hightower, Aurie F. McCabe, and Leonard Wells, and, without question, to the young men who passed through the "600" schools.

Other friends, colleagues, and former University students who contributed somewhere along the line to this book include Frank C. Aquila, Roy K. Bartoo, Harold Bass, Jerry and Claudia Collins, Mary A. Davis, Leo DiMarco, Stephen J. DeGarmo, Denise Esposito, Philip Fanone, Harriet Ferrer Goldberg, Dean Robert J. Grantham, James K. Holder, Domenic J. Mettica, Joseph E. Moreus, Geraldine S. Mycio, Naomi Ploshnick, David A. Pratt, Judson T. Price, Jr., Michael R. Romance, Joseph Shanahan, Amelia Sherrets, George Singfield, Jonathan Treible, Kathleen Voigt, and Maggie Wright. Also, the staff of the New York City Fire Library. And, finally, those Buffalo school personnel who have worked with our students giving unselfishly of their time and experience.

The writing of two men also helped me develop my ideas for this book. They are Thomas Kochman with whom I have corresponded, and Roger D. Abrahams whom I have never met.

Foreword

Our great cities usually offer all the advantages of our American culture. It is ironic that most of these cities are being abandoned by our middle class to the poor, the disadvantaged, and the alienated minority groups. This then leaves to the educators in the cities the challenging task of educating the children who are products of our society's ills.

Many books have been written about this. Some are good, but many offer no real insight into the problem. Therefore, it is especially gratifying to those of us who are attempting to meet the challenge of these children who need so much for one of our own who has loved, lived with, and taught them, to come forth with a book that deals with the *Reality* of the problem.

It is no panacea, and does not purport to be. It is, instead, a very real picture of "how it is," written by a man who is on the scene, and has devoted all his teaching career to recognizing and helping solve the problems of inner city school children.

Dr. Foster's book is unique in many ways. He has shown an understanding and insight into the *Reality*—that unrecognized dilemma—that no other author has really discussed or even recognized. He has accomplished this with sensitivity, understanding, and clarity. He also makes *Reality* suggestions to improve student-teacher relations and student learning. This, too, few other books about inner city schools have done.

His *Reality* examples of the "ribbin', jivin', and playin' the dozens" will provide most of our inner city teachers and administrators with wholly new insights about what they have been experiencing without understanding; similarly for his chapter on verbal communication problems (Chapter Four). I wonder how many inner city educators would pass Foster's Jive Lexicon Test?

Never being one to run from a problem, Dr. Foster's chapter on discipline (Chapter Six) is also unique in its dealing with the gut issues teachers in inner city schools face all the time. His discussion of the conflict between the teachers and inner city students' life style reflects an intimate knowledge of the situation. The discussion of classroom sexuality also opens new areas for consideration and discussion. His chapter on discipline will doubtless be read and reread by many.

Because Dr. Foster is idealistic while being pragmatic, his last chapter presents many ideas for teacher education that should be replicated across the country. Additionally, his book draws not only from education but from a variety of sources in linguistics, pop culture, literature, anthropology, sociology, and psychology.

It is with a great deal of pride that I write this foreword. We in special education in New York City as well as the entire state, have been proud of Dr. Foster. First, because he is one of us; second, because he is in the position to transmit to fledgling teachers our ideas and views on interaction between student and teacher. He is constantly in touch with us for sharing our views on all of his publications.

On a personal level, I have known Herb since 1953. He and I taught, studied, and worked in various programs for the disadvantaged and emotionally and socially maladjusted youngster. I can recall that he started the first Boy Scout troop for troubled youngsters in our state. He molded that troop into a fine group of youngsters. In the main, they became successful students; one is now a teacher of Special Education, four own thriving businesses in our city, and one is a radiology technician.

I have always pointed out Herb to my teachers when some say that "maybe white teachers can't relate to black and Puerto Rican children in the inner city" as one who could, and does.

As an Adjunct Assistant Professor of Long Island University, I have used many of his innovative ideas with young teachers. His ideas have been extremely helpful. Besides being an involved and excellent teacher, he is the most humane person it has been my privilege to know.

Coy L. Cox
Principal and
Vice President, New York Association of
Supervisors in Special Education

Ribbin', Jivin', and Playin' the Dozens

Chapter One

Introduction—Getting It Off My Chest

THE STREETCORNER

...If you were going to stay in control, you had to be in the street.

The street is where young bloods get their education. I learned how to talk in the street, not from reading about Dick and Jane going to the zoo and all that simple shit.

Sometimes I wonder why I ever bothered to go to school. Practically everything I know I learned on the corner.

—H. Rap Brown, *Die Nigger Die!*

...in the center of a major American city,...in the heart of a Negro slum area, on a corner where men can be seen lounging all hours of the day and many hours of the night.

—Elliot Liebow, *Tally's Corner*

On the streetcorner, "failures are rationalized into phantom success and weaknesses magically transformed into strengths." In many ways, the streetcorner man is a con man and a faker. Much of his behavior is "his way of trying to achieve many of the goals and values of the larger society, or failing to do this, and of concealing his failure from others and from himself as best he can."

...they were persons who were not going anywhere and they knew it. Seriously flawed or severely handicapped by lack of education and skills, and inadequate income, they moved about in...limbo—in a social milieu between that of the relatively stable and upwardly mobile lower-middle-class workingmen, and that of the derelict and bum.

—Hylan Lewis, Howard University,
Forword to *Tally's Corner*

The behavior of the streetcorner male is a natural pattern of masculinity with which ghetto dwellers grow up and which to some extent they grow into.

—Ulf Hannerz, "Another Look At
Lower Class Black Culture," in *Soul*

There are three underlying reasons why we have not been able to educate more urban black children. The first is institutionalized white racism:[a] The second is the fear people have of those exhibiting unfamiliar and different life styles. The third, related to and to some extent a consequence of the first two, is that urban educators are playing the game of teaching and learning in inner city schools by the wrong rules.

Many reasons have been suggested for our failure to educate more urban black children and many suggestions have been made for ameliorating this situation. To date, however, neither the reasons nor the suggestions have either reflected an accurate understanding of what is happening in inner city schools or really come to grips with the "gut" issues: *the issues involved when a few black, urban, lower class youngsters use streetcorner behavior to test their well-intentioned middle class teacher's worth.* Most often, the teacher fails this test and disruption and educational disaster result. Mind you, I am talking about only a few youngsters in each class who may use streetcorner games to test their teachers.[b]

[a]According to *The Random House Dictionary of the English Language* (Stein, 1966, p. 1184) racism is: "1. a belief that human races have distinctive characteristics that determine their respective cultures, usually involving the idea that one's race is superior and has the right to rule others. 2. a policy of enforcing such asserted right. 3. a system of government and society based upon it." Institutionalized racism as reflected in our schools is sometimes overt, sometimes subtle, and often perpetrated by whites who have been conditioned since childhood in ways of white racism so that they do not even realize that they are acting in a racist way.

This racism is reflected in textbooks that ignore the contributions of blacks, in white school personnel who consider black youngsters inferior to all white youngsters and, therefore, don't push them to learn. It is seen also in the pictures of whites only on the bulletin boards in a school with an all-black student body; or in a high school reading list without any books by black authors being used in a school with an all black student population; or where the white teachers and administrators coming from all-white backgrounds do not know how to relate to blacks as equals because the only blacks they knew cleaned their homes or their cars or served in similar "menial" positions.

Consequently, the whites are patronizingly racist when they try not to be—i.e., the principal who considers himself devoid of racism because his staff has pictures of blacks on the bulletin boards, has books by black authors on reading lists in the library, and has schoolwide participation in Negro History Week, but calls all his white teachers by their first names and all his black teachers by Mr., Ms., Miss, or Mrs., and their last names, and never reprimands black teachers as loudly as he reprimands white teachers.

[b]See Chapter Two for a breakdown of the categories of student behavior found in inner city classrooms.

REALITY 1

Picture this. This is your first teaching job. You are white and grew up in a middle class urban or suburban area. Neither you nor your parents ever had any blacks whom you could call friends. You have just completed your teacher preparation where you took the usual courses and did a fairly good job of student teaching. You consider yourself a liberal, having been involved in a number of civil rights and antiwar protests. You even successfully tutored some black youngsters on a one-to-one basis in a special program. You feel blacks have been wronged and you want to help them. You even feel your students should call you by your first name. You are aware of a lot of racist teachers who are not really teaching black youngsters; you intend to be different.

In the main, however, you have always been in a dependency role. Your parents, up to now, have always administered and provided for your needs. Tomorrow, just about overnight, you are expected to go from your student's dependency role to the supervisory role of a teacher. Of course, you don't expect any problems because you like black kids; you are not like "those other teachers."

You are ten minutes into your first class. Most of your students are seated when a big kid with a big, wild Afro and a shirt open to the waist walks into the room. You try to ignore him, figuring he will sit down. Finally, he walks toward you. You smile and want to know why he is late. When you are eyeball to eyeball with him he says, so everyone in the classroom can hear, "Get the fuck out of my way."

What do you do? You never discussed this in teacher preparation. Do you get out of his way? Do you panic and punch him? Do you make a joke of what he said? Do you start crying? Do you tell him to go to the office? Do you ask him why he said that to you because you want to like him, and you want him to like you, and you are not prejudiced against his people, and you want to help him? Do you tell him to get the fuck out of *your* way? Or, do you wonder whether there was something about the way you acted toward him that caused him to do what he did?

If you are lucky and show neither fright nor panic, your intuition may help you through the confrontation. You may make it as a teacher in an inner city school, and you may even come to like working there.

Similar incidents happen every day. They happen because white school personnel neither understand nor know what is *really happening from the black youngster's point of view.* Therefore, school personnel are frightened; and, as a result, some black youngsters are allowed to disrupt their fellow student's education. White school personnel allow black children to get away with behavior that white children are not allowed to get away with.

This happens regardless of the quantity or quality of the supplies, the age of the school building, the curriculum, or even who controls the school patronage in the community. Once a teacher faces his students, some youngster, sooner or later, will begin to test him. Whether the teacher remains or leaves, will depend, to a large extent, on how he or she handles this testing.

Furthermore, because only a few urban teachers, fewer administrators, even fewer education professors involved in teacher education, and hardly any of the editors who determine what is printed in our "better" educational journals and influential news weeklies have the ability to combine idealism and pragmatism, there rarely has been a realistic discussion of inner city school problems. And because there has not been an accurate discussion, we have not been able to solve the real problems. Therefore, the *reality* for most inner city teachers is described in this excerpt from a statement of the Ad Hoc Education Committee of the Joint Commission on Mental Health of Children (Tannenbaum, 1968).

> V. *Teachers in ghetto schools frequently find the classroom an unmanageable administrative unit for purpose of instruction.*
>
> There is no doubt that the problem of disruptive behavior in the classroom has discouraged large numbers of teachers from planning long professional careers in ghetto schools. It has been responsible in significant measure for the huge turnover rates in these schools and for the crippling morale problems among professionals who stay on for any length of time. The extent to which disruptiveness has spread in inner-city classrooms is not known, but some practitioners estimate that roughly 30 to 35 per cent of the school population displays serious behavior disorders. From a mental health point of view, the problem has serious implications despite the fact that its origin may not be intrapsychic. . . . The teacher is so preoccupied with his tense, disciplinary vigilance that children see him only in that role. He does not have the opportunity to present himself as a companion, critic, an instructor and counselor, and a stimulator of ideas and values.
>
> Efforts at calming the learning environment in ghetto schools have not met with notable success. Experimentors have gone into these classrooms with a sincere desire to establish rapport by demonstrating to the pupils an abiding interest in their innermost concerns. They have worked with the children in small groups and, on occasion, on a one-to-one basis, in order to win their confidence and provide supportiveness in the most permissive manner possible. . . . The object of (one such) experiment was "to surround children with a team of adults who were sensitive to their needs and concerned with designing learning experiences to meet those particular needs." Unfortunately, these objectives were never met. The project director blamed the bureaucratic rigidity of the school system rather than

student misconduct for the defeat of the experiment, while the school principal became disenchanted with the air of permissiveness which he felt led to chaos. . . . The professionals from the university were no better able to make headway in modifying behavior or stimulating learning than were the school officials. After repeated failure, the spirit of despair began to tarnish initial enthusiasm and the project staff resorted to futile improvisation to quell the disruptive behavior.

Administrative solutions have not fared much better. . . .

From all indications, it would seem that no solution to the problem of disruptive behavior in ghetto schools is currently discernible. . . . The classroom as we know it may not be manageable enough to sustain ghetto children in learning activity (pp. 35-39).

Unquestionably, the phenomenon of testing teachers contributes to these conditions. It takes place in the inner city, the suburbs, and in rural area schools. The rules governing the various testing and challenging games, however, differ in each setting from the inner city to the suburbs. The life style and expectations of the teachers and students are further apart in the inner city schools than they are in the suburban schools.

In the inner city, teachers and students do not respect the same rules. Many of the youngsters want their teachers to play the game of teaching and learning by the rules and regulations they know and understand, and that are important to them—not by the rules that are important to their teachers. They want their teachers to be humanly and emotionally tough enough to make them control their behavior, since they in fact gain strength to behave from the emotional strength of their teachers. They want teachers who will "make me work and not let me get away with anything" (told to me and my university students by innumerable so-called inner city school "discipline problems").

For the teacher's rules to count, he must have control of his class. By "control" I mean the teacher's ability to nonpunitively control the behavior in the classroom so that each student may relax and " . . . allow himself to be motivated to learn (Foster, 1964, p. 23)." Youngsters can do this only when they sense that their teacher is in charge and no one is allowed to bother them, to steal from them, or to shake them down; hence they feel safe, secure, and relaxed in their classroom.

Some inner city youngsters often test their teachers according to the rules governing their streetcorner behavior rather than by their teacher's middle class rules and expectations. This testing by streetcorner rules happens to teachers and administrators in inner city schools every day. And most of the teachers and administrators neither realize nor understand what is happening. Indeed, until you actually experience this testing—when all your middle class niceties do not count a damn and you wonder why this kid is doing this to you because you are not prejudiced as the others and you really want to help blacks—it will be hard, if not impossible, for you to understand emotionally what I am talking about. I am referring to the way the aforementioned junior high school youngster I knew tested every new teacher's worthiness (Reality 1). Remember, I am talking about a few youngsters in a class of 30.

Whereas earlier conflicts in the schools involved ethnic and religious groups (Covello, 1970; Gans, 1962; Levine & Levine, 1970; Patri, 1923), today's conflicts are exacerbated to a large extent by skin color. White educators, sometimes racist, and generally unfamiliar with and often fearful of black school children, allow these children to create a violent and fearful school atmosphere in which learning is impossible. In response, black groups accuse school personnel of practicing genocide and "menticide" (miseducation) for allowing black children to get away with conduct they would not condone in white children. White educators then suspend supposedly disruptive children. In response, blacks indict the schools for acts of wanton suspension and for treating black children as colonial subjects.

The charges and countercharges are often made by well meaning, sincerely interested individuals. At other times the combatants are only interested in patronage, the maintenance or attainment of position, control, and/or power, or because they are either black or white racists. The consequences, however, for most inner city school personnel and their students is a school beset with disorder and disruption; students, teachers, parents, and outsiders physically attacking other students and teachers; shakedowns, false fire drills, bomb threats, and stealing by a small group of students—all interfering with and preventing instruction (Bailey, 1970; Foster, 1969, 1969, 1971; Assaults, 1972).

With a little effort on the part of some teachers, administrators, and professors in teacher education programs, we can reverse this trend. We need neither new buildings nor the latest media or books to accomplish this. What we need are more teachers capable of recognizing and understanding the reality of the consequences of institutionalized white racism, how it affects their behavior and how it prevents them from understanding the streetcorner behavior that sets the informal rules under which the teaching and learning is taking place in inner city schools. This is what the problem is about in inner city schools. It is that simple. We must also understand that it is institutionalized white racism in the form of discrimination in housing, employment, and unions that have created the ghetto conditions that have given rise to the development of "streetcorner behavior."

Improvements *can* be made in inner city schools. I will discuss how to accomplish this by writing on the affective areas and ideas that to date none of the other books or articles on inner city schools have addressed. I can do this because my experiences have been different from the experiences of most of the others who have written or spoken about inner city schools, with an occasional exception, such as Dr. Esther Rothman's *The Angel Inside Went Sour*. Most of what has been published has been written by those who taught for a year or two in the elementary schools or by professors who have "visited" inner city schools but never taught in them.

Almost all my teaching and administrative experience has been with the urban lower class black youngsters whose streetcorner life style and supposed emotional problems contribute to most of the inner city school problems. Furthermore, my experience has been predominately on the secondary school level, most of it being in the "600" schools, which were organized in 1944. Since 1966 they have been designated as Schools for the Education of Socially Maladjusted and Emotionally Disturbed Children. There are now seventeen of these schools—one high school for girls; three high schools for boys; thirteen schools for boys, grades 5 through 8. Of these seventeen schools, seventeen are day schools; five are hospital schools; ten are institution schools and some are located in correctional centers, residential centers, narcotics centers, and day treatment centers. There are presently 968 teachers for 6,900 students.

In my seven years at the University of Buffalo, I have directed Teacher Education Centers located in inner city and urban schools to prepare undergraduates for inner city teaching positions. Indeed, although a university professor, I am still in inner city schools. For two years I also directed a New Teacher and Teacher Aide Project for beginning secondary teachers of the disadvantaged and teacher aides that set a national record by retaining all the 130 teachers in the program.[c]

My first public school teaching position was at Haaren High School in New York City's Hell's Kitchen. I had rushed through my undergraduate work in industrial arts at New York University's School of Education in three years to make up for time spent in the Army. After taking both regular and substitute examinations in industrial arts, I was offered a position for teaching mechanical drawing and blueprint reading at Haaren High School in Manhattan. It was there that in my first two days I underwent my "rite of passage" as a teacher.

REALITY 2

I went to Haaren and was interviewed by the department chairman. He showed me my room, which contained four or five large tables around which my forty-five students would sit. When I proposed taking the T-squares and drawing boards off the tables, he suggested that I just tell the students not to use them until I gave the word.

Next, we walked to his room where I noticed that each student had his own work table. He told me that I shouldn't give my students too much too fast because they were slow. As he bid me goodby, he suggested that I come in

[c]The New Teacher and Teacher Aide Project was funded by the Office of Urban Teacher Corps, the State Department of Education, Albany, New York, under contract number C-37075 and C-45609 (see Chapter Seven for a description of the program).

on the following day and mentioned that I was the sixth substitute for this class since the regular teacher resigned a few weeks ago. I started working on Friday, November 3, 1950, at $13.25 per diem.

I managed to get by the homeroom period and the next double period. After lunch, about 10 to 15 minutes into the first of three periods, I noticed a youngster run out of the back door of my classroom. When I closed the back door, another youngster ran out of the front door of my classroom also leaving it open. After briefly watching some of my students run in and out of the front and back doors, I realized that they were the same ones who were going in and out of the doors. They were not running out and leaving. (In New York City you are required to lock the door to your room if it is empty; you are not allowed to lock the door if a student is inside. As I became a more experienced teacher, I taught with my door open. If you went to see *Up the Down Staircase*, you will see what my room looked like, for although Bell Kaufman did not write her book about Haaren, the movie was shot there.)

Next, I discovered a new word—"Teach." One of the youngsters walked up to me and said, "Hey, Teach, we work a period, read comics a period, and then take off the last period—OK?" To which I responded with something like, "Look, I'm a vet and I'm the teacher now. I intend to stay, and we are going to work all three periods."

From then on everything seemed to happen at once. Someone crumpled up a piece of paper and threw it at me with a near miss. I thought of my Psychology I and II courses ("make a joke out of things"—or—"decontaminate through humor") so I said, "If that's the best you can do, you better hang up." Whereupon all hell broke loose. The class was going to show me they could do better!

Students ran across the table tops throwing T-squares and drawing boards. Others ran in and out of the room. The noise was deafening. T-squares and drawing board missiles flew through the air. The classroom was not only noisy but dangerous. And do you know what I did? You know that section that is cut out of the teacher's desk where the teacher puts his legs when he sits down? I hid there—in the kneehole.

Suddenly, five or six teachers stuck their heads into the room to see what was going on. I looked up sheepishly from my shelter without saying a word. Since the din continued even with their presence, they threw both doors open and my students took off.

I will never forget the weekend that followed. All my life I had known that I wanted to be a teacher. Here was my first chance. I had just spent three years in college getting an education that was supposed to prepare me to teach. I had failed on my first job. What could I do with my life? I was distraught; I actually considered suicide. You get a funny feeling in your stomach when you think you have known what you wanted to do all your life and the first time you try it you fail. It was a shattering experience.

Some of my university students laugh when I talk about this today. I have to remind them that in 1950 and 1951 you *had* to get a job. There were few if any graduate school fellowships and assistantships. And, if it were not for World War II and the G.I. Bill, it is questionable how many of my generation would have gone to college. At best, it would have taken us many years of night school.

Actually, my feelings were not too much unlike those experienced by Jerome Weidman in writing of his boyhood in *Fourth Street East.*

> The funny thing about growing up in the Great Depression was that while money was the most important factor in your life, because without money you didn't eat, it wasn't really money you worried about. What you worried about was what you were going to be, what you were to do with your life, and whether, by doing what you were doing now, you were on the right track (p. 217).

REALITY 3

I went back to Haaren on Monday, after a rather shaky weekend. The first youngster from my homeroom to see me said, "Hey, Teach, you back!"

I don't recommend that other new teachers do what I then did with each of my classes. I don't know why I did it. I don't think I was really too angry at my students. Perhaps, it was because I grew up on the streets of Brooklyn and to some extent I was fighting for my emotional life. If I couldn't make it there—where could I go—what could I do?

What I did was to put my name on the board. Then, when about half of the class was in the room and seated, I waited for someone to make fun of my name by mispronouncing it. As soon as one of the students made fun of my name, I walked to the front of the room, picked up about a two-foot-long stick I had found in the room, and walked up to him. I gripped his shirt front and picked him up out of his seat. In a calm and moderate voice that somehow did not give away my shaking knees, I said, "Read that name to me."

The class sat transfixed awaiting the outcome—*waiting to join the winner.* Ten to 15 seconds elapsed; he did not say a word. I dropped him back into his seat, turned my back on him, walked to the board, put down the stick, and started to teach. I repeated this *act* with each of my classes. In none of my classes did any youngster actually read my name to me.

Would you believe that this turned out to be the easiest teaching job, from a discipline point of view, I ever had? Later, as I reflected upon this incident, I realized that in not actually forcing anyone to read my name, I had given each of the students I had picked up a way out. Each had been provided with a way of saving face with his buddies if he had the need. If his friends challenged him, he could always say that he had never actually read my name.

Fortunately, we all could relax now. *They had tested me and I had shown how far I would allow myself to be pushed.* I had also shown that I could bounce back; I had shown that I was not afraid physically and that if "push came to shove," I would be able to hold my own with them physically. (Many of my friends and fellow professionals are bothered by my use of the word "physically" and its implications. I will go deeper into its role in Chapter Six.)

A few years later, as I read Arthur Schlesinger's description of the secret discussions held during the Cuban crisis, that second day of teaching came to mind. The psychology I intuitively had applied during my rites of passage into teaching was similar to the thinking that guided our approach to the U.S.S.R.: if you corner someone and you don't give him a way out, he may be forced to fight you against his will in order to save face with his friends. Schlesinger quotes Governor Harriman as suggesting: "We must give him (Krushchev) an out . . . if we do this shrewdly, we can downgrade the tough group . . . which persuaded him to do this. But if we deny him an out, then we will escalate this business into a nuclear war (Schlesinger, 1965, p. 821)." Schlesinger also writes of President Kennedy's praising Liddell Hart's *Deterrent of Defense* philosophy.

> Keep strong, if possible. In any case, keep cool. Have unlimited patience. Never corner an opponent, and always assist him to save face. Put yourself in his shoes—so as to see things through his eyes. Avoid self-righteousness like the devil—nothing is so self-binding. Liddell Hart was addressing these remarks to statesmen; they work as well for historians (p. 110).

I should add, for teachers too.

There is a difference between a teacher who meets his testing challenge as I did once or twice and then quickly achieves control and humanizes his classroom approach, and the teacher who regularly uses punitive measures, either corporal punishment or a more covert form of punishment which is often a manifestation of racism and inhumanism.

There is also the teacher who is not introspective enough to see what is happening to his classroom and allows his students to create so much disorder and disruption that no one learns. My students at Haaren understood my reaction because it was on a level with which we were all familiar and secure. It was something they and I had learned in the streets. If I had to do every day what I had done that second day, I would not and should not have continued as a teacher. Actually, the students would not have allowed me to remain, either.

Also, interestingly, what happened points up one of the gaps that separates many of today's "liberal-minded" new teachers from black children and their parents. This factor also separated the immigrants of the 1880s and 1900s from the educational reformers of those eras. What I am referring to is an unwillingness on the part of most educators and college professors to come to grips with the lower class urban ghetto child's life style—a way of life that courts violence and physical aggression. Indeed, urban lower class black parents are also part of this culture, share its values, and expect their children's teachers to be tough disciplinarians. More than one black parent has told me, "You are a man. Why did you let him do that?" or "Why did you let him get away with it?"

There is a dichotomy between the expectation of lower class parents and children in relation to firm discipline—physical discipline if necessary—and the new teacher's concept of his role. Some of my pacifist and liberal students and friends have become extremely angry with me when I have suggested the need for ghetto teachers to be tough but humane in establishing control over a class. They feel love and freedom will solve all problems. For some reason they either refuse or are unable to face the *reality* of the inner city classroom. For many of them, lower class life style as it is played out in the classroom, and the teacher's feelings about it, is an off-limits area for investigation or even discussion.

To deal with such issues as violence or even to recognize its existence in the inner city culture is often seen as prima facie evidence of racism. Hence the conflict between the lower class expectancy of physicalness and toughness in discipline and the middle class ideal of permissiveness and nonviolence remains unresolved.

Thus on the one hand we have students challenging their teachers physically, with their parents having a specific view of how the teacher should respond to this challenge.

> The black parent approaches the teacher with the great respect due a person of learning. The soaring expectations which are an important part of the parents' feelings find substance in the person of the teacher. Here is the person who can do for this precious child all the wonderful things a loving parent cannot. The child is admonished to obey the teacher as he would his parents and the teacher is urged to exercise parental prerogatives, including beating. To this the parent yields up his final unique responsibility, the protection of his child against another's aggression. The child is placed in the teacher's hands to do with as he sees fit, with the sole requirement that she teach him. . . . The parent tells of a child both beloved and beaten, of a child taught to look for pain from even those who cherish him most, of a child who has come to feel that beatings are right and proper for him, and of a child whose view of the world, however gently, it persuades him to act toward others, decrees for him that he is to be driven by the infliction of pain. . . .
>
> . . . [B]lack parents will feel that, just as they have suffered beatings as children, so it is right that their children be so treated. . . . (Grier & Cobbs, 1968, pp. 137-138).

On the other hand we have administrators telling teachers, "never touch a youngster under any circumstances," with the higher education academics adding their support to this hands-off position. Neither differentiates between corporal punishment and the physical restraint of a child who has lost control of his behavior and may be threatening a fellow student or teacher, and interfering with instruction. Or the teacher's wanting to become physical in desperate frustration or fear—how can teachers express physical and emotional strength without hitting their students? What role does the teacher take when he is challenged physically or aggressively? And somewhere in between the knowledge that ". . . disadvantaged youngsters equate the worker's willingness to use nonpunitive physical force with caring and warmth, and they (disadvantaged youngsters) perceive fear as prejudice (Foster, 1971, p. 61)." These are some of the tabus educators refuse to face.

Because of this we also find desperate teachers and administrators using corporal punishment, with innumerable studies establishing that increasing numbers of teachers and administrators use and want to use corporal punishment as a tool for altering what they perceive as negative behavior. Of course, the bigger and older the student the less school personnel want to administer corporal punishment.

Instead of facing this dilemma and attempting to resolve it, we have statements (Jablonsky, 1971) that leave us further in limbo with added feelings of guilt and frustration.

> In these last decades of the twentieth century, in this assumed enlightened country, infant and child abuse continues to deform large numbers of our young physically, intellectually, and emotionally. When a frequently disturbed or harrassed parent inflicts his hostility upon his child it is a sad and criminal act. When a supposed professional, a principal, teacher, guidance counselor, or other staff member beats a child, insults him, or diminishes him in any way he and the whole system bear responsibility for the act. . . .
>
> An interesting dichotomy of children's feelings is presented in the following quotation from the interview. It does not, however, represent their general resentment against those who beat them.[d]
>
> Dr. Jablonsky: What is a good teacher like?
>
> Boy: We have a good teacher. She says she is not doing it for her, but she wants to see us when we grow up, about ten years from now, that we can do things and . . . that we get a good education.
>
> Girl: Like if you don't do your work or something; and your mother sends you to school to work and not to play. If you don't do it, she come over and hit you. And then, if you still don't do your work, so then she start beating you. If you did your work, she'll never do nothing to you.

---

[d]Dr. Jablonsky does not make it clear whether this was her perception of the children's feelings or whether they told this to her.

Dr. Jablonsky: And you say she is a good teacher and she beats you?
Boy: She doesn't beat you. She just hits you to make you do your work.
Dr. Jablonsky: Has she ever hit you?
Boy: Yes.
Dr. Jablonsky: And you still think she is a good teacher because she cares and makes you learn?
Boy: Yes, because when she talk to you she tell you that when you grow up she don't want to see you like ten years from now scrubbing other people's floors, or doing something like that.
Dr. Jablonsky: Is this teacher a white teacher or a black teacher?
Boy: She is black.
Dr. Jablonsky. Do you think that that is another reason why you feel good about her—because she is black?
Boy: No, I like that teacher because she makes us learn (p. 19).

Unfortunately, we also have in-service programs that run away from touching base with a teacher's true feelings, emotions, and anxieties that in any way relate to the aggression and violence of lower class life styles or the teacher's feelings of aggression and violence.

REALITY 4

I was asked to lead a Saturday morning workshop for inner city secondary school teachers in a large city. I led the workshop informally. We sat in a circle talking and sharing experiences. There were about fifteen teachers and the district's supervisor responsible for my workshop. All were white.

I discussed student-teacher aggression and lower class life style. When the question of corporal punishment came up, I announced that I was against it. One of the new young male teachers talked about how he hit his students and said that he felt this was an acceptable way to achieve order in his classroom, if not the only way. His words and feelings began to loosen up some of the other participants. Many began to express their feelings quite strongly in agreement with him.

At this point the supervisor became noticeably anxious over the direction of our discussion. After looking at her watch a few times, she informed us that it was time for the coffee break. During the break she cornered me. In an anxious whisper she insisted that we change the direction of the discussion. When we reconvened, she took over and led the conversation in a different direction. The group went to sleep. I have never been asked back to run any other Saturday workshops in that district.

Such refusal to face the problems of life style openly and honestly results in a buildup of guilt and frustrations for inner city staff and hampers teaching and learning. Chapter Six will discuss further this quandary of discipline, corporal punishment, nonpunitive physical intervention, and the clash of life style expectations in relation to discipline. And, of course, the question that is basic to any discussion of discipline, *Is the teacher's role in teaching passive or is it participatory?* Many teachers feel that their role in discipline is nonexistent. Their students should enter their classroom ready to learn; they merely transfer knowledge to them or show them where it can be found.

I finished the term at Haaren and never had any other real problems. I even managed to assist other teachers who were having discipline problems. On one occasion I commented to some students that someone had stolen two of the hubcaps from my car—not near school but home in Brooklyn. The next day when I arrived in school four hubcaps were on my desk.

It was also at Haaren that I experienced my first argument with a teacher about "lowering yourself to their level." I remember at Haaren one of the aloof male teachers always spoke negatively of his students because, according to him, his students couldn't understand what he was trying to teach them.

It was the first of many disputes of this type that I have had with teachers, administrators, college and university professors, laymen, and students. I would suggest that perhaps anyone who thinks that way or even raises the question of "lowering oneself" should not be working with disadvantaged youngsters. Good teachers of disadvantaged youngsters discipline and motivate their students without worrying about "lowering themselves." *Motivation has to start where the youngster is, with something he or she can relate to, not where you wish they were; or else you will never be able to take them where you want them to go.* The good teacher ". . . must relate his teaching to the world of his students as it is, not as he would like it to be (Foster, 1964, p. 23)."

This question of whether one should "lower oneself" has arisen before in other contexts. One such arguments developed at the height of Russian Jewish immigration to the United States between Jewish immigrant radicals and Abraham Cahan, who organized and became the editor of the *Jewish Daily Forward*, a leading Yiddish newspaper in New York City.

According to Manners, Cahan, who could ". . . identify and empathize with the uneducated Jewish immigrants (p. 274)," loved Yiddish, which he saw as

> . . . "a veritable linguistic ugly duckling." Yiddish was not even acceptable in early Yiddish theater companies which fastidiously chose a broken-German, broken-Yiddish "refined" blend known as *deitchmerish*, a dialect spoken by the socially ambitious in an attempt to pass as German Jews. Heroes often spoke straight German, and only the low comic spoke Yiddish (p. 275).

Under Cahan's leadership the *Forward* was printed in Yiddish "clear as chicken soup." When Cahan and his reporters were reproached for their use of

Yiddish, a language with "no status at all," and for dealing with the real immigrant problems rather than more elevated topics, he often repeated an analogy which suggested his feelings about helping the newly arrived Jewish immigrants adapt to American life: "If you want to pick a child up from the ground, you first have to bend down to him. If you don't, how will you reach him. (Manners, 1972, p. 28; Sanders, 1969, p. 265)."

No matter how much we don't want to believe it, lower class youngsters start with a different frame of reference in relation to discipline than do middle class youngsters. And teachers must attempt to enter that frame of reference if we are to make contact with them.

If what I did on my second day of teaching annoys you, give me credit for being honest. I had to describe the incident for a number of reasons. The first reason is that since this is an honest book about the way I see teaching in inner city schools, I must tell about the experiences that brought me to what I now believe. There are already too many teachers full of guilt because their fellow teachers, supervisors, and college professors (who may not really know) denied that these testing incidents actually happened to them or to anyone. How many teachers, feeling dejected after a tension-filled confrontation with a disruptive student, walk into the teachers' room looking for solace and a little compassion and help, only to be told by a colleague, "I can't understand why that happened to you. He never gives *me* any trouble."

The "official" image presented by the nonprofessional educational critics is that America is an all-loving, classless society always engaged in a war against those who do evil. The offspring of the lower classes are represented as "dead-end kids" whose wrongdoing is somehow related to Robin Hood acts. All they need is love, understanding, and some affection, and somehow good intentions will prevail against all evil. Of course this is not true; it is *bullshit*.

There are distinctions in child-rearing practices, and a myriad of other areas that to a large extent are the result of *class differences* rather than the result of *color differences*. There also happen to be quite a number of seriously disturbed and aggressive acting-out youngsters as well as physically handicapped children inhabiting our schools. All it takes is one acting-out youngster in a class of 30 and the teacher is in trouble. Although acting out can be a symptom of emotional disturbance, *it may be a streetcorner behavior that is being used to test a teacher.* Because the average middle class teacher is not familiar with lower class streetcorner behavior, most often it frightens him. Too often, though, the teacher considers it a manifestation of emotional disturbance or mental retardation and mislabels the child. However, the youngster's behavior may also be a healthy adaptation to the effects of racism and poverty.

To survive discrimination and poverty, many minority group youths adopt a life pattern which in itself perpetuates the cycle of poverty. Motivation is stifled by a society which apparently prefers to support the poor with welfare payments which keep them at a level of bare subsistence rather than to allow minority groups an equal opportunity within the economic structure. The marginal activities of the ghetto, the reservation, the barrio, or the depressed rural sections are the only social settings in which many opportunities exist for enhancing self-esteem. Large families are at once a burden and a supportive group. Education may correlate with economic advancement, but the school institution tends to push out those children who cannot conform to the goals established by the school. Such life circumstances may be accepted in a pattern of ennui, hopelessness, and despair. A healthier adaptation may be rebellion (Joint Commission, 1970, p. 220).

Because idealistic new teachers are not told the truth about how lower class behavior is played out in the classroom to test them, they are ill prepared for the rigors of the testing games to which they are subjected. The result has been observable. Not enough of the new teachers who do remain are able to move beyond their fixation at the disciplinary level and true teaching never begins. Hence we continue to dehumanize and discourage more lower class urban black children.

Or, as the Joint Commission has reported, "Discipline becomes a major preoccupation of the teacher (p. 231)."

The role of the teacher in a child's life is of vital importance. Not only is a year of the child's education in her hands, but she may also have a crucial effect on his mental health. Many teachers are neither educationally nor emotionally prepared for this responsibility. The behaviors learned by children living in a slum may be repugnant and even terrifying to the teacher. Some teachers become intolerant of ethnic differences after a frustrating year of struggling to teach effectively in a ghetto or barrio school. Others bring to the classroom a stereotyped preconception of what the black, brown, or red child is capable of achieving (p. 232).

Another reason for my telling the story of my first and second days of teaching is that too many in educational leadership positions, and too many editors of the more influential magazines and newspapers, either have not been aware of or have refused to recognize reality. Whether they have acted from political, psychological, or other reasons is a matter for speculation. However, because they control so much of what is discussed and what gets printed—which, in turn, generates public opinion—we have not been able to deal with the real problems involved in inner city schools. The publicized rationales have been wrong for the most part. Consequently, we have not been able to solve our inner city schools' problems. Typical of this inability to recognize and come to grips with reality was Bosley Crowther's review of the movie "The Blackboard Jungle" when he wrote:

> Evan Hunter's *Blackboard Jungle*, which tells a vicious and terrifying tale of rampant hoodlumism and criminality among the students in a large city vocational training school, was sensational and controversial when it appeared as a novel last fall. It is sure to be equally sensational and controversial, now that it is made into a film.
>
> For this drama of juvenile delinquency in a high school, which, ... is no temperate or restrained report on a state of affairs that is disturbing to educators and social workers today, it is a full-throated, all-out testimonial to the lurid headlines that appear from time to time, reporting acts of terrorism and violence by uncontrolled urban youths. It gives a blood curdling, nightmarish picture of monstrous disorder in a public school. *And it leaves one wondering wildly whether such out-of-hand horrors can be . . .* [my emphasis] (p. 21).

At the time of the review, I was already teaching in the New York City "600" schools, and was experiencing incidents like those depicted in the movie. Soon afterwards Claire Booth Luce, our Ambassaor to Italy, prevented the movie from being shown in an Italian film festival.

As recently as 1967, Hechinger, then education editor of the *New York Times* continued in this tradition when he reviewed the movie version of *Up the Down Staircase.*

> School people are relieved to see that earlier motion picture image of 1955—*Blackboard Jungle*—superseded by something less sensational, more honest. At the time of this violence-packed "portrayal" of an alleged vocational high school, the *New York Times* film critic Bosley Crowther said: "And it leaves me wondering wildly whether such out-of-hand horrors can be (p. E 19)."

Although we can excuse Mr. Crowther for his comments because he wrote as a movie reviewer without any special knowledge of inner city schools, Mr. Hechinger is an education editor and should know better. Nor can I understand why Mr. Hechinger and so many others refuse to come to grips with the reality of inner city schools. After all, quite a literature has been developed on the lower class or slum life style. Why hasn't anyone discussed how this life style is played out in the classrooms of our inner city schools? For reasons unknown to me, no one seems to be able to take the next logical step that will lead them to the real issues. Of course if they did this, their excuses will have run out.

What is so regrettable about this state of affairs is that this approach generates endless books, articles, and theories that are nothing but smoke screens clouding the real issues and problems. Possibly some of the more militant black critics are right; maybe it is just another manifestation of institutionalized white racism. Indeed, if we continue to talk and write but refuse to deal with the real problems and issues, we can continue to keep blacks and other minorities in their present state without too much guilt. Or, perhaps it is the guilt that keeps us from dealing with the real issues.

Another example of this unwillingness to come to grips with the real problems of the schools and thereby help the schools can be seen in the reports of the National Commission on the Causes and Prevention of Violence. As far as children and their schools are concerned, the reports were simply another exercise for academicians to contribute, primarily, as a source for an additional listing on a vita or a source for citations for future papers, lectures, books, and speeches.

On June 10, 1968, President Johnson launched the greatest single effort of organized research in the area of violence that has ever been attempted when he issued Executive Order 11412 and established the National Commission on the Causes and Prevention of Violence ". . . to undertake a penetrating search into our national life, our past as well as our present, our traditions as well as our institutions, our culture, our customs, and our laws (National Commission, 1969, p. 1)."

To accomplish their charge the Commission divided its research into seven areas and created a Task Force to inquire into each area. Included were Task Forces on: (1) Historical and Comparative Perspectives, (2) Group Violence, (3) Individual Acts of Violence, (4) Assassination, (5) Firearms, (6) the Media, and (7) Law and Law Enforcement.

An eighth Task Force was organized to investigate the then violent events on which no other adequate factual records had been made. While the various Task Forces proceeded, the Commission met and studied reports and articles. They held public hearings and sponsored conferences in which the views of more public officials, scholars, experts, private citizens, and religious leaders were heard. More than 140 research projects and special analyses were undertaken for the Task Forces by outside experts and scholars.

On January 9, 1969, after six months and 29 days, the Commission submitted a progress report that *established a relationship between youth and violence* (National Commission, 1969).

> The key to much of the violence in our society seems to lie with the young (my emphasis). Our youth account for an ever-increasing percentage of crime, greater than their increasing percentage of our population (p. 6).
> Recent research suggests the possibility of identifying the youths most prone to violent or antisocial behavior, . . . These . . . youths accounted for the major cost to society from juvenile crimes. Clearly

these chronic offenders merit special attention and study, especially as a means for judging when and how society might best take preventive and therapeutic action.

The Task Force is assessing the factors that motivate and stimulate the young to act, . . . and the manner in which factors that motivate peaceful behavior might be encouraged (p. A-21).

The Commission also investigated and gave special consideration to corrections institutions, rehabilitation of convicted offenders, and adjudicated delinquents, and reported that

The theme of the inadequacy of penal institutions as agents for rehabilitation has been reiterated by many of the witnesses appearing before the Commission (p. A-22).

Some of the points made by the Commission included: First, the imperativeness of working with the youth of the nation to solve the problems of violence. ("The key to much of the violence in our society seems to lie with the young (p. 6). . . . juvenile arrest rates for crimes of violence are rising . . . rapidly (p. A-21).") Second, we do have reasonably valid tools for identifying potential delinquents: "Recent research suggests the possibility of identifying the youths most prone to violent or antisocial behavior, especially those prone to commit the more serious crimes (p. A-21)." Third, the longer we wait to help the troubled child, the harder it is to help him: "It will always be difficult to rehabilitate the young person who had already been in trouble and been labeled a delinquent (p. A-22)."

The Commission was also aware of the very high rates of recidivism and wrote:

The Commission has given a great deal of attention to the question of prevention of juvenile delinquency and violence before it happens. . . .

In an F.B.I. survey of a large number of arrests in 1966 and 1967, approximately 75 percent of those arrested for violent crimes were "repeaters" . . . (p. A-22).

After reading all the aforementioned and knowing that there were 183 titles that the Commission's consultants and experts worked on, how many of those 183 titles do you think were related directly to the largest social agency we have for working with youth—the schools? Would you say 30, 15, 5? *Would you believe ONE?*

The Task Force on Individual Acts of Violence contracted with the United States Office of Education for a "Review of Education Legislation, Survey of Requirements Necessary to Improve Educational Environment."

Isn't this hard to believe! The final staff report of the Task Force on Individual Acts of Violence (Mulvihill, D.J. & Tumin, M.M., 1969) also refused to deal with the problems of the schools—except, that is, to suggest the schools' shortcomings.

> The public school should be a major institution for the transmission of legitimate values and goals of society. Recent commissions and studies, however, have pointed out that the system is failing to reach all youth equally and is thus contributing to low achievement and school dropouts (p. xxxiv).

What is interesting is that the Task Force on Individual Acts of Violence, in addition to all the data linking youth and violence, came up with a number of findings that should have suggested a greater effort on their part in investigating the problems related to youth and the schools. The Task Force reported that

> As part of the age cycle, youth has a higher probability than any other period for engaging in protest, overt expression of grievance, or rebellion. Psychologically, and in terms of the sheer distance to biological termination, the young have a greater tendency to strike out vigorously for or against something (p. 603).

The Task Force reported also that our correctional system is a failure; that the "goal of rehabilitation must be given first priority (p. xlvi)." They also reported

> . . . that if the question of social intervention is posed in terms of the greatest amount of offense reduction registered between groups, it is clear that preventing poor nonwhite boys from committing crimes after their first offense would produce maximum delinquency reduction. By focusing resources and attention on lower-class, nonwhite offenders, not only would the general rate of delinquency be affected, but the incidence of serious violent acts would be most drastically decreased (p. 611).

Additionally, the Task Force went back further and even recognized where we should place a larger share of our effort.

> We do know that our public educational system, overburdened and inadequate as it may be for the tasks, remains the major single instrument for opening opportunities for success, influencing patterns of future behavior, and recognizing and answering specific individual problems and needs before they become dangerous. Teacher training, school-community relations, programs for dropouts and educationally handicapped adults, and many other areas of

education deserve more research and national support for the roles they can play in diminishing violence in America (p. xliii).

Why did the Task Force on Individual Acts of Violence do exactly the opposite of what they suggested should be done? Why did they not place a greater effort into the schools? After all, no one dictated to them what or where they should investigate. Actually, their charge was open:

> That scholarly research is predominant in the work here presented is evident in the product. But we should like to emphasize that the roles which we occupied were not limited to scholarly inquiry. The Directors of Research were afforded an opportunity to participate in all Commission meetings. We engaged in discussions at the highest levels of decision making, *and had great freedom in the selection of scholars, in the control of research budgets, and in the direction and design of research* [my emphasis]. If this is not unique, it is at least an uncommon degree of prominence accorded research by a national commission (p. xvi).

With this unique freedom to move, it is interesting to note that *no* public school educator was brought in on the initial planning by the commission. "In early July a group of 50 persons from the academic disciplines of sociology, psychology, psychiatry, political science, history, law and biology were called together on short notice to discuss for two days how best the commission and its staff might proceed to analyze violence (p. xv)."

When an official from the Task Force on Individual Acts of Violence called me about a paper I had written (Foster, 1968), I asked why the Task Force had not done more on the schools. His response was, "We just didn't think about it." What does *that* tell us?

Perhaps I am being too harsh in my criticism. Possibly those who determine what gets published and those who write most of what gets published are limited in their ability and feelings to deal in concrete terms with educational realities. The insights and understandings required to deal with line level, pragmatic solutions may be beyond the range of their liberal arts education, training, and experiences. Their psychological set, education, and training may not have provided them with the ability to function at the level of the reality faced by the teacher in the inner city classroom.

What I am talking about is analogous to the rear echelon World War II staff officers who were infuriated by Bill Mauldin's realistic front line "Willie and Joe" cartoon characters. The staff officer's experiences of their interpretation of their experiences kept them from the understanding required to comprehend "Willie and Joe," or that there actually could be real Willies and Joes.

What this book is all about is reality on the teachers' level—not the reality understood at the staff or academic level. Those in academia used to dealing with educational issues on a philosophical level, and those in school staff positions, may not identify with this book. They may not even be capable of understanding or relating to it at all. To them it may be something wholly foreign, a fantasy, a dangerous book, even a racist book.

But those teachers who get up early every morning and fight a feeling in their stomachs, as well as most of the teachers who can't wait to get into their inner city classrooms, and the majority of urban blacks, who are at home with their blackness, will recognize the book for what it is—a true statement about the reality of inner city schools. It is a statement about what I have seen, what I have experienced, and what I continue to see and experience.

Most of the book, therefore, will deal with the lower class urban black male's streetcorner life style, and how it is played out in the classrooms and schoolyards of our northern inner cities. The book will discuss how teachers and administrators can deal with this behavior in the affective areas to create the safe, secure, relaxed atmosphere necessary for teaching and learning. If inner city school personnel could come to understand, and learn to work positively with, children possessing this life style, most of our inner city school discipline problems would disappear, and teachers could turn to their role of educating black youngsters in our inner city schools. Indeed, educating black youngsters would become the primary role of teachers in inner city schools, and discipline a secondary or a taken-for-granted role.

NOTES TO CHAPTER ONE

Assaults on Teachers. *Today's Education* 61(2): 30-32, 69, 70-71, 1972.

Bailey, S.K. *Disruption in Urban Public Secondary Schools.* Washington, D.C.: National Association of Secondary School Principals, 1970.

Covello, L., and D'Agestion, G. *The Teacher in the Urban Community.* Totowa, N.J.: Littlefield, Adams, 1970.

Crowther, B. Delinquency shown in powerful film. *New York Times*, March 21, 1955, p. 21.

Foster, H.L. Teaching industrial arts to the emotionally disturbed student. *Industrial Arts & Vocational Education* 53(1): 22-23, 1964.

Foster, H.L. The inner-city School: A different drumbeat. *University Review* 2(2): 28-32, 1969.

Foster, H.L. The inner-city teacher and violence: Suggestions for action research. *Phi Delta Kappan* 50: 172-175, 1968.

Foster, H.L. To reduce violence: The interventionist teacher and aide. *Phi Delta Kappan* 53: 59-62, 1971.

Gans, H. *The Urban Villagers: Group and Clans in the Life of Italian-Americans.* New York: The Free Press of Glencoe, 1962.

Grier, W.H. and Cobbs, P.M. *Black Rage.* New York: Basic Books, 1968.

Hechinger, F. Schools, teachers, and images. *New York Times*, August 20, 1967, p. E 19.

Herbers, J. Discrimination held main cause of income inequality. *New York Times*, February 25, 1970, p. 18.

Jablonsky, A. Man's inhumanity to the young. *IRCD Bulletin* 7(1&2): 19, 1971.

The Joint Commission on Mental Health of Children. *Crisis in Mental Health: Challenge for the 1970's*. New York: Harper & Row, 1970.

Levine, M. and Levine A. *A Social History of Helping Services: Clinic, Court, School, and Community*. New York: Appleton-Century-Crofts, 1970.

Manners, A. *Poor Cousins*. New York: Coward, McCann & Geoghegan, 1972.

Mulvilhill, D.J., Tumin, M.M., and Curtis, L.A. *Crimes of Violence: A Staff Report Submitted to the National Commission on the Causes and Prevention of Violence*, Vols. 11, 12 & 13. Washington, D.C.: U.S. Government Printing Office, December 1969.

National Commission on the Causes and Prevention of Violence. *Progress Report of the National Commission on the Causes and Prevention of Violence to President Lyndon B. Johnson*. Washington, D.C.: Superintendent of Documents, U.S. Government Printing Office, 1969, 0-311-949.

Patri, A. *A Schoolmaster of the Great City*. New York: Macmillan, 1923.

Rothman, E. *The Angel Inside Went Sour*. New York: David McKay, 1970.

Sanders, R. *The Downtown Jews: Portraits of an Immigrant Generation*. New York: Harper & Row, 1969.

Schlesinger, Jr., A. *A Thousand Days: John F. Kennedy in the White House*. Boston: Houghton Mifflin, 1965.

Stein, V. (Ed.) *The Random House Dictionary of the English Language: The Unabridged Edition*. New York: Random House, 1966.

Tannenbaum, A.J. *Education and Mental Health*. Washington, D.C.: Joint Commission on Mental Health of Children, a statement by the Ad Hoc Education Committee. Unpublished manuscript, October 15, 1968.

Weidman, J. *Fourth Street East: A Novel of How It Was*. New York: Random House, 1970.

Chapter Two

The Unrecognized Dilemma of Inner City Schools

Over the mountain,
   across the street.
There's a bad mutha fucka,
   named Stackolee.
He wore baggie pants,
   wore hustler's shoes.
Talked more trash,
   than the Daily News.

                                 –taped in Brooklyn, New York

"The feelings of brotherhood on The Streetcorner never stopped astonishing me."

                                –Mezz Mezzrow, *Really the Blues.*

In addition to institutionalized white racism, most of our problems in inner city schools come about because only a few educators are playing the game of teaching and learning by the right rules. Few urban educators are either aware of or understand the *real* rules guiding the teaching and learning game being played in their classrooms and schools. They think they are setting the rules for the game but they are not. Their formal organizational rules do not count; what does count are the informal organizational rules that urban lower class black youngsters are superimposing on the school's formal organizational rules.

The informal organizational rules are neither middle class nor Marquis of Queensberry. They are the rules that evolve from the urban lower class black male's culture and life style as it is played out in the ghetto's streets and street corners and in its barber shops or wherever lower class black males meet.[a]

[a]Street and/or corner behavior will hereafter be referred to as streetcorner behavior.

25

This phenomenon is true not only for the schools. It was also visible when the late Dr. Martin Luther King brought his Southern, acceptable-to-whites, religious style civil rights movement to the Northern urban black ghettoes. We saw a confrontation between the rules of the ghetto and the rules that guided Dr. King's middle class behaviored and supported movement. We also saw an expression of male role expectancy as reflected in the ghetto black's feelings toward Dr. King as compared with his feelings toward Malcolm X. Henderson points this out.

There was also something in the personality and background of the man—the mere fact that he was a preacher and formally educated man [Dr. King]—which, while no obstacle to the loving, suffering black multitudes in the South, made it difficult for the Northern, urban, hip young blacks to identify with him. The abstractions of brotherhood and universal love were difficult to believe in after a day with the Man,[b] or a night with the blues.

Chicago signaled the dimensions of the urban alienation. In addition to a powerful political machine, theology stood in the way. *Nonviolence was not natural. Self-defense was* [my emphasis]. And then we remember the terrible anguish that King endured as he tried to come to grips with the power of black power, we realize that there was some limitation in his early life which precluded his solving the problem in time. *That limitation was insufficient knowledge of black ghetto life* [my emphasis]. Of course, he knew the poverty, and he deliberately subjected himself to it; and he knew immense suffering and anguish. Of course, he sympathized with and loved the poor people, the common people; he was like Langston Hughes in this, and he never tired of quoting the poet's "Mother to a Son," with the line, "Life for me ain' been no crystal stair." And it hadn't been, with his beautiful mind and raw courage and his pride. *But he didn't know the pimps and the whores and the dope pushers* [my emphasis] that black poets both love and hate and try to change—the "konk-haired hipsters wig-wearing whores."

Malcolm X Shabazz knew them. He had been a konk-haired hipster and he had been a pimp and he had been a hustler and a dope addict. But he went through changes. Rough changes! And paid more dues than any man on record. And he was baptized into blackness and repudiated his slave name (Little—how inappropriate!) and became Malcolm X—indicating the lost part of his life and history. He went through more changes—beautiful changes—and became, after his pilgrimage to Mecca, El-Hajj Malik El Shabazz. In some ways, his death was more tragic than King's, for the Movement had moved North and he had the potential of unifying elements in the black community that King could not reach (pp. 110-111).

[b]In jive talk, the Man is the white man. The term may refer to anyone from an employer, to policeman, to white society as a whole.

The rules governing streetcorner behavior that cause problems for urban educators obviously also caused problems for Dr. King. These rules are related closely to what Kiel (1970, p. 1) refers to as the "... expressive male role within urban lower class Negro culture—that of the contemporary blues-man (p. 1)."

To provide an understanding of the "expressive male role" as it applies and relates to black school children and their middle class teachers, we must look at three concerns that have their roots in the urban lower class black males' streetcorner life style.

THREE CONCERNS OF STREETCORNER BEHAVIOR

1. The rules, regulations, and conditions of the ritual coping and survival techniques that urban lower class black males have developed and refined to survive in the Northern white racist society.
2. The additional behavior involved in urban lower class black male streetcorner life style, e.g., language, mode of dress, running a game, aggression (sometimes only perceived as such by whites and sometimes real), physicalness, putting someone down before he puts you down, the put-on or front, playing either the "cat" or "gorilla," the importance of style, and a flare for drama.
3. The urban lower class black's concept and expectation of men's and women's behavior and role as related to a teacher's behavior and role, and the juxtaposition of these expectations with the middle class male and female teacher's concept and expectation of his or her teaching role.

FOUR CATEGORIES

To point up the degree to which these three areas affect the rules governing the teaching and learning in inner city schools, four categories of student behavior are suggested as operating in secondary school classrooms housing large numbers of urban lower class black children. It is through these four categories of student behavior that the rules, regulations, behaviors, and style embodied in the above three areas of concern set the informal organizational rules superimposed on the school's formal organizational rules. These four categories of student behavior, however, should not be considered as suggesting a similarity to the urban lower class black adult population.

1. Youngsters with middle class life style and behavior.
2. Youngsters who have adopted the life style and the behavior of the streetcorner, but have the potential for middle class life style and behavior.

3. Youngsters who are emotionally and/or physically handicapped. Because of the inner city environment, the disturbed inner city child often exhibits an aggressive acting-out syndrome.[c]
4. Youngsters who are religious or politicized. These youngsters may adopt streetcorner behavior to achieve their objectives.

There is some movement by youngsters among categories 1, 2, and 4. The behavior of any youngster on any particular day may depend upon his teacher or teachers, his home situation, what may have happened on the way to school, as well as how he feels on that day. And, of course, how the teacher feels that day. (Chapter Six, dealing with discipline, will go into this in more detail.)

Though the parameters of behavior are to some extent fluid, there are central tendencies of behavior within each category. Additionally, the unknowing middle class teacher or administrator may improperly classify youngsters who exhibit streetcorner behavior as emotionally disturbed or socially maladjusted. In fact, in the N.Y.C. "600" schools I found many youngsters classified as emotionally disturbed or socially maladjusted who were merely practicing streetcorner behavior.

To explain my hypothesis of differentiated inner city classroom behavior, a brief exposition of the four classifications of behavior follow which should provide the reader with insight into the consequences and importance of which rules are governing the teaching and learning in inner city schools, as well as making the reader aware that there are large differences in student behavior in inner city classrooms.

1. Youngsters with Middle-Class Life Style and Behavior

This behavior will be discussed briefly because middle class black and white youngsters behave pretty much the same. The youngsters who behave this way usually learn regardless of the teacher and his methods. However, these youngsters learn very little, if anything, when they are in schools with large numbers of urban lower class black youngsters. This is because these classrooms and schools are chaotic and disruptive; because our society has not opened up to provide them with the motivation for achieving in spite of the disruptive ones; and because racism has prevented their parents from moving into middle class neighborhoods.

Middle class behavior is compatible with the way the schools are

---

[c]These youngsters may fit into Ulf Hannerz's "swingers" classification. In his ethnographic study of a black neighborhood in Washington, D.C., Hannerz found four descernible life styles within the ghetto social system: mainstreamers, swingers, street families, and streetcorner men. As many of these youngsters achieve adulthood, they will undoubtedly fall within his streetcorner men category.

organized presently. It is also the behavior with which most of our teachers, guidance counselors, and administrators feel secure. This is the behavior that is reflected in the ability of the youngsters to sit still for reasonably long periods of time; to use and be secure with pen and pencil; to understand the importance of time and structure; to be oriented toward the importance of reading and writing; and to be conversant in "Standard English." This is the behavior that tends to inhibit and internalize aggression, physicalness, and sexuality.

The middle class youngster is still fearful of a "blue slip" or whatever other system is used for reporting misbehavior. These youngsters usually behave when you threaten to call their parents. This is also the group that must be educated to develop a black middle class. If pressure of law, court action, militant physical action, and growing numbers can continue to force economic opportunities and accompanying middle class or suburban housing for this group, our schools will be integrated through social and economic movement instead of busing. To add support to the possibility of this contention, a recent survey found more white ethnic Americans favoring integration than ever before, even though they continue to oppose busing (Fried, 1971).

Another important point is that this group has the behavior compatible with middle class white American behavior. Their moving to the suburbs or better neighborhoods, after initial fear and some selling by whites, will begin to show whites who have never known blacks on their own social, educational, or economic level personally, that the middle class life style of blacks and whites is similar except for skin color. I would suggest that one of the contributors to inner city school problems is the institutionalized white racism which has prevented most black and white middle class Americans of reasonably similar social, educational, and economic level or background from meeting and knowing one another. Black and white school personnel with three or more years of teaching in inner city schools estimate this group of youngsters as representing approximately 17 percent of the black inner city school population.

2. Youngsters Who Have Adopted the Life Style and the Behavior of the Streetcorner but Have the Potential for Middle Class Behavior

This is the behavior that most middle class black and white school personnel neither understand, nor relate to, nor even know exists. This is the behavior that many youngsters use to test their teachers. The streetcorner youngster to a large extent sets the informal organizational rules and regulations that override the formal organizational rules and regulations set by the teachers and administrators. It is behavior that many white school personnel consider to be symptomatic of emotional disturbance and/or social maladjustment, often resulting in the improper placement of these youngsters in programs for the emotionally disturbed or sometimes the retarded. It can also be argued that these school personnel act out of guilt, racism, or ignorance.

This is the behavior you read about in Brown's *Manchild in the Promised Land* and *The Life and Loves of Mr. Jiveass Nigger*; Bullins's *The Reluctant Rapist*; Cain's *Blueschild Baby*; Heard's *Howard Street*; Liebow's *Talley's Corner*; Meriwether's *Daddy Was a Number Runner*; Pharr's *The Book of Numbers*; Smith's *A Walk in the City*; Thomas's *Down These Mean Streets*; Williams's *The Man Who Cried I Am*; Wolfe's *Radical Chic & Mau-Mauing the Flak Catchers*; Wright's *Lawd Today*; and Yurick's *The Warriors*, to name a few. (See Notes to Chapter Two.)

This is also the behavior you read about or see in many of the plays of Ed Bullins, Immamu Amiri Baraka (Leroi Jones), and J.E. Franklin. Or in Melvin Van Peebles movie, *Sweet Sweetback's Baadasssss Song*, or his play, *Ain't Supposed to Die a Natural Death*. This is also sometimes the behavior that urban blacks use to "run a game on the man." It is the defensive behavior that, to some extent, some blacks have been forced to adopt to help them survive in a white racist society.

Although this behavior takes place on streetcorners in the black ghetto, in books, is acted in plays, is presented in night club acts, is found in songs and records,[d] and was seen by many in the movies *M*A*S*H* and *Putney Swope*, there is very little in the educational literature discussing this behavior.

Abrahams (1970a, 1970b), Dollard (1939), and Kochman (1969, 1970, 1973) must be credited with providing the best material to date by placing aspects of this behavior in some perspective and order. However, even they have not placed streetcorner behavior in an inner city school setting. A literature placing streetcorner behavior in a school setting does not exist, although Kotchman (1970) writes that, "it would be . . . difficult to imagine a high school student in a Chicago inner city school not being touched by what is generally regarded as 'street culture' in some way (p. 162)."

Such a literature should: (1) describe and report it as an organized behavior with guidelines, (2) place it in a school setting and perspective, (3) offer suggestions to the educator to assist him or her to cope with the behavior, and (4) suggest methods and techniques for using the behavior for positive educational effect.

Despite the paucity of reporting of streetcorner behavior, the streetcorner is where many lower class blacks are really educated. H. Rap Brown (1969) talks about the importance of the streetcorner as the locus for educating black youngsters.

[d]For example: "The Rudy Ray Moore Album: Eat Out More Often," COM S 1104; "The Second Rudy Ray Moore Album," KST-002; Oscar Brown, Jr.'s "Sin and Soul," CS 8377; "The Best of Lou Rawls," SKAO 2948; and Melvin Van Peebles's "Ain't Supposed to Die a Natural Death," SP 3510.

Sometimes I wonder why I even bothered to go to school. Practically everything I know I learned on the corner (p. 30). . . . If you were going to stay in control, you had to be in the street. . . .

The street is where young bloods get their education. I learned how to talk in the street, not from reading about Dick and Jane going to the zoo and all that simple shit. The teacher would test our vocabulary each week, but we knew the vocabulary we needed. They'd give us arithmetic to exercise our minds. Hell, we exercised our minds by playing the Dozens."[e] . . . And the teacher expected me to sit up in class and study poetry. . . . If anybody needed to study poetry, she needed to study mine. We played the Dozens for recreation, like white folks play Scrabble.

In many ways, though, the Dozens is a mean game because what you try to do is totally destroy somebody else with words. It's the whole competition thing again, fighting each other. . . . Those that feel humiliated humiliate others. The real aim of the Dozens was to get a dude so mad that he'd cry or get mad enough to fight. You'd say shit like, "Man, tell your mama to stop coming around my house all the time. I'm tired of fucking her and I think you should know that it ain't no accident you look like me." And it could go on for hours sometimes. Some of the best Dozens players were girls (pp. 25-27).

Playing the dozens, for example, is one of the prime streetcorner contributers to school discipline problems. I have observed youngsters playing the dozens in innumerable ways to test teachers. I have witnessed the dozens being played by students and ending in some horrible fights and classroom disruptions. At other times, playing the dozens had no negative effects whatsoever because the teacher knew the game and knew how to handle it.

Realities 5 and 6 are two examples of the dozens being played in school. In Reality 5, the dozens was played with an almost deadly result. In Reality 6, it had very little negative effect because the student teacher upon whom it was being played had been taught about the dozens as part of his undergraduate teacher education program.

REALITY 5

The dean of boys was in his office talking with a student. Suddenly, there was loud screaming and cursing coming from the other end of the building. The noise grew louder. One of the seniors was running through the hall cursing, screaming, and crying. Students and teachers gave him a wide berth. In one hand he held a whisky bottle, jagged edges showing where the top had been broken off; in his

[e]See Chapter Five for an explanation of the dozens.

other hand he held two four-foot sticks. "I'm gonna kill that mutha fucka who sounded on my moms," he screamed. He was 17 and stood about six one.

The dean ran from his office and grappled with the youngster. When he realized that the youngster didn't really want to fight him, he grabbed the youngster's hand that held the bottle with both his hands, twisting and hitting it against the top of a bench back, forcing the youngster to drop the bottle. The youngster was then isolated in the dean's office and held for about 20 minutes until he gained control of himself.

After the youngster had calmed, he explained his action as retaliation against another boy who had said something about his mother.

REALITY 6

The student teacher was working his way around the room helping children with their work. It was an eighth grade social studies class. As he neared the back of the room, one of the bigger students said, "Hey, I saw your mother on Jefferson Avenue last night."[f] A number of the nearby students stopped working and listened.

"I don't play that dozens game," the student teacher responded.

"You know how to play the dozens?" the student said slowly with his eyes wide open.

The students nearby who had been listening chuckled. One of them pointed a finger at the student involved and said, "Hey, he got you."

Everyone went back to work—including the youngster who had asked the question.

Streetcorner behavior is expressed in many ways in addition to playing the dozens. Some of the additional streetcorner behavior is demonstrated through such verbal games as "signifying," "shuckin' and jivin'," and "ribbing." The streetcorner is also where some young blacks learn to "run a game," to act in a physical way to achieve something, to "put someone down," or how to play on someone's fears or fantasies for personal, emotional, financial, or sexual gain, or for other kinds of exploitation of another.

Another aspect of streetcorner behavior that causes problems in school is the physicalness that can explode or be provoked into acting-out aggressive or sometimes violent acts. Claude Brown (1968) writes of the street pressures that put many young blacks into the position of always having to act tough and crazy and to be willing to fight *from the jump*.

> They'd ask me, "You kick anybody's ass today?" I knew that they admired me for this, and I knew that I had to keep on doing it. This was the reputation I was making, and I had to keep living up to it

[f]Two points: (1) Jefferson Avenue is the main street of the black community of Buffalo, New York; (2) the statement implied that the student teacher's mother was out whoring the night before.

every day that I came out of the house. Every day, there was a greater demand on me. I couldn't beat the same little boys every day. They got bigger and bigger. I had to get more vicious as the cats got bigger. When the bigger guy started messing with you, you couldn't hit them or give them a black eye or a bloody nose. You had to get a bottle or a stick or a knife. All the other cats out there on the streets expected this of me, and they gave me encouragement (p. 259).

Fighting was the thing that people concentrated on . . . we all had to make our reputations in the neighborhood. Then we'd spend the rest of our lives living up to them. A man was respected on the basis of his reputation. The people in the neighborhood whom everybody looked up to were the cats who'd killed somebody. The little boys in the neighborhood whom the adults respected were the little boys who didn't let anybody mess with them (p. 256).

H. Rap Brown (1969) also writes of growing up and always fighting to survive or to get ahead.

Once I'd established my reputation, cats respected it. . . . If I went out of my neighborhood, though, it was another story. I'd be on somebody else's turf and would have to make it or take it over there. So there was always a lot of fighting and competition among the young brothers (p. 15).

If you acted like a child, you didn't survive and that's all there was to it. Hell, you be walking home from school and up comes some high school dude who'd jack you up and take the little dime your mama had given you to buy some candy with. So what'd you do? Jump some dude who was younger and littler than you and take his dime. And pretty soon you started carrying a razor blade, a switchblade or just a pocketful of rocks so you could protect yourself as a man. You had to if you were going to survive (p. 18).

According to Heard (1968) there are few options of behavior available to someone who is black and poor and living in a black ghetto. "For in a black slum if one is not loud-mouthed and aggressive, then one is mean, a square or a punk (p. 26)."

Additionally, for the highly mobile ghetto youngster, moving back and forth from one neighborhood to another takes on the additional problem of always having to prove yourself physically in each new neighborhood. Piri Thomas (1967) relates the problems he encountered as he moved again—back to Spanish Harlem, to 104th Street.

You're torn up from your hard-won turf and brought into an "I don't know you" block where every kid is some kind of enemy.

Even when the block belongs to your own people, you are still an outsider who has to prove himself a down stud with heart (p. 47).

Thomas (1967) then describes how he planned to fight his way into acceptance on the block where he knew he had to take on the leader of the local gang. *"I've got to beat him bad and yet not bad enough to take his prestige all away."* They fought—they punched and bit. Then it was time to talk peace.

I had to back up my overtures of peace with strength. I hit him in the ribs, I rubbed my knuckles in his ear as we clinched. I tried again. "You deal good," I said.

Then it was over, almost as soon as it had started.

"You too," he muttered, pressuring out. And just like that, the fight was over. No words. We just separated, hands half up, half down. My heart pumped out. *You've established your rep. Move over, 104th Street. Lift your wings, I'm one of your baby chicks now* (p. 50).

Streetcorner behavior appears to be more highly developed in the Western and Northern urban areas. White racism in urban areas appears to perpetuate the streetcorner behavior and life style, causing it to become such a destructive school force. Whereas members of most of America's earlier ethnic and religious groups, after initial overt bigotry, were allowed to move out and up economically and educationally, this has not been the case with blacks. Hence, in frustration, many blacks have tended to direct their drives and energies into developing streetcorner behavior and life style.

Furthermore, those who become involved in the streetcorner behavior would become at least aggressive salesmen, businessmen, or politicians under the conditions experienced by the earlier white ethnic and religious minorities. But to understand the depth of racism we must realize that earlier ethnic and religious minorities eventually controlled the crime in their neighborhoods. Blacks, however, have not even been allowed to achieve this degree of autonomy.[g] Hence, because of a lack of successful middle class adult models to emulate, too often the black child's model for emulation becomes the hustler, the pimp, the murphy man, the preacher, the athlete (only recently), and the bluesman. Tom Wolfe writes:

In the ghettos the brothers grew up with their own outlook, their own status system. Near the top of the heap was the pimp style. In all the commission reports and studies and syllabuses you won't see anything about the pimp style. And yet there it was. In areas like Hunters Point boys didn't grow up looking up to the man who had a solid job working for some company or for the city, because there

[g]There is some indication that certain areas of dope traffic, etc., are gradually moving into the hands of blacks, though the higher levels of crime are still under white control.

weren't enough people who had such jobs. It seemed like nobody was going to make it *by working*, so the king was the man who made out best by *not working*, by *not* sitting all day under the Man's bitch box. And on the street the king was the pimp. . . . The pimp is the dude who wears the $150 Sly Stone-style vest and pants outfit from the haberdasheries on Poll and the $35 Lester Chambers-style four-inch-brim black beaver fedora and the thin nylon socks with the vertical stripes and drives the customized sun-roof Eldorado with the Jaguar radiator cap. The pimp was the aristocrat of the street hustle. [He] . . . might be into gambling, dealing drugs, dealing in stolen goods or almost anything else. They would truck around in the pimp style, too. Everything was the street hustle. When a boy was growing up, it might take the form of getting into gangs or into a crowd that used drugs. . . . The pimp style was a supercool style that was much admired or envied (Wolfe, 1970, pp. 130-131).

Keil, (1966) in writing about lower class Negro life, adds to the importance of the hustler's life in the ghetto.

On the basis of my own limited research into lower class life, I would go further, suggesting that the hustler (or underworld denizen) and the entertainer are ideal types representing two important value orientations for the lower class Negro and need not be distinguished from the lower class as a whole. Both the hustler and the entertainer are seen as men who are clever and talented enough to be financially well off without working.

Most ways of making good money without working are illegal, and Henry Williamson has explored many of these ways in *The Hustler*. The most striking thing about his autobiography is not the thoroughly criminal character of his life, from the white American point of view, but that within his culture he is very well adapted, successful (when out of jail), and even enjoys "doin' wrong."

. . . Aside from hustlers, entertainers, and rare individuals like Malcolm X (who began his career as hustler) or Reinhardt (the archetypal preacher-hustler in Ellison's *Invisible Man*), few Negroes wear their image in real comfort. Those black men who are comfortable in this sense become logical career models for those who aren't. If we are ever to understand what urban Negro culture is all about, we had best view entertainers and hustlers as culture heroes—integral parts of the whole—rather than as deviants or shadow figures (p. 20).

Even Malcolm X turned to hustling when his drives were thwarted. However, his later short-lived leadership of ghetto blacks reflected his brilliance that was earlier devoted to hustling. In his autobiography (Haley, 1966) he wrote of the night he turned to hustling.

On that night I had started on my way to becoming a Harlemite. I was going to become one of the most depraved parasitical hustlers among New York's eight million people—four million of whom work, and the other four million of whom live off them (p. 75).

Horton (1970) interviewed 25 black males who had sporadic unsatisfactory work and unemployment. Many turned to hustling whenever necessary or possible.

When I asked the question, "When a dude needs bread, how does he get it?" the universal response was "the hustle." Hustling is, of course, illegitimate from society's viewpoint. Street people know it is illegal, but they view it in no way as immoral or wrong. It is justified by the necessity of surviving. As might be expected, the unemployed admitted that they hustled and went so far as to say that a dude could make it better on the street than on the job. "There is a lot of money on the street, and there are many ways of getting it" or simply, "This has always been my way of life." On the other hand, the employed, part-time hustlers, usually said, "A dude could make it better on the job than on the street." Their reasons for disapproving of hustling were not moral. Hustling meant trouble. "I don't hustle because there's no security. You eventually get busted." Others said there was not enough money on the street or that it was too difficult to "run a game" on people.

Nevertheless, hustling is the central street activity: It is the economic foundation for everyday life. Hustling and the fruit of hustling set the rhythm of social activities.

The best hustles were conning, stealing, gambling, and selling dope. . . . To "con" means to put "the pump" on a "cat," to "run a game" on somebody, to work on his mind for goods and services.

Hustling means bread and security but also trouble, and trouble is a major theme in street life. The dudes had a "world of trouble"— with school, jobs, women, and the police.

Keeping cool and out of trouble, hustling bread, and looking for something interesting and exciting to do created the structure of time on the street. The rhythm of time is expressed in the high and low points in the day and week of an unemployed dude. I stress the pattern of the unemployed and full time hustler because he is on the street all day and night and is the prototype in my interviews (pp. 37-39).

According to Dennis (1972), "Hustling, as a profession, has been adopted by many black men as a way of life, a means of survival, requiring a degree from the streets (p. 16)." Although hustlers have varied educational backgrounds, "they believe the only relevant education is that which is learned in the streets (p. 57)." Hustling offers the black man who has his desires blocked the avenue for acquiring all the material accoutrements and symbols of white American success. Indeed, this can be accomplished by the full time qualified hustler without having to " 'work,' that is work defined in terms of holding a regular legitimate job (p. 18)."

Dennis also reports that the "qualified" hustler usually participates in two or more of the five major categories of hustling, i.e., loan sharking, playing the con game, pimping, drug sales, and the selling of stolen goods. Dennis also suggests that,

> Hustling offers an oppressed man a chance to advance financially. It gives him an opportunity to feel and be important among his peers. The hustler must demonstrate his success through his material gains in order to remain on top in his profession (p. 19).

Certainly some black youngsters who are exposed to the hustler will envision him as a role model to emulate. Therefore we can expect some of these youngsters to practice their hustling ability by running their hustling game on their teachers and fellow students. Indeed, the youngster who successfully hustles his teachers will gain the respect of his peers.

If you look at the streetcorner closely, there really is not too much difference between the desires of the streetcorner man and the desires of the middle class man—to some extent, they both want the same things. The difference comes about in what each perceives as a logical road to travel to reach the objectives his subculture has set as a concept for "making it."

Many streetcorner students share in the desires and actions of streetcorner men. Heard (1968) spells out where students of the streetcorner are at.

> "Do you know that if you gave any one of the people you see a hundred dollars, he wouldn't buy food if he was hungry? The whores'd give it to their pimps and the men'd go buy a suit and a pair of long shoes.
>
> "... Y'see, long shoes are success. They're the keen-toed design, right for kickin' a whore in the behind with when she comes up with short money or gits outta line. Some of the guys that got whores do kick 'em in the ass. The ordinary cat, though, is just satisfied to show off the shoes and quote the high price of 'em. It'd take too long to really run it down to you, man. Just say that long shoes means that the cat wearin' them is into somethin', er, if he ain't an outright pimp, he's doin' good, dig?
>
> "... Like I was saying about the hundred bills: the suit and shoes would run about eighty bill, right? So he'd have twenty left, which his rent would take if he'd pay it all. But he wouldn't do that: he'd give the landlord maybe ten, then he'd bring the other ten to Howard Street and party with it. As for eatin'—he can always beg a

sandwich somewhere. Anything that ain't showy don't impress him, see? He's got three main ambitions . . . one is to drink and look sharp; two is to fuck as much as he can; and three is to have as much dope as he wants without workin' for the money to buy it with. In a word, his ambition is to ball. . . . (p. 177)"

The style and abilities required for success on the streetcorner and in hustling suggest that the participants are gifted. Accordingly, it is hypothesized that had not racism forced black males to develop and exploit this illegal outlet for the preservation of masculinity and ego, and the wherewithall for monetary reward, many of the players would have shown extreme giftedness in their pursuit of middle class, socially acceptable means for gaining economic success.

We could say that the high pressure television or automobile salesman is really a hustler. The difference is that his method of hustling or his hustle is socially acceptable. The parallel development of black and white societies in the South supports this contention. Indeed, where black males have been allowed to earn economic rewards through middle class endeavors and rewards, a highly organized streetcorner society appears not to have developed; whereas in the North's and West's urban areas, a highly organized streetcorner society has developed.

It is also hypothesized that those blacks who left the South may have had more drive and ambition than those blacks who remained. Consequently, when the black man's drive for middle class economic success within the overall Northern communities was thwarted by racism, the streetcorner life style evolved and developed as an outlet for these drives. Some support for this overall argument can be found in nine inmates earning high school diplomas (9, 1972) and a black prisoner, Victor Taylor, earning an undergraduate degree *magna cum laude* at a United States Penitentiary at Merion, Illinois. He earned a normal four-year undergraduate degree in 21 months with cumulative grade point average of 4.89. Dr. Walter G. Robinson, Jr. claims that "there are Vic Taylors at every institution," . . . and "there is an abundance of brain power sitting out there behind those walls (Vecsey, 1972, p. 1). Victor Taylor may be a typical example of the intelligent black man who becomes thwarted by racism or imagined racism and turned to extreme streetcorner behavior—crime.

In his talk, Taylor recalled family fights, frequent separations and constant poverty. He also recalled the torment of integrating a posh Jesuit high school in Dallas, spending three years envying his classmates' convertibles while he rode public buses—and then quitting school.

He recalled how he wanted to be a Navy pilot but was disqualified because of his slight color-blindness. Feeling that the Navy had deceived him, he and a buddy held up a Navy bank and were caught in Mexico. After four years in jail, he was paroled back to Dallas, where his peers "already had college degrees, wives and families, embarked on successful careers."

Within 90 days he went on a robbing spree ("I guess I was trying to get myself killed"). The resultant jail term was so long that he tried to escape twice (Vecsey, 1972, p. 60).

Mezz Mezzrow (1964, pp. 193-194), a white clarinetist jazzman and one of the few whites accepted by black jazzmen, describes his feelings about the giftedness of streetcorner hipsters. His reporting brought to life the street language and feelings of the 1930s and '40s as an outlet for blocked dreams and desires.

Once and for all, these smart Northern kids meant to show that they're not the ounce-brained tongue-tied stuttering Sambos of the blackface vaudeville routines, the Lazybones' of the comic strips, the Old Mose's of the Southern plantations. Historically, the hipster's lingo reverses the whole Uncle Tom attitude of the beaten-down Southern Negro. Uncle Tom believes he's good-for-nothing, shiftless, sub-human, just like the white bossman says he is. Uncle Tom scrapes and bows before his ofay 'superiors,' kills off all his self-respect and manliness, agrees that he's downtrodden because he doesn't deserve any better. Well, the kids who grew up in Northern cities wouldn't have any more of that kneebending and kowtowing. They sure meant to stand up on their hind legs and let the world know they're as good as anybody else and won't take anybody's sass. They were smart, popping with talent, ready for any challenge. Some of them had creative abilities you could hardly match anywhere else. Once they tore off the soul-destroying straitjacket of Uncle Tomism, those talents and creative energies just busted out all over. These kids weren't schooled to use their gifts in any regular way. So their artistry and spirit romped out into their language. They began out-lingoing the ofay linguists, talking up a specialized breeze that would blow right over the white man's head. It gave them more confidence in themselves.

"Deny the Negro the culture of the land? O.K. He'll brew his own culture—on the street corner. Lock him out from the seats of higher learning? He pays it no nevermind—he'll dream up his own professional doubletalk, from the professions that *are* open to him, the professions of musician, entertainer, maid, butler, tap-dancer, handyman, reefer-pusher, gambler, counterman, porter, chauffeur, numbers racketeer, day laborer, pimp, stevedore. These boys I ran with at The Corner, breathing half-comic prayers at the Tree of Hope, they were the new sophisticates of the race, the jivers, the sweet-talkers, the jawblockers. They spouted at each other like soldiers sharpening their bayonets—what they were sharpening, in all this verbal horseplay, was their wits, the only weapons they had. Their sophistication didn't come out of moldy books and dirty colleges. It came from opening their eyes wide and gunning the world hard. Soon as you stop bowing your head low and resting your timid, humble eyes on the ground; soon as you straighten your spine and look the world right in the eye, you dig plenty. . . . Their hipness, I could see, bubbled up out of the brute scramble and sweet living. If it came out a little too raw and strong for your stomach, that's because you been used to a more refined diet. You didn't come of age on the welfare, snagging butts out of the gutter. You can afford the luxury of being a little delicate, friend.

You know who they were, all these fat-talking kids with their four-dimensional surrealist patter? I found out they were the cream of the race—the professionals of Harlem who never got within reaching distance of a white collar. They were the razor-witted doctors without M.D.'s, lawyers who never had a shingle to hang out, financiers without penny one in their pokes, political leaders without a party, diplomatless professors, and scientists minus a laboratory. They held their office-hours and made their speeches on The Corner. There they wrote prose poems, painted their word pictures. They were the genius of their people, always on their toes, never missing a trick, asking no favors and taking no guff, not looking for trouble but solid ready for it. Spawned in a social vacuum and hung up in mid-air, they were beginning to build their own culture. Their language was a declaration of independence (pp. 193-194).

In reading this section on streetcorner behavior in the schools, the reader must understand that we are talking about a percentage of students. Exactly how many we do not know, although estimates by inner city black and white school personnel with three or more years of experience in inner city schools put the number at 60 percent.

However, we must be realistic and understand that if a teacher has only two or three youngsters in a class who exhibit this behavior and adhere to its standards, the teacher may be in trouble if he or she cannot cope with the testing techniques. When this happens and the teacher starts to panic, other students join in playing the disruptive game, and no one in the class learns. The teacher becomes involved in discipline only. Sadly, it is almost a self-destructive action on the part of black youngsters. What we are doing is allowing black school children to use their creativeness to destroy themselves and one another. It is the same destructiveness that H. Rap Brown (1969) wrote about.

It's one of the things that keeps us fighting ourselves instead of the enemy. Black people have always been ready to shoot and cut each other up. The weekend is always wartime in the Black community. Every week when Friday rolls around, you know that somebody is goin' to get killed before church time Sunday morning (p. 17).

3. Youngsters Who Are Emotionally and/or Physically Handicapped

At least two factors and one question must be considered in a discussion of the youngsters who are emotionally or physically handicapped. The two factors are: (1) the numbers of emotionally or socially handicapped youngsters in inner city schools, and (2) the numbers of physically handicapped youngsters in inner city schools. The one question is whether middle class personnel unfamiliar with streetcorner behavior can diagnose accurately, or differentiate, streetcorner behavior from either emotionally disturbed, socially maladjusted, or mentally retarded behavior—particularly the borderline child's behavior.

Numbers of Emotionally or Socially Handicapped Youngsters. The first area to be considered are the numbers of emotionally and socially handicapped youngsters in inner city schools. The latest reporting of data concerning emotionally handicapped children comes from reports of the Joint Commission on Mental Health of Children, Inc. (1969, 1970). Glidewell and Swallow (1968), gathered data for the Commission concerning maladjustment of children enrolled primarily in public elementary schools that emphasized the results from research performed in the United States since 1922. They found that

> Within the limits of the validity of the data available, the best approximation of the prevalence of maladjustment in elementary schools is that 30% of the children show at least mild, sub-clinical problems in adjustment. Of that 30%, there are about 10% who need professional attention. Of that 10%, there are about 4% who would actually be referred to clinical facilities if they were available. The age differences in the prevalence of maladjustment are not great. There is some increase in anti-social behavior as adolescence is approached, and some decrease in developmental problems. The rate for boys is about three times as high as that for girls. Social class differences are difficult to isolate, but the lower classes show somewhat higher rates. The social class differences were more marked for boys. Race differences have not been carefully investigated.

Additionally, Glidewell and Swallow (1968) reported finding 5 to 25 percent of the school children having subclinical symptoms of intrapersonal tension and distress with no clear differences in social class. Up to 30 percent of the school children were found to exhibit symptoms of interpersonal ineptness. These findings were less prevalent in girls who manifested inappropriate withdrawal. However, these symptoms were more prevalent in boys who manifested inappropriate aggression. One to 30 percent of the children exhibited some form of antisocial behavior. Though less prevalent than in other adjustment problems, antisocial behavior was found to be more prevalent in the lower classes and in boys (pp. 66-67).

The studies they reviewed were based primarily on the reporting of teachers. Though some may question the validity of teacher ratings for maladjustment, Glidewell and Swallow (1968) pointed out that ". . . although teachers do not equate distress at school and mental illness, they do make reports about children's distress which are in as much agreement with clinicians' reports as clinicians are in agreement with each other (p. 9)."

The Joint Commission in reporting on emotionally disturbed and mentally ill children and youth in its *Digest of Crisis in Child Mental Health: Challenge for the 1970's* (1969) found:

> *At least 10 million* of our young people under 25 are thought to suffer from mental and emotional disorders. It is estimated that .6 percent are psychotic and that another 2 to 3 percent are severely disturbed. An additional 8 to 10 percent are in need of some kind of help from knowledgeable persons (p. 28).

Additionally, the Commission, (1970) in the first of its final reports, *Crisis in Child Mental Health: Challenge for the 1970's*, reported, "At least 1,400,000 of our youngsters under eighteen need immediate psychiatric care. This National Institute for Mental Health estimate is considered by that institute and most mental health professionals to be a conservative figure (p. 250)."

The Commission (1970) found basically the same in its larger report.

> Estimates vary as to the number of mentally ill children and young people in this country. It is estimated that about .6 percent are psychotic and that another 2 or 3 percent are severely disturbed. It is further estimated that an additional 8 to 10 percent of our young people are afflicted with emotional problems (neuroses and the like) and are in need of specialized services. However, only about 5 to 7 percent of the children who need professional mental health care are getting it. . . . However, more than 10,000,000 young people under age twenty-five need knowledgeable help (pp. 253-254).

The next question is how do these figures relate to black disadvantaged children? Although there is mention in the literature of increased numbers of emotionally and physically handicapped youngsters within slum, lower class, poverty, or disadvantaged groups, there apparently have not been many studies reported in this area. There are a few studies which should be cited, however.

For example, an analysis of Head Start children showed at least 10 percent, by the age of four, who were judged to be crippled in their emotional growth. This figure is estimated at 20 to 25 percent in some cities. In a typical black district in Chicago, one study found that 70 percent of several thousand first graders were mildly to severely maladapted to the psychological requirements of the first grade. When compared to a well adjusted white group, by the end of the school year these youngsters ran a 9 to 1 risk of developing psychiatric symptoms. Some 10 percent of the youngsters between 7 and 17 years of age in the same district came to the attention of authorities each year because of delinquent behavior. Similarly, in New York City, the early results of a study of emotional and mental disorders among children showed a much higher rate for poor children and for children from oppressed minority groups (Joint Commission, 1969, p. 25).

Glidewell and Swallow (1968) also report greater emotional problems associated with slum areas.

> The data from Turner (1962) and Kellam and Schiff (1967) indicate that school maladjustment rates in urban slum schools may be as high as 60% or as low as 30%. By implication from other studies, the rate of clinical maladjustment in urban slum schools falls between 9% and 18%. These approximations, however, must be considered to be tentative. Additional, more careful, social class comparisons are necessary for firmer approximations.
>
> In summary, results of social class comparisons have been inconsistent, in part due to the inclusiveness of the term, "maladjustment." Generally, however, teachers rate more lower class children as maladjusted. It seems likely that social class differences influence different behavior problems differentially, but data available are not clearly interpretable in these terms. It should be reemphasized that one bias in the approximations for total populations in this report is that most of the data used to estimate clinical maladjustment in children were collected in middle class schools. Thus, it is likely the general approximations will underestimate behavior problems as perceived by teachers (pp. 47-48).

One of the problem areas related to discussions of disadvantaged children is that too many equate the term disadvantaged to mean black disadvantaged only. Additionally, the negative aspects related to the black disadvantaged child are most often considered as related to his or her race rather than to his or her social class. Glidewell and Swallow (1968) point out this misconception in relation to race differences.

> Of all the data available, those indicative of race differences in maladjustment are the least extensive and the least satisfactory.
>
> The data available, sparse and unsatisfactory as they are, reflect very small race differences, if any, in non-achievement problems when sex and social class are constant. They also tend to support the widely reported observation that problems in conforming to class-

room management demands—authority acceptance and concentration, for example—are more frequent among lower-class Negroes than among middle-class Negroes. *These are, however, social class differences, not race differences, as they are often incorrectly assumed to be* [author's emphasis] (pp. 47, 49, 51).

Glidewell and Swallow (1968) found additional reports of maladjustment that are interesting in relation to males and aggressiveness in the areas of interpersonal ineptness and antisocial behavior. They found that clinicians and teachers were commonly able to recognize problems in developing interpersonal skills. It is typical for interpersonal ineptness to be manifested on the one hand by timidity, withdrawal, shyness, or submissiveness, and on the other hand by dominance, aggressiveness, acting-out, or assertiveness. These kinds of problems were emphasized by most of the research reports they reviewed.

Their reporting stressed the importance of distinguishing the forms of withdrawal and aggressiveness in interpersonal relations from aggressive antisocial behavior and from antisocial withdrawal and isolation. These difficulties do not result from conformity pressures from adults or to authority. Instead these difficulties are derived from a lack of interpersonal skill with peers.

The problems surrounding interpersonal ineptness may be closely related to the classroom problems associated with some of the aspects of streetcorner behavior. For example, continual aggressive "ribbing" of one child by another in relation to his or her clothing may be a manifestation of interpersonal ineptness. (Chapter Five discusses the concept of "ribbing" in more detail.)

As noted earlier, the studies investigated by Glidewell and Swallow (1968) dealt with middle class elementary school children primarily. It is with this in mind that we look at their reporting in relation to antisocial behavior.

Rebellion against authority or social conformity pressures is perhaps the most dramatic and the *least* prevalent of the several classes of behavior problems at school.

It is not identical with delinquency. In the elementary school years, it includes lying, cheating, stealing, destructiveness, truancy, and sexual behavior deviations which violate social norms but represent no violation or only very minor violations of laws. It does not include the few delinquent acts punishable by law, such as vandalism and petty theft. . . .

The data show a very wide range of prevalence rates—too wide for really satisfactory single estimation, but the central tendency approaches 10%. It may well be that, in any social system at all, judged by its own standards, 10% of the members resist the norms enough to cause concern by the agents responsible for socializations. These data suggest that 14% of the boys and 2% of the girls present anti-social behavior to their teachers, but they are not well supported by other findings. It seems likely that there is a significant variation in time and place in what teachers consider to be anti-social behavior.

In spite of variations from one study to the next, there is quite consistent evidence that anti-social behavior is more frequent. It is also more frequent in the lower classes, especially the deprived lower classes. The more marked the breach of laws, the closer is the social class relationship. In community data on delinquency in adolescents there is a tendency for delinquency to be underreported in the middle classes. In elementary schools, however, most of the anti-social behavior surveyed occurred at school, observed by the teacher. Underreporting by teachers, while perhaps operative, is much less extensive. The existence of the social class relationship is clear; the *extent* of the relationship is, as yet, in doubt. It would seem likely, however, *that a large proportion of the social class influences on general maladjustment, as rated by teachers, can be accounted for by anti-social behavior* [my emphasis] (pp. 62-63).

Physically Handicapped. The second area to be considered is the numbers of physically handicapped children in the United States as well as in schools serving disadvantaged populations. These reports and figures, of course, must also be looked at in light of reports that there are fewer programs for the physically handicapped in schools serving disadvantaged populations as compared with schools serving middle class populations.

According to the Joint Commission on Mental Health of Children, Inc. (1969), disadvantaged children exhibit high rates of cumulative educational retardation. Estimates suggest that 85 percent of Harlem's eighth grade students are "functional illiterates." These youngsters typically come from understaffed, ill-equipped, and dilapidated schools (p. 25). Further studies suggest a close correlation between low socioeconomic status and prematurity, and between high rates of infant mortality and low birth weight, and such serious handicaps as mental retardation, blindness, brain damage, and other disabilities. Data also shows that large proportions of poor mothers, most often nonwhite mothers, receive inadequate obstetrical care at delivery and no prenatal care (p. 25).

The Joint Commission (1969) also reported that of the 3 percent of the mentally retarded children, 75 percent have few physical handicaps and show no obvious brain damage. Commonly, these apparently nonorganic cases come from census tracts where the median income is $3,000 or less a year (p. 25).

A report from Great Britain has found much the same physical and medical problems associated with the lower class groups as has been found in the United States (Weinraub, 1972). A survey of 17,000 children born in one week in 1958 in Great Britain found that "working-class children are more likely to have a squint, a speech defect or poor physical coordination and are even shorter than middle-class youngsters (p. 2)."

The inferences and reporting, therefore, suggest large numbers of emotionally and physically handicapped youngsters in inner city classrooms who, in response to their handicaps, may exhibit an aggressive acting-out syndrome. The child with a learning or physical problem or disability may act-out to divert attention from, for example, his inability to read. Further reporting also suggests too few programs for emotionally and physically handicapped youngsters as well as normal youngsters in inner city areas. Also, inner city schools have fewer experienced teachers able to cope with acting-out youngsters.

We must also include in this category of emotionally and physically handicapped youngsters those with hearing and learning problems or other physical disabilities.

Differentiating Between Streetcorner Behavior and Emotionally Handicapped Behavior. The third area to be considered here was mentioned earlier. This is the question of whether middle class school personnel who are unfamiliar with streetcorner behavior can diagnose accurately and differentiate between streetcorner behavior and emotionally handicapped or retarded behavior.

Many of the black youngsters I became friendly with in the New York City "600" schools were either big and tough, or small and tough, or wise in the ways of the streets. When these youngsters were with teachers who were not physically afraid of them, they generally behaved well and also learned their school skills. This is interesting when you consider that so many of these youngsters had been assigned to the "600" schools for overt acts of verbal or physical aggression and assaults against teachers. However, when you understand streetcorner behavior and the workings and conditioning of racism, you observe incidents precipitated every day. You see the black youngster involved being penalized punitively for acting in a streetcorner way toward a teacher, an administrator, other school personnel, or even a fellow student. In school, most often the youngster's streetcorner behavior draws a reaction from school personnel that is different from the reaction he would draw in the street. Very often, the school personnel overreact or underreact because of factors varying from fear, to racism, to a lack of knowledge, to a lack of understanding of streetcorner behavior and what to do about it, to completely panicking. Often one incident leads to another and a youngster soon develops a "loser" syndrome, because he is punished out of proportion to his supposed misdeed. I refer to this as the Emmett Till syndrome.[h]

[h]Emmett Louis Till was a 14-year-old black youngster from Chicago who went to Mississippi to visit with his relatives. While visiting he was lynched for not "knowing his place."

According to the *Times* (2 held, 1955, p. 19),

Till's body, a bullet in his head and a 100-pound cotton gin fan tied to his neck to weight him down, was pulled from the Talihatchie River Wednesday.

The streetcorner conditions some black youngsters to act in a certain way. Similarly, the teacher's middle class background directs or conditions him or her to act in a particular way, too. The actions and expectations of each do not mesh and often lead to a conflict that only a few are capable of avoiding.

When the streetcorner child is in school and acts in the way that his environment has rewarded, he often gets into trouble; sometimes a great deal of trouble: for the kinds of physical, sexual, and aggressive acts that he is rewarded for on the streetcorner, he is condemned for in the schoolhouse. Indeed, the kinds of acts that are rewarded on the streetcorner are the antithesis of what is rewarded in school.

Often his streetcorner acts lead him into greater trouble in school, with greater punitive consequences. This leads the streetcorner youngster to fall prey to the Emmett Till syndrome. Thus the first supposed offense is simple but draws a disproportionate punitive response, and so on until the youngster is considered a hard core discipline problem; whereupon he and his teachers create and act in roles pursuant to each other's expectation of the other. What is so sad is that he should have been so severely punished for the first negative act. If the teacher had known how to cope positively with his actions, he would not have been reported in the first place. The following anecdotes will provide the reader with some illustrations.

REALITY 7

This incident took place in a Northern inner city elementary school. Those involved included a fifth grade black male student and an exceptionally attractive white female teacher, a Southerner who had resided in the North only a few years. She was a personable young teacher and spoke with a decided Southern drawl. A number of the youngsters recognized her Southern dialect and talked with her about where she came from and developed a good relationship with her.

The boy . . . was kidnapped three days earlier from his uncle's home where he had been vacationing.
Young Till allegedly whistled or made "ugly remarks" to Mrs. Bryant.

Although Mrs. Bryant, a 21-year-old white woman, never testified about what Emmett Till allegedly did, according to Popham (1955, p. 15), Emmett Till entered her store and,

made a purchase and when she held out her hand for the money he grabbed her hand and she had to tug to get free. She said he followed her to the cash register, grabbed her around the waist and said "How about a date? I've been with white women before."

Later, according to Popham, Till was pulled out of the store and onto the porch by another black youngster where Till "wolf-whistled" at Mrs. Bryant.

Roy Bryant, 24, and his half-brother J.W. Milan, 36, were indicted for murdering Till. However, the all-white jury in LeFlore County, Mississippi acquitted them for murder and refused to indict them for kidnapping.

One day as she was walking in the hall, one of the youngsters she was friendly with called to her, "Hi, Country," and she waved back to him smiling.

The principal heard the youngster call out, "Hi, Country," and suspended him from school. The teacher found out about the suspension and interceded to clear the case. However, not all children are usually this lucky.

The point here is that the expression "country" is used to refer to someone who is newly arrived in the city.[i] It is not necessarily an insulting or threatening term. The term often is used as a kidding term. In this incident, it was used with feeling and affection. The principal, lacking an understanding of the streetcorner life style and language of his pupils, saw this friendly exchange as some form of insult that deserved punishment.

The following background information is provided to give the reader some insight into Reality 8, below.

George is a junior high youngster who runs in the streets. In the streets he has learned that physical behavior has brought him and his friends rewards. George is also quite involved in using females in the way streetcorner men use them. According to Liebow (1966), the streetcorner man views himself as an economic and sexual exploiter and user of women.

> ... in a world where sexual conquest is one of the few ways in which one can prove one's masculinity, the man who does not make capital of his relationship with a woman is that much less a man (p. 150).[j]

Additionally, according to Liebow (1966), the streetcorner man is often reinforced for acting physically and forcefully with his women.

> The husband who sometimes responds to this testing and challenging by slapping his wife's face or putting his fist in her mouth is frequently surprised at the satisfactory results. . . . Leroy . . . was going home to see what "Mouth" (Charlene) wanted. She probably wanted a whipping, he said; she seems to beg him to beat her. Afterwards, she's "tame as a baby, sweet as she can be. . . ."
>
> For Charlene, like Lorena, wanted some tangible evidence that her husband cared about her, about them as a family, and that he was willing to fight to establish and protect his (nominal) status as head of the family. She openly envied Shirley who, when things were going tolerably well for her and Richard, took pleasure in boasting to Charlene, Lorena and other women that Richard pushed her

---

[i]See the movie *The Jungle*, produced by Churchill Films, 662 North Robertson St., Los Angeles.

[j]See also N.C. Heard's *Howard Street* New York: The Dial Press, Inc., 1968; and "Street Corner Hustler's Blues," The Best of Lou Rawls, Capital SKAO 2948.

around, insisted she stay off the street, and enforced the rule that she be up early every morning, dress the children and clean the house. For evidence of this kind of concern, Charlene would gladly pay the price of a slap in the face or a pushing around (pp. 134-135).

Furthermore, Liebow (1966) reported that the streetcorner man was always ready to look elsewhere for sexual gratification, even though he might already have a good sexual relationship with a willing partner, be it his wife or someone else.

> *Sexual Infidelity as a Manly Flaw—*. . . One of the most widespread and strongly supported views the men have of themselves and others is that men are, by nature, not monogamous; that no man can be satisfied with only one woman at a time. This view holds that, quite apart from his desire to exploit women, the man seeks them out because it is his nature to do so. This "nature" that shapes his sex life, however, is not human nature but rather an animality which the human overlay cannot quite cover. The man who has a wife or other woman continues to seek out others because he has too much "dog" in him.
>
> "Men are just dogs! . . . hopping around from woman to woman, just like a dog."
>
> This pronouncement from Sea Cat met with unanimous agreement from the men on the corner. Another occasion brought forth similar unanimity. . . . Tally cooed at the women as they walked by.
>
> One woman, in response to Tally's "Where you going, baby?" approached the car and looked the five of us over carefully, each in turn. "Walking," she said, and turned away. We watched her saunter across the street, her hips lurching from side to side as if they were wholly independent of the rest of her body. "That's real nice," said Tally, "that's real nice." There was a chorus of yes noises from the others.
>
> It don't matter how much a man loves his wife and kids," said Clarence, "he's gonna keep on chasing other women. . . . A man's got too much dog in him." The others agreed with Clarence and remained in complete agreement throughout the discussion which followed.
>
> The dog in man which impels him to seek out an ever-expanding universe of sex is a push-pull affair. A "new" woman is, by common consent, more stimulating and satisfying sexually than one's own wife or girl friend. The man also sees himself performing better with "new meat" or "fresh meat" than with someone familiar to him sexually. Men in their late twenties or older pooh-pooh the suggestion that they are not as good sexually as they were in their late teens or early twenties, maintaining that their performance in any given sex encounter depends less on age or any other personal fact or

than on the woman they happen to be with. Variety is not only the spice of sex life, it is an aphrodisiac which elevates the man's sexual performance. The point is perhaps best made by a standard joke which frequently appeared when the subject of sexual competence came up. It was told more as a fact of life than as a subject of humor.

An old man and his wife were sitting on their porch, rocking slowly and watching a rooster mount one hen, then another. When the rooster had repeated this performance several times, the old woman turned to her husband and said, "Why can't you be like that rooster?" "If you look close," the old man said, "you'll see that that rooster ain't knockin' off the same hen each time. If he had to stick with the same one, he wouldn't do no better than me" (pp. 120-123).

With this background suggested as George's frame of reference, we should look at the reporting of Reality 8. Before we do this, however, one further point dealing with discipline. This point relates to the effects of conditioning and will be discussed in greater detail in Chapter Six.

A veteran, a former Green Beret, killed his friend in a barroom brawl where ". . . dazed and thinking he had just killed an attacking Viet Cong, was stripping the body so that it could not be rigged with booby traps (Violent, 1972, p. 45)."

The veteran was eventually acquitted. His acquittal was based on the testimony primarily of Harvard Sociologist Charles Levy, who reported on interviews with returning combat veterans who experience also a "kind of psychological disorientation . . . after returning from Southeast Asia (p. 45)." Levy reported that

. . . he discovered a common tendency on the part of his subjects to carry into civilian life the unbridled violence that served them well in combat. "They have learned to react violently, spontaneously and without premeditation . . . it's a situation that keeps them alive over there but gets them into prison back here (p. 46)."

Levy also found that often veterans learned to: ". . . admire the courage and skill of the Communists, and often vent their anger against their South Vietnamese comrades, whom they see as inept, and against their own officers, sometimes brutally injuring or killing them (p. 46)." Then, when discharged and home, ". . . some of the veterans still treated allies like enemies. Relatives and friends often took the place of officers and South Vietnamese as targets for misdirected hostility (p. 46)." Levy conceded that some of his veterans were probably violent before they entered the armed forces. However, he finds now that their violence ". . . has no boundaries (p. 46)."

What is being suggested is that there are to some extent behavioral similarities between these veterans and some inner city school children. Many of the school children are conditioned to act in certain physical, aggressive, and sexual ways. They are also used to a strong physical control. Their behavior has also been conditioned and reinforced to act his way. Therefore, when such a youngster comes to school and his teacher does not act in the way he expects a man or woman to act, he is disoriented and does not understand the behavior. This often throws him out of sorts. Indeed, if the situation becomes sticky or crisis, most often he will revert to his streetcorner behavior; he acts-out in the way he has been conditioned to act. This should be kept in mind when reading Reality 8 and this book.

REALITY 8

School has just ended. George is sitting on the steps in the school running a strong rap[k] with a number of girls. A female teacher comes down the steps and hears him say, "How about a kiss, baby?"

The teacher's face reddens and she slaps his face. He, in turn, kicks her backside. She is white; he is black.

Investigation reveals that the teacher was a good teacher who had a rough week. She had accidently been knocked down by a running student while she was walking in the hall as well, and experienced a few other unsettling incidents. George, for his part, said he was talking to one of the girls.

George, who had had a reasonably good school record, was acting in typical street fashion for which, we must realize, he has been reinforced with the street rewards he and his peers value. The teacher, because she had had a rough week, acted the way her background had taught her to act. The principal, knowing the need to support teachers, did what he felt he had to do—suspend the youngster assault charges against the youngster were drawn up, too. At the last moment, however, the teacher decided not to sign the charges.

If the teacher had not been out of sorts, she could have parried his repartee and no one would have considered it an incident worth much more than talking about in the lunch room or in some graduate course, if at all.

This may not excuse the youngster's asking, "How about a kiss?" loud enough for the teacher to hear, which was what he probably intended. However, it must be understood that from his frame of reference, it was not meant as a threat but more likely a form of compliment.

[k]The earlier definition of "rapping" or "running a strong rap" had sexual connotations. The object was for the rapper to get the girl's nose. When a male has a female's nose, she is in his power, which usually means she is his to do with as he pleases sexually.

Actually, if the female teacher were a "scab" or a "fish"[1] the student probably would have ignored her. This teacher, however, was a "phat tip."[m] By making a big play in front of the girls, he was paying her a compliment.[n]

Realities 9, 10, and 11 will provide the reader with insight into how three adult white males reacted to a reasonably similar incident. The actions of the youths in these incidents are typical of the way streetcorner youngsters may physically test a new teacher or almost anyone who is unknown to them—a test of the machismo of someone he knows or who he may think is weak. The action reflects the streetcorner, where "might makes right" and where you must put the other person down first or he will put you down.

REALITY 9

A new teacher was walking the hall on his way to his room from lunch. As he turned a corner, two students came toward him. When the student closest to him was about a foot from him, he suddenly reached out and put his hand against the wall. The teacher said, "Hey, what are you trying to do?" The student responded by keeping his hand on the wall and leering at the teacher.

The teacher, not sure of what was happening except that he felt uncomfortable and fearful, was unsure as to whether he should bend and walk under the outstretched arm or walk around both boys. He opted to go under the boy's arm (actually I have observed teachers doing both); whereupon, teacher and students went on their way.

The next time the boys saw the teacher, they greeted him with, "hi faggot." Before too long, most of the school population called the teacher Mr. Faggot rather than by his proper name. He soon left the school after too many classroom problems.

Before this teacher transferred, he told everyone in the school that he did not come here to hit kids. When asked, "Who do you see hitting kids?" he could not name anyone. What he was saying was that he was afraid physically of the students.

Because the teacher reacted improperly, a number of negative behaviors were reinforced for the teacher and the two students. The teacher's and students' negative feelings about each other were reinforced; all black kids are "animals" and all whites are "faggots." The students were allowed to continue learning how to manipulate their environment or life space both negatively and physically. Indeed, they were allowed to use their creative powers

[1]In jive lexicon or street language a "fish" or a "scab" is an ugly girl. Also, a female who is a "phat" is a beautiful girl or woman.

[m]My informants tell me that the letters in "phat" stand for "pussy," "hips," "ass," and "tits," or a "pretty hole at times." I am sure that there are also some others. "Tip" is a Buffalo word meaning a girl or woman.

[n]See Chapter Five for further explanation of street or corner behavior as related to cat and gorilla roles.

to contribute to their own destruction. When the teacher reacted the way he did, he reinforced the youngsters' manipulative behavior, and the youngster, observing the incident, saw this behavior reinforced.

REALITY 10

This incident started out about the same as Reality 9. However, when the teacher asked what they were doing and they continued to laugh and leer, the teacher panicked. He hit the youngster who had his arm against the wall. This youngster, in turn, punched the teacher in the face. The incident was terminated with the student being suspended. Of course, it was never brought out that the teacher hit the youngster first.

Additionally, as in Reality 9 both the teacher's and the students' negative feeling about one another and how one is supposed to act were all reinforced.

REALITY 11

This example is similar to Realities 9 and 10 except that the teacher was more experienced and reacted differently. An experienced inner city school teacher was walking in the hall of a junior high school. As he walked, six students came toward him. The first youngster in line moved over close to the wall to block the teacher's path. He smiled, grabbed the youngster's outstretched arm while pressing his thumb into the pressure point, moving him to the side out of the way, and in a loud clear voice said, "Excuse me," while smiling and walking on.

The biggest student in the group observing this incident saw that the teacher's "game" was the stronger and joined his side. He indicated this by saying to his friend so that everyone could hear, "Hey Jiiim, what you tryin' to do to that man? You tryin' to make him walk around you?" With that everyone laughed and continued on his respective way.

In this incident neither the youngsters' nor the teacher's negative feelings about each other were reinforced. Additionally, the students did not see any positive reinforcement for their friend's behavior, and the student involved was not allowed to use his creativity to destroy himself. The situation was handled without any negative or punitive aggression, violence, or reporting of the student.

Actually, this youngster is now ready to listen to this adult because the adult gained his respect for the way he carried himself in the streetcorner machismo competition. Additionally, the youngster's negative behavior was stopped in a way that did not make him lose face. The student, therefore, does not have the need to retaliate with an even more aggressive act.

Another point must be mentioned but cannot be explored in depth here. This is the type of testing that teachers in inner city schools are being subjected to. To some extent, this testing has reached the point at which it may be in violation of the civil rights of teachers and of the students whose education is being interrupted by the resulting disruption.

Because teachers are being tested so physically and because they are unprepared to deal with it, we have an unhealthy teaching-learning environment. Do we blame streetcorner youngsters for testing the way they do? Or do we blame the teachers for their inability to pass the tests the students impose on them? This question is discussed further in Chapter Six.

Black and white school personnel with three or more years of teaching in inner city schools estimate that 18% of their students are emotionally or physically handicapped.

Youngsters Who Are Religious
or Politicized

The youngsters who are religious or politicized may fall into any of at least five categories that I have been able to identify. The first two categories are those who may belong to the Black Panthers or the Black Muslims. The third category includes youngsters who may act in a political way and have some formal political or religious affiliation other than the Black Panthers or the Black Muslims. The fourth category consists of those youngsters who are regular churchgoers. And the fifth category includes those youngsters who are organizationally uncommitted but militant and antagonistic to whites or to the system.

All five groups of students can affect the school's teaching and learning in many ways. The first three groups, Black Panthers, Black Muslims, and affiliated politicized students may affect the school through similar types of actions. They may even receive assistance in the form of political expertise and advice, strikers, and propaganda, fliers from outside sources such as white college, or high school, third world, radical, or Communist students.

The fourth group of students who are conventional churchgoers may affect the teaching and learning in a completely different way. They may become the butt of jokes, pranks, and physical abuse because of their middle class behavior, dress, and actions. Hence, they may cause problems not because of any particular overt actions but rather as targets for the acting out of the frustrations of others. Similarly, some youngsters may be bullied because their parents belong to the Jehovah's Witnesses, Seventh-Day Adventists, or other religious groups that support middle class life styles.

Elenore Lester (1971) in discussing the works of J.E. Franklin and Ed Bullins, writes of the frustration, helplessness, and self-hate that makes ghetto "hoods" and others act-out against symbols of "upward mobility."

> . . . the implicit concept in . . . Ed Bullins' play, *Clara's Ole Man*, for example, . . . typically makes the young college man in a suit the

victim of a brutal attack by young hoodlums who view his gentle manners, school attendance and fondness for poetry as symptoms of Uncle Tomism (p. D 5).

The first three groups can affect the schools in any number of ways. Youngsters who are Black Muslims may want alternative meals made available whenever pork is served in the school's cafeteria, or to wear a fez in school, or refuse to salute the flag for religious reasons. The politicized student may also refuse to stand and salute the flag, or he may want soul food served in the school cafeteria. Additionally, these youngsters may also want the school closed to commemorate the birthday of Martin Luther King or other black leaders. (In many school districts with large numbers of black students, the schools are already closed on some of these days.) Others may organize protests to compel the establishment of black studies programs or demand that a teacher they consider racist be fired despite his tenure.

Certain nonaggressive acts may be construed as threatening by racist or unknowing white personnel. For example, the black student's pride in his or her blackness may in itself frighten many white school personnel who look upon Afros and dashikis as signs of aggression against themselves as whites. This also takes place outside of school.

In one example, a black stewardess with United Airlines lost her job because she refused to cut her Afro. According to *Newsweek* (Airline, 1969), "Some whites fearfully see Afro hair-do's . . . as a symbol of anger and rebellion. But United says it was simply a matter of enforcing the airline's traditional standards of good grooming (p. 104)."

Some youngsters may wish to organize a black student club or union that would exclude whites in violation of school or board of education rules. In other cases, students may just wish to start the club and leave it open to all, black or white. Reality 12 provides an example of how a simple request for a Black Students Club ended in a political fracas that went beyond the school.

REALITY 12

Black students in a school with a 99.9 percent black student body made a request to their principal (also black) to organize a Black Student Club. The principal was not noted for acting with dispatch. First, the principal held his students off for awhile. This increased the students' militancy. They threatened boycotts of the school and disruption of the board of education offices. Finally, they held a sit-in at the school.

The principal at this point requested a decision of the superintendent of schools. By this time the newspapers and city council were aroused by the issue and the superintendent of schools passed the buck to the board of education. After public hearings, recriminations, and the building of more black and white ill feelings, the board moved that the club be organized in compliance with the rules of the board of education concerning school clubs.

This is a typical example of an administrator's refusal to act, causing old wounds to open and new ones to be cut. Had he moved as he should and could have, the public recriminations and ill feelings would not have had to come about.

In some schools, some youngsters may wish to fly the red, black, and green flag of the Republic of New Africa alongside of or in place of the flag of the United States on the stage, in each classroom, in the halls, or on the school's main flagpole.[o]

In the city of Newark, New Jersey, the Board of Education passed a ruling that the Republic of New Africa flag should "... be hung in all public schools and classrooms where black students are in the majority (Jersey, 1971; School, 1972; Sullivan, 1972; Black, 1971). Eventually State Education Commissioner Marburger ruled that the Newark Board of Education must "... desist from implementing its own resolution to fly black liberation flags (State, 1972, p. 1)." Of course, readers must also remember that many other black and white teachers and students have also been involved in protests concerning the saluting and/or standing for the Pledge of Allegiance as well as the singing of the Star Spangled Banner. These acts are not a black militant phenomenon (Budder, 1970; Florida, 1970; Principal, 1970c; Sinn, 1971; Teacher, 1971a; Teacher, 1971b; Michigan, 1972).

These religious or politicized students and the streetcorner youngsters may have their fingers on the pulse of what is happening in the school. If teachers and administrators will work with these youngsters, positive changes could be made in such areas as curriculum, staffing, disciplinary policies, the purchasing of black products for school use, and the displaying on school bulletin boards materials relevant to blacks, to name a few (Thompson, 1970; National, 1969). For example, at Woodlawn Junior High School in Buffalo, "Lift Every Voice and Sing," which is popularly known as the Black National Anthem, is sung every morning by the students. Additionally, the school is organized by "Houses" based on African culture.

I have observed and have had described to me incidents where honest, friendly, and respectful relations between school personnel and the streetcorner, the religious, and the politicized students were used to prevent minor scuffles or fights between black students or black and white students from exploding into major disruptions. Where school personnel have worked and shared some of their power with these youngsters, they have prevented walkouts and strikes over irrelevant demands and issues of a few students vying for power.

[o]U.N.I.A. Black Liberation Flag. The flag came into contemporary use about ten years ago. The "liberator" tristar originated with Marcus Garvey's black nationalist movement.

To the politicized youngster and to many Black Muslims everything related to blacks may be "political." For example, everything read or discussed in the civics, social studies, and history curriculums and classes may be looked upon as political. The reasoning offered for this position is that the condition and position of blacks in America is either the outcome of institutionalized white racism, the political inequality of black people in America, and/or the economic and political deprivation of black Americans (Fraser, 1971; Brown, 1971).

Sometimes, even where administrative and teaching decisions are sound, outside-of-school problems may have an impact on the school. For example, many community organizations in ghetto areas go through internal upheavals. Sometimes these schisms can result in confrontation and violence (Delaney, 1972). A school located in a large ghetto area may often have students who have family, relatives, or friends who are connected with opposing factions fighting for control of the various community organizations. These problems of outside-of-school organizations therefore sometimes affect the teaching and learning despite sound educational policy.

The last and most important point related to this classification of behavior is that the politicized and religious students often use streetcorner behavior to achieve their goals. The behavior of the adult black militant groups has not been lost on the school-aged youngsters; they have learned their lessons well.

There is a most important issue related to this notion. That is, because of sometimes uncompromising political and educational leadership refusing to share any power with black adults or students; and because of school and outside-of-school conditions continuing to perpetuate institutionalized white racism; and outside-of-school groups continuing to fight for power and patronage in many instances, we are at that point in history where blacks now demand and are willing to fight to achieve their objectives. (To some extent this holds true for white groups too.) Often the blacks' tactics take the form of streetcorner behavior. This has become a new power wedge used by blacks in the confrontation and in fighting to achieve their stated or unstated demands. Actually, this behavior has provided a new dimension for what whites call "gut politics."

Streetcorner behavior has been observed and reported in use by adults as well as students in testing devices in school confrontations and bargaining sessions with whites and sometimes middle class blacks on many college campuses, in public schools, in city halls, in governmental agencies, and in many of the encounters dealing with community control. Often, by using streetcorner behavior, the blacks have attempted to achieve their ends by intimidating the middle class blacks and whites with whom they are bargaining.

Tom Wolfe (1970) describes these streetcorner behavior tactics beautifully. He writes about San Francisco blacks "mau-mauing the flack catchers," for financial gain. Or, in other words, how some San Francisco blacks and their friends would turn their streetcorner behavior games and tactics into playing on the fears and fantasies of the white governmental functionaries to secure federal poverty funds. To some extent, this is the same way many inner city youngsters "run their game" on their teachers.

REALITY 13

Going downtown to mau-mau the bureaucrats got to be the routine practice in San Francisco. The poverty program *encouraged* you to go in for mau-mauing. They wouldn't have known what to do without it. The bureaucrats at City Hall and in the Office of Economic Opportunity talked "ghetto" all the time, but they didn't know any more about what was going on in the Western Addition, Hunters Point, Potrero Hill, the Mission, Chinatown, or south of Market Street than they did about Zanzibar. They didn't know where to look. They didn't even know who to ask. So what could they do? Well . . . they used the Ethnic Catering Service . . . right . . . They sat back and waited for you to come rolling in with your certified angry militants, your guaranteed frustrated ghetto youth, looking like a bunch of wild men. Then you had your test confrontation. If you were outrageous enough, if you could shake up the bureaucrats so bad that their eyes froze into iceballs and their mouths twisted up into smiles of sheer physical panic, into shit-eating grins, so to speak—then they knew you were the real goods. They knew you were the right studs to give the poverty grants and community organizing jobs to. Otherwise they wouldn't know (pp. 97-98).

Blacks who play these confrontation games usually know exactly what they are doing. In many cases they have their tactics down to an art; even as what to wear.

"Now don't forget. When you go downtown, y'all wear your *ghetto rags* . . . see. . . . Don't go down there with your Italian silk jerseys on and your brown suede and green alligator shoes and your Harry Belafonte shirts looking like some supercool tooth-picking-noddin' fool . . . you know. . . ."

"Don't nobody give a damn how pretty you can look . . . You wear your *combat* fatigues and your leather *pieces* and your shades . . . your *ghetto rags* . . . see. . . . And don't go down there with your hair all done up nice in your curly Afro like you're messing around. You go down with your *hair stickin' out* . . . and *sitting' up!* Lookin' wild! I want to see you down there looking like a bunch of *wild niggers!* (pp. 99-100)."

Mau-mauing usually frightened the whites. And mau-mauing, or similar tactics, in the schools usually frighten inner city school personnel. (This now also happens in schools of higher learning, too.) However, the whites upon whom the games are being played are usually not in any danger. The danger comes about when they begin to act irrationally—irrationally, that is, in the sense of ghetto expectations. To quote Wolfe again:

Ninety-nine percent of the time whites were in no physical danger whatsoever during mau-mauing. The brothers understood through and through that it was a tactic, a procedure, a game. If you actually hurt or endangered somebody at one of these sessions, you were only cutting yourself off from whatever was being handed out, the jobs, the money, the influence. The idea was to terrify but don't touch. The term *mau-mauing* itself expressed this game-like quality. It expressed the put on side of it. In public you used the same term the whites used, namely, "confrontation." The term mau-mauing said, "The white man had a voodoo fear of us, because deep down he still thinks we're savages. Right? So we're going to do that Savage number for him." It was like a practical joke at the expense of the white man's superstitiousness (p. 124).

Abrahams (1969) suggests that these tactical games have

... become a central aggressive technique used by black militants in confrontations with whites. Because this aggressive technique of interpersonal behavior has as its aim playful aggression and coercion, and because it is almost solely used by blacks and is aggressive, whites read it as hostility (which it may be in certain cases).
... Whites carry certain expectations into these confrontations which blacks have learned to counteract immediately, and thus they disarm whites and make them play their own game (generally without whites even knowing it).... However, we deem such behavior inappropriate for high-tension encounter occasions.... Consequently, white arbitrators, who come from the sector of the establishment most insistent about its concepts of decorum, are embarrassed and threatened and they fall to their barest displays of power as they resort first to call for 'reason' (really a white plea to permit power-play and coercion in their terms), then to silence and rumination, then to appeal to the rules of society (made for all to be accepted by all) and finally to the whole law-and-order dimension of the argument (p. 53).

These gamelike tactics continue to confound and frighten innumerable whites who have come to fear blacks. Many middle class blacks fear ghetto blacks, too. The tactics are to a large extent an enlargement and refinement of the tactics or games many school children have been using to test their teachers. Actually, Abrahams' description is also reminiscent of the middle class teacher's plea to the black child to try to get him to cease and desist his testing of him.

Reality 14 and 15 provide additional examples of black confrontation tactics. Reality 14 describes a black vs. black confrontation, and Reality 15 describes a black political confrontation with the white power structure.

REALITY 14

In 1968, as part of the stormy controversy in Ocean Hill-Brownsville and New York City between the United Federation of Teachers and the Ocean Hill Governing Board, the services of nineteen teachers were "terminated." This action precipitated a most disruptive conflict between teachers and community, between teachers and teachers, and between communities. Mayer (1969) describeş the meeting at which streetcorner behavior was used in a threatening way to sway a vote helping to terminate the services of the nineteen teachers.

> Over the weekend before, Assemblyman Wright had pleaded with the governing board not to take arbitrary action on personnel during the week the State Legislature was to begin its consideration of decentralization bills. Nevertheless, when the governing board met that Tuesday evening in executive session the report of the personnel committee was called up for approval. Professor Lockwood opposed the report, and urged that the board at least call the accused staff before it to talk over the charges before acting. Especially when complaints relate to behavior rather than to competence, he argued, people must be given a right to some kind of hearing. Moreover, if the teachers refused to appear at the meeting, they would be automatically guilty of insubordination. Several of the parent members stirred uneasily while Dr. Lockwood spoke.
>
> *Presently, as though on signal, the door to the meeting room burst open and 15 to 20 militants rushed in and ranged themselves against the wall. This was a community board they said, and they were the community, and they were there to see that the board did what the community wanted. ("At this point," the minutes of the meeting say gallantly and rather glumly, "the community entered the room.") In this atmosphere, the report of the personnel committee was approved, and McCoy was ordered to write letters to the 19, "terminating their services" in the district* [my emphasis] (p. 42).

REALITY 15

On September 11, 1968, the New York City teachers returned to work after summer vacation. To quote Mayer again:

At J.H.S. 271, a group led by Sonny Carson of Brooklyn CORE, who is widely regarded as terrorist in his inclinations and does nothing to discourage that opinion, had blocked the front door against the returning teachers. Principal William Harris had come out, and with the help of police had escorted the teachers into the building. There he told them, as the other principals were telling the other U.F.T. teachers through the district, to report to the I.S. 55 auditorium for an orientation session with McCoy. When the teachers arrived at the auditorium, they found about 50 Negro men, some wearing helmets, carrying sticks or with bandoleers of bullets, who shouted curses at them. The 83 teachers clustered in the center of the auditorium, terrified, and McCoy entered. As he started to speak, choruses of jeers from the men drowned him out, and after a few minutes he left. The lights in the auditorium were then flicked on and off, and the teachers were told from the crowd that if they came back to the district they would be carried out in pine boxes. Finally, McCoy returned. If the teachers still insisted on returning to the district, he said, they should report to their schools at 1 o'clock.

The teachers left the auditorium, caucused, and decided to go through with what they had come to do. When they reported to their schools again, they found they had been given no teaching assignments and there were no time cards for them to punch. J.H.S. 271 pupils were encouraged to leave the school by some nonunion teachers and members of the governing board. On their way out, they jeered at the union teachers, and, in some cases, maneuvered as though to assault them. Harris locked the teachers into a room for their own protection, and arranged a police escort for them out of the building at 2:15. That afternoon, the Ocean Hill teachers reported on their experiences to the executive board of the union, which exercised the option in the motion which had ended the preceding strike, and called for the city's teachers to walk out again on Friday (Mayer, 1969, p. 58).

REALITY 16

In the City of Buffalo, New York, there is an all-black, Saul Alinsky-organized community action organization, BUILD, which stands for Build Unity, Independence, Liberty, Dignity.[P] In their early days, the organization employed streetcorner tactics and games at public hearings (some of which were televised) in an attempt to achieve their goals.

BUILD's appearance at most public hearings followed a reasonably

[P]Just before organizing BUILD in Buffalo, Alinsky's organization had helped Rochester organize FIGHT. It was suggested that the fear of whites for the name FIGHT prodded those involved in Buffalo to reach for a more positive and less fearful name, BUILD.

similar pattern of behavior. Whenever one of their speakers rose to address the meeting, a number of "big guys," some in dashikis, Afros, goatees, and sunglasses would jump to their feet and stand big and tall with hands folded on their chest. Two or three other men or women would stand in similar manner and dress behind their speaker. Most often these tactics were successful in frightening the whites who watched.

While writing the above, I discussed the incident with someone who had worked for a poverty agency in a large Northeastern city. When I gave her the excerpt to read, she began to chuckle and told me of her experiences.

REALITY 17

"It seems that every time a new budget was coming up for approval—which was about every nine months—there would always be a problem because our program wasn't one of the priority programs. It was a tutorial program. It was always to be one of the program that would be cut.

"The State didn't realize that our program included about 150 community people. So when the people from the Office of Economic Opportunity and the State office would bring their budgets and let us know that we either had been cut out completely or cut down, we would get together as many people as we could—not only people employed in our program but everybody, their friends, and their relatives. We would go down to City Hall and rap. I would always stay in the background because I was one of the few whites there. Some of the black women who had had long experience in dealing with institutions because of welfare and the schools and so on would be in the front and be the speakers.

"We would always get that whole thing—the routine. The man in charge couldn't see us because he was in an important meeting. They would send some second grade flunky out to talk with us and the women would say, 'No, we're only talking with the boss,' and eventually the boss would leave his meeting and come out and talk. They would, in very plan down-to-earth, street people way, let the guy know that this was a program that they intended to have . . . and we always got funded. In fact, it is one of the few tutorial types of programs that is still going on in New York State and they are still doing it, still using the same tactics to keep the program funded."

The fifth and last type of youngster suggested is the one who is organizationally uncommitted but militant and contemptuous of whites. This is the youngster who does not belong to any particular religious, politicized, or civil rights group. He is ready, nevertheless, to take on any administrator or teacher whom he feels is racist; often he feels all whites are racist until they have proved they are not. Quite often this youngster comes from an intact home where:

1. Parents may be active in a militant organization that is contesting the white political structure openly.
2. He or she has been affected by the step-by-step advance of the civil rights movement from legal cases, to sit-ins, to marches, to street confrontations.
3. He (or she) has become resentful of his middle class parents who he thinks have denied their black heritage by playing "the man's" game.
4. His or her middle class parents have just discovered their blackness and are attempting to make amends by a hatred of whites, which they pass on to their children.
5. His or her parents, who always looked negatively at their blackness or never expressed their true feelings about racism, begin to vicariously relive their lives through his acting-out against the schools and the system.

Often this youngster openly shows his dislike and outright hatred for whites. Sometimes he may cause more problems in school than the militant organization youngster because he does not have any organizational discipline to guide and set limits for him. Indeed, he may physically or verbally attack either school staff or his fellow students.

Furthermore, while not denying the very real negative and destructive effects of white racism, this youngster's actions more often result from internal conflicts that can only be resolved by warm and feeling staff who do not become racially defensive in response to his actions. I am not suggesting giving in to this youngster just because he is black. He will not be helped to resolve his problems by adults who give in to him continually and indiscriminately. What he needs are warm, understanding black and white teachers who will help him resolve his conflicts, some real and some not so real; to help him to grow into adulthood while still retaining some of his feelings of militancy and idealism.

Black and white school personnel with three or more years of teaching in inner city schools estimate that 6 percent of their students fall within the religious or politicized category.

CONCERNING MIDDLE CLASS VALUES
AND BEHAVIOR

Whenever I present my four classifications of student behavior in inner city classrooms to university students or to teachers, the more radical ones accuse me of making a value judgment that middle class behavior is more desirable than is lower class behavior. They also say that "the trouble has been that we have been forcing middle class values down the throats of black kids."

When these accusations are made, I plead *nolo contendere* to the charge that middle class behavior and values are more desirable than are lower class behavior and values, and ask my accusers to list the negative aspects of middle class life or values that they are referring to. Their response usually refers to the supposed middle class drive to accumulate money and the subsequent purchase of material goods.

I then remind my class that the poor black men and women whose ghetto existence they are romanticizing, desire all the material items the middle class talk about denying while wallowing in them. After all, if they have these items, why deny them to the poor! Additionally, ghetto residents lead fearful lives trying to keep their children free from drugs and from becoming victims of violence. If ghetto life is so exemplary, why are we so involved in trying to improve the conditions of the poor or disadvantaged?

These students and new teachers then figure they can get me by asking me to list the middle class values or skills that I think are so good. Whereupon, I list or call off such saleable skills and values as learning how to read so that one can read a street sign to get off a bus and get to work, or to read street signs and numbers to make a delivery; or to be able to read a plan or blueprint, or to be able to read well enough to advance to a better job. I also mention getting to know how to use an alarm clock to get up to go to work; or learning how to use a bank account to save money. And of course I talk about being able to write, and to do mathematics also.

These students and new teachers then respond with, "Then maybe we ought to change the system. Why should we continue to perpetuate this system?" To which I suggest, "Good idea, but *you* change the system. Don't use black youngsters to change your system—it sounds to me as though you are trying to keep them out and from getting the material things you have."

It is really amazing how many teachers with middle class skills, bank accounts, and even job tenure, want to use black youngsters to change the system instead of teaching them how to read, write, and do mathematics so that they can take advantage of the good of the system. Once inner city youngsters grow into adulthood knowing how to read, write, and do arithmetic, they have the option to do as they please with their saleable skills. It is the teachers' job to provide them with these skills.

To get back to the charge that "we have been forcing middle class values down the throats of black kids," I would suggest that these young people are confusing the plight of inner city black students with their conflicts of growing up in a family amidst an abundance of material good without ever having had to assume any responsibility. What they are really talking about is racism that has neither taught nor allowed that black is also beautiful and that blacks should be prideful too.

In actuality, these radical students and teachers are acting in a racist way toward the black children they profess to help. They are doing this by not pressing black children to learn to read, write, and do math, to do homework, and to study. In spite of their paternalistic rhetoric, they are saying that black youngsters really are slower than whites, and therefore we don't have to pressure them to learn and do all the academic things we expect from middle class white youngsters.

Many of these white college students and teachers—the offspring of materially dominated, middle and upper class homes—are still caught up in the dilemma of growing and maturing into adulthood, and tend to take the stance that (1) glorifies and romanticizes the pimps, the whores, the hustlers, and the abject poverty of ghetto blacks and rural poor; (2) talks of doing away with poverty and racism; and (3) attacks *all aspects* of middle class life while unable to verbalize any comprehensive meaning of "middle class life." All while they indulge themselves in academic lives of some study; summers abroad; unlimited hi-fi equipment and supporting tapes, records, and rigs; lower air rates; and automobiles that their parents' middle class behavior has provided for them. Or they might have the opportunity to "drop out" in England or somewhere else for a year or two "to find oneself" rather than going to work, to school, or to the armed forces. The new teacher frequently sports a new car, and Christmas, Easter, and summer vacations based on the pay scales secured by the "establishment" they condemn.

Sadly, many of these "idealistic" and rebellious undergraduate students and new teachers cannot separate their insecurities and feelings from their teaching role, and they spread these insecurities and conflicts to their urban black lower class students, who continue to pay the bills long after their radical teachers have gone on to graduate school, to write a book about their experiences, or something else. Unquestionably, older teachers, too, have these problems, but the young who see and verbalize the negative aspects of society should not make the same mistakes.

Such a stance is a contradiction, and actually bespeaks of the need of some college students to be helped into adulthood. Too often, though, some of my older and younger colleagues cannot understand this behavior and become jealous of the new teachers' or university students' alleged wild, erotic lives, condemning them without any understanding. In addition, some younger professors and teachers themselves, caught up in their own conflicts and uncertainties, rhetorically feed their students' insecurities.

Instead, what is needed are more professors and teachers who are understanding, empathetic, warm adults, willing to help young people into adulthood with some of their idealism still intact. This responsibility and need was pinpointed in Richard Schickel's (1971) review of *The Last Picture Show*.

> . . . what the picture says, ever so softly and ever so intelligently, is that the way out of adolescence that always carries with it the threat of becoming perpetual is through decent connections with those few adults who, whatever their other problems, have at least made this journey successfully and are willing to show and tell what it's like. The movie says what we all know—that too few adults are willing to perform these vital initiatory functions—but it adds a point that, in our present romanticizing of rebellious youth, we often forget that a youth has to reach out to them, make known in some civil way his pain and need (p. 14).

SUMMARY

Almost all school children challenge their teachers. However, when some urban lower class black youngsters challenge their teachers with streetcorner behavior, most school personnel become frightened and react improperly. Most often, this improper reaction to their students' testing escalates a testing game into ongoing disorder and disruption. In turn, the resulting disruption and disorder prevents youngsters from learning as much as they are capable of learning, if anything at all.

Whether school children should be condemned for their testing games that result in disorder, or whether the educational staff should be condemned for allowing this state of affairs to continue, is questioned. Better yet, who will take the first real step to solve the problem? The Emmett Till syndrome of negatively marking and stigmatizing youngsters for small misdeeds continues to be perpetuated, and the destruction and waste of additional humans is continued.

Urban educators and administrators have not solved the problem of how to educate more lower class urban black children because neither they nor the urban professors have come close to understanding what is causing this problem. Sadly, most urban school and university educators have neither an understanding nor appreciation of lower class black male social behavior. Too often, where there is some knowledge, the response is either contempt or, at the other extreme, romantic idealization. They are not aware that the informal organizational rules affecting every aspect of inner city school life are derived from the streetcorner. Consequently, until they learn to understand these informal rules and regulations—the rules under which the schools are really run—and learn to use them for educational change and advantage, they will not be able to educate urban black youngsters.

The discussion in this chapter, the game of teaching and learning in inner-city schools as related to the manner in which the three concerns of streetcorner behavior are played out in the classroom through at least four categories of student behavior, should not be considered as suggesting that all school personnel must play the game by streetcorner rules.

Just as each teacher should develop his or her teaching style based on his or her personality, so should each teacher relate his or her personality to the playing of streetcorner games. Those who can play and teach that way, may; those who cannot play and teach that way should not. All teachers, however, must become aware of and learn the rules and regulations of the games they are involved in every day in their schools. If this can be accomplished, school personnel may not be so upset by their students' actions. And, hopefully, we may then be able to get on with the teaching and learning in inner city schools.

It goes without saying, though, that if we could do away with the underlying racism that permeates our society, urban lower class black youngsters would learn in spite of all of us.

My reporting of only the negative aspects of urban lower class black youths is done for a reason. However, readers must be reminded again that there are many black youngsters with middle class behavior in inner city classrooms. These youngsters, by and large, are not the perpetuators of the testing and disruptive tactics; they are rather the ones who are being deprived of the education they are legally and morally entitled to. Consequently, the emphasis must be placed on understanding and reaching those who are involved in the tactics or games that are creating the disruption that is interfering with the teaching and learning. Teachers must learn to hear and understand that different drumbeat to which the streetcorner youngster responds. That is what this book attempts to say.

NOTES TO CHAPTER TWO

Abrahams, R.D. Feedback from our readers: Rapping in the black ghetto. *Trans-Action* 6(7): 53, 1969.

Abrahams, R.D. *Deep down in the jungle . . . : Negro Narrative Folklore from the Streets of Philadelphia.* Chicago: Aldine, 1970.

Abrahams, R.D. *Positively Black.* Englewood Cliffs, N.J.: Prentice Hall, 1970.

Airlines: A question of style. *Newsweek*, October 6, 1969, p. 104.

Black flag. *Time,* December 13, 1971, p. 10.

Brown, C. *Manchild in the Promised Land.* New York: Macmillan, 1965.

Brown, D. *The Life and Loves of Mr. Jiveass Nigger.* New York: Fawcett World, Farrar, Strauss & Giroux, 1969.

Brown, H.R. *Die Nigger Die!* New York: Dial Press, 1969.

Brown, M. New breed of inmate considers himself to be political prisoner. *Buffalo Evening News,* September 23, 1971, p. 1.

Budder, L. Education board curbs use of nonofficial flags. *New York Times,* December 10, 1970, p. 56.

Bullins, E. *The Reluctant Rapist.* New York: Harper & Row, 1973.

Cain, G. *Blueschild Baby.* New York: McGraw-Hill, 1971.

Delaney, P. Internal struggle shakes Black Muslims. *New York Times,* January 21, 1972, p. 1.

Dennis, L.A. The hustler. *Black America* 2(6): 16-18, 57, 1972.

Dollard, J. The dozens: Dialect of insult. *American Imago* 1(1): 3-5, 1939.

Ellison, R. *Invisible Man.* New York: Signet Books, 1947.

Florida teacher tries to keep job lost in fight on flag oath. *New York Times,* December 27, 1970, p. 41.

Fraser, C.G. Black prisoners finding new view of themselves as political prisoners. *New York Times,* September 16, 1971, p. 49.

Fried, J.P. Study finds steady rise in whites' acceptance of integration. *New York Times,* December 8, 1971, p. 34.

Glidewell, J.C. and Swallow, C.S. *The prevalence of maladjustment in elementary schools.* Chicago: University of Chicago, July 26, 1968.

Haley, A. *The Autobiography of Malcolm X.* New York: Grove Press, 1966.

Hannerz, U. *Soulside.* New York: Columbia University Press, 1969.

Heard, N.C. *Howard Street.* New York: Dial Press, 1968.

Henderson, S.E. Survival motion. In M. Cook and S.E. Henderson (Eds.), *The Militant Black Writer.* Madison, Wisc.: The University of Wisconsin Press, 1969.

Horton, J. Time and cool people. In L. Rainwater (Ed.), *Soul.* Chicago: Aldine, 1970.

Jenkins, R.L. Motivation and frustration in delinquency. *American Journal of Orthopsychiatry* 27: 528-537, 1957.

Jersey slates hearing on black flag issue. *New York Times,* January 11, 1972, p. 41.

The Joint Commission on Mental Health of Children, Inc. *Digest of crisis in child mental health: Challenge for the 1970's.* Washington, D.C.: The Joint Commission on Mental Health of Children, Inc., Fall 1969.

The Joint Commission on Mental Health of Children. *Crisis in child mental health: Challenge for the 1970's.* New York: Harper & Row, 1970.

Keil, C. *Urban Blues.* Chicago: The University of Chicago Press, 1966.

Kellam, S.G. and Schiff, S.K. Adaptation and mental illness in the first-grade classrooms of an urban community. *Poverty and Mental Health, Psychiatric Research Report,* No. 21, 1967, pp. 79-91.

Kochman, T. "Rapping" in the black ghetto. *Trans-Action* 6(4): 26-33, 1969.

Kochman, T. *Rappin' and Stylin' Out.* Chicago: University of Illinois Press, 1973.

Kochman, T. Toward an ethnography of black American speech behavior. In N.E. Whitten, Jr. and Jr. F. Szwed (Eds.), *Afro-American Anthropology: Contemporary Perspectives.* New York: The Free Press, 1970.

Lester, E. Growing up black and female. *New York Times,* July 11, 1971, p. D 5.

Liebow, E. *Tally's corner: A Study of Negro Streetcorner Men.* Boston: Little, Brown, 1966.

Mayer, M. The full and sometimes very surprising story of Ocean Hill, the teachers' union and the teacher strikes of 1968. *New York Times Magazine,* February 2, 1969, pp. 18-23, 42-43, 45, 48, 53, 56, 58, 62, 64-71.

Meriwether, L. *Daddy Was a Number Runner.* Englewood Cliffs, N.J.: Prentice-Hall, 1970.

Mezzrow, M. and Wolf, B. *Really the Blues.* New York: Signet Books, 1964.

Michigan reinstates teacher who sat during Anthem. *New York Times,* April 30, 1972, p. 14.

National School Public Relations Association. *High School Student Unrest.* Washington, D.C.: National School Public Relations Association, 1969.

9 tomps inmates awarded high school diplomas. *New York Times,* October 12, 1972, p. 51.

Pharr, R.D. *The Book of Numbers.* New York: Doubleday, 1969.

Popham, J.N. State rests case in youth's killing. *New York Times,* September 23, 1955, p. 15.

Principal accused of pledge coercion. *New York Times*, December 12, 1970, p. 18.

Rogers, C.R. Mental-health findings in three elementary schools. *Educational Research Bulletin* 21: 69-79, 86, 1942.

Sanders, R. *The Downtown Jews: Portraits of an Immigrant Generation*. New York: Harper & Row, 1969.

Schickel, R. Some lessons in growing up. The last picture show. *Life*, October 15, 1971, p. 14.

School trustee sues over flag. *New York Times*, December 3, 1971, p. 49.

Sinn, J.I. Pledge of Allegiance causes school problems. *Buffalo Courier-Express*, April 4, 1971, p. 43.

Smith, D. *A Walk in the City*. New York: World Publishing, 1961.

State school chief overrules Newark on black flag plan. *New York Times*, January 27, 1972, p. 1.

Sullivan, J.F. Argument heard on blacks' flag. *New York Times*, January 15, 1972, p. 35.

Teacher suspended over flag pledge: Community stirred. *New York Times*, October 24, 1971, p. 95.

Teacher upheld on flag pledge. *New York Times*, February 28, 1971, p. 43.

Thomas, P. *Down These Mean Streets*. New York: Alfred A. Knopf, 1967.

Thompson, S.D. A perspective on activism. In R.L. Hart & J.G. Saylor (Ed.), *Student Unrest: Threat or Promise*. Washington, D.C.: Association for Supervision and Curriculum Development, N.E.A., 1970.

Turner, V.H. Teachers' judgments of children's functioning by sex and social class of different social class and racial composition. Unpublished doctoral dissertation, Washington University, St. Louis, 1962.

2 held for trial in slaying of boy. *New York Times*, September 7, 1955, p. 15.

Vecsey, G. A scholar in the new Alcatraz. *New York Times*, October 2, 1972, pp. 1, 60.

The violent veterans. *Time*, March 13, 1972, pp. 45-46.

Weinraub, B. Poorer children in Britain found to lag both in health and mental development. *New York Times*, June 6, 1972, p. 2.

Williams, J.A. *The Man Who Cried I Am*. Boston: Little, Brown, 1967.

Williamson, H. *Hustler!* New York: Avon Books, 1965.

Wolfe, T. *Radical Chic and Mau-Mauing the Flak Catchers*. New York: Strauss & Giroux, 1970.

Wright, R. *Lawd Today*. New York: Walker and Company, 1963.

Yurick, S. *The Warriors*. New York: Holt, Rinehart & Winston, 1965.

Chapter Three

A Historical Perspective Concerning Inner City Conditioning Experiences

It is a community where rage always lurks just below the surface and often erupts in acts of seemingly mindless violence. It is a place where a dissenter at a meeting of a model cities policy committee was murdered by being dragged into the street and thrown under a moving car. It is where a youngster outside intermediate school No. 155 on Jackson Avenue in Mott Haven was nearly stomped to death in an argument over a bottle of soda pop.

> —M. Tolchin, "South Bronx: A Jungle Stalked by Fear, Seized by Rage," *New York Times* (January 15, 1973), p. 19.

In some neighborhoods boys went to and from school in parties, to insure safety against attack by gangs of enemies or toughs slightly older. Tenth and Fourteenth Warders on opposite sides of the Bowery were hereditary enemies. A boy from one ward ventured into the other only at the risk of black eyes, split lips, and ruined clothing. Pitched battles were fought across the frontier along the Bowery itself; and when word flashed up and down the street, "De Tent' and Fourteent' is fightin' again!" loyal partisans joyously hastened from all quarters to the fray. Stones, brickbats, and oyster shells flew like hail, to the great menace of noncombatants—until at last came the crash of a merchant's window or a cry of "cheese it, de cop!" and the armies vanished like fog before the sun.

> —A.F. Harlow, *Old Bowery Days*, 1931.

As suggested in Chapter Two, there are at least four classifications of student behavior in inner city classrooms housing large numbers of lower class urban black youngsters. It must also be emphasized that not all these children are either emotionally disturbed, socially maladjusted, or retarded. Many of them are very middle class.

All inner city children, however, are exposed to some degree to negative conditioning experiences that include, among others, racism, delinquency, gangs, poor housing, crime, violence, drugs, and lower class physicalness.

Unquestionably, many inner city children are also exposed to positive conditioning experiences. However, we must realize that continual exposure to the maladies associated with lower class or slum life style must have some effect upon the child's behavior, particularly as it is played out in the inner city classroom.

Indeed, those life styles that are most predominant among the very poor tend to be most damaging to a child's mental health. Although these life styles are adaptive to poverty living, "the patterns interact with many stresses of economic deprivation and tend to limit the growing child's opportunity for positive mental health (Joint Commission, 1970, p. 265)." Research findings, although inconclusive and fragmentary, suggest the seriousness of the problem.

> An overview of related studies strongly suggests that very poor people, to a greater extent than others, often fail to adopt child-rearing and family life patterns which research indicates are associated with children judged to be mentally healthy in our society (Joint Commission, 1970, p. 265).

With this in mind, it is foolish to believe that all inner city children will behave: (1) one way in the streets and another way in school, and (2) like middle class children. It is inevitable that some inner city children will bring their streetcorner life style into the school. This is particularly true in a crisis of unfamiliar situation where those involved in the altercation or misunderstanding may revert to their more familiar behavior or provoke others to act. Salisbury (1958), in writing about gang problems, points out how uncertainty about this behavior can affect teaching and learning.

> ... when you have large numbers of these youngsters in a school, when they have, like Pavlov's dogs, been subjected to so many bewildering shocks by life that their reaction patterns become erratic, unpredictable and frequently dangerous to themselves and others, you introduce a very uncertain factor into the classroom. Trouble may break out at any time—and for no reason which even an alert teacher necessarily observes. It may have a source far away from the study section. Knowledge that she is conducting her lessons in a situation which may suddenly explode can unnerve a teacher—to the point that she herself triggers the outburst by revealing a lack of certainty of control (pp. 136-137).

It is because we have denied the possibility that this streetcorner life style is being played out in the classrooms that we have contributed to our problems in inner city schools. We have been influenced too much by the advocates of the simplistic "there are no bad boys," or "all you need is a well planned lesson," or "that is not our responsibility. Suspend them." We have to become more realistic and pragmatic in our attempts at educating inner city or poor youngsters. To this end we must look at the factors that affect the inner city youngster's life space—the factors, in addition to his family, that mold and shape his behavior.

Three of the many negative inner city life style conditioning experiences that affect this child, and which in turn affect his classroom behavior, are (1) juvenile delinquency and crime, (2) gangs, and (3) physicalness and violence. These are the areas that appear to cause consternation among middle class adults and school personnel. Hence, they cause problems in school which interfere with instruction.

GANGS

There is some disagreement over the amount of crime and violence that juvenile gangs and groups are responsible for. Nevertheless, the Task Force on Individual Acts of Violence (Mulvihill, D.J. & Tumin, M.M., 1969) reported significant involvement by gangs in certain areas of crime and violence.

> These figures are crude, and more refined work is obviously necessary. When combined with the foregoing literature, however, the information does lead us to believe that gangs and groups are responsible for a very small proportion of the urban criminal homicides and aggravated assaults in this country, but that they are involved in a significant percentage of all robberies and, to a lesser extent, of all forcible rapes. The implication, in turn, is that the dominant form of serious violence committed by juvenile or youthful gang is much more likely to be robbery than murder, assault, or rape (pp. 609-610).

Recently there has been increased reporting of violent crimes that are allegedly related to gang conflicts. Supposedly, gangs and the problems they cause have returned to our larger Northern and Western cities—if, in fact, they were ever gone. Gang violence appears to follow a cyclical pattern through the years with some differences in each cycle. In the early '50s we had the "bopping" or fighting gangs with mass fights or "rumbles" between gangs as they guarded their "turf," territory, or neighborhood. In the mid '50s, drugs and street workers appeared to be taking over and the gangs supposedly began to wane.

According to Miller (1969), however, gangs have always been with us; ". . . the urban adolescent street gang is as old as the American City (p. 11)."

. . . Gangs in the 1910's and the 20's were attributed to the cultural dislocations and community disorganization accompanying the mass immigration of foreigners; in the 30's to the enforced idleness and economic pressures produced by the Great Depression; in the 50's to the emotional disturbance of parents and children caused by the increased stresses and tensions of modern life. At present, the existence of gangs is widely attributed to a range of social injustices; racial discrimination, unequal educational and work opportunities, resentment over inequalities in the distribution of wealth and privilege in an affluent society, and the ineffective or oppressive policies of service agencies such as the police and the schools (Miller, W.B., 1969, p. 12).

In discussing the gangs of the late '50s, Salisbury (1958) also notes some earlier New York City gangs. A generation earlier, such gangs as the Navy Street Boys, the Red Hook Boys, the Coney Island Boys, and the Garfield Boys used bricks, sticks, and fists to rule their areas. "They used to haul ashcans of cinders and broken glass up to the roofs of the four-story houses and dump them on passersby (p. 9)."

Historically, there were gangs in New York City as early as 1728. White boys formed the Vly gang (from the Vly Market), the Broadway Boys, and the Bowery Boys. Negro boys formed the Fly Boys and the Long Bridge Boys, the name for the latter coming from either the bridge at the foot of Wall Street, the Coffee House Bridge, or the bridge over the sewer at the foot of Broad Street. The reporting of the earlier gang fights sounds similar to the reporting of gangs of later and probably earlier generations of gangs, though the weapons are different.

> There were great hills of tanbark in the swamp district which the warriors utilized as lookouts and redoubts. Their conflicts, especially when they fought with slings and stones, sometimes became a serious menace, not only to their own persons but to those of innocent bystanders. When they clashed in Pearl Street or Maiden Lane, shopkeepers hastily put up shutters over their windows and pedestrians fled for their lives (Harlow, 1931, p. 185).

Just as today, gangs organized alliances to ward off encroaching powers. The Broadway Boys gang allied with the Smit's Vly Boys to fight the Bowery Boys gang from the North,

> . . . with whom they had each separately contended, the dissemination of whose principles they dreaded, and whose strength, from the rapid increase of population in that quarter, threatened to overwhelm their southerly and more civilized neighbors. The battles between the allies and the Bowery Boys were frequently fought on and around Bunker Hill, sometimes with armies of twenty to fifty

on a side. The Grand Streeters and the Spring Streeters were two other youthful clans who fought many a lively skirmish in the early decades of the century (Harlow, 1931, p. 186).

During the first ten to fifteen years of its existence, the Five Points area was a relatively peaceful and decent place: one policeman could preserve order. By about 1820, however, " a regiment would have been unable to cope with the turbulent citizenry of Paradise Square, and rout the gangsters and other criminals from the dens and burrows (Asbury, 1970, p. 9)." Respectable families began to leave the area and freed slaves and "low class" Irish began to move in as part of the first big wave of post Revolutionary War immigration. "They crowded indiscriminately into the old rookeries of The Points, and by 1840 the district had become the most dismal slum in America (p. 9)."

The tenements, dance halls, and saloons were the genesis of the original Five Points gangs. About 1825, greengrocery speakeasies opened and in their back rooms these gangs were organized into working gang units.

> This room became the haunt of thugs, pickpockets, murderers, and thieves. The gang known as the Forty Thieves, which appears to have been the first in New York with a definite, acknowledged leadership, is said to have been formed in Rosanna Peers' grocery store, and her back room was used as a meeting-place, and headquarters by . . . eminent chieftans (p. 21).

Such gangs as the Kerrigonians (from County Kerry, Ireland), the Roach Guards, the Chichesters, the Plug Uglies, and the Dead Rabbits[a] were organized and met in various grocery stores, "and in time these emporiums came to be regarded as the worst dens of the Five Points, and the centers of its infamy and crimes (p. 22)."

Just as today's gangs wear the "colors," the Five Points gangs had their colors too. The Dead Rabbits wore a red stripe on their pantaloons and when they went into battle a guidon (flag) with a dead rabbit was carried. The Roach Guards adopted only the red stripe on their pantaloons as a battle uniform. The uniform of the Shirt Tails obviously was shirt tails hanging outside their trousers. The Plug Uglies,[b] mainly big Irishmen, received their name from the enormous wool and leather stuffed plug hats they wore pulled down over their ears to serve as a battle helmet. In the ranks of the Plug Uglies were some of the toughest fighters of the time.

[a]A rabbit was a rowdy in the slang of that time. Originally, the Dead Rabbits were a faction of the Roach Guards. During a stormy meeting of the Roach Guards, marked by internal dissension, a dead rabbit was thrown into the center of the meeting room. Whereupon, one of the dissident factions took it up as their name and standard.

[b]The term *plug ugly* has carried over to today's slang. According to Wentworth & Flexner (1960, p. 398), a *plug ugly* is "a hoodlum; a tough or ugly-looking ruffian . . . a strong, ugly, uncouth man; a rowdy; a tough guy" (p. 398).

> Even the most ferocious of the Paradise Square eye-gougers and mayhem artists cringed when a giant Plug Ugly walked abroad looking for trouble, with a huge bludgeon in one hand, a brickbat in the other, a pistol peeping from his pocket and his tall hat jammed down over his ears and all but obscuring his fierce eyes. He was adept at rough and tumble fighting, and wore heavy boots studded with great hobnails with which he stamped his prostrate and helpless victim (Asbury, 1970, p. 22).

Most of the gang members were young men, some of them being mere boys (Headley, 1971, p. 131). Five Pointer gangs fought in their undershirts after removing their shirts and coats. Although the Five Points gangs fought each other, they made common cause when fighting the Bowery or waterfront gangs, or the police.

Gradually, the Bowery superseded the Five Points as an amusement area, and gangs began to form in the Bowery too. The O'Connell Guards, the True Blue Americans, the American Guards, the Atlantic Guards, and the famous Bowery Boys were the most important gangs in the Bowery's early days, according to Asbury. The primarily Irish gangs of the Bowery were not as ferocious as were the Five Points gangs, although they were good fighters.

During the 1850s such street gangs as the Forty Thieves, the Hudson Dusters, the Plug Uglies, the Dead Rabbits, and the Slaughter Housers, held whole areas of New York City in their grips. Savage battles were fought by these gangs in the streets in which it was not uncommon for fifteen to twenty to be killed. The police were often fearful of entering some of their neighborhoods. The police were sometimes unable to stop the gang fights and had to call for the aid of the National Guard or the Army.

The Dead Rabbits and the Bowery Boys had many bitter fights, and maintained a vicious feud. Rarely did a week pass without at least one brawl. These gangs participated in the greatest gang fights of the nineteenth century.

> Sometimes the battles raged for two or three days without cessation, while the streets of the gang area were barricaded with carts and paving stones, and the gangsters blazed away at each other with musket and pistol, or engaged in close work with knives, brickbats, bludgeons, teeth, and fists. On the outskirts of the struggling mob of thugs ranged the women, their arms filled with reserve ammunition, their keen eyes watching for a break in the enemy's defense, and always ready to lend a hand or a tooth in the fray (p. 29).

One such fight between the Dead Rabbits and the Bowery Boys occurred on July 4th and 5th, 1857, and turned into a riot when the gangs and their allies made common cause first against the police and then against the police and the Army. At times the fighting was hand-to-hand and bloody. Clubs, bludgeons, muskets, paving stones, axes, pistols, brickbats, knives, and pitch-forks were used.

The riot was touched off when the Five Points gangs, except for the Roach Guards led by the Plug Uglies and the Dead Rabbits, started their Fourth of July celebration by raiding No. 42 Bowery, which was the clubhouse of the Bowery Boys and the Atlantic Guards. The Bowery gangs managed to repulse and drive the attacking gangs back to the Five Points.

The next morning, however, the Five Points gangs, now joined by the Roach Guards and armed with large paving blocks and iron bars, attacked the Green Dragon, a favorite hangout of the Bowery Boys and other Bowery gangs. The Bowery gangs were surprised and the Five Pointers wrecked their barroom, ripped up the dance floor, and drank all their liquor. The Atlantic Guards, and other Bowery gangs who owed their loyalty and allegiance, now joined the Bowery Boys. The Five Points and Bowery gangs joined in battle at Bayard Street in downtown Manhattan, and "began the most ferocious free-for-all in the history of the City (Asbury, 1970, p. 113)."

> Barricades were now erected, behind which the mob rallied, and the contest assumed the aspects of a regular battle. . . . Captain Rynders came on the ground, and attempted to restore quiet. Not succeeding, however, he . . . told Commissioner Draper, if he had not police force enough to disperse the mob, he should call out the military. The latter replied that he had made a requisition on Major-General Sanford, for three regiments, and that they would soon be on the ground. . . . The police then in two bodies of seventy-five men each, and supported, one by the Seventy-first Regiment and the other by the Eighth, marched down White and Worth Streets. This formidable display of force overawed the rioters, and they fled in every direction. This ended the riot, although the military were kept on duty during the night (Headley, 1971, p. 133).

During the two days of fighting, at least eight men were known killed and over a hundred were injured; at least fifty of these remained hospitalized for treatment. It was believed that many more dead were secretly carried away and buried by the gangs (Asbury, p. 116).

June Lazare (1966), in her "Folk Songs of New York City," sings of the fight between the Dead Rabbits and the Bowery Boys.[c]

> They had a dreadful fight, upon Saturday night,
> The papers gave the news accordin',
> Guns, pistols, clubs, and sticks, hot water, and old bricks,
> Which drove them on the other side of Jordan.

[c]June Lazare, "Dead Rabbits Fight with the Bowery Boys," *Folk Songs of New York City*, Folkways Record Album No. FH 5276.

Then pull off the old coat and roll up the sleeve,
Bayard is a hard street to travel.
Pull off the old coat and roll up the sleeve,
The Bloody Sixth is a hard ward to travel, I believe.

Like wild dogs they did fight, this fourth of April night,
Of course they laid their plans accordin'.
Some were wounded, and some killed, and lots of blood was
    spilled
In the fight on the other side of Jordan.

The new police did join the Bowery boys in line,
With orders strict and right accordin',
Bullets, clubs, and bricks did fly, and many groan and die.
Hard road to travel over Jordan.

When the police did interfere, this made the Rabbits sneer,
And very much enraged them accordin'.
With bricks they did go in, determined for to win,
And drive them on the other side of Jordan.

At last the battle closed, yet few that night reposed,
For frightful were their dreams accordin'.
For the devil on two sticks was a marching on the bricks,
All night on the other side of Jordan.

Many of the women were ferocious fighters. During the Draft Riots
the women inflicted some of the most horrendous and fiendish tortures upon
the soldiers, policemen, and Negroes who were unlucky to be captured by the
mob. The women sliced their flesh with butcher knives, ripped out tongues and
eyes, and "applied the torch after the victims had been sprayed with oil and
hanged to trees (Asbury, 1970, p. 19)."

In the slums, the gang boy's elders also were organized into gangs.
Although these groups were small at first, they soon grew in size. These gangs
started as petty thieves who also fought for their neighborhoods for the fun of
fighting. Gradually, however, some of them became very much involved as
predators and as tools of politicians (Harlow, 1931).

In the early days before the Civil War, the composition and
objectives of the gangs began to change. In the 1830s district and ward political
leaders began to purchase saloons, dance houses, and the greengrocery speakeasies in which many of the gangs congregated, while also taking houses of
prostitution and gambling under their protective wings. Hence we had the
beginning of the amalgamation of the underworld of the gangs with the
politicians.

The underworld thus became an important factor in politics, and under the manipulation of the worthy statesmen the gangs of the Bowery and Five Points participated in the great series of riots which began with the spring election disturbances of 1834 and continued, with frequent outbreaks, for half a score of years. In this period occurred the Flour and Five Points riots, and the most important of the Abolition troubles, while there were at least two hundred battles between the gangs, and innumerable conflicts between volunteer fire companies (Asbury, 1970, p. 37).

From about 1731, when the first two fire engines were brought to New York City from England, until 1865 when the New York City fire department was municipalized, there appear to have been ongoing physical and violent conflicts between various volunteer fire companies (Botkin, 1954, p. 251), gangs, and guard target groups. Most often, the gangs were members of the fire companies, while many of the guard groups grew from the fire companies. According to Botkin, the fire company rivalries heightened during the 1830-1850 riot era when election and abolition disturbances and outbreaks by the criminal gangs of the Bowery and the Five Points tore New York City.

The volunteer fire companies were an odd lot. In addition to their membership of Bowery, Five Points gangs, and other area gangs, their membership consisted of many eminent personages. Indeed, the volunteers were powerful politically. In addition to the gang members, important politicians such as William M. (Boss) Tweed also belonged to the volunteer fire brigades. And for a short period while he resided in New York City, George Washington was head of the New York Department (Asbury, p. 31).

Costello (1887, p. 19), reported on the political power of certain politicians who refused to punish those who had caused problems for the fire brigades. In particular, Costello wrote about Chief Carson's 1843 report, that was

> ...mainly taken up with the troubles existing among certain inharmonious bodies of fire brigades. From this it appears that William M. Tweed, the one-time boss, and then foreman of Engine Company No. 6, was expelled for leading in an attack on Hose Company No. 31, and his company suspended for three months. The Common Council, however, to the deep disgust of Chief Carson, failed to ratify this sentence, and Mr. Tweed was let off with a suspension of three months (p. 19).

Another complaint of Chief Carson was against "the outrageous spirit of rowdyism of certain clubs of desperate fighting men called 'Short Boys,' 'Old Maid's Boys,' 'Rock Boys,' etc. . . . ." Apparently these gangs or clubs were patterned after similar groups in London and Paris. They appeared to have spent a goodly amount of time attacking the firemen. According to Chief Carson, these clubs

> . . . make deliberate and bloody attacks on our firemen while going to and returning from fires, destroying the apparatus, and often, by stratagem, putting certain companies in collision with each other, individual members against each other, and creating in every way endless broil and confusion in the Department. . . . I have had many of these villains . . . arrested for upsetting our engines, cutting the hose, beating our firemen almost to death, etc., but they were no sooner in prison than the captains of police, the aldermen, and judges of police, would discharge them, to commit fresh attacks on the firemen the following night. . . . "But why," he asks, desperately, "recount these daily and daring outrages, when these bloodthirsty creatures are thus encouraged and liberated by aldermen, on whose conscientious watchfulness and unsullied integrity the people rely for the incarceration and severe punishment of these abandoned and heartless fiends" (Costello, 1887, p. 118).

In the summer of 1842, suggestions were made to prevent young men and boys who were not members of the Department from interfering with the firemen performing their duties. Even where some volunteer companies were disbanded for fighting and rioting, their members attached themselves to other companies and there, too, caused problems.

> Serious and disgraceful fights and riots had occurred in the autumn of 1843 between different fire companies, principally originating with low and violent characters whose respective companies had been disbanded and broken up by the corporation, and who attached themselves to others on occasions of fires, to create fights and disorder, thus degrading the character and impairing the usefulness and discipline of the Fire Department (Costello, 1887, p. 107).

In an attempt to overcome such outrages against the firemen, Chief C.V. Anderson requested the establishment of a twenty-man fire police group. However, nothing seemed to help. The volunteers fought over everything. They fought as they ran to the fires, and they even fought over the hydrants. According to Botkin (1954) the firemen even organized special groups of tough fighters who would run to the fire ahead of their engine. Once at the fire, they would place a small barrel over the hydrant or cistern to wait until their crew arrived. Needless to say, the firemen often spent more time fighting one another than they did fires. Many instances of fighting among the fire departments have been recorded.

> The possession of a hydrant convenient to the fire was greatly to be desired, and frequently the occasion of disturbance between rival

claimants. Many have been the hydrant-fights which were settled by the superior prowess of one of the claimants, or by the opportune arrival of an engineer or the police (Sheldon, 1882, p. 170).

A fireman has been known to cover a hydrant with a convenient barrel, thus concealing it from rival companies, and keeping it until his own company should arrive. Woe be to him if his rivals should detect the artifice (Costello, 1887, p. 171)!

Like a flash through a train of powder, the fray was joined all along the ropes, a distance of nearly a block, and near a thousand men were fighting. The din was frightful—curses, yells, the whack of huge fists against hard skulls and massive torsos, the roar of the onlooking mob, greedy for action and gore. The fighters were so crowded that a defeated brave scarcely had room to fall, and more than one man knocked cold was held upright by the jam around him. If he fell, he was in danger of being trampled to death by the boots of friend and foe (Botkin, 1954, p. 68).

During the year 1853 several extremely violent fights took place between fire companies. Pistols and other dangerous weapons had been brought into requisition, and the apparatus upset and nearly destroyed (Costello, 1887, p. 123).

Traversing Chatham Square it was evident that the conflict was imminent, and both sides began to "peel" for it, some even taking off their shirts. Jim Jeroloman removed his earrings and put them in his pocket. As they passed into the narrow bottle neck at the beginning of the Bowery, the pressure of the crowds on either side forced the two lines into collision. Instantly Jeroloman dropped his rope and swung at McClusky, and the battle was on (Botkin, 1954, p. 68).

In one battle on July 26, 1846, five companies of volunteer firemen fought.

The battle had raged all the way to Canal and Hudson Streets, and attracted an immense crowd of citizens (Costello, 1887, p. 173). . . .

The rowdies have for a long time remained quiet and it was hoped that the Department would not again be molested by them. But of late three attacks had been made. In one case Engine Company No. 41 was proceeding at great speed to a fire, when they were set upon by these miscreants with clubs, slung-shots, and stones. . . . Another, . . . [was] attacked while attending to their duty, the men driven away, and the carriage upset in the street. The third was an attack . . . by a gang of rowdies. It was useless to look to the police justices for redress, for it was well known they dared not grant it, the political influences of the gangs being so great (Costello, 1887, p. 134). . . .

There were many fights, and hot ones, too, in the old department, but they grew out of a natural emulation and were not lacking in a certain rugged element of chivalry which promoted manhood, though somewhat at the expense of public order. The murderous revolver and assassin-like disposition which now mark its use were unknown in those days. The combats were fair hand-to-hand fights between man and man, and he who resorted to any other weapon than those which nature supplied was accounted a ruffian or a coward (Costello, 1887, p. 172).

In addition to fighting and rioting, some of the volunteer firemen also participated in thievery. According to Campbell (1892), when there was a fire, the firemen would strip many of the stores in the neighborhood of their contents, particularly if one of the stores happened to be a clothing store. It was just thievery on the part of Bowery "roughs," "toughs," or "Bowery b'hoys" that helped legislate the volunteer fire departments out of existence.

While a bill for the abolition of the volunteer fire department was before the State Assembly, with some doubt about its passage, a fire broke out in a large clothing-store. During the conflagration several firemen were killed by falling walls; when their corpses were taken from the ruins some of them were found to have on overcoats from which the dealer's tickets inside the collars had not been removed. This circumstance at once secured the passage of the bill through the Legislature, as it sustained one of the charges that had been made against the old organization (Campbell, 1892, pp. 529-530).

The Gulick Guards, who took their name from Chief Engineer James Gulick, had as their motto "Firemen with Pleasure—Soldiers at Leisure." From 1855 through 1861, guard groups going on target "excursions" were a great feature in New York City. When the Civil War call to arms came to New York City, in 1861, there existed a "considerable hodgepodge of militia and of unofficial military and target companies, in various stages of drill and equipment (Harlow, 1931, p. 337)."

As noted, many of these guard units had their origins with various fire companies (Costello, 1887, p. 190) and dated back to the 1840s. And many of the Bowery and Five Points gangs assumed names such as the American Guards and the O'Connell Guards. Asbury (1970, p. 38) reports on a fight between them.

The Bowery gang known as the American Guards, the members of which prided themselves on their native ancestry, was soon devoted-ly attached to the Native Americans party, and responded joyfully to the appeals of its ward heelers and district leaders. During the summer of 1835, about a year after the election riots, bitter enmity developed between this gang and the O'Connell Guards, which had been organized under the aegis of a Bowery liquor seller, and was the particular champion of the Irish element of Tammany Hall. These gangs came to blows on June 21, 1835, at Grand and Crosby Streets on the lower East Side. The fighting spread as far as the Five Points, where the gangsters of Paradise Square took a hand and the rioting became general throughout that part of the city. The Mayor and the Sheriff called out every watchman in the city, and the force managed to stop the fighting without the aid of soldiers, although several companies were mustered and remained in their armories overnight (p. 38).

John Allison (1948) immortalized the "goings-on" of the various pre-Civil War gangs, volunteer firemen and guard groups through his song "The Bowery Grenadiers."[d]

> We're a gal-lant bunch of he-roes,
> We've been or-ganized ten years,
> We're known a-bout the cit-y as the BOWE-RY GREN-A-DIERS.
> We've had three fights with the Hoo-li-hans
> And won ten-thou-sand cheers, . . .
>> We can lick the Brook-lyn guards
>> If they on-ly show their cards,
>> We can run like the dev-il (When the ground is lev-el) for about
>>> four hun-dred yards . . .
> (Should the) la-dies be in dan-ger
> When the flames a-round them roar,
> We're the lads who fight through fire and smoke for a res-cue safe
>> and sure.
> But when we march of Sun-day
> And the Mul-li-gans beat ta too,
> We're good old stock with a cob-cle rock and a length of gas
>> pipe too. . . .
> We're the toughs with the cuffs,
> We're THE BOWE-RY GREN-A-DIERS![e]

[d]Mr. John Allison, who was 88 years of age in January 1973, reports that "the item done by Mitch Miller is a patched together job from the memories of both my friend Ted Dibble and myself. He and I heard it back in about 1924 as done by a Dr. Holmes in Englewood, New Jersey. The doctor used to bat it out in his key-of-C chords on the Holmes piano for the amusement of us youngsters. . . . I have no idea where Dr. Holmes heard the song—it may even be that he dated back to those days of the fire laddies. . . ." (from personal correspondence with Mr. John Allison).

[e]"The Bowery Grenadiers," *Mitch's Greatest Hits*, Columbia CL 1544.

While the members of the Dead Rabbits, Bowery Boys, and similar gangs were often thieves, and occasionally murderers, they were primarily street fighters and brawlers and partook of their battling openly in the streets. The newer gangs, however, were thieves and killers first.

Following the post Revolutionary War wave of immigration, by about 1840 the wealthier residents had already moved northward. Rows of rundown tenements replaced the mansions of the wealthy. By 1845, the Fourth Ward was a hotbed of crime. River gangs such as the Patsy Conroys, Short Tails, Swamp Angels, Hookers, Buckoos, Daybreak Boys, Border Gang, and the Slaughter Housers ravaged all who entered the area. According to Asbury (1970, p. 49), "No human life was safe, and a well-dressed man venturing into the district was commonly set upon and murdered or robbed, or both, before he had gone a block."

Howlet and Saul, who became captains of the Daybreak Boys in 1850 and terrorized the East River until 1859, had joined the gang when they were fifteen and sixteen. Many of the other gang members were even younger, some as young as ten and twelve. None of the gang members was older than twenty years when they had already gained reputations as cutthroats and murderers, according to Asbury (p. 67). The police finally succeeded in driving the gangsters and gangs out of the Fourth Ward by the end of the Civil War. By 1900 the Steamboat Squad, which was organized in 1876, had managed to drive the organized gangs out of the waterfront.

As America grew through immigration, and ecological use changes came about in the cities, new gangs arose, remained awhile, and then disappeared. In some cases, remaining gang members joined up with the newer gangs, became independent criminals, or took over the leadership of criminal groups.

There were the Honeymoon gangs that operated in the middle East Side's Eighteenth Ward in 1853. And in 1855 it was estimated that 30,000 men were aligned with the gang leaders and through them to the corrupt political leaders of Tammany Hall, Native American Party or Know Nothing Party as they plundered the New York City treasury (Asbury, 1970, p. 104-105).

Those who are appalled at today's gang actions or the rioting of students, the blacks, or the police, should look closely at the Draft Riots in New York City in July 1863. The riots lasted for five days and were started when the Black Jack Volunteer Engine Company No. 33 attempted to destroy the records and wheel used in picking their leader's draft number (Asbury, 1970, p. 127).

It was estimated that between 50,000 and 70,000 rioters were engaged in looting, burning, and killing during the week of rioting, and that some of the individual mobs were made up of at least 10,000 men and women. The majority of the rioters were Irish because the criminal and gangster elements of New York City then were mostly Irish.

For the most part they were the human sweepings of European cities who had been packed into ships during the forties and fifties and dumped in ever-increasing numbers upon American shores. A vast majority landed in New York and remained there, and soon found their natural levels in the great gangs of the Bowery, the Five Points and other areas into which the gangsters had spread and become firmly entrenched. It was these gangsters swarming from their holes at the first indication of trouble that formed the organized nuclei around which the rioters rallied (Asbury, 1970, p. 120).

Amassed against the rioters were 2,297 men of the Metropolitan Police Force, and between seven and ten thousand Army and National Guard troops. Also included were approximately a dozen artillery batteries that poured grape and cannister (shot) into the mobs surging through Manhattan. Although the casualties of fighting were never figured exactly, they were estimated to be as high as some Revolutionary battles and even such Civil War battles as Bull Run and Shiloh.

Conservative estimates were about 8,000 wounded and 2,000 killed. Most of these casualties were rioters. Although only three policemen were killed, almost every man on the force was wounded. The armed forces had about 300 wounded and 50 killed. The rioters hanged eighteen Negroes; 70 others were reported missing. The law authorities confiscated 11,000 firearms such as pistols and muskets plus a few thousand bludgeons and other weapons. The estimate of property loss was five million dollars. Over 100 buildings were burned and about 200 were damaged and looted (Asbury, 1971, pp. 169-170).

In New York City after the Civil War a gang known as the Whyos arose, supposedly from the Chichesters of the Old Five Points, and lasted into the middle nineties. The gang was made up of sneak thieves, burglars, pick-pockets, and murderers. The Whyos also advertised murder and mayhem for money. For example—punching for $2.00; stabbing for $25.00; and doing the "big job $100.00 and up (Asbury, 1970, p. 28)."

During this period New York had such gangs as the Rag Gang, the Hartly Mob, and The Molasses Gang. And, in about 1868, the Hell's Kitchen Gang was organized. Meanwhile, such gangs as the Stable Gang, the Silver Gang, and Potashes, and the Boodle Gang were operating on the lower West Side of Manhattan.

From many of the ethnic and racial gangs in immigrant neighbor-hoods came the criminals and hoods of the next generation. In the early 1900s, under Tim Sullivan, there arose two great racial mobs, Jews under Monk Eastman operating from the Bowery, and Italians under Paul Kelly operating in the Fourth and Sixteenth Wards just west of the Bowery. "Out of these two groups came the majority of the vicious criminals who pestered and disgraced New York during the first two decades of the century. . . . (Harlow, 1931, p. 501)," and who educated the next generation of thugs and criminals.

Unquestionably, the adult gangs had an effect on the footloose children of the immigrants who roamed their neighborhoods. Asbury (1970), writing in 1927, reported an "enormous increase in the number of Juvenile gangsters, who were to provide material for street gangs of the nineties and the early part of the present century (p. 238)." Prior to the Civil War, adult and juvenile gangs operated largely in the Bowery, the Five Points, and the Fourth Ward,

> ... simply because these were the congested and poverty stricken areas of the city; as the slums increased in extent, gangsters of all types and ages multiplied in numbers and power. By 1870 the streets throughout the greater part of New York fairly swarmed with prowling bands of homeless boys and girls actively developing the criminal instinct which is inherent in every human being. While all of these gangs chose their titular leaders from their own ranks, a majority were at the same time under the domination of adult gangsters or professional thieves, who taught the children to pick pockets, snatch purses and muffs, and steal everything they could lay their hands upon, while they masked their real business by carrying bootblack outfits, baskets of flowers, or bundles of news-papers. They lived on the docks, in the cellars and basements of dives and tenements, and in alleys and area ways; and when their masters could not feed them, which was often, they ate from swill barrels and garbage pails (pp. 238-239).

The Reverend J.F. Richmond (1873), although not mentioning gangs per se, also wrote about the large numbers of children roaming the streets of New York City and about the institutions responsible for juvenile delin-quents.

> Every great city contains a large floating population whose in-dolence, prodigality, and intemperance are proverbial, culminating in great domestic and social evil. From these discordant circles spring an army of neglected or ill-trained children, devoted to vagrancy and crime, who early find their way into the almshouse or the prison, and continue a life-long burden upon the community. It becomes the duty of the guardians of the public weal to search out methods for the relief of society from these intolerable burdens, and the recovery of the wayward as far as possible. That a necessity existed for the establishment of this institution, appears from the fact that two companies of distinguished philanthropists ... arose in the autumn of 1849, to inaugurate some movement for the suppression of juvenile crime. ... they were happily united, and after ... re-peated appeals to the Legislature, the New York Juvenile Asylum was incorporated June 30, 1851 (pp. 328-329).
>
> The children who come under the care of the society are between the ages of five and fourteen, and may for the sake of brevity be divided into two general classes. First, the truant and disobedient;

secondly, the friendless and neglected. The first are either voluntarily surrendered by their parents for discipline, or committed by the magistrates for reformation. The second class found in a state of friendlessness and want, or of abandonment, or vagrancy, may be committed by the mayor, recorder, any alderman or magistrate of the city (p. 330).

. . . of the fifteen thousand three hundred and thirty-six children admitted since its opening in January, 1853, only sixty-three have died, and during 1864-65 but one death occurred.

The correctives applied are mainly moral, the rod being very rarely employed (p. 331).

Reverend Richmond (1873) also reported on the Society for the Reformation of Juvenile Delinquents.

The House of Refuge, under the control of the "Society for the Reformation of Juvenile Delinquents," . . . was incorporated in 1824. . . . Thousands of children in our great cities and towns are constantly growing up in ignorance and neglect, many homes being little less than schools of vice. A consciousness of guilt, attended with imprisonment and disgrace, crushes what little of self-respect and laudable ambition may yet remain. To hurl these truant youth into a penitentiary, filled with mature and expert criminals, is but to cultivate their treacherous tendencies, and insure their final ruin (p. 568).

Richmond (1873) also reported on the institutions on Hart Island in New York City. One was The Industrial School and The School Ship.

The number of vagrant, vicious, and adventurous children around New York is so great, that a new institution for their correction and reformation springs up every few years, . . . the buildings are always full, and the supply well nigh inexhaustible. for years past a class of large vicious boys have been thrown on the hands of the Commissioners of Charities and Corrections, for whom it has been difficult to well and suitably provide. If sent to the Workhouse or Penitentiary, they would be further steeped in evil, and if sent to the Nurseries, their insubordination incited the younger and more dutiful to mischief and demoralization. Hence, after the purchase of Hart Island, which occurred in May, 1868, they were placed there in the capacity of an *Industrial School* (p. 572).

. . . The school began late in the year 1868, and on the 31st of December, 1868, the warden reported the reception of 504 boys. The utter neglect under which they had thus far grown up appears in the fact that seventy-five per cent of them could neither read nor write, fifteen per cent able to read only, leaving out ten per cent in tolerable possession of the rudiments of an education.... During the last year 972 boys were received into the school.

Many boys in each generation are wild and adventurous in their natures, fond of excitements and dangers, and who will not sober down to the quietudes of ordinary industry. Neglected, they become the roughs, harbor thieves, pirates, and fillibusterers of the world. As early as 1812, Rev. Dr. Stanford, chaplain of the penal institutions of New York, recommended the separation of the youthful criminals from those more advanced, and urged the importance of training this adventurous class in a nautical ship for service on the sea.... The boys, whose features for the most part show their foreign origin and treacherous tendencies, are all clothed in bright sailor's uniform, and governed on the apprenticeship system of the United States Navy (p. 573).

The Reverend L.M. Pease arrived in the Five Points in 1850 and found a connection between the fighting and thieving adult gangs and the juvenile gangs. The Dead Rabbits had their Little Dead Rabbits, The Forty Thieves had their Little Forty Thieves, and the Plug Uglies had their Little Plug Uglies, all emulating the older gang members in action and speech, and wherever possible in dress. Along the waterfront in the Fourth Ward youngsters of eight to twelve were in the Little Daybreak Boys. Most of these youngsters strove to emulate and aid their elders in their criminal activities and act as lookouts, participants, and decoys. They also engineered their own escapades. The police believed that these juvenile gangs had also committed a number of murders. Interestingly, some of these earlier juvenile gangs also had female leaders (Asbury, 1970, p. 239).

With the Civil War over less than ten years, the slums of New York grew beyond the Bowery and the Five Points and so did the juvenile gangs. On the lower West Side, around Washington and Greenwich Streets, a group of sneak thieves and small beggars made life miserable for the householders and the merchants.

Of course the adult and juvenile gang activity had some effect upon the schools too. Harlow (1931, p. 444) reported on some of the problems faced by youngsters who wanted to to to school.

In some neighborhoods boys went to and from school in parties, to insure safety against attack by gangs of enemies or roughs slightly older. Tenth and Fourteenth Warders on opposite sides of the Bowery were hereditary enemies. A boy from one ward ventured into the other only at the risk of black eyes, split lips, and ruined clothing (p. 444).

Asbury (1970, p. 246), summed up the actions and activities of the pre-1900 gangs of New York City.

The character of the juvenile gangs changed in proportion to the increased activity of welfare agencies, better housing conditions, greater efficiency of the police and, especially, to reforms in the educational system which permitted effective supervision and regulation of the children of the tenement districts. It is quite likely that there are as many juvenile gangs in New York today as there have ever been. For forming in groups and fighting each other is part of the traditional spirit of play, but in general they have become much less criminal. Until recent years, when the custom has fallen somewhat into disuse, the election-night bonfires were a prolific source of fights between the juvenile gangs, for when one group ran short of material it raided the blazing heaps of wood around which another gang capered. These fights always resulted in a more or less permanent enmity, and election nights were followed for several weeks by frequent battles as the despoiled gang sought revenge. In many parts of the city, particularly the Harlem and upper East Side districts, the boys fought with wooden swords and used wash-boiler covers for shields. But invariably the excitement of battle overcame them and they resorted to bricks and stones, with the result that a few heads and many windows were broken (p. 246).

Most of the criminals and racketeers of the years from about 1900 to the 1930s spent their formative years prowling and fighting with juvenile gangs. Al Capone, for example, was born in Brooklyn, in 1899, and joined the waning Five Pointers while in his mid teens (Kobler, 1971).

The stark reality of gang activities and fighting is something that most urbanites and suburbanites fear but have very little experience with. Most of their experience has been vicarious. Sometimes the vacarious experience was visual and auditory, such as observing the Jets and the Sharks battling on the stage and screen in the musical *West Side Story*. The theory of social causation of gang participation was satirized as gang members analyzed themselves in "Gee, Officer Krupke!"

> Dear kind-ly Ser-geant Krup-ke,
> You got-ta un-der-stand,
> It's just our bring-in' up-ke
> That gets us outa hand.
> Our moth-ers all are junk-ies,
> Our fath-ers all are drunks.
> Gol-ly Mo-ses, nat-cher-ly we're punks!
> Gee, Of-fi-cer Krupke,
> We're ver-y upset;
> We nev-er had the love that ev-'ry child ought-a get.
> We ain't no de-lin-quents,

We're jus mis-un-der-stood.
Deep down in-side us there is good!

Transcriptions from some of my own tapes made with Brooklyn gang members in the '50s sound different.

"On the Corner of Honky Tonk Street
Out jumped the Chaplains in a black sedan
Pull out a shotgun ready to cheat
Make a Corsair cop a bad plea."

. . .

"In a 1941 the might Bishops
They had just begun."

. . .

"1, 2, and 3, 4,
We are the Chaplains,
Mighty, Mighty, Chaplains"

. . .

"Bishops on the corner
Three Four Five
Doin' what we wanna."

A very realistic presentation of gang activity and fighting ("20 minutes and 14 seconds of uncompromising ugliness and waste") is a movie called *The Jungle* (Stone, 1968, p. 16D). *The Jungle* was written, acted in, and directed by black street gang youngsters from 12th and Oxford Streets in Philadelphia.[f]

Sorenson (1959) taped "six boys in trouble" singing gangland and street rhythms. One of the gangland rhythms is entitled "gang fight" and ends with,

We never . . . . , We never go without a fight,
Because we can't lose any fight,
That's why they call us the Teen . . . Teen Agers,
The Alligator Lords,
We rumble, we tumble, we fight all night,
We never, we never, we never give up,

[f]"The Jungle" may be rented or purchased from Churchill Films, 662 North Robertson Street, Los Angeles, California 90069.

We always fight, we never lose,
We always get somebody 'fore we go,
Because we are the winner Teen Ager Lords.[g]

More recently, gangs, fraternities, cliques, organizations, and "rat packs" have again begun to be reported. New York, Chicago, Los Angeles, and Philadelphia report an increase of street gangs (Janson, 1972). One of the supposed differences between today's gangs and the gangs in the '50s is that the gang members are now older—some in their early 30s and some Viet Nam veterans (Southside, 1972; Stevens, S., 1971).

Janson (1972) reports some 200 gangs ranging in size from large consolidated organizations to small corner groups in predominantly Puerto Rican Southeast Bronx in New York City: ". . . more than 70 'cliques' or 'organizations' have formed in the past year (Southeast, 1972, p. 17)." Weingarten (1972) also reports at least 70 street gangs in the Bronx. Further, he suggests that the gangs vary in size from two dozen to 200 members, with a total membership guessed at 4,000. Broyan (1972) reports that police records show there are 85 gangs with ". . . a verified male membership of 5,300 (p. 48)." She also reports that 25 of these cliques or organizations have female affiliates with ". . . 160 verified members and 750 to 1,000 unverified members (p. 48)." This reporting is reminiscent of the "deb" affiliates of the gangs in the '50s. Janson (1972) reports New York, Philadelphia, Los Angeles, and Chicago are each supposed to have from 4,000 to 6,000 gang members. Markham (1972) reports approximately 80 gangs throughout the Bronx, ten in Brooklyn's Williamsburg, 30 throughout Washington Heights and Harlem, and half a dozen in Chinatown.

Police Lieutenant Appier (Wright, 1972) reports 150 gangs in Los Angeles now as compared with approximately 75 gangs in the fifties. Most of these gangs are black or Mexican-American with from 10 to 1,000 members. Gang members range in age from 11 years to about 18, with most of the gang members males, but with fast-forming female auxiliaries. According to the police, (Wright, 1972) New York City has 285 identifiable gangs varying in size from 35 to 100 members with 9,000 total gang members. New York City police (Tolchin, 1973) report some 9,500 "clique" members, ages 13 to 30, in the South Bronx.

Where the gangs of the '50s used knives, clubs, zip guns, chains, and fists, today's gangs are reported to have arsenals consisting of such additional weapons as ". . . molotov cocktails, rifles, shotguns, and, say youth workers, hand grenades and machine guns (Southside, 1972, p. 18)." Additionally, Wright (1972) reports "sophisticated" shotguns and automatic pistols replacing the zip guns of the '50s.

According to Weingarten (1972, p. 34),

[g]Gang Fight, *Street and Gangland Rhythms*, Folkways FD 5589.

Today there is scarcely a gang in the Bronx that cannot muster a factory made piece for every member at the very least, a .22 caliber pistol, but quite often heavier stuff: .32s, .38s, and .45s, shotguns, rifles, and—I have seen them myself—even machine guns, grenades, and gelignite and explosive. One gang, The Royal Javelins, has acquired some walkie-talkie radios (p. 34).

Weingarten (1972) also reports that right after *The Daily News* ran a story of gangs organizing a coalition called the Brotherhoods,

... munitions salesmen dispatched by the organized black under-world, some gang members are convinced—were filtering through the Bronx ready to deal in handguns, machine guns, grenades, and explosives. Earlier this month, a large clique in the Northeast Bronx concluded a deal—one of the gang insists it was with the Black Panthers—for four high-powered rifles and "several" .38 revolvers. Reported price just under $300 (p. 35).

There may be a parallel between the Black Panthers allegedly selling these guns to the gangs and the way the SDS and some third world groups sold drugs to college students to earn money to keep their cause going a few years ago.

Another major difference is that as "... the racial composition of America's slums has shifted from white to black, so has the makeup of America's gangs (Return, 1969, p. 51)."

To this should be added the reporting of Chinese gangs in San Francisco and New York City killing, mugging, bullying, and extorting (Arnold, 1970; Beware, 1971; Kneeland, 1971; Foreign-Born, 1971; Hanley, 1972). Many reasons are presented for these Chinese gangs, reasons related somehow to the change of the United States laws allowing orientals to immigrate in increased numbers. In New York City the 1960 census reflected 20,000 residents of Chinatown. The estimates for 1970 were 45,000 people (Arnold, 1970, p. 23). In San Francisco the Chinese population has doubled in the last decade to an estimated 70,000 residents (Kneeland, 1971, p. 33). It may be that because of sudden immigration of Chinese into the United States that the Chinese are experiencing the problems related to immigrants.

During the past 30 or 40 years the Chinatowns in the United States' urban areas experienced little crime, juvenile or otherwise. Now, however, with increased immigration by large numbers of marginal poor Chinese with few saleable skills, these immigrants are experiencing the same family and juvenile problems experienced by earlier occidental immigrant groups. In New York City,

These youths either immigrated alone, or came with parents who both must work to make ends meet in America. . . . Unable to cope in school or in the job market because of language difficulties,

several hundred youngsters age 14 to 22 have taken to the Chinatown streets, forming gangs with names such as White Eagles and
Black Eagles (Winship, 1973, p. 28).

Meanwhile, the other racial and ethnic gangs set neighborhood
improvement goals that included cleaning streets and backyards, registering
voters, and a dedication to driving the junkies from their neighborhoods. Some
of the gangs, however, have killed and raped in the process (Southeast, 1972;
Janson, D., 1972).

In Philadelphia, for example, 160 killings in the four years prior to
April 1972, as well as many maimings, were attributed to gang warfare (Janson,
1972; 1972a). As of June 24, 1970, in Chicago's Black South Side there were
". . . 38 gang-related homicides and 316 gang shootings with 398 wounded. . . .
(Chicago, 1970, p. 13)."

New York City Police Inspector Robert H. Johnson (Tolchin, 1973),
leader of the 90-man Bronx youth gang task force reported that the 130 gangs in
the East Bronx had accounted for more than 22 attempted homicides, 30
murders, 300 assaults, 124 armed robberies and ten rapes, with 1,500 gang
members arrested.

Although most of the victims of this gang warfare have been
members of rival gangs, some of the victims have been innocent bystanders.
Janson (1972, p. 30) reports that in Philadelphia, "Resulting violence has
terrorized merchants and householders, forced early store closings and required
parents to convey fearful children to and from school ." Janson (1972a, p. 58),
reports further that packs of youths have been beating, raping, robbing, and
occasionally killing, "sometimes entering homes to do so," in Watts and in other
sections of Los Angeles, with widespread fear being instilled by the terror.
Janson (1972a, p. 58) reported Mr. Billy G. Mills, ". . . council president pro tem,
said that the increase in murders, robberies and assaults had imposed a 'crisis of
intimidation and fear' on parts of Los Angeles 'by roving groups of young people
ranging in age from 10 to 30.' "

There are some similarities between today's gangs and the earlier
gangs of the Five Points and the Bowery. One similarity is that today's gangs
have "colors." The colors, for example, of the Cypress Bachelors consist of a
"top hat, cane and white gloves on a red and green field (Tolchin, 1973, p. 28)."
The gangs also have names that are presumed to inspire fear—Black Assassins,
Savage Nomads, Warlocks, Brothers of Satan, Spades, Dirty Dozen, Black
Spades, and Majestics.

Hart (1973) reports similarities and differences between today's
gangs and the gangs of the '50s. Membership includes males and females from
elementary school age into the '30s. Often, today's gang uniform is derived from
that of the motorcycle gangs, and when the fighting gets serious, automatic
weapons are often used. Whereas an earlier gang leader was the toughest of the

gang, today's leader is supposedly the brainiest. He may hold a regular job, he may be a veteran, and he is usually a good organizer. He refers to himself not as a gang leader but as a social theorist or politician. However, it is easier for him to point up the problems than it is for him to suggest alternatives and solutions.

Salisbury (1958) points out a misconception concerning the comparisons of the ages of present gang members with the ages of the earlier gangs.

> There is an impression today that the street gangs of the past were "adult" gangs whereas those of today are "adolescent" gangs. This is a misconception. One hundred years ago little distinction was made between the adolescent and adult. A boy strong enough to work was regarded as an adult. Boys of fourteen or fifteen started out in life on their own. Physical maturity and strength, not chronological age, were the test. The street gangs of the last century were made up of the same age groups as those of today. This is not the first era in which society, particularly the adolescent segment, has been badly disturbed and shaken up (pp. 9-10).

Certainly, it is obvious that the gangs have some effect on the inner city communities within which they range, upon the schools that are located within the inner city area, and on the schools to which inner city youngsters are bussed.

In the City of Buffalo, during the past few years, gangs have had a definite effect upon the schools. In some cases the threat of sudden gang incursions so permeated the school that the staff and students were in a constant state of fear of the gangs. Often, rumors would spread through the school that it was about to be raided by a particular gang. At times, gangs would bring all teaching and learning to a halt as they would ring a school suddenly. Then, just as suddenly, they would leave, with rumors spreading that they were on their way to another school.

According to Hart (1973), gang presidents sometimes speak with school authorities concerning the conduct of a gang member, thus taking on the *in loco parentis* role. Additionally, gang ethos sanctions the use of force as a means for solving problems and grievances.

Although Hart reports that gangs do not generally operate in the schools, schools have been paralyzed and operations disorganized by the fear of gang reprisals. Misdemeanors go unreported; assault charges are not filed; students who should be suspended are not; school resources are diverted from educational considerations; and extracurricular activities are curtailed.

Many students have reported being shaken down. Some parents have transferred their children because they were afraid they would be shot or stabbed. At other times, gangs actually entered schools in a very violent and real way. Reality 18 describes an inner city school teacher's experience with a gang from another school. He was on morning duty near the door to give out late passes.

REALITY 18

"My early morning assignment went regularly until one of my students warned me of an imminent invasion by a youth gang known as the Manhattan Lovers. The gang supposedly was armed with broom handles, chains, knives, and so on. Since the student in question had a very poor attendance record—he was absent from school at least 120 days up to that time—and since he did absolutely no work for me, nor for any of his other teachers, I did not place much confidence in his information. Indeed, I initially laughed it off and dismissed the young man. . . .

"As the homeroom period slowly drew to a close I decided to tell our principal what I had been told. . . . I went to see the principal to report my news. But he was unavailable. . . .

"As I was leaving the main office, I noticed a group of boys approaching our school from the direction of———Junior High School. The boys were armed with broomsticks, bats, chains, and so on. Since at this time I was in the relative safety of the main office, for some reason . . . I saw fit to try to intercept the young men and lock the front door to prevent their entering.

"When I reached the hall, I was too late. The boys already had entered and I saw one youngster pick up my briefcase, which was heavy with books and reports, and slam it into one of our display cases which housed trophies and various articles.

"The glass shattered and the noise . . . brought many people into the halls to see what the problem was. At this moment, I was out of the main office directly in the path of the invaders. I had no time to dash back to the main office. Therefore, I made a right turn and sought the safety of the elevator. Unfortunately, the elevator was on a different floor and the door was locked.

"At this time the boys all passed me. At no time did I approach, speak to, or try to prevent any of them from entering our school. . . . Since I was alone, . . . I did not feel I was in any position to prevent their progress into the school.

"As the boys went by me, . . . no youngster made a threatening gesture to me nor did they look at me in any dangerous way. However, the last youngster in line had a black glove on. As he approached me, I saw out of the corner of my eye that he was swinging at my face. I decided to . . . prevent this from happening. . . . I brought my right elbow up to protect myself, and as I did so, his punch missed my mouth area and nose . . . and just grazed my right upper cheek area. In fact, my blocking action prevented pretty much serious injury to this part of my face.

"A swelling developed which was . . . taken care of by an ice pack provided by our office nurses.

"After the boys had passed by me, they proceeded to the second floor. . . . They attacked a teacher who had opened his door to see what the commotion was. . . . A youngster hit him in his eye and caused a cut and some injury. . . .

"After the boys had entered the second floor, they decided to leave the building. . . . The police arrived about ten minutes after the boys left the building.

"One of our assistant principals took me and the other teacher to the hospital where extensive x-rays were taken.

"The next day, many of our teachers in the school, fearful of their safety and health, did not report."[h]

In some Buffalo high schools where black youngsters were being bussed, black and white gangs, clubs, and fraternities, often goaded by parents, sometimes battled one another. At other times, the gangs kept everyone in a constant state of fear in anticipation of renewed hostilities.

Because of the threat of gangs, some PTAs found it impossible to have evening meetings because parents were fearful of venturing out at night. One school had to turn to Saturday morning meetings—which, by the way, proved very successful.

In some schools, because parents feared for their children's safety at after-school remedial and advanced programs, the attendance at these programs fell off. When rumors circulate through a neighborhood that gangs have invaded a particular school, many parents rush to the school to take their children home.

Further reporting by Janson (1972a) found additional school-gang problems affecting the teaching and learning in New York, Philadelphia, Los Angeles, and Chicago. For example, gangs attacked children going to and from school. At Stevenson High School in the Bronx, parents have kept 350 children home while other parents transferred their children to parochial and private schools (p. 58).

Pupils in some New York schools are afraid to go to the toilet for fear of being assaulted or robbed. Additionally, some principals have suggested that their teachers not remain alone in their classrooms. Across the country, innumerable schools now employ security guards and a "Safe Schools Act" has been introduced in Congress.[i] Furthermore, many principals have to take teachers from their teaching responsibilities to have them patrol in and around the school.

·Montgomery (1971, p. 30), reported I.S. 162 in New York City closed in protest over the lack of police protection from a gang after ". . . an average of two or three students a day have been mugged, assaulted or

[h]Transcribed from a taped interview by the author.
[i]The Safe Schools Act of 1971, 92nd Congress, 1st Session H.R. 3101. Introduced by Jonathan B. Bingham, U.S. House of Representatives, 22nd District, New York State.

threatened on the way to school." Maeroff (1972, p. 36) also wrote of a new high school in New York City where assaults, numerous robberies, and acts of intimidation have taken place around and in the school. Half the school's lavatories have been locked so that the school security guards had less area to cover. The white students were so apprehensive that "if someone wearing a jacket approaches one of them, they feel a whole gang is confronting them rather than an individual."

Fasso and Wetherington (1972) reported a battle in which nine youths were stabbed, one critically, inside the school yard of Junior High School 71 on the lower East Side of Manhattan. The fight lasted for about 20 minutes and some 40 to 50 students were involved. According to police, rocks and stones were thrown, and fists were used before the knives were drawn. As a result of the stabbings, school was dismissed for the day. According to Markham (1972) a 17-year-old student was clubbed on the head with a pistol butt and stabbed in the spine outside George Washington High School in upper Manhattan. The stabbing and beating allegedly was the outcome of fights between two gangs. After the stabbing, a hunting knife, a pellet gun, and a butcher's knife strapped to a youngster's leg were confiscated by the police.

Additional gang related problems included youngsters being beaten if, for example, they did not carry a leaf or similar item in a certain pocket. Sometimes gang members would force nongang members to carry their knives or guns into school. In the late '50s and early '60s, some gang members stopped carrying weapons. However, they would walk close to the curb. If attacked, they would break off a car antenna and use it as a weapon. Gang and nongang members often threatened teachers, with, "I'll get my gang after you."

For me, two incidents out of many with gangs or students who belonged to gangs stand out. They stand out because of the numbers of school-aged youngsters involved. And, because of what could have happened if I had not been so lucky.

REALITY 19

Our school was on West 93rd Street and Amsterdam Avenue in New York City. We had just opened the school after closing the one for drug users on North Brothers Island.

The principal called me into the office and introduced me to a detective, who informed me that one of the students on my going-home line was the war counselor of a gang responsible for the stabbing of a youth from another gang.[j] The stabbed youth had just been released from the hospital and would probably try to retaliate against the student on my line. Should my student spot him, I was supposed to notify the principal, who would call the police.

[j]In the "600" Schools, students were escorted to the bus or subway to make sure they were on their way out of the neighborhood of the school. Supposedly, the "600" Schools were organized in nongang neighborhoods so that the gangs would have to travel quite a distance to get anyone in the school.

About two days later, another teacher and I started our fifteen students toward the subway. Just as we left the school building one of our students yelled, "There he is!" and pointed to one of a group of about eight teenagers standing there.

I called to the fellow they had pointed to, "What do you want—this is still school property?"

"Fuck you!" he yelled.

As he ran toward me holding a bat that I had not noticed earlier, suddenly about 30 more teenagers popped up from behind parked cars. I turned and shouted to the other teacher, "Call the cops!" I tried pushing and yelling at our students to go back the fifteen feet or so to the school.

One of our bigger students ran off to the side, reached into his inside jacket pocket, pulled out a large serving spoon, and yelled, "Come on mutha fuckas—over here." The gang leader and two others then ran past me to get to him. When two of them reached the sidewalk, they bent down and picked up a bat and metal window frame they had stashed, and went after him. Almost unbelievably, he beat the three of them off.

As I think back, he probably saved my life, or at least saved me from getting a good beating by attracting the three boys to him and away from me.

For the next few minutes, I still don't know how long, we all cursed, screamed, dodged, ran, punched, shoved, kicked, and swung out. Then suddenly, as quickly as it started it was over; the attackers took off running.

The police arrived about 15 minutes later and told us to go to the station house while they hunted for the other gang. While we were sitting in the station house waiting, one of my students turned to me and asked, "Hey, what would you have done if he had hit you in the head with the bat?"

"What do you mean?" I asked.

"Man, when you turned around and told us to get into school, he missed your head by about that much with the bat as he ran by you," he responded, holding two fingers about an eighth of an inch apart.

After a wait of about 20 minutes, the police brought in four members of the gang and asked us to identify them. Although the gang leader had been less than 20 feet from me, I was not sure. I turned to one of my students and asked, "That him?"

He nodded.

I turned to the policeman and said, "That's him." They were booked, and I ran to catch my car pool.

A month later we were called to Family Court on 23rd Street. We went before the judge and all the reports were read. The judge asked whether I had been hit or hurt with the bat. When he was told no, he let all four go without even a reprimand. Interestingly, we learned the gang leader was playing hooky from another "600" School the day they jumped us.

As we were leaving, the judge called the three students who were with me as witnesses. He leaned across the table, pointed his finger at them, and snarled, "If I see you punks down here again, I'll put you all away."

As we walked away, I turned to my students, shook my head, and apologized.

REALITY 20

We were on the G.G. Independent Subway on our way to Red Hook Stadium for an afternoon of track and field events with about 60 students from our after-school program. Six teenagers loped through the train eyeing everyone.

They halted and pointed at two brothers among our students. "You Eagon's brother?" one of them asked.

Before either of the brothers could answer, they ran to the next car, had a quick and excited conversation, and got off the train at the next stop. Our seven staff members got together to talk over what had happened as our students began to get fidgety. One of the staff informed us that our students' brother was an important member of a Brooklyn fighting gang; he had beaten up someone from another gang the week before.

We got off the train at Smith and 9th Street and began about a six-block walk to Red Hook Stadium. We walked hurriedly, everyone looking about apprehensively. As we neared the stadium, about 20 teenagers then nearly two blocks away, came toward us. They carried sticks, pipes, chains, bottles, and anything that would make a good weapon.

We filed into the stadium and sent someone to call the police. When the gang kids reached the stadium, they stopped outside so we decided to go on with our track meet. Our students sat in the stands. We seven faculty went down to the track to organize things. We had just finished our opening ceremonies when we noticed our students moving away from the Eagon brothers.

As if by signal, the gang had come into the stadium through a hole in the chain link fence and entered the stands. They formed a line from the bottom of the stands to the top and began walking toward our students.

I was dead on my feet. I was scared. I thought, "Shit, what the hell am I doing here—I have a kid now."

Suddenly one of our staff, a short wiry guy, yanked his jacket off, grabbed a bat, yelled "Come on," and took off running for the stands. The rest of us faculty moved after him. He turned and faced the gang as they walked slowly toward him. We lined up on either side of him and formed a line between the gang and the two Eagon brothers and our students.

The teacher who had moved first began to shout and gesture with the bat. The gang was then about seven or eight feet from us.

"You mother fuckers," he yelled, "touch one of our kids and we'll kick everyone of your fuckin' asses! This is a school function and we'll defend the two brothers."

The gang president must have realized we were serious. He took the smart way out. "We didn't know it was a school meet. We'll get them some other time."

In almost a single file, the gang walked to the top of the stadium and tossed their weapons over the stadium wall. They slowly walked out of the stadium and hung around on the outside.

By then, two police cars had arrived, and the policemen agreed to take the brothers out of the neighborhood. However, the brothers refused to go until they ran in their races. We therefore rearranged the schedule and ran their race. The brothers won their races, got into the squad cars, and were on their way out of the neighborhood. When the gang saw them leave, they too left.

This was the first time that our students had not stuck together. And, this was the last time we went to Red Hook.

The youngsters who belong to gangs may fall into any of my four categories of behavior. The middle class student may join a gang because his survival on his or nearby streets necessitates joining. The streets in his neighborhood may be controlled by a gang, and peer gang pressures as well as the need to walk the streets in his or other neighborhoods may require his joining a gang. Also, the gang may give him the security, belonging, and action he craves and needs.

This reminds me of a newspaper story I read twenty years ago. At a social worker conference, the participants were arguing over defining a neighborhood. After listening for about 45 minutes, a Puerto Rican social worker took the floor.

"I don't know about you guys," he said. "But where I come from a neighborhood is the place that if you walk out of it you get beat up."

Of course, whether gangs really fight or not becomes of little consequence. The fearful atmosphere they create permeates the community and its schools, interfering with the teaching and learning and sometimes tying up the downtown administrators for weeks. This is true for the City of Buffalo, and it is true for many other cities where gangs guard their territory physically or pose the threat of violence. Indeed, the gangs' continued existence is also noted by their graffiti markings on the school buildings that declare their territory or turf. (See Chapter Four for section on graffiti.)

JUVENILE DELINQUENCY AND CRIME

Unquestionably, there is underreporting of the misdeeds of middle class children. However, even this underreporting would not explain the increased rates of delinquency on the part of lower class groups.

Studies by Congers and Miller (1966) indicated higher delinquency rates among certain lower class groups, particularly those in socially disorganized areas. Whether or not delinquency and emotional disturbance should be equated is still being debated. However, even where such subgroup behavior is considered "normal," it is not likely to produce emotionally healthy results.

Despite the biases in reporting of youthful crime and delinquency, there appear to be some substantial conclusions. In a staff report to the National Commission on the Causes and Prevention of Violence (Mulvihill, D.H. & Tumin, M.M., 1969), some factual perspectives were presented concerning crime.

> The conclusions nonetheless emerged that the true rate for each of the four major violent crimes—homicide, rape, assault, and robbery—appears considerably higher for those aged 18-24 and 15-17 than for the other age groups. The juvenile and youthful population is growing at a greater rate than other age groups; thus, we found that about 12 percent of the increase in the rate of the major violent crimes combined between 1950 and 1965 was attributable merely to increases in the population aged 10-24. Uptrends over the last 10 years were reported for all age groups in each of the major violent crimes . . . (p. 607).

Further reporting on crime by the Task Force on Individual Acts of Violence concerning race, sex, and the inner city found,

> Most youthful offenders are male, and there is a disproportionate representation of Negroes. FBI estimates in 1967 suggested a reported criminal homicide arrest rate for the Negro 10-17 age group of 22 per 100,000, approximately 17 times greater than the white 10-17 age group. The reported forcible rape rate for Negro juveniles was 12 times higher than the corresponding rate for white juveniles; the reported robbery rate 20 times higher, and the reported aggravated assault rate 8 times greater. Even when considerable reporting problems are taken into account, these figures imply large differentials in the true rates of juvenile violence when broken down by race (Mulvihill, D.J. & Tumin, M.M., 1969, p. 607).

According to Stevens (1971, p. 92) there has been more than a 300 percent increase in reported incidents between the police and juveniles. In one police division taking in much of Harlem in New York City, juvenile-police incidents have more than doubled in the past decade. In New York City in 1970, there were 17,944 arrests. Of this number more than 10,000 were for felonies. In addition 49,000 referrals were made dealing with juveniles under 16 years of age.

Further, according to Mulvihill & Tumin (1969),

> The locus of delinquency and youth violence is more likely to be the urban ghetto than any other place. A 1960 study of Minneapolis

showed that ghetto delinquency rates were twice as high as in the rest of the city. The same differential appeared when the Hough area was compared to Greater Cleveland in 1961. A 1961 study conducted in a St. Louis ghetto area, where 60 percent of the population is Negro, showed a delinquency rate 3 times higher than in the rest of the city. In 1962, the delinquency rate for Harlem was 109 per 1,000 population between the ages of 7 and 20, while New York City taken as a whole the rate was 46 per 1,000 for the same age group. In 1963 statistics gathered in a ghetto area of greater Boston where most of the city's Negro population resides showed delinquency to be four times greater than for Boston as a whole (p. 607).

The Commission in reporting these figures realized that there is some aspect of bias in arrests and in the reporting of ghetto crimes as compared with middle class white crime. However, taking this into consideration they found,

There is some bias in these figures because, among other things, slum offenders are more likely to be arrested than urban or rural offenders. Although it would be naive to say that inner-city youth have a monopoly on violence when middle- and upper-class delinquency are considered, it is still safe to conclude that delinquency remains primarily a slum problem (Mulvihill, D.J. & Tumin, M.M., 1969, pp. 607-608).

VIOLENCE AND PHYSICALNESS

The National Commission on the Causes and Prevention of Violence (1969) provided much documentation in relation to youthful crime and violence in the ghettos. For example,

The key to much of the violence in our society seems to be with the young. Our youth account for an ever-increasing percentage of crime, greater than their increasing percentage of the population. The thrust of much of the group protest and collective violence on the campus, in the ghettoes, in the streets—is provided by our young people (p. 6).
    Studies over the past decade show that the heavy concentration of crime is among the poor, the ethnic minorities who dwell in the city ghettoes; that the areas of lowest per capita income and highest unemployment, or lowest level of average educational attainment, of poorest housing, and of highest infant mortality rate are also areas of high crime (p. A-20).

The Commission makes an interesting point in relation to the instigation of ethnic and religious violence in America. Whereas earlier ethnic and religious violence in the United States came about when those groups further up on the economic scale resisted the advances of the newer group lower down on the economic ladder, today's racial violence has been instigated by those same groups who had their way blocked by the earlier groups.

> Ethnic and religious violence has also occurred frequently in the United States, involving the Irish, Italians, Orientals, and—far most consequently—Negroes. Only in the last decade, however, has it become common for such ethnic groups to initiate violent conflict. Historically the violence resulted when groups farther up the socioeconomic ladder resisted the peaceful upward progress of particular ethnic and religious groups toward higher positions in the social order. Those who felt threatened by the prospect of the new immigrant or the Negro getting 'too big' and 'too close' resorted to defensive violence (p. A-5).

Criminal and violent attacks upon citizens are not committed by the emotionally disturbed only. However, there is a great deal more crime and physical assault in lower class socioeconomic areas when compared with middle class or upper class areas. In a staff report (Mulvihill & Tumin, 1969, p. 707) submitted to the National Commission on the Causes and Prevention of Violence, the difference between the ghetto residents' contact with physical assault as compared with the suburbanites' contact with physical assault was reported: "A recent survey in Chicago concluded that the chances of physical assault for a Negro ghetto dweller were 1 in 77, while the odds were 1 in 10,000 for an upper middle-class suburbanite (p. 707)."

The Federal Bureau of Investigation uniform crime report for 1971 (Greenhouse, 1972), established that in the 57 cities with populations greater than a quarter-million people, crimes of violence rose 7.5 percent over 1970. The suburbs for the same period experienced a rise in violent crime of 13.4 percent.

Although the rate of increase for crimes of violence was greater in the suburbs, the suburban population is greater than the big city population by 56.9 millions to 42.6 millions (p. 12). Therefore, in relation to a person's chances of being exposed to a violent crime these figures show, "For every 100,000 people in the suburbs, 206 were victims of violent crimes. In the large cities the number was 1,048 (p. 1)."

Furthermore, in the ghetto ". . . violence is a common means of solving problems among the adult models that the young emulate (National Commission, 1969, p. A-21)."

In a recent study in New York City (Burnham, 1972), a life style of violence was reported. Dr. Marvin E. Wolfgang, director of the Center for Studies in Criminology and Criminal Law at the University of Pennsylvania, offered a possible reason for the high rates of robbery and murder in the slums as contrasted with the rest of New York City.

"In some of these communities," he said, "a subculture of violence had developed. In addition to the drug scene and the unbelievable poverty, there is a life-style of organized violence and physical aggression sometimes looked on as machismo or manliness.

"It's sort of corny to say," Dr. Wolfgang added, "but there is a violence born into generations. Life has become terribly cheap (p. 16)."

When a university professor was mugged and killed near Columbia University in New York City recently, a resident's comments expressed the acceptance of violence as part of the routine of living in that area.

". . . there are so many muggings and purse-snatchings in daylight on the street that such incidents have become part of the neighborhood scene, like the sound of the cars and trucks (Arnold, M., 1972, p. 48)."

In a hot dog establishment frequented by prostitutes, pimps, and junkies and just off New York City's Times Square, knife-wielding has become so common that even the police ignore it.

"It's normal," said the restaurant supervisor . . . "It wouldn't be normal if someone didn't come in here with a naked knife."

And even as he spoke, in low, guarded tones, another man walked in, also wielding a knife. Within an hour, a third man walked in waving a knife (Knife-Wielding, 1972, p. 42).

From another point of view, in America the pathology of the black urban slum has developed over long years and many ecological pattern changes. The slum culture provides some black disadvantaged children with a "frame of reference" or code of behavior that is different from that of the middle class teacher.

The disadvantaged child's lower class life is violent, hostile, aggressive, anxious, and unstable. Often he turns his aggression on himself, his peers, and authority figures. He learns to fight for everything; he learns that might does indeed make right. As a child, his discipline tends to be physical and custodial, with the use of threats and punishment as common means of control rather than the gentler psychological and emotional approaches of the middle class (Keller, 1965).

If you have read Claude Brown's (1965) *Manchild in the Promised Land*, and Piri Thomas's (1967) *Down These Mean Streets*, which deal with growing up in Harlem and Spanish Harlem, you will recall how, time and time again, the authors make the same point: to make your reputation and not succumb, you had to act crazy and prove yourself with your fists.

Brown writes,

Fighting was the thing that people concentrated on. In our childhood, we all had to make our reputations in the neighborhood. Then
we'd spend the rest of our lives living up to them. A man was
respected on the basis of his reputation. The people in the neighborhood whom everybody looked up to were the cats who killed
somebody. The little boys in the neighborhood whom the adults
respected were little boys who didn't let anybody mess with them
(p. 256). . . . It seemed as though if I had stayed in Harlem all my
life, I might never have known that there was anything else in life
other than sex, religion, and violence (p. 281).

Finally, there is physicalness in lower socioeconomic groups. Whereas middle class youngsters, in both subtle and unsubtle ways, are taught to
sublimate or hold back their feelings, emotions, and attitudes concerning
physicalness, lower class youngsters are not. Consequently, many lower class
children are very physical. Aggression and violence are lower class problem
solving techniques. Most often this physicalness frightens members of the middle
class, particularly school personnel. Quite often the teacher interprets physicalness as aggression; and it is normal for an adult to fear an aggressive child.

Such lower class physicality is depicted in such works as Greene and
Ryan's (1966) *The Schoolchildren: Growing up in the Slums*; Kohl's (1967) *36
Children*; Le Roi Jones's (1963) off-Broadway production of *The Toilet*; the TV
special and now movie entitled *The Way It Is* (1967), which depicted the N.Y.U.-
Jr. High School fiasco in Brooklyn; and Herndon's (1965) *The Way It Spozed To
Be*. Anyone who has lived in an inner city, lower class neighborhood or worked
in an inner city school has also experienced or observed such behavior.

Tennenbaum's (1963) "The Teacher, The Middle Class, The Lower
Class," describes how one house of lower class inhabitants unknowingly terrified
and frightened an entire block of middle class residents on the west side of
Manhattan.

Boys and girls mixed and it was difficult to think of them as single,
individual children. They shouted, they screamed, they pushed, they
fought. In the midst of play, they would suddenly get into individual
fights and collective fights. Violence, aggression, play and friendliness seemed all mixed up. Every wall on the block was used, either
to play ball on or throw things at. The streets became cluttered with
debris, especially broken glass (p. 82).
. . . what frightened them, was the violent, hostile way in which
lower-class families found their amusement. An almost palpable
atmosphere of aggression and violence hovered over the street. The
children would attack an automobile—literally attack it as locusts
attack a field—climb on top of it, get inside, and by combined,

cooperative efforts shake and tug until they left it a wreck (p. 83).
. . . even their innocent, friendly play was violent. Suddenly, strong, tall, gangling adolescent boys would dash pellmell down the street, like stampeding cattle, shrieking and screaming, pushing, shoving, mauling each other (p. 83).

Like my neighbors, teachers remain in a perpetual state of fear of these children, at their acting out, their defiance of discipline, their destructiveness and vandalism. . . . Many teachers feel trapped, frightened, helpless (p. 85).

Brill (1971), in reporting on a rent strike, adds support to the view of a lower class black life style that is threatening, aggressive, and loud; they were expressive but not effective. They appeared to be continually searching for stimulation which begot behavior that was frantic, highly impulsive, sometimes frightening, and also dramatic.

The middle class teacher who has played competitive sports is usually better able to deal with this physicalness. Given certain positive personality attributes and attitudes, this professional has the potential for becoming a good inner city teacher. Because this person is more secure with physicalness and his or her body, he or she is usually capable of separating hostile aggressive acts from playful lower class physical activity or streetcorner behavior. Additionally, the physical teacher may not be fearful of another physical person, or may not feel threatened and insecure by a student's physical actions. These feelings are often instinctual reactions on the part of this professional who is physical. Also, the physical child senses the teacher's physicalness, which he can relate to and be secure with. (Chapter Six, "Discipline," discusses this point.) Reality 21 is an example of lower class physical activity that did not frighten two middle class teachers and ended positively.

REALITY 21

Two male teachers were standing and talking at the bottom of the steps in an inner city, all-black, junior high school. A male student was standing a few feet from them. Suddenly, another male student let out a banshee scream and leaped, as though propelled, at least five or ten steps onto the back of the other youngster. They started pummeling one another.

The teachers barely took time from their conversation. One of them, however, turned to the supposed battling youngsters and said, "Hey fellas, give it some slack."

The youngsters looked at the teachers, flung their arms around one another's shoulders, and walked down the hall talking.

The majority of teachers and administrators, however, are frightened and repelled by such physically aggressive behavior. Hence, all physical activity becomes a threat to them. And, their fears create problems. Reality 22 is just such an example. It is identical to Reality 21 except in its outcome.

REALITY 22

Two male teachers were standing and talking at the bottom of the steps in an inner city, all black junior high school. A male student was standing a few feet from them. Suddenly, another male student let out a banshee scream and leaped the last five or ten steps onto the back of the other youngsters, whereupon, they both started pummeling one another.

The teachers stopped their conversation and yelled at the boys to stop. When the boys continued their roughhousing, one of the teachers ran over to them and attempted to stop them physically, whereupon, they both ganged up on him. There was a lot of cursing, hollering, and threats, when suddenly, the boys broke away, ran down the hall, and yelled, "Fuck you, you white fuck."

Too often, the teacher who has the positive instinctual feelings about the streetcorner physical behavior ends up feeling guilty about his instincts to become physical with his students in a positive, nonpunitive way. What this person needs is a good college or in-service course, or contact with a good supervisor who will help him (1) feel good and not guilty about his or her physical instincts; (2) help him or her develop this physicalness in a teaching style; and (3) help him or her to be at ease with lower class streetcorner behavior.

You may argue that our entire society is becoming more violent. There is a difference, however, between the violence of the middle class and that of the lower class. For those in the middle class or upper class, most violence is experienced vicariously, safely, and at a distance by the half hour or hour from movies, reporting of crime and war on TV, and Sunday afternoon professional football. For many disadvantaged children, violence is a way of life. It is very real; and to cope with it is to survive.

Realities 23, 24, 25, and 26 describe my personal experience with lower class physicalness that may provide the reader with additional insight into what is being referred to as physicalness and how it affects those from the middle class.

REALITY 23

I was directing a large day camp campground within which were sixteen decentralized day camps. My elder daughter, at the time about eight years old, wanted to go to one of the camps. I picked the camp with the best director and program for my daughter to attend.

The camp drew its population from a neighborhood which was in flux. Most of the middle class inhabitants had moved and had been replaced by lower class black and Puerto Rican families whose children now made up the majority of the campers.

After two days in camp my daughter demanded vehemently to be taken out. No amount of talking or questioning on my part could either get her back or uncover the reason for her departure. Indeed, it wasn't until months later that I found out why she refused to go back to camp.

Her reasoning went something like this: "You know, Daddy, everytime my counselor put out cookies or crayons or milk, or anything else, all the kids were rough and would fight and yell and shove and grab and I would never get any milk or cookies or crayons or anything, and the counselor never did anything about it."

Because my roots were in the city streets and because of my experiences in the "600" schools, the physicalness of the black and Puerto Rican campers seemed natural to me. Not so, however, to my daughter, accustomed to a quiet, calm, suburban, almost rural, life style. It frightened her and she didn't want any part of it.

REALITY 24

My family was in Manhattan one weekend visiting with relatives in the West 80's. My daughters and I decided to cross Broadway to purchase some ices at one of the pizza places on the East side of Broadway. Traffic was not too heavy as we crossed to the East side of Broadway. Suddenly, as we came close to the East side sidewalk, my daughters pressed close to me holding my hands tightly. It was as though they were trying to climb into my pockets.

I looked at them and then around to see what was going on. They tried to get closer to me as we walked South on Broadway. Suddenly, I realized what was happening. All around us were dozens of kids of all sizes and shapes. They were running, pushing, shoving, laughing, jumping, yelling, and generally playing as urban lower class youngsters do. No one was being beaten or hurt, but many had dirty faces and hands, their shirts or tee shirts were torn or open, dirty and flapping as they ran. It was not unlike Tennenbaum's (1963) description. All the physicalness had frightened my middle class suburban daughters.

In relation to Realities 21 and 22, it was not the blackness of many of the youngsters that my daughters feared. We had middle class black friends with children with whom we exchanged visits, therefore blackness was not something my daughters feared. But constant aggressive physical behavior was something that frightened them, and they could not relate to it.

This clash of divergent socioeconomic life styles is the phenomenon that has been causing many of our school problems. For some reason we fear unfamiliar life styles. In addition to the middle class fear of aggressive physicalness, we also have differences in dress that cause fear and problems.

Greenfield (1971, p. 1) makes this point as he describes his "terror" in visting the unfamiliar ground of the Brooklyn Paramount to see a rock show.

REALITY 25

Terror. Perhaps you think you can define it. It is sitting in a jet fighter cockpit, plummeting to a crash landing in a hostile country. It is losing footing on a mountain ledge in the midst of a blizzard. It is walking down a deserted city street in the dead of night, with the sudden sound of footsteps behind you.

No, that is not terror. I will tell you what terror is. Terror is waiting on line at 6:30 in the morning on a school holiday in 1957 for the Brooklyn Paramount to open for Alan Freed's rock and roll revue.

You have been up since 5:30 on your first day of vacation. Christmas or Easter (Hanukkah or Passover in my set). You have staggered into the darkness, found your friend Alan (another normal, neurotic Jewish kid) and weaved your way into the subway. There you pass interminable time, speeding past unfamiliar stops, emerging into the sullen dawn in downtown Brooklyn (downtown Brooklyn?). There, about a block away, is the Brooklyn Paramount, a huge movie palace built to hold the thousands who do not go out to movies anymore. On the marquee are big red letters: "Ten Days Only! Alan Freed's All-Star Rock 'n' Roll Revue!"

You walk to the theater, past the shuttered luncheonettes and cheap clothing stores. There is already a knot of kids waiting on line, even though the doors will not open for 2 hours and 45 minutes. And now you will begin to learn the meaning of fear.

There people are different. They do not look the way I do. They do not talk the way I do. I do not think they were born the same way I was. All of the males are six feet, seven inches tall. The last six inches is their hair, carefully combed into a pompadour. They are lean, rangy, even scrawny (except for one who is very, very fat). They have the hard faces of the children of the working poor. They read auto specs at night, not college catalogues. They wear St. Christopher medals, white T-shirts with their cigarette packs held in the left sleeve which is rolled up to the muscles. They have muscles.

The girls are all named Fran. They have curlers in their hair and scarves tied around their heads. They chew gum. They wear jeans and sweaters, and their crucifixes bounce on their breasts, some of which are remarkable examples of stress under pressure.

The conversation is guttural, half-sentences and grunts, with innuendos and veiled hints of lubricity. "Eh, that party, eh, Fran? Remember, heh, heh? Han, she don' remember nuthin." Fran is giggling, blushing. There is about these people an overwhelming sense of physical force, the same sense exuded by the students of Ascension High who chased the Jews home from school every afternoon: they hit other people a lot. Every joke, every insult, every question, is followed by open-handed jabs to the face, punches on the arm, slaps which barely miss being punches. It is like watching Leo Gorcey and Huntz Hall in the Bowery Boys movies.

At this point, there is only one stark thought in my mind: what in God's name am I doing here? These people are going to kill me and steal my five dollars and I will not be found for days. Consequently, the strategy of waiting on line at the Paramount is clear. You do not talk with your friend about your grades on the Social Studies test. You do not talk about where you are going to college. You do not engage in precocious argument about socialism. You keep your big mouth shut.

The vow of silence makes time go slowly, so you look at the posters over the theatre entrance, the pictures of the stars blown up on cardboard, the names spelled out in letters glittering from the gold and silver dust. There is Buddy Holly and the Crickets; the Cleftones, in white dinner jackets and red slacks; Jo Ann Campbell, "the blonde bombshell" who wears high-heeled shoes and very tight skirts, and whose biggest hand comes when she turns her back to the audience.

If you talk at all, it is in grunts to the others. "Yeah, Frankie Lyman, I saw him—seen him—last year. You heard the new Fats Domino?" You wait for the doors to open, for the sanctuary of the dark theater, for the Terror to go away (p. 1).

Here we saw "Terror" resulting not only from the phenomenon of divergent socioeconomic life styles, but also from a different speech pattern, dress, and even hair style. Indeed, these problems resulted from differences within white groups; blacks were not even involved. The divider was life style and social class—not color.

REALITY 26

Reality 26 came about as my wife and I observed another instance of the contrast between lower class and middle class life styles when we walked along the crescent-shaped shore of Lake Welch in the Bear Mountain Harriman State Park.

At one end of the lake, we observed bathers in what appeared to be less expensive bathing suits, milk in glass containers, people sitting on towels or occasionally beach blankets, a preponderance of adult females. The water was in endless turmoil as kids with few adults around yelled and screamed, jumped and shoved, and ran after one another screaming. No one was really hurt or crying, though.

As we continued along the water's edge and neared the middle of the crescent-shaped beach, we observed a different order of things. On the beach were men, women, and children sprawled on chaise longues or on big towels or blankets. The bathing suits looked more expensive. Food was continually being withdrawn from large ice chests and eaten. Juice, iced tea, and iced coffee poured from insulated coolers, not glass jars. In the water there were a notcieable number of adults, particularly fathers playing with their children. If by some slip of the mind a father lifted his child onto his shoulders or someone flipped some water at someone else, the life guard's whistle soon brought them back to the middle class reality and they ceased breaking the rules.

When fear of physicalness is combined with a fear of blacks, the fear can become hate. Norman Podhoretz (1963) explains his special "twisted" fear, envy, and hatred of Negroes as compared with other immigrant groups. While growing up in Brooklyn in the 1930s, he alternately envied, feared, and hated blacks because they ". . . were tougher than we were, more ruthless, and on the whole they were better athletes (p. 93)." And, they ". . . do not seem to be afraid of anything," and ". . . act as though they have nothing to lose (p. 94)."

> What mainly counted for me about Negro kids of my own age was that they were "bad boys." There were plenty of bad boys among the whites—this was, after all, a neighborhood with a long tradition of crime as a career open to aspiring talents—but the Negroes were *really* bad, bad in a way that beckoned to one, and made one feel inadequate. *We* all went home every day for a lunch of spinach-and-potatoes; *they* roamed around during lunch hour, munching on candy bars. In winter *we* had to wear itchy woolen hats and mittens and cumbersome galoshes; *they* were bareheaded and loose as they pleased. *We* rarely played hookey, or got into serious trouble in school, for all our street-corner bravado; *they* were defiant; forever staying out (to do what delicious things?), forever making disturbances in class and in the halls, forever being sent to the principal and returning uncowed. But most important of all, they were *tough*; beautifully, enviably tough, not giving a damn for anyone or anything. To hell with the teacher, the truant officer, the cop; to hell with the whole adult world that held *us* in its grip and that we never had the courage to rebel against except sporadically and in petty ways (pp. 97-98).

Even today, Podhoretz points to aspects of physicalness as being central to his feelings towards blacks.

> But envy? Why envy? And hatred? Why hatred? Here again the intensities have lessened and everything has been complicated and qualified by the guilts and the resulting over-compensations that are the heritage of the enlightened middle-class world of which I am now a member. Yet just as in childhood I envied Negroes for what seemed to me their superior masculinity, so I envy them today for what seems to me their superior physical grace and beauty. I have

come to value physical grace very highly, and I am now capable of aching with all my being when I watch a Negro couple on the dance floor, or a Negro playing baseball or basketball. They are on the kind of terms with their own bodies that I should like to be on with mine, and for that precious quality they seem blessed to me (p. 99).

SUMMARY

The object of this chapter is to demonstrate the additional conditioning experiences that poor or inner city youngsters are exposed to whenever they are in their neighborhoods. Certainly, continual exposure to the negative conditioning of gangs, juvenile delinquency, crime, and violence must have an effect on inner city children. Therefore, when you talk about inner city schools you must consider the social and economic realities of their community.

It must also be remembered that the inner city youngster's willingness to become aggressive and violent has not been lost on either the black ghetto child or his teacher. Indeed, the inner city youngster is more willing to initiate classroom disturbances or to challenge his teacher today than he was even ten years ago. And from a historical point of view, this willingness to become aggressive and violent is positive, for a study of American history will reveal that almost all ethnic, religious, and racial groups had to go through a period of violent confrontation with those who preceded them as one of the final steps required for achieving economic and political power.

The pictures of the violence and the disturbances in the ghettos accompanied by racist fantasies linger in the minds of school personnel; many come to school fearful of blacks. And many black children come to school with their fantasies and fears of whites. This fear, dislike, and sometimes hatred of poor blacks by school personnel is rather obvious to the poor black child. In turn, these feelings expressed by school personnel provoke the streetcorner-conditioned youngster to act-out even more. For ghetto living teaches you to take advantage of, manipulate, abuse, or even destroy those who are weaker, or who fear or dislike you.

Another point that must be remembered is that historically, as the earlier Irish, Italian, Jewish, and other ethnic and religious immigrants struggled through their urban immigration rites of passage, to a large extent they had similar incidents and experiences to those reported in this chapter. Though blacks were nonvoluntary immigrants, racism has kept them in an economic, legal, and social state of immigration since the American Civil War. Therefore, the incidents of crime, gangs, and overcrowded housing are manifested and perpetuated by social class behavior and racism rather than by one's blackness.

NOTES TO CHAPTER THREE

Arnold, M. Teen-age gangs plague merchants in Chinatown. *New York Times*, August 5, 1970, p. 33.

Arnold, M. Where violence is part of life's routine. *New York Times*, September 22, 1972, p. 48.

Asbury, H. *The Gangs of New York: An Informal History of the Underworld.* New York: Capricorn Books, 1970.

Beware the Wah Ching! *Newsweek*, August 30, 1971, pp. 63-64.

Botkin, B.A. *Sidewalks of America.* New York: Bobbs-Merrill, 1954.

Brill, H. *Why Organizers Fail: The Story of a Rent Strike.* California: University of California Press, 1971.

Broyan, N. For hundreds of girls in city, street gangs offer a way of life. *New York Times*, May 9, 1972, p. 48.

Burnham, D. A wide disparity is found in crime throughout city. *New York Times*, February 14, 1972, p. 1.

Burns, H. Can a black man get a fair trial in this country? *New York Times Magazine*, July 12, 1970, pp. 5, 38, 44-46.

Campbell, H. *Darkness and Daylight; or Lights and Shadows of New York Life, a Woman's Story of Gospel, Temperance, Mission, and Rescue Work.* Hartford, Conn.: A.D. Worthington, 1892.

Chicago: Turning against the gangs. *Time*, July 27, 1970, p. 13.

Conger, J., and Miller, W. *Personality, Social Class, and Delinquency.* New York: John Wiley & Sons, 1966.

Costello, A.F. *Our Friends: a History of the New York Fire Department: Volunteer and Paid.* New York: Augustine F. Costello, 1887.

Fasso, F. and Wetherington, R. Nine stabbed in fighting at a junior high. *New York Daily News*, June 9, 1972, p. C 3.

Foreign-born gang terrorizing Chinatown in San Francisco. *Buffalo Evening News*, October 27, 1971, p. 34.

Greene, M.F. and Ryan, O. *The Schoolchildren: Growing Up in the Slums.* New York: Pantheon Books, 1966.

Greenfield, J. "But papa, it's my music, I like it." *New York Times*, Hi Fi Recordings, March 7, 1971, Section 13, p. 1.

Greenhouse, I. Violent crimes rise in suburbs. *New York Times*, October 9, 1972, pp. 1, 12.

Hanley, R. Unrest vexes youth in a torn Chinatown. *New York Times*, January 31, 1972, p. 37.

Harlow, A.F. *Old Bowery Days: The Chronicles of a Famous Street.* New York: D. Appleton, 1931.

Hart, C. Street gangs. *New York University Education Quarterly* 4(2): 30-31, 1973.

Headley, J.T. *The Great Riots of New York 1712 to 1873: Including a Full and Complete Account of the Four Day's Draft Riot of 1863.* New York: Dover Publications, 1971.

Herndon, J. *The Way It Spozed to Be.* New York: Simon and Schuster, 1965.

Janson, D. Gangs face drive in Philadelphia. *New York Times*, February 13, 1972, p. 30.

Janson, D. Violence by youth gangs is found rising in 3 cities. *New York Times*, April 16, 1972, pp. 1, 58.

Jones, L. The toilet. *Kulchur* 3(9): 25-39, 1963.

Keller, S. *The American Lower Class Family.* Albany, New York: State Division for Youth, 1965.

Kneeland, D.E. Young hoodlums plague San Francisco. *New York Times,* September 5, 1971, p. 33.

Knife-wielding is reported common at site of a midtown slaying. *New York Times,* October 8, 1972, p. 42.

Kobler, J. *Capone: The Life and World of Al Capone.* New York: G.P. Putnam's Sons, 1971.

Kohl, H. *36 Children.* New York: New American Library, 1967.

Maeroff, G.J. Anxiety growing at Stevenson High over gangs and violence at school. *New York Times,* March 21, 1972, p. 36.

Markham, J.M. Stabbing of Washington High School student points a resurgence of youth-gang violence in city. *New York Times,* April 19, 1972, p. 29.

Miller, W.B. White gangs. *Trans-Action* 6(10): 11-26, 1969.

Montgomery, P.L. School closing over gang threat asked in Bronx. *New York Times,* December 21, 1971, p. 30.

Mulvihill, D.J., Tumin, M.M., et al. *Crimes of Violence, Vol. 11, 12, & 13: A Staff Report Submitted to the National Commission on the Causes and Prevention of Violence.* Washington, D.C.: U.S. Government Printing Office, 0-399-809, 1970.

The National Commission on the Causes and Prevention of Violence. *Progress Report of the National Commission on the Causes and Prevention of Violence to the President Lyndon B. Johnson.* Washington, D.C.: U.S. Government Printing Office, Superintendent of Documents, 1969.

Podhoretz, N. My Negro problem—and ours. *Commentary,* 35:93-101, 1963.

Return to the rumble. *Newsweek,* September 8, 1969, pp. 51-52.

Richmond, Rev. J.F. *New York and Its Institution, 1609-1873,* (Rev. Ed.). New York: E.B. Treat, 1873.

Salisbury, H.E. *The Shook-Up Generation.* New York: Harper & Brothers, 1958.

Sheldon, G.W. *The Story of the Volunteer Fire Department of the City of New York.* New York: Harper & Brothers, 1882.

Silberman, C.E. *Crisis in black and white.* New York: Vintage Books, 1964.

Southeast side story. *Time,* April 3, 1972, pp. 17-18.

Sowell, T. A black professor says . . . colleges are skipping over competent blacks to admit "authentic" ghetto types. *New York Times Magazine,* December 13, 1970, pp. 36-37, 39, 42, 44, 46, 49-50.

Stevens, S. The "rat packs" of New York. *New York Times Magazine,* November 28, 1971, pp. 28-29, 91-95.

Stone, J. The best thing we knew was gang war. *New York Times,* October 13, 1968, p. 16 D.

Tennenbaum, S. The teacher, the middle class, the lower class. *Phi Delta Kappan* 45(2): 82-86, 1963.

Tolchin, M. Gangs spread terror in the South Bronx. *New York Times,* January 16, 1973, pp. 1, 28.

The way it is. National Educational Television Journal (Channel 13, 9:00-10:00 p.m.), May 1, 1967.

Weingarten, G. East Bronx story—return of the street gangs. *New York* 5(13): 31-57, 1972.

Wentworth, H. and Flexner, S.B. *Dictionary of American Slang.* New York: Thomas Y. Crowell, 1960.

Winship, F.M. U.S. Chinatowns now are torn by gang violence. *Buffalo Courier-Express,* July 15, 1973, p. 28.

Wright, R.A. Rise in youth gang killing alarms police in 3 cities. *New York Times,* November 27, 1972, pp. 1, 53.

Chapter Four

Jive Lexicon and Verbal Communication Problems

"If you signify you qualify."

—Streetcorner philosopher

"The only language of education is the language which people can understand—no matter where it originates."

—Covello, *The Heart Is the Teacher*

Genesis: "Come let us go down, and there confuse their language that they may not understand one another's speech."

"The heavy thing in the black community is the con and conversation."

—A black student

Teacher-student communication is vital to the teaching-learning process. This communication may come about through such modes as language in the form of verbal symbols or words modified by tone and emphasis, by nonverbal body movements, motions, gestures, shrugs, head movements, facial expressions, and the touching or holding of one person by another.

Our schools, however, are highly developed verbal institutions where language consisting of Standard English verbal symbols is the main instrument of communication. Teacher-student and student-teacher communication depends upon the student's and the teacher's ability to understand what each is saying to the other.

When people from the same social class or region of the country communicate, differences in dialect cause little difficulty. But when members of different social classes or sections of the country interact, dialectical differences may cause communication problems.

117

Because schools are verbal institutions, the middle class child's language and life style are compatible with the way our schools are organized. Accordingly, most middle class children succeed in school regardless of the teacher and methods.

For the disadvantaged child, however, his language and life style work against school success. His segregated environment ill prepares him for the rigorous Standard English demands of our schools. Despite his verbal problems in school, however, he is able to communicate without apparent problems in his home, with his peers, and in his neighborhood.

It appears that these problems existed between the children of earlier immigrant groups too. The following outlines some of the problems faced by Italian immigrant children in Greenwich Village in New York City from 1920 through 1930. C.V. Ware observes:

> The literary material to which the child was exposed often lacked reality. . . . While children drew the bulk of their experience from movie attendance, the subjects and the attitudes contained in the movies were ignored by the schools. The same was true of language and speech. All the schools of the locality reported that they laid special stress on the teaching of English—"the teachers almost break themselves trying to make the children talk right" because of the importance of having children from foreign homes learn the English language. But the language which is taught was not that which had vitality for the children—the accent of the street, the diction of the movies, and the vocabulary of the tabloid press. To talk in the manner prescribed at school was to act the part of a "sissy" or to "put on airs" (Ware, C.F., 1965, p. 338).

A major source of problems in inner city schools is the breakdown in student-teacher communication that often results from these differences in verbal usage. This is particularly true in today's inner city schools where initial student—teacher relationships are often precarious. Bernstein (1958, p. 169), writing about English working class children, points out that "this may lead to a situation where pupil and teacher each disvalues the other's world and communication becomes a means of asserting differences." The words of Bagdikian (1965, pp. 185-186) are also appropriate and related.

> Nothing in the usual background and training of the American schoolteacher prepares her for the special problem of the slum child. Nothing in the background of the child prepares him for the teacher. They are strangers to each other, commanded by law to be mutually present a certain number of hours a day, but they part, usually, still strangers and even bitter enemies. When by chance there is established the communication needed to teach and learn, it is a tenuous line easily broken.

This chapter will not discuss Black English from a technical or linguistic view. Instead it will discuss pragmatically communication in general and in particular where communication problems may be caused by differences in definition or knowledge of the other's lexicon as related to: (1) double or nonstandard meaning; and (2) crisis or emotional stress situations. This chapter will combine the theoretical with the empirical. I argue for the school's unconditional acceptance of the black, disadvantaged, urban child's dialect as the first step toward his acceptance of the school. This argument must not be considered, however, as suggesting that black urban students should not be taught Standard English.

Realities 27 and 28 are examples of teacher-student communication problems resulting from the teacher's ignorance of jive lexicon (discussed later in this chapter). Both examples are related to the word "trim." This story was told to me by this teacher after hearing my lecture on jive lexicon in which the double meaning of "trim" was discussed.

REALITY 27

A black, middle class, middle-aged, female teacher was conducting a lesson on poetry with her all-black inner city students. The teacher was giving the students the correct pronunciation of the different terms used to measure a line of poetry.

The teacher said, "A line of poetry with two measures or two feet is called dimeter and it is pronounced dim-e-ter. Now class, repeat each syllable." The class repeated the term. Then she went on.

"The line of poetry with three measures or three feet is called trimeter—trim-e-ter. You know how to say trim-e-ter, I'm sure."

The class began to giggle and whisper among themselves and it took some time for the puzzled teacher to get the class to order again.

REALITY 28

This incident took place in an inner city junior high school language arts class about a week before the Christmas vacation. During a lull in the class, two black male students approached their white female teacher and asked, "Miss Frank, what does *trim* mean?"

Miss Frank, unsuspectingly, responded with, "Oh, I guess to hang ornaments on the Christmas tree."

With that, one youngster turned to his friend, grinned, put out his hand for some skin,[a] and the class burst into laughter.

[a]To give "skin," "five," or "dap" is to slap the palms of one another's hands. The viewer of TV sporting events will often observe black athletes, and whites too now, giving skin after a home run, a touchdown, or at the start of a basketball game. Giving skin

In this incident, too, it took the teacher quite some time to get the class to order again.

Now let us see what meaning *trim* had that could cause these two classroom incidents.

According to *The Random House Dictionary of the English Language*, (Stein, 1966, p. 1514) there are 32 definitions for the word trim. The most common is "to put into a neat orderly condition by clipping, paring, pruning, etc." According to Wentworth and Flexner (1960), trim is "to defeat an opponent or opposing team, as in a game, esp. to defeat by a narrow margin (p. 554)."

These dictionary definitions aside, in the jive lexicon of the black ghetto junior high school youngsters described above, trim means sexual intercourse or vagina. Had either of the teachers been familiar with jive talk or jazz or blues vocabulary, they may have understood the game the youngsters were "running" on them. For example, H.L. Mencken (1963, p. 745) in reporting on jive and jazz vocabulary: "Trim is sexual intercourse enjoyed by bedding down." Gold (1964, pp. 327-328) reports trim as "To possess (a woman sexually)." Sadly, none of the glossaries that I know of that are written or published by blacks, contain the word trim. One glossary by Hermese E. Roberts, a black public school principal, distributed widely to industrial firms, not only ignores the word but adds the following for other "off color" definitions.

---

is a physical gesture of approval, agreement, paying a compliment, a greeting, or even parting. To some extent it could be considered equivalent to a slap on the back or a nudge on the arm or shoulder.

According to Burley (1944, pp. 59-60), giving skin originated in Chicago, in 1939, at the time of the Tony Galento-Joe Louis fight, and jive-conscious blacks almost universally understand it.

> The act of "Gimme-some-skin" involves some theatricals, an intricate sense of timing, plenty of gestures. For example: You are standing on the corner. You see a friend approaching. You bend your knees halfway and rock back and forth on your heels and toes with a swingy sway like the pulsing of a heartbeat. You hold your arms closely to your sides with index fingers pointing rigidly toward the sidewalk. You say to your friend as he comes up: "Watcha know, ole man, whatcha know?" He answers:
> "I don't know, ole man, whatcha know?" Then he says: "Gimme some skin, ole man: gimme some of that fine skin!"
> You bend your knees in a gentle sag. Your upper right arm is held close to your side, but the forearm, with the palm of the hand open, is thrust out like a motorist flagging on a left turn. You both swing around and your palms collide in a resounding whack (pp. 59-60).

Malcolm X (Haley, 1966, p. 79), describes going back to visit Michigan. "My appearance staggered the older boys I had once envied; I'd stick out my hand, saying 'Skin me, daddy-o!' . . . wherever I went, I was the life of the party. 'My man! . . . Gimme some skin!' "

For a contemporary exposition of giving or getting skin see Cooke (1972, pp. 32-64).

Many of those of the more earthy or "gut" variety, and many of those preempted by the broader language community and now in general use may not appear in this collection. Where an entry is included, but some aspect of its connotation is omitted, we have indicated this omission with an asterisk (*) (Roberts, 1971, p. 2).

In Reality 27, the word trim had another meaning that was unknown to the teacher. Her students realized this and interrupted the class. Probably they were surprised to find a black teacher who did not know what trim meant. In Reality 28, the word trim was used deliberately to upset the teacher, to wrest control of the class, and to cause a diversion from the lesson. Realities 27 and 28 are further examples of the breakdown of student-teacher communication.

DIALECT AND JIVE LEXICON

When I lecture about student-teacher communication problems in inner city schools, I usually use my Jive Lexicon Test (Foster, 1972) as a motivational tool.[b] My talk usually goes something like this.

"You shouldn't have any problem with the test you are about to take. As you know, in most cases, you must pass a standardized aptitude or achievement test to get into most graduate schools."

"An analogy test is often used as a separate test or as an important part of a battery of tests. Analogy questions are important parts of such well known testing instruments as the College Entrance Examination (Scholastic Aptitude Test), The Graduate Record Examination, Medical College Admission Test, and Miller Analogy Test.

"Remember, the major variables in analogy test items include vocabulary, relationships, and word associations. Analogy questions test your ability to see relationships to additional words and ideas. The test indicates your vocabulary knowledge and your ability to think things through clearly, based on the influence of your past associations.

"Some of the relationships analogy tests ask you to think through include: (1) antonym, (2) synonym, (3) part-whole, (4) part-part, (5) cause-effect, etc. To test these relationships, analogy test items are usually designed so that the correct response is secured through: (1) true or false, (2) multiple choice; (3) blank space, or (4) matching answers. With this as background, I have designed *Foster's Jive Lexicon Analogy Test Series II* on which I have tested about 1000 adults.

[b]On my first version of the test (Foster, 1970), with a white population of 322 and a black population of 90, blacks scored higher and race was significant at the < .0001 level.

"I might add that I am working on the University of Buffalo's testing service people to have my test replace the Miller Analogy Test as a requirement for admission to our Education graduate faculty. I already require it of my students.

"Oh, one more point. As you know, the argument has been presented that our standardized tests are culturally biased. The words, experiences, and ideas used in the makeup of these standardized achievement tests suggest a white, middle class frame of reference. Therefore, when the disadvantaged child is tested on the standardized test model, he is being tested on an unfamiliar model.

"Supposedly, members of any disadvantaged population would score higher if tested on references to their experiential background. Whether blacks would score higher than whites on tests reflective of the black experiential background is another question that appears not to have been tested."

Instructions are then given for taking the test. Participants are given 20 minutes. Here is an example of one of the questions from *Foster's Jive Lexicon Analogy Test, Series I:*

> CHUMP CHANGE (small amount of change) is to YARD ($100) as TOGETHER (good, a person who is all right) is to:
>
> (1) tack (someone who does not know what is going on)
> (2) fox (a pretty girl)
> (3) freak (good, nice)
> (4) work (to fight, to dance, or do something with gusto)

This item requires an answer related to opposites. "Chump Change" means small change and is quite different from "yard," which refers to $100. Hence, "together," which means good or a person who is all right or dressed stylishly, requires an opposite response. The proper response is, therefore, "tack," which is used to describe someone who does not know what is going on.

Another example of the usage of "together" is shown in this dialogue. A youngster was bemoaning the grade he had received in an English course. He explained how he played around, neither doing his homework nor participating in class discussion. About three-quarters of the way through the course, he realized what he was doing and attempted to make amends. However, as he stated, "I got myself together, but it was too late."

Once the test is undertaken, blacks in the group usually begin to smile and chuckle. Most of the whites look disgusted, uncomfortable, annoyed, and some laugh nervously. The group is asked for their feelings when the test is completed.

Invariably, a few sullen white teachers immediately argue that the test is phony and that the words do not exist. In a middle school with a majority of black students, where I gave the test to the staff, one white male teacher jumped up, waved his hand at me, and yelled.

"Look, I've been working with black kids for twelve years; eight years in this place. I never heard one of these words. You trying to tell me that these words exist and these kids know them?"

When this happens, I usually suggest he not take my word, since I don't work here, but that he ask one of the black teachers.

"Why don't you ask him?" I suggest, pointing to one of the black teachers I had noticed smiling during the test.

Most often, the white teacher then asks, "Do the kids in this school really know and use words like those on the test?"

The black teacher usually responds with, "They use them—they sure do." while his face says *if you really liked these kids you would have heard some of these words.*

Everyone usually then starts yelling and talking at once. When everyone is calm, I steer the discussion toward the recognition that all languages could be considered a dialect consisting of: (1) phonology (the way we pronounce words), (2) syntax (grammar), and (3) lexicon (word meaning and vocabulary).

The group is provided with an example of phonology when those from New York City, Utica, Rochester, and Buffalo are asked to pronounce "apple," demonstrating the difference between an up-state and a down-state pronunciation. The group is also reminded of the way our Presidents have spoken with their regional dialects.

Two of the many phonological characteristics of Black English that are mentioned briefly are: (1) sometimes the *r* is dropped before vowels—example: Carol-Cal; and (2) some final consonant clusters are simplified—*t, d, s,* or *z*—example: hold-hol.

Syntax or grammar is discussed next. A number of examples of syntactical differences between Black English and Standard English are offered, for example: (1) I been washin' the dishes, (2) I be washin' the dishes, and (3) I wash the dishes.

The point is stressed that educators working with disadvantaged youngsters must be aware of these Black-Standard English differences for communication as well as curriculum.

I then suggest a number of books that can be read for insight into the phonology and the syntax of Black English, such as (Dillard, 1972; Vetter, 1969; Fickett, 1970; Williams, 1970; Aarons, 1972; The Florida FL Reporter, 1972).

We next get to the urban, black, disadvantaged child's functional peer vocabulary, which I call the jive lexicon but which has also been referred to as slang, cant, idiom, metaphor, Afro-Americanism, colloquial expression, patois, and vernacular.

To bring the lexicon discussion closer to home, I use the overhead projector to show a bottle of soda, ice cream on a stick, and a common flying insect. Everyone is asked what they call these items. Usually the New York City folks call ice cream on a stick a pop while to the Buffalonians it is the soda that is called pop. The insect is called any number of names such as a darning needle, dining needle, an ear sewer, etc.

As one moves from one region to another, improper use of regional expressions can sometimes prove discomfiting. This begins to get the realization across that our vocabulary may depend upon where we grew up or where we live now. Hence, vocabularies may be regional; there may not be only one correct word for a particular item. From here the group becomes a bit more receptive to the concept of Black English and even begins to admit that it exists. The audience is then provided with the answers to the test and a good discussion ensues.

We discuss the fact that vocabularies of the black and white teacher and student are "borrowed" from many sources. Their Standard English vocabulary includes regionalisms and, most often, other distinctive vocabularies. For example, most social, religious, ethnic, professional, and trade groups have distinctive vocabularies that operate within the framework of Standard English and are understood primarily by members of that group. Educators and members of most professions and organized sports also have their particular vocabularies. For centuries, criminals and drug users have used and still use their secret argots and lingos. With each war, each advance in technology, or each development of new industries, also come new vocabularies. For example, space flight enthusiasts know that "burn" is the firing of a spacecraft's rocket engines in flight, and that EVA is a space walk or extravehicular activity (Glossary, 1969). Presently, as a particular sport achieves prominence and a following, a special language is often born. Surfers know that a "wipe-out" is what happens when you are knocked off your board, and the "curl" is the top of a wave when it crests (Cady, 1966).

The Department of Defense, in addition to other material, published an eleven-page mimeographed pamphlet to provide returning Vietnam prisoners of war with "a head start, and perhaps bring you up to date, on the current slang expressions being used by the young people of America." The glossary was compiled from the slang expressions suggested by the prisoner's sons, daughters, and wives as being used in their houses and community.

Our nation's immigrants, too, have contributed "borrowings" from their language to today's American English vocabulary. From the Dutch we have borrowed sugar, butt, and waffle; from the Spanish, mosquito, calaboose, and corral; from the French, chowder and levee; from the Germans, kindergarten, burger, and delicatessen; from the Italians, spaghetti; from the Jews, bagel and blintz; from the Turks, chisel; from the Chinese, chow mein; and from the Swedish, smorgasbord, to name a few. We are indebted to the American Indian for hickory, hooch, pow-wow, moccasin, and skunk (Shuy, 1967; Wentworth & Flexner, 1960).

These examples suggest that the teacher speaks a form of Standard English that includes any number of vocabularies. These vocabularies may include: (1) a regional form of Standard English; (2) a language used in his profession, avocation, hobby, or sport interest; (3) an earlier language shared with childhood, adolescent, or college peers; or (4) an earlier ethnic or religious vocabulary brought from the home country of his parents or grandparents. In addition, the middle class speaker knows the appropriate social situation in which to use each vocabulary. He acquired this facility through a middle-class conditioning process of imitation and correction through the mediating forces of parents, brothers, sisters, relatives, and teachers; that is, from his total milieu.

Although some middle class urban black children possess typically middle class Standard English vocabularies, personal observations and a review of the pertinent literature suggest that a large proportion of urban blacks do not. These youngsters have their own fully developed and structured linguistic system, containing its own non-Standard lexicon. Moreover, although the middle class teacher's vocabulary includes many lexicons, the words and definitions in his vocabulary are often different from the words and definitions contained in his disadvantaged black student's jive vocabulary. For example, the white male teacher may say, "She's a sharp lookin' chick (or broad)." His black student may say, "Jim, she fly," or "She a phat chib," or "She a boss tip."

It is important to realize that the black disadvantaged child's jive lexicon may be the only language he possesses. He may not have any additional stock of vocabulary words from which to choose. Therefore, at certain times and under certain conditions, it is possible that neither the child nor his teacher possesses a vocabulary that is compatible with the other's.

The streetcorner youngster is probably the one who is most often jailed for various crimes. He is also the youngster who is most often in trouble in school. Additionally, he probably associates most often with other streetcorner inhabitants.

Clemmer (1940) has discussed the development of a particular jail or prison vocabulary. He reported that in prison, whether the inmates use the words or not, they all know the meanings of the argot. "It is even probable that some mental defectives know as much of the prison jargon as they know of common language (p. 90)." Clemmer also suggested that language is one of the most important media for expressing a culture, ". . . therefore, it is necessary for us to understand those aspects of language which are characteristic of our prisoners since, by its use, various contacts and relations develop and the culture is reflected (p. 88)."

Maurer (1964) in a study of the technical argot of the pickpocket with his behavior pattern, reported that most pickpockets assiduously avoid the use of their argot in general conversation and rigorously avoid its use when being observed by nonpickpockets. However, lower level pickpockets "think, speak and live the argot," and they can't avoid its use and would be inarticulate without it. "To pickpockets of this class, standard English is virtually a foreign language (p. 43)."

These teacher-student language incompatibilities play an important role in exacerbating communication problems arising from (1) double meaning or non-Standard word meanings, and (2) crisis or emotional stress situations.

DOUBLE OR NON-STANDARD WORD MEANINGS
AND UNKNOWN WORDS

Problems can be caused from double word meanings and unknown words either unknowingly or purposely. In some cases, the teacher may innocently use a word for which his students have another meaning, often with sexual connotations or overtones. On the other hand, a student may use such words to playfully test his teacher's "hipness," or to deliberately destroy the teacher's effectiveness by student ridicule with a resulting loss of class control. At other times, a word spoken innocently may cause a problem. Thus problem situations may come about when:

1. The teacher does not know all the meanings or nuances of certain words he or she is using.
2. Children purposely use particular words to embarrass or test the teacher, or to wrest control of the class from the teacher.
3. Students use certain words to insult, taunt, or make fun of other children.
4. Children unknowingly use words that cause problems.
5. Students do not know what a Standard English word means.
6. A student does not have another word in his repertoire to use in a particular situation.

There is precedence in Afro-American culture for black urban youngsters' applying a second (often sexual) meaning to a Standard English word. The blues, which to a large extent is based on black folk songs, is replete with double meanings of a sexual nature.

Johnson (1927) divided the double meanings into two general groups: "(1) those meanings pertaining specifically to the sex organs and (2) those relating to the sex act or to some other aspect of sex life (p. 13)." Though his breakdown is into two groups, there is still continual overlapping.

Gold (1964) writes that throughout the history of jazz there runs an opposition and rejection of the "dominant modes of thinking and feeling (p. xviii)." And, that this was often expressed through the "deliberate and significant reversal of the conventional connotations" of certain vocabulary. Gold feels that this usage by Negro jazz men expresses their belief in the hypocracy of conventional white morality. Therefore, the terms with which the white man expresses his morality must be also hypocritical.

> . . . in addition, the puritanical equation of sex with sin has re-
> inforced the Negro's suspicion that the in-group is supremely
> mistaken in its judgments of good and bad, and that standard
> designations of disapproval have been attached to things that are, by
> sensible standard, perfectly good—for example, earthiness and viril-
> ity. Hence, the Negro retains the standard terms of designation, but
> gives to these an interpretation which reverses their value (p. xix).

For example, the term "to jazz" has an American folk speech definition of participating in sexual intercourse (Mencken, 1963, p. 742). According to Oliver (1969), the recorded blues was seldom an outspoken song of protest. Negro self-assertiveness, however, was often manifested through sexual concepts in the blues.

> Above all other subjects there is in blues a preponderance of lyrics
> about sexual love, or merely sex. A complex language of metaphors,
> often domestic or culinary, camouflaged a multitude of sexual
> references. "I want my biscuits in the daytime and my jelly at
> night," declares one singer. "My stove's in good condition, this is the
> stove to brown your bread," his woman replies. A swaggering list of
> the singer's physical attributes was common, with women no less
> than with men. "I'm a big fat woman with meat shakin' on the bone,
> and every time I shake it a skinny woman leaves her home." Sexual
> virtuosity is the subject of scores of blues and the singer played a
> game with the censor and hence with "the Man" when he sang *The
> Dirty Dozen* or *Shave 'Em Dry*. His words were heavily bowdlerized
> but were clear enough to his listeners. Sometimes a more specific
> code would be used—the number combinations of the "policy
> racket"—a kind of "housey-housey"—in which the figures 3 - 6 - 9
> would mean excreta or 4 - 11 - 44 would mean a phallus. In his
> sexual prowess, real or imagined, a man could realize himself; he
> knew and asserted the maturity as a man which segregation and race
> legislation deprived him of within the total society. In sexual blues
> the spirit of revolt was canalised; the blues singer did not care
> whether he was fitting popular stereotypes about the Negro: "I'm
> blue, black, and I'm evil; and I did not make myself," he declared
> coldly (p. 104).

Few symbols are found for sex organs in the blues. Where one is found, however, it is usually "worked to the utmost." One of the most commonly used of these terms is "jelly roll." The term refers to the vagina, the female genitalia, or sometimes sexual intercourse (Johnson, 1927).

A recent reissue of Bessie Smith's earlier records is available and the reader can hear her "Nobody in Town Can Bake a Sweet Jelly Roll Like Mine," "I Need a Little Sugar in My Bowl," and others.

The term *transvaluation* is used by Abrahams (1972) to describe the process of assigning a definition and feeling to a word that is "sometimes diametrically opposed to the accustomed (Standard English) meaning (p. 33)." Abrahams points out that the techniques of using words in this way is a dramatic trait in a "performer-centered word play." The use of such words is an important attribute of a good talker's repertoire because of the affective value. The audience must listen closely to decipher the tone of voice as well as the context to gain the full meaning of the story or presentation.

According to Grier and Cobbs (1968), the slaves brought to America were divided so that none speaking a similar African tribal dialect would be together. This arrangement was made to prevent slaves from communicating and conspiring. Additionally, slaves were not allowed to learn to read or write. Therefore, what English words they learned were garbled and mispronounced and usually understood only by those on the same plantation.

The slaves, however, reversed the purpose of the language as it was given to them, which was what the slave owners did not want. Though the slaveowners laughed at their slaves' misunderstandings and mispronouncements, a secret language began to be developed from the "patois."

> Language was used with a particular emphasis on double meanings. In fact, multiple meanings were imposed on language, as, for example, in the spirituals. To the uninformed listener the words spoke of religious longing; the singing provided a harmonious accompaniment to their work, and to the viewer all was piety and submission. The true meaning of the spirituals, however, involves a communication from one to another regarding plans for escape, hostile feelings toward the master, and a general expression of rebellious attitudes (p. 123).

Inversion is the term Holt (1972) uses to describe the verbal defense mechanism developed by blacks to fight white psychological and linguistic domination. Blacks gradually developed this inversion process as their way of resisting the white man's domination through the use of his language. Furthermore, since the whites' language was also an expression of their caste system, blacks, by mastering the system, would "in effect . . . consent to be mastered by it through the white definitions (p. 154)." By using the inversion process blacks were able to take advantage of the unknowledgeable white opponents.

Blacks took standard words and phrases and reversed or changed their function and meanings. Because the whites were unaware of the dualism, denotations, and connotations that blacks were developing linguistically, whites were unaware of the new interpretations. Consequently, the black and white understanding of a linguistic event were dissimilar. Therefore, blacks were and are able to:

> deceive and manipulate whites without penalty. This protective process, understood and shared by blacks, became a contest of matching wits, the stake in the game being survival with dignity. This form of linguistic guerrilla warfare protected the subordinated, permitted the masking and disguising of true feelings, allowed the subtle assertion of self, and promoted group solidarity. The purpose of the game was to *appear to but not to* (p. 154).

According to White (1970), any discussion of language and the black experience is complicated because historically words were used simultaneously to conceal and express meaning with hidden meanings, nuances, and intuition. Some ideas had to be conveyed to slaves while being hidden from the slavemasters.

> The slavemaster . . . listening to . . . singing "steal away, steal away to Jesus, steal away home" were deceived into believing that the (slaves) were thinking only about Heaven. The real message was about stealing away and splitting up North (p. 50).

Schechter (1970) also discusses the double meanings attached to Bible stories and jazz terms. He writes that "Negroes transformed the accepted (e.g., Bible Stories) into their own unique culture (p. 60)." He uses the term double-entendre to describe the indecent blues expressions that "often approached or reached obscenity (p. 69)" (for example the words "angel cake" and "jelly roll," which referred to female sex organs). Because the words were known to blacks and unknown to whites, blacks laughed when whites unknowingly used any of these expressions.

In addition, blacks used music and humor as outlets in their spirituals and slave work songs where "courageous *double-entendre* lyrics . . . provided a small measure of comic relief from the cruelty and hardships of slavery (p. 26)." Drums, rhythms, and slave work songs also carried ominous warnings and important messages.

With the aforementioned in mind, the reader may begin to understand how the following incidents resulted in classroom disruption of the teaching learning processes.

REALITY 29

The following incident took place in a junior high school language arts class being taught by a young white female teacher. A number of female students were at the board practicing sentence structure skills. One of the students wrote, "Everybody knows Jean is a ho."

Jean jumped up, yelled, "See what she wrote about me!" and attacked the writer. A wild hair-pulling, cursing, and punching fight raged through the school's halls, as a result.

In this incident, a junior high school youngster taunted her classmate by using a word the teacher knew nothing about. Had the teacher known that "ho" meant a whore or prostitute, she could have interceded immediately on behalf of the wronged youngster and the wild, upsetting race through the halls might have been avoided, to say nothing of the loss of another forty-five minutes of instruction.

Actually, had the teacher been doing her homework and keeping up to date with the latest literature by blacks, she might have read Nathan C. Heard's *Howard Street* (1968): "Whut is you? Nuttin' but a 'ho! Seem like t'me you oughta be glad t'have a man want you fuh his woman 'steada his 'ho (p. 95)."

REALITY 30

Another form of testing practiced by many students is to ask a new or experienced teacher who thinks he is "hip," what a certain word means. Sometimes, if the word has an off-color meaning and the teacher is too embarrassed or becomes angry, the children have won even if the teachers knows the definition.

In this incident, handled successfully by a guidance counselor, two junior high school male students asked their guidance counselor, "Do you eat at the 'Y'?"

He responded by playfully pushing them out of his office and saying, "Do you think I was born yesterday!"

Of course, everyone knows that "Y" is short for either Young Men's or Women's Christian Association (Y.M./Y.W.C.A.) or Young Men's or Women's Hebrew Association (Y.M./Y.W.H.A.). As used by these youngsters, "Y" meant "Do you practice cunnilingus?" Had they asked the question of a female teacher they would have been referring to fellatio. This phrase has been observed in use by both blacks and whites. [c]

In Realities 31 and 32 a disadvantaged black high school youngster did not understand the Standard English word used by a middle class school administrator.

[c]This ploy is also used by teachers to taunt new teachers. Two incidents that I know of involved suburban school staffs.

A sign was placed on the teachers' room bulletin board—"All those who want to eat at the Y, sign below."

In the second incident, a male teacher sent a student to new female teachers with a note asking whether they would like to eat at the Y.

REALITY 31

The student had worked for many weeks completing an excellent woodworking project. The teacher picked up the project and called the youngster, as he started for the principal's office. Once in the office, the teacher praised the youngster for his work and complained that the youngster would not allow him to place the project on *display*. Suddenly, the youngster grabbed his project, bolted from the school, and went home. The next day, after a lengthy conversation, it was discovered that the youngster did not know what the word *display* meant. He thought that the woodworking teacher wanted to keep the project that he had worked on for so long.

REALITY 32

A youngster was being questioned by a school administrator concerning a rash of incidents of urinating on the radiators. The suspected youngster was uncooperative and gave the questioning administrator a rough time. Upon questioning the youngster later, it was ascertained that he thought he was being charged with stealing, as he did not know what the word "urinate" meant.[d]

REALITY 33

This incident describes how a black disadvantaged junior high school student, unknowingly, created a problem for himself by using the word "crib." With permission, he walked into the office and politely asked the secretary (who also happened to be black), "Do you mind if I call the crib?"

The harried secretary responded with, "What did you say?"

"May I please call the crib?" he responded once again.

She turned and asked whether he thought he was a wise guy. Luckily, a knowledgeable teacher came by and explained to the secretary that "crib" meant the youngster's home.

REALITY 34

In this next incident, the student did not have another word readily available to use that would describe what he was talking about. He was making a speech as a candidate for school office and ended his presentation with, "No matter what I say, you guys gonna vote for the fellas you *down with*."

The next day when asked what he meant by "down with," he responded, "You know, the guys they drink with, smoke pot with."

[d]See Rowe, M.D., Science and soul, *The Urban Review*, 1969, 4(2), 31, for an article that reports on inner city and suburban upper middle class youngsters verbalizing their observations of guppies defecating.

When asked why he didn't use another word, he said, "Man I don't know no other word. And, anyway, those cats know what I meant."

Reality 35 provides examples of how two teachers handled the same incident where a commercially purchased ditto master caused an interruption of the teaching-learning process. In the first example, the teacher lost the class completely. In the second, because the teacher knew the lexicon, she was able to recoup and get on with the lesson.

REALITY 35

The junior high school language arts teacher was using a commercially purchased ditto master to conduct a class on critical reading. She distributed the dittoed copies to her students and signalled for them to start reading.

After a few minutes, students began to laugh and giggle. The teacher tried to calm the class but finally gave up in desperation. Her students joked and played for the remaining class time. To this day, she is still not sure of what happened.

The material she was using told the story of an Indian chief and his raiding party returning from an unsuccessful raid. Many of his braves had been killed. "The chief was very sad. He was returning to his village in disgrace. He had no booty; he had no scalps."

An innocent appearing sentence? The word "booty" caused the upset. Neither Wentworth and Flexner (1960) nor Stein (1966) list the definition for booty that could explain the students' reactions to the word. Stein (1966, p. 171) provides three reasonably similar definitions for booty, all of which are what middle class students would assume—"spoils taken from an enemy in war; plunder; pillage." Wentworth and Flexner (1960, p. 55) list *bootie* as a 1929 definition meaning a bootlegger. However, the youngsters involved in Reality 35 defined booty as backside, buttocks, or sexual intercourse in their usage.

A similar incident happened to a second teacher using this material. She reacted differently, however, because she was hip to the lexicon.

She just said, "Look, I'm sure this is not talking about *that* definition." After a few more chuckles, the class got back to work. The incident had passed without any real interference with the teaching and learning.

EMOTIONAL STRESS OR CRISIS SITUATIONS

This area takes on almost frightening importance because of the tensions and explosiveness of the atmosphere prevailing in many inner city schools as well as many of the schools receiving bussed youngsters. Within these schools, because of the prevailing conditions, calm, unemotional, nonracist, good intentions can inadvertently deteriorate and explode into crisis. One of the factors working against conflict resolution in these situations is the possibility of linguistic switching or the misreading of cues under emotional stress or crisis.

Among the psycholinguistic factors that may cause problems in this area are: (1) too large a difference between the teacher's language and his student's language, which may lead to alienation and behavior problems (Sheviakov & Redl, 1964); (2) in crisis or emotional stress, those involved may revert to their native, more secure language and/or lexicon (Edwards, 1918; Frazier, 1966; D'Evelyn, 1957; "Tshombe, 1967); (3) for conflict resolution, continual communication is imperative regardless of the topic (McNeil, 1961; Redl, 1964; Redl, 1959); and (4) one may be able to express oneself only through his non-standard dialect or lexicon (Cohen, 1959; Maurer, 1964; Clemmer, 1940; Temple, 1967).

These psycholinguistic behaviors must be considered as they interact with the prevailing life styles of the children in our inner city schools. For example, for many black disadvantaged children, their life is often poverty-stricken, hostile, violent, aggressive, anxious, and unstable. Further, Finn (1969) has found that lower class children "refer more to violence" when compared with upper and middle class children.

Because the child's life style cannot be kept out of the school, confrontation and crisis has become a way of life in many of our inner city and urban schools and universities. Therefore, the potential for further escalation of an already volatile school atmosphere is increased by additional ramifications resulting from psycholinguistic behavior in crisis and emotional stress situations. These may play a crucial role in either the resolution or escalation of a crisis or emotional stress situation.

Morgolis (1970) reported what might be considered a classic example of an escalation of crisis because a white college student unknowingly used a word that had negative meanings to his black protagonist. Actually, this incident reflects the interaction of language and social class, with ethnic overtones.

REALITY 36

A white student in a letter to the editor of Wesleyan University's *The Argus*, referred to a black student as a "punk." Because the white student was unaware of the black student's definition of punk, and that the black student came from a social class background that settled problems with fists, the following escalation ensued:

> In Black argot, and unknown to Berg, 'punk' means homosexual. That night about a dozen Blacks went to Berg's room and threatened

him with physical harm if he did not retract his statement. The next night Walker paid another call on Berg, found him taking a shower, and beat him up.

As racial tempers continue to reach a boiling point, the possibility of misunderstood lexicon increases.

REALITY 37

A white high school administrator, giving out late passes to a black student who appeared tired and red-eyed, said, "Boy, you look beat up and tired."

Whereupon, the young man jumped back, threw up his hands and yelled, "Who's beat up?"

The comment, innocent from the administrator's point of view, was interpreted as a challenge to the manhood of the youngster. He interpreted the comment to mean that he had just been beaten up in a fight. Luckily, the school administrator did not overreact to the youngster's challenge. Instead, he questioned him and then explained what he had meant.

REALITY 38

In this incident, a black student was annoying his teacher when his teacher said, "Stop buggin' me."

The youngster responded by running into the hall, throwing off his coat, and challenging the teacher to a fight by yelling, "You better check yourself before you wind up by yourself."

The teacher became fearful and words and threats began to be exchanged between the teacher and his student when a school administrator appeared. The administrator calmed the incident and it was then resolved when he elicited from the youngster the fact that *buggin'*, in his neighborhood meant "let's go—let's fight."

REALITY 39

In a similar incident, a student had followed his new program which contained an error made by the school's office. A school administrator was trying to straighten out the mistake with the youngster. However, the young man began to verbally play with and harass the administrator. Whereupon, the administrator said, "Come on, I'm not playing now."

With this, the student jumped up out of his seat, ran into the hall, and yelled that he was ready to fight. The administrator, who had been on reasonably good terms with the youngster, calmed him down and found that the youngster had interpreted "I'm not playing now," as a challenge to a fight.

In Reality 40, a white female guidance counselor could have prevented what started out as a low key verbal encounter from escalating into a regrettable incident had she understood her student's language.

REALITY 40

Two black female students in a special college skills program were engaged in verbally aggressive argument. The guidance counselor realized that something was wrong and walked between the girls. However, as the argument heated, the girls lapsed further into their dialect, using a lexicon which the counselor did not understand. The counselor just watched without knowing how threatening to each other the girls had become. The resulting fight, during which one of the girls was severely hurt, took her completely by surprise.

REALITY 41

This incident took place in a high school for emotionally disturbed youngsters. A white teacher was working with a student. Suddenly, the door burst open and one of his students rushed into the room and demanded his coat, which was locked in a metal closet. Since it was too early for the student to go home, the teacher told the youngster to wait until he the teacher finished his work with the other student.

The youngster then lost control of his behavior and began kicking and smashing the metal closet doors while pulling the closet from the wall. The teacher rose from his seat, pushed the closet back against the wall, turned, and started to speak to the out-of-control youngster.

He jumped back and said, "You gonna *off* me?"

Since the teacher knew the lexicon, he responded with, "If I have to."

Whereupon the youngster sat down and waited calmly.

The word "off" was popularized a few years ago in such usages as "Off the pigs." Off can mean anything from kill, beat up, destroy, to "waste" (lexicon to beat up or kill). In the above incident it meant that the teacher would have intervened by physically restraining the youngster. The school where the incident took place forbade corporal punishment, while staff used nonpunitive physical restraining techniques. In this incident, the situation was ameliorated because the teacher knew his student's lexicon.

Two interesting examples of linguistic switching are reported in Realities 42 and 43.

REALITY 42

As a teacher was describing an incident in her classroom, she became excited and switched her linguistic style to her earlier dialect. When she had completed the story, she was asked whether she realized that she had switched linguistic styles?

She responded, "When I get hot, I don't have time to think—I say the first thing that comes to my mind."

The second example is similar to the first in many respects. A teacher was describing a school incident when she said, "I tol' im, I'd hit 'em on the *butt*."

I looked at her and said, "Do you realize you used the word *butt*?"

She responded by saying, "When they get me provoked, I don't have time to say 'behind'! I don't have time to think. I was talkin' that way all my life."

Linguistic switching can be observed not only in an overt crisis situation, but also in the classroom as students and teachers become positively involved in an emotional discussion. In Yurick's (1968) *The Bag*, one of the main characters switches his linguistic style as he deteriorates emotionally. Very often, black civil rights leaders will switch to their dialect when giving an emotional speech. In labor bargaining sessions in the French areas of Canada, the bargaining begins in English. However, as the discussions become heated, linguistic switching takes place and French becomes the language. Edwards (Frazier, 1966) reports that when his maternal grandmother, who came to this country as a slave and who could speak the African language "became angry, no one could understand what she said (p. 11)." Interestingly, when Moise Tshombe, the late former president of the Congo, was brought to Algeria and injected with sodium pentothal, he confounded his captors by speaking in his tribal dialect (Tshombe, 1967).

Apparently there is a difference between the anxiety of an athletic contest and the anxiety generated in a court of law. A well known All-American black basketball star went before a judge for a speeding ticket. Although the judge thought she was taking the athlete's basketball schedule into consideration when she fixed a trial date, the judge set a wrong date. According to the newspaper report, supposedly the following verbal switching occurred:

REALITY 43

At this point Lanier, acting as his own lawyer, should have worked up an objection to the date with such phrases as "Your honor" and "May it please the court" and other time-worn stereotyped expressions.

Instead, he blurted out: "I won't be here, baby."

This brought a broad smile from Judge Mikoll, who usually goes about her work with a rather set solemn manner.

"I am not your baby," she answered (O'Grady, 1969, p. 31).

The following anecdote describes how a Polish-speaking Jew lived through Gestapo torture and was not deported to a gas chamber.

He was "passing" as a Christian when a former neighbor informed the Gestapo that he was Jewish. In such cases it was Gestapo practice to torture the suspect until the pain became so unbearable that he could no longer control his language and would cry out in Yiddish, which was the primary language of most East European Jews. In this instance, however, though the person was Jewish, Yiddish had not been spoken in his upper class Warsaw home. Consequently, even under torture he continued to cry for help in Polish. Having schooled himself to behave like a Christian, he repeatedly called out to Jesus, Mary, and the Christian Saints, convincing the Gestapo that he was not Jewish. He was eventually released and survived the war.

ADDITIONAL CONSIDERATIONS

The language we use to communicate and to be understood can be called an arbitrary system of vocal symbols. What is appropriate or inappropriate depends upon the social group and context within which we are attempting to communicate. Because of many factors, most black disadvantaged youngsters do not possess either Stokely Carmichael's or the late Dr. George Wiley's middle-class ability to switch to the appropriate verbal code, and hence social role, as described.

> In the four months that I traveled with him I marveled at his ability to adjust to any environment. Dressed in bib overalls, he tramped the backlands of Lowndes County, Alabama, urging Negroes, in a Southern-honey drawl, to register and vote. The next week, wearing a tight dark suit and Italian boots, using the language they dig most—hip and very cool. A fortnight later, jumping from campuses to intellectual salons, where he was equally damned and lionized, he spoke with eloquence and ease about his cause, quoting Sartre, Camus and Thoreau (Parks, 1967, p. 77).

> "We demand $35,000. We demand it now and that's that." A moment later, talking to a reporter, Dr. Wiley shifted from anger to a scholarly calm that belied the tense atmosphere in the convention hall, as it reflected his academic background.
>
> And then, turning next to the Negro youths who were still barricading the hall because Dr. Wiley had not yet told them to desist, he slipped into the vernacular of the street, obviously retaining their confidence with it.
>
> The ease with which the 38-year-old leader established the several relationships illustrated one of the major assets of a black militant who speaks with mounting national power for an increasing number of impoverished Americans (Borders, 1969, p. 32).

For many black disadvantaged youngsters their dialect, and particularly their lexicon, may be their only mode of verbal communication. Their language is an integral part of them; to deny their language and its use is to deny them. Language is egocentric. Indeed, certain hypotheses can be made in relation to lexicons.

1. The social structure and attitudes of a group are reflected in its lexicon (Clemmer, 1940; Marckwardt, 1958; Sapir, 1956);
2. Lexicons are developed, at times, by subcultures to maintain or develop privacy, selectivity and/or status (Bernstein, 1958; Brewer, 1966; Calitri, 1964; Clemmer, 1940; Guitar, 1963; Heffron, 1962; Hibbert, 1963);
3. Lexical terms and definitions change and may vary according to city, area, neighborhood, or even from school to school or class to class (Brown, 1965; Evans & Evans, 1957; Foster, 1966, 1968);
4. Some forms of lexicon are used by all levels of society, professions, and occupations (Evans & Evans, 1957; Kelly, 1962);
5. A nonstandard lexicon may, in some cases, be the only verbal language known to a particular individual (Goldberg, 1964; Kelly, 1962);
6. The use of a special vocabulary is perfectly acceptable and often the only method of verbal communication in certain subcultures (Maurer, 1964); and
7. With time, certain words of a group's nonstandard lexicon may become acceptable English (Hibbert, 1963; Nelson, 1964).

Furthermore, lexicons are always in a state of flux.

1. Words change meaning.
2. New words are born.
3. Some words lie fallow only to grow in use at a later date.
4. Word usage and definition sometimes differ from city to city—even neighborhood to neighborhood.
5. The definition of a word may depend upon who is using it and the context of the conversation in which it is being used.
6. The way a word is pronounced, and even the syllable on which the emphasis is placed, may also have to be considered before certain words can be defined.
7. With time, some words become shortened.
8. A school youngster's definition or understanding of a word may vary from that of a more sophisticated adult, of an older or younger child, or even that of the child's parents. For example:

> Sometimes I would try to tell Mama things in the slang terms. They had their down-home slang expressions. I couldn't understand theirs too much and they couldn't understand ours. The slang had

changed. In this day when someone would say something about a bad cat, they meant he was good (Brown, 1965, p. 28).

Despite these lexical variations, the student's language and, in particular, his lexicon, must be considered as being integral to improving student-teacher communication. I have used my student's lexicon successfully in curriculum materials, the binding of student-teacher relationships, the easing of student-teacher and student-peer tensions, and the improving of teacher-student articulation.

Many of the riots in the black ghetto a few years ago were, to some extent, caused by the inability of white officers to differentiate between a real threat and ghetto rhetoric. Similarly, the fuse for the Attica prison riot in New York State, was ignited when a guard misinterpreted horseplay.

The top ranking black police officer in Detroit, Deputy Chief Inspector George Harge, points up the problem white officers face in differentiating between repartee and a real threat.

> Language is the biggest barrier. White policemen find it hard to differentiate between riot language and horseplay language. Some black talk implies an imminent riot to whites, but to blacks it is a way of life. A rash decision by a patrolman based on language that he believes is offensive can precipitate instead of quash a riot (The Anguish, 1970, p. 14).

Another manifestation of this controversy was brought out when *Time* (The Panthers, 1970) reported on the disagreement between the F.B.I. and the then Attorney General, Ramsey Clark. The F.B.I. wanted to bug the Panthers and Clark turned them down as a "local law-enforcement problem, not as a national menace.... 'Life,' said one veteran of those days, 'is full of chances. The question is whether you're going to exhaust yourself guarding against dangers that don't exist (p. 30).' "

However, John Mitchell's Justice Department looked upon the Panthers as more of a national threat.

> If a Hilliard threatens the President, said one Panther specialist there, we can't afford to sit back and say, "That's just rhetoric." They have the capability of killing any government official, and I'm not going to get into the position of having to walk around apologizing after they do it (p. 30).

In the same article, *Time* pointed out that the Panthers are engaging in "guerrilla theater masterfully done—so masterfully that, at a point, everybody began to believe them and to be frightened of them (p. 26)."

In my doctoral dissertation (Foster, 1969), one of the few studies related to the black disadvantaged student's dialect and lexicon, I studied the effect of introducing non-Standard English dialect and lexicon upon the black disadvantaged 10th grade high schools student's ability to comprehend, to recall, and to be fluent and flexible in providing titles for verbal material.[e]

Examination of the data revealed the students scored higher in response to non-Standard English stories than they did to the Standard English stories. Furthermore, the results, at least as they relate to recall, flexibility, and fluency, suggest that the subjects obviously think better in their language when they are: (1) cued in some semblance of their language, (2) not limited to preset written responses, and (3) allowed to respond verbally, freely, and to interpret as they proceed. The test also suggested that in an uninhibiting situation, the black disadvantaged youngster can be more verbal and intellectually creative in his own language than he can be in Standard English.

STREET CULTURE, GRAFFITI, AND CURRICULUM

Graphic arts is an ideal subject area for bringing student street culture and lexicon into the school's curriculum. Student street culture can provide the motivation for achieving curriculum objectives. Three of the many street related curriculum areas I have worked with are (1) wolf tickets, (2) party announcements and tickets, and (3) graffiti and L.A.M.F.

Wolf Tickets

About ten years ago, my students started using the words *wolf* or *woof* interchangeably in a number of ways.

A student might say, "Mr. Foster, he's woofin' on me."

This may have meant anything from he is challenging me to a fight, to he is making fun of my clothing or my mother. Accepting a "wolf ticket" was accepting a challenge to fight (see Chapter Five).

One of my students cut a wolf's head out of linoleum, another set some type, and thousands of wolf tickets were printed. (Illustration 1 in Chapter Four) Printing wolf tickets gave my shop status with students. By printing wolf tickets that were related to my students' street culture: (1) working in my shop took on new meaning, (2) many students increased their work in the shop, and (3) some ended up working in the graphic arts industry. Of course, students had to master preliminary skills before they were allowed to print the tickets.

[e]Dillard (1972, p. 241) reports that "The lengthiest treatment of ethnic slang known to me is a dissertation at Columbia University Teachers College by Herbert Foster, who was steered onto the subject as a study of the 'cant' of 'emotionally disturbed' youngsters and discovered that it was not cant and that the youngsters were culturally different rather than emotionally disturbed."

Wolf Ticket

This person is allowed to
wolf anyone or anything
whenever he pleases.

This card, however, is not valid on the Sabbath.

Illustration 4-1.

Party Announcements and Tickets

My students printed invitations and announcements that usually contained a rhyme announcing their parties, sessions, sets, or gigs. (Illustration 2 in Chapter Four)

Taking pictures of Harlem graffiti, I came across a rhyme on a wall similar to those printed on the above cards. (Illustration 3 in Chapter Four)

Later, as I read Negro history, I discovered that the rhyming cards had historical significance for my students. A Southern custom, the Friday night fish fry or house rent party, moved North during prohibition and the depression. In Chicago, these parties were called a "parlor social," "gouge," "struggle," "percolator," "too terrible party," or the "skiffle." Most often though, they were just called a house rent party or a boogie. During the worst of the depression days these parties "provided a substitute for open saloons, being mounted in back-rooms in ten thousand apartments all over the South Side (Oliver, 1969, p. 83)."

In Harlem, the parties were also referred to as whist parties or dances. They were held to raise rent money, and "to have a get-together of one's own, where you could do the black bottom with no stranger behind you trying to do it, too (Hughes & Bontemps, 1958, p. 596)."

Langston Hughes (Hughes & Bontemps, 1958) writes that these parties

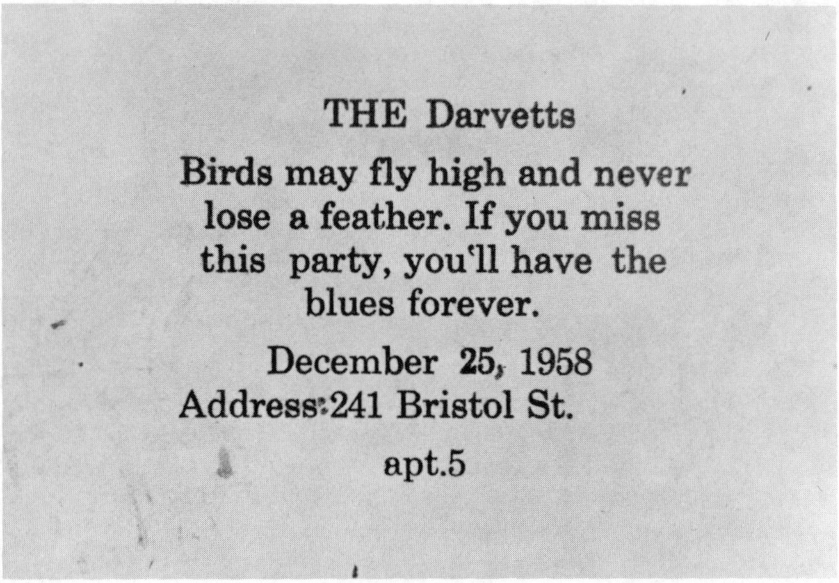

THE Darvetts

Birds may fly high and never lose a feather. If you miss this party, you'll have the blues forever.

December 25, 1958
Address: 241 Bristol St.

apt. 5

Illustration 4-2.

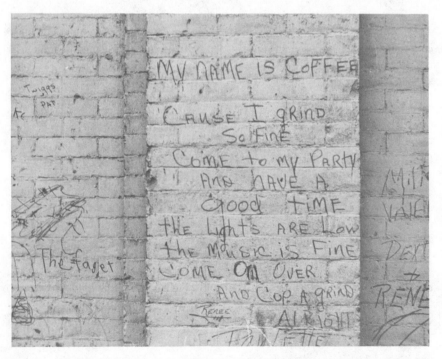

Illustration 4-3.

... were often more amusing than any night club, in small apartments where God knows who lived—because the guests seldom did—but where the piano would often be augmented by a guitar, or an old cornet, or somebody with a pair of drums walking in off the street. And where awful bootleg whisky and good fried fish or steaming chitterlings were sold at very low prices. And the dancing and singing and impromptu entertaining went on until dawn came in at the windows (p. 597).

These parties were usually advertised or announced by "brightly colored cards stuck on the grills of apartment house elevators. Some of the cards were highly entertaining in themselves (p. 597)." (Illustration 4 in Chapter Four)

Malcolm X (Haley, 1966, p. 76) also reminisces about the "rent-raising parties," and people giving out little cards announcing the parties. One that he went to had about 30 to 40 guests eating, dancing, sweating, drinking, and gambling. They were all together in a run-down apartment, "the record player going full blast, the fried chicken or chitlins with potato salad and collard greens for a dollar a plate, and cans of beer or shots of liquor for fifty cents."

Graffiti and L.A.M.F.

I became interested in graffiti when one of my students printed a card that caused quite a stir. My policy allowed anyone who printed a card to tack it up for all to see. One youngster printed a card with his name and the letters L.A.M.F. (Illustration 5 in Chapter Four)

Winding and Grinding like the old Dutch Mill,
The Boys do the work while the Girls stand still

A SOCIAL PARTY

Given By

THE ADELERETTE'S S. C.

At 170 West 136th Street   Apt. 12

SATURDAY OCTOBER 6, 1956   9 Until?

Donation 50 Cents   Free Cocktail

Illustration 4-4.

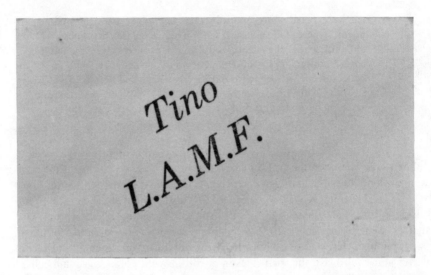

Illustration 4-5.

This card was up for two weeks when I realized that there was some snickering and guffawing over the card. Upon investigating, I discovered that L.A.M.F. meant "Like a Mother Fucker." Further investigation, however, disclosed a different type of meaning from that related to fornication.

This youngster was boasting, in his own way, that he was proud. Since then I have seen L.A.M.F. affixed to individual and gang names or even such as "black–L.A.M.F." Often when used with gang names L.A.M.F. is usually accompanied with D.T.K. which means "down to kill." (Illustration 6 in Chapter Four) More recently, in my travels to Brooklyn, I have noticed the same L.A.M.F.–D.T.K. in what were Jewish and Italian middle class neighborhoods. Whether blacks and Puerto Ricans have moved into these neighborhoods or Jewish and Italian youngsters have picked up the graffiti, I don't know.

L.A.M.F. has shown up in a number of other places. A rock record by Bunky and Jake is titled *Bunky & Jake L.A.M.F. The New York Times* (Roberts, 1967) and the *Herald Tribune* (No landlord, 1962) ran pictures showing walls on which L.A.M.F. was written. The *Star Journal* (Button, 1965) reported, as part of the button craze a few years ago, students at Queens College in New York City, wearing buttons that had the inscription L.A.M.F. According to button wearers, L.A.M.F. meant "Let's All Make Friends," and "Look At My Face."

In its own way, today's L.A.M.F. and D.T.K. graffiti may compare with the blustering masculine epic yell, roar, brag, boast, holla, scream, or boasting chant of the Mike Finks, The Davy Crocketts, and the hosts of

raftsmen, cowboys, riverboat men, mountain men, bullies, and pseudo bad men
of the American frontier.

> West of the Mississippi the scream of the backwoods boaster and
> bully passed into the howl of the pseudo or mock bad man, who, in
> his boasting chants and yells, proclaimed his intestinal fortitude with
> more and more weird anatomical details. . . .
> No one liked to play bad man more than the cowboy on a
> spree; . . . But if a would-be desperado announced that it was his
> time to howl, this was chiefly for the benefit of the uninitiated. For
> the rest knew that with the true bad man or killer the rule was:
> "Shoot first and talk afterward."
> On the frontier, however, "apparent rage" and "vigorous lan-
> guage" had their uses in bluffing or blustering one's way out of a
> tight place as well as in letting off steam (Botkin, 1944, pp. 51-52).
> "Bad men," of the "I eat humans for breakfast" kind functioned
> in the presence of tenderfoots by fierce looks and snorts, by savage
> remarks, and sometimes by the recital of speeches ferocious in
> phrase and committed to memory. These men would "wild up"
> whenever they obtained an impressionable audience, and their
> braggadocio often was picturesque, even though made up at least in

Illustration 4–6.

part from strings of stereotyped Western anecdotes (Botkin, 1944, p. 60).

Typical of this form of bravado was David Crockett's brag.

"I'm that same David Crockett, fresh from the backwoods, half-horse, half-alligator, a little touched with the snapping-turtle; can wade the Mississippi, leap the Ohio, ride upon a streak of lightning, and slip without a scratch down a honey locust; can whip my weight in wild cats—and if any gentleman pleases, for a ten dollar bill, he may throw in a panther—hug a bear too close for comfort, and eat any man opposed to Jackson (Botkin, 1944, p. 56)."

Bragging or boasting has always been part of the make up of the hero. The same holds for the streetcorner youngster. The fantasy and transparent world of the streetcorner is similar to Botkin's (1944, p. 3) feelings about the backwoods boaster.

[He] seemed more interested in making claims than in living up to them. Moreover, since boasting, like bombast, contains in itself the seeds of its own travesty, it became hard to distinguish bragging from windy laughing at bragging and serious from mock or burlesque boasts.

Although graffiti can tell you who is going with whom, who claims the territory, turf, or neighborhood of the school, what someone's nickname is; can be used to boast without any immediate put up; and is usually found all over the school, there is not too much that has been reported in the professional literature. Unfortunately, most educators consider graffiti as defacing the school rather than reporting what has been happening in the school and the neighborhood; few are able to decipher the graffiti.

In Yurick's *The Warriors* (1966), he describes Hinton making his graffiti mark.

Hector told Hinton to leave their mark. Hinton took out the Magic Marker and put the Family sign on the tomb, Dominators, LAMF, DTK and told the Junior, "I leave this for them ghosts" (p. 50).

Wambaugh, in his *The New Centurions* (1970, p. 111-112) dramatically and realistically describes the actions of members of the Los Angeles Police Force. His writing takes officers to the Mexican barrio where officers also observe graffiti.

This was a gang neighborhood, a Mexican gang neighborhood, and Mexican gang members were obsessed with a compulsion to make their mark on the world. . . . Serge read the writing on the wall in black and red paint from spray cans which all gang members carried in their cars in case they would spot a windfall like this creamy yellow irresistible blank wall. There was a heart in red, three feet in diameter, which bore the names of "Ruben and Isabel" followed by *"mi vida"* and there was the huge declaration of an Easystreeter which said *"El Wimpy de los Easystreeters,"* and another one which said "Ruben *de los Easystreeters*," but Ruben would not be outdone by Wimpy and the legend below his name said *"De los Easystreeters y del mundo,"* and Serge smiled wryly as he thought of Ruben who claimed the world as his domain because Serge had yet to meet a gang member who had ever been outside Los Angeles County. There were other names of Junior Easystreeters and Peewee Easystreeters, dozens of them, and declarations of love and ferocity and the claims that this was the land of the Easystreeters. Of course at the bottom of the wall was the inevitable "CON ʹSAFOS," the crucial gang incantation not to be found in any Spanish dictionary, which declared that none of the writing on this wall can ever be altered or despoiled by anything later written by the enemy (pp. 111-112).

In my study of cant (Foster, 1967) no mention was made of ghetto graffiti per se. However, D.T.K. and L.A.M.F. were reported with definitions. My dissertation (Foster, 1969) provided some material on graffiti. More recently, Kohl (1969; 1972) has provided graffiti material. Salisbury (1958) refers to graffiti as "a living newspaper of the streets."

Here are the threats and taunts of rival gangs, the challenges and defiances. Here is word of neighborhood romance, old flames and new loves. Here bids are staked for leadership. Here bulletins are posted on the rumbles (p. 4).

Goldstein (1973) described the graffiti blitz of New York City subway cars. And, *New York Magazine* (The Graffiti, 1973) inaugurated the Taki Awards (to be known as I.A.s) for the graffiti conquest of the New York City subways.

The Taki award was spawned by the *New York Times* ('Taki 183,' 1971). The *Times* reported on a 17-year-old high school graduate named Taki (Taki is a traditional Greek diminutive for Demetrius, his real first name) who lived on 183rd Street between Audubon and Amsterdam Avenues in New York City, and using a Magic Marker, wrote "Taki 183" all over New York City. Taki claims he took the idea from "Julio 204," who did it for a few years until he stopped when busted. Taki started leaving his mark in the summer of 1970. He began by sneaking his name and street onto ice cream trucks in his neighborhood.

"I didn't have a job then," he said, "and you pass the time, you know. . . . I just did it everywhere I went. I still do, though not as

much. You don't do it for girls; they don't seem to care. You do it for yourself. You don't go after it to be elected President. . . .
"I don't feel like a celebrity normally," he said. "But the guys make me feel like one when they introduce me to someone. 'This is him,' they say. The guys knows who the first one was (p. 31)."

Graffiti writing in New York City really took off after the article, and subway graffiti became the vogue. Earlier subway graffiti was confined primarily to station advertising and placards.

The onslaught of ink and paint has spread to steel and tile walls, to route maps in cars, to station ceilings and to trackside walls reachable only through subway windows or by standing between the cars of stopped trains (Prial, 1972, p. 33).

More recently, the graffiti has spread to what is referred to as "grand design" or "masterpiece graffiti." "The masterpiece is a large, usually multicolored, inscription, applied on the side of a subway car with cans of paint spray, that may cover half or more of the car's length (Fight, 1973, p. 39)."

Most of New York City's over 6,000 subway cars have been "hit" (to hit something is to write on it) with graffiti (The graffiti, 1973). It costs the Transit Authority more than $1.3 million a year for the "defacing" of subways and busses (Shirry, 1972). Philadelphia, meanwhile, spends about $4,000,000 a year trying to curb graffiti. (Philadelphia graffiti, with its lean geometric letters with little platforms—the fancier, the more hip, the more ego boosting—has been the undisputed graffiti capital of the United States.) An antigraffiti law was finally passed in New York City in 1972 (Stiff, 1972; Lindsay, 1972).

Stocker (1971) suggested schools develop graffiti fences of paper to combat school graffiti. Others use graffiti corners, graffiti bulletin boards, and a number of school libraries that I know of have conducted graffiti contests.

Ghetto youngsters coming to the University bring their graffiti with them. Thus graffiti in the University of Buffalo's Norton Union called for "Girl Needed to Pull a Train—Call (a number was provided)."

To "pull a train" is for a female to have consecutive sexual intercourse with numbers of males. The female pulling the train may do so voluntarily for financial remuneration, forcefully, or out of fear. Synonyms are a "gang bang" or a "gang shag."[f]

[f]Brown (1965, p. 16) wrote that "They thought I was one of the guys who had pulled a train on their sister in the park the summer before." Iceberg Slim (1967, p. 312) defines *train*, n, as "mass rape" and describes his participation.
 Yurick (1966, pp. 106-110) in his *Warriors* described a street gang pulling a train. Heard (1968, pp. 75-78) described an almost similar incident. This time, however, the train is pulled in the Newark ghetto—and the teenager who rode the train twice discovers it was his mother.
 One of my students told me that he had once been a "caboose" on a train. Another student described a gang bang that he had taken part in with twelve boys and the

The following picture of graffiti was observed in Buffalo. (Illustration 7, Chapter IV) In addition, on some buildings, the knowledgeable teacher can interpret the graffiti just as an archeologist discovers bones and artifacts located in various horizons.

LANGUAGE ARTS

Of all the inner city school teachers who should know jive lexicon and black dialect, the most important is the language arts teacher. To be realistic, though, so should all suburban and urban language arts teachers understand and know jive lexicon as well.

Many suburban and urban districts have introduced black studies programs and have placed books by black authors on their reading lists and in their libraries. Some teachers take their students to see plays by Afro-American authors. If they are not truly hip to black streetcorner culture and language, they, probably inadvertently, will be feeding their students misinformation and possibly racism. Indeed, a large amount of the present works by black authors is based on their streetcorner experiences.

Tom Wolfe (1970), provided an example of this in his usual style. He described an English class at San Francisco State where the white female "Peter, Paul, and Mary-type" intellectual instructor read aloud to her class of predominately liberal white students from Cleaver's (1968) *Soul On Ice*. She read to her students in a "pure serene tone." When finished, she closed *Soul On Ice* just like a preacher closing the bible. Her eyes shone, her chin was up, and she had a soulful look on her face.

She had read with heavy emotion, letting it all sink in. She had her students all thinking they were in a college cell block, and that revolution was the only thing that could change the damn system.

She asked for comments. A ghetto blood raised his hand to speak, and she recognized him "with the most radiant brotherly smile the human mind imagines and says, 'yes?' " The brother put her and all the white students down and told them that ghetto folks would probably laugh at what she just read.

> You try coming down in the Fillmore doing some *previously dabbling* and talking about Albert Camus and James Balwin. They'd laugh you off the block. That book was written to give a thrill to

---

girl was there voluntarily. It was at Coney Island in the back of a truck. The eleventh in line discovered the girl was his sister. Whereupon, according to my informant, "he picked her up, smacked her in the face, and kept screaming at her." As I think back, it was never clear whether he discovered it was his sister before or after he rode the train.

Trains are pulled everywhere. Thompson (1967, pp. 247-248) described the Hell's Angels getting a young lady to pull a train for more than fifty men including her former husband. Tom Wolfe (1969, p. 157) appeared to describe the same train at a bash at Ken Kesey's place in LaHonda, California. Selby (1967, pp. 96, 112-116) described Tralala pulling endless trains in Brooklyn.

white women in Palo Alto and Marin County. That book is the best su*burb*an jive I ever heard. . . . and don't preevy-dabble the people with no split-level Palo Alto white bourgeois housewife Buick Estate Wagon backseat rape fantasies . . . you know? . . . " (p. 128).

He completely destroyed their "black hero trip" before they really had a chance to get into it. They are really confused, they cannot talk against what he just said because he looks and talks like real ghetto. "So mostly this fellow is trying to blow their minds because they are being smug and knowing about The Black Man. He's saying, "Don't try to tell *us* who our leaders are, because you don't know (p. 129)."

Reading the above reminded me of a story a black woman college student told me about a language arts class she had been in in high school. Her white female teacher was reading some prose about the British soldiers during the Revolutionary War.

REALITY 44

"This teacher was reading us this story, and she came to, "The soldiers in their red uniforms and black *boots, boots, boots!*"[g]

"All the guys and girls started crackin' up and laughing." "She just stood there and couldn't figure out what had happened that we were all laughing."

"Why didn't someone tell her why you were all laughing?" I asked.

"Oh, I don't know," she responded, "We were kind of ashamed to do it." "We had tried to tell her other things but she just would look at us."

Reality 45 is part of a taped conversation I had with a black high school student who was both laughing and disgusted about all the books in his school by blacks and about blacks but that were unintelligible to his white teachers, thereby almost making everything useless because the white language arts teachers could not interpret or even understand many of the writings.

REALITY 45

"We got all these books but the teachers don't understand them."

"It's in the book, you know." "The latest one out on blacks." "It concerns the point of the story." "A short story concerning this fellow going into town and the white man arresting him for no reason and he turns around and shoots this cop, and he speaks about a monkey on his back."[h]

[g]*Boots* is used to refer to blacks or Negroes, usually in a pejorative sense.

[h]The term, "monkey on my back" was popularized back in the late '40s and early '50s by Nelson Algren's *Man with the Golden Arm*. A movie was produced based on the book, which dealt with heroin addicts.

"You know, killing the monkey to feed my habit."

"And, she swears this means killing the white man to survive in a racist society. This is not it. It's not it at all!" "You know, to kill a monkey, to feed my habit—it is slang for a junkie. . . ."

"Yeah, but you can't convince her of it."

What is going on in some schools is a reversal of the usual role of the English teacher. Traditionally, the teacher knows and the student does not know the context clues. However, if the middle class teacher is not "into" Afro-American literature, her black students will understand the context clues and she will not.

Realities 46 and 47 are reasonably similar. However, Reality 46 took place in Vietnam and Reality 47 took place in an urban high school in New York State.

REALITY 46

The South Vietnamese finally closed down a comic strip entitled "Bich Bop." The comic strip stories usually ridiculed the officers and men of the Army of the Republic of South Vietnam in their struggles with the Vietcong—who usually came out on top.

The stories in Vietnamese slang contained frequently lewd obscenities, were always ungrammatical, and were popular with the youth of Saigon. Because of the slang, it took a long time for the Ministry of Information to catch on. At first, they chiseled out the word balloons over the characters' heads. A few months later, they closed the comic strip down altogether (Just, W., 1966).

Too often, middle class language arts teachers feel their responsibility to their students ends when they put the black authored books on their reading list, or provide the books. Real involvement goes beyond this token approach. Real involvement means reading the books and learnings what they are saying. It seems not enough middle class teachers are able to do this.

Reality 47 is part of another taped conversation with a black high school youngster. The conversation concerns a book that the teacher had provided for the class and which he did not understand.

REALITY 47

Student: "Well this was one that they produced at ———High School. They were laughing at the teacher for . . . because he didn't even understand what we were really getting across to him."

Adult: "Was the book made by the youngsters at ————High School?"

Student: "No, this is one [that] one of the teachers had given to the kids." "The kids were laughing at him because they, you know, they would get to various slang words and various expressions and the teacher couldn't explain it."

Many black authored books have been published in the past decade that are heavy with jive talk. A few are Haley's (1966) *The Autobiography of Malcolm X*, Pharr's (1969), *The Book of Numbers*, Brown's (1965) *Manchild in the Promised Land*, Cain's (1970) *Blueschild Baby*, Reed's (1972) *Mumbo Jumbo*, Heard's (1968) *Howard Street*, and Brown's (1969) *The Life & Loves of Mr. Jiveass Nigger.*[i] (See notes to Chapter Four for full references.)

Also lately, books by white authors contain jive talk too. Some of these are Bonham's (1971) *Cool Cat*, Wambaugh's (1970) *The New Centurions*, Stevens's (1971) *Way Uptown in Another World*, Knebel's (1969) *Trespass*, Cooper's (1969) *Black Star*, and Mezzrow's (1964) *Really the Blues*. There are also books like Malamud's (1971) *The Tenants* where you have to know both jive talk and Yiddish (see Notes).

In addition to jive lexicon, the language arts teacher should also know what such sentences as " 'Lesser, I have to pull your coat about a certain matter (Malamud, 1971, p. 55),' " or, what words such as *megillah* (p. 43), *shiksa* (p. 33), and *chutspah* (p. 29) mean. If you are listening to records by black authors, how would you interpret "When the man runs his game, he sure runs it mean"?[j]

Many black poets are using and have used jive talk as an expression of blackness.

By the end of the 1960's there were indications that Black artists and intellectuals were picking up Black English and making it a symbol of Black unity. Today an impressive school of Black poets is producing poetry in Black English and expressing pride in the expressive power of the language (Dillard, 1972, p. 114).

Imamu Amira Baraka (LeRoi Jones) (Baraka & Fundy, 1970) use jive lexicon and Black English creatively as a form of expression. Some of the jive lexicon used includes "vine," "main man," "fly," and "a do rag." According to Ron Welburn, (1971) Baraka uses language and Fundi (Billy Abernathy) uses images that blacks understand and whites have problems understanding.

The language is rich, but never inflated or esoteric; it abounds with

[i]An early book introducing Negro dialect into American fiction was Hugh H. Brackenridge's *Modern Chivalry* (Part I, 1972). Tremaine McDowell (1930) in writing "Notes on Negro Dialect in the American Novel to 1821," spells Negro with a small n and also uses the word "negress."

[j]*Ain't supposed to die a natural death,* by Melvin Van Peebles, Advantage Sound Studios, N.Y.C., A & M Records, SP 3510.

verbal images that only blacks are likely to interpret effectively. There are no concessions made to the nonblack reader. . . . Couched in the language of the streets and intoned with the rhythms of jazz, it is both an expression and evocation of the rudiments of blackness, which whites may find perplexing (p. 11).

Welburn (1971) also points out to the nonblack reader that the title of the book, *In our Terribleness,*

. . . is derived from black slang, in which reversing the white standard, "bad" and "terrible" are synonymous with "good" and "superb" (p. 10).

In Jones and Neal's (1970) *Black Fire: An Anthology of Afro-American Writing*, jive lexicon is used throughout in the poetry and short stories. Such jive words and expressions as "toms," "grey," "gimme five," "outta sight," "stone," "fox," "run it down," "shades," and "buns" are used. James T. Stewart (Jones & Neal, 1970, p. 202) uses "half a man" and "buns" in "Announcements." Marvin E. Jackman (Jones & Neal, 1970), in his *Flowers for the Trashman*, employs such jive lexicon as "hittin'," "stone fox," "rapped," "run it down to me," "gimme some slack," and "light'n up on me."

John O. Killens (1972) writes of the conflict a young black female experiences as she tries to find her black identity while being pressured to fulfill her mother's bourgeois aspirations. The author-narrator states he must write in Afro-Americanese, using a rhythm, an idiom, nuances, a style, truths, and exaggerations that are all black.

Paul Carter Harrison and Ed Bullins (Couch, 1971) use the black idiom to do more than entertain their audience. In *Tabernacle*, Harrison's selection of language articulates the verbal aggression ghetto blacks experience and sometimes express. Bullins also uses jive vocabulary to illustrate the counter-culture and consciousness of blacks.

Bullins, (1971, p. 188) in "Goin'a Buffalo," provides the reader with a picture of the aggression and violence of prison life. To help paint the picture, he uses such black lexicon as "agitatin'," "signifyin'," "rank," "ofays," "sucker," "jive-sucker," "shit started really going down," and "got themselves together."

Henderson (1969, p. 78) presents one of LeGraham's poems and writes that his poem "shouts his own black beauty in his own black language." In discussing further LeGraham's "The Black Narrator" and Sonia Sanchez's "Righteous Brothers," he writes,

There should be no doubt in anyone's mind that these poems are not intended for white readers and white audiences, that their purpose was direct address to the black community, to get us together to

TCB. If there is any doubt in anyone's mind, Don L. Lee dispels it. He states that his poetry is not directed to "white boys and girls" but to black people. . . . His poetry speaks for them and to them—to "the man with the wine bottle and processed hair"—about rat-infested slums and the spiritual corruption they breed. His poetry is a weapon for his people at the same time that it draws upon them for strength. It is "like daggers, broken brew bottles, bullets, swift razors from black hands cutting through slum landlords and Negro dope pushers." It will confront "pimps and prostitutes and aid in the destruction of their actions." He says, "Black poems are a part of the people: An energy source for the people's life style."

HISTORY OF JIVE LEXICON

There appears to be some controversy concerning the origins of jive lexicon. Dan Burley (1944) former editor of Harlem's *Amsterdam News*, reports that Negroes began to use jive about 1921 in Chicago, to play the dozens. It meant to scoff, to taunt, to sneer—it was an expression of sarcasm (p. 62).

> Like the tribal groups of Mohammedans and people of the Orient, Negroes of that period had developed a highly effective manner of talking about each other's ancestors and hereditary traits, a colorful and picturesque linguistic procedure which came to be known as 'putting you in the dozens.' Later, this was simply called 'Jiving' someone (p. 62).

Eventually, ragtime musicians adopted the term and it soon began to mean any number of things. Since the '30s, the "jitterbug" population has used the term jive as the trade name for "swing." The dozens concept of jive no longer exists today; it is no longer a term of opprobrium related to one's appearance, one's parents, or one's knowledge. Today, jive is "a term of honor, dignity—class (p. 62)."

Burley also suggests that "Jive talk came into being because of the paucity of words and inadequacy of the vocabularies of its users (p. 66)." Jive is also the result of slang parlance from the hamlets, the villages, and from the cities wherever Negroes come together. The jive lexicon undergoes a continual "purifying process" in which expressions are used and retained or tried and discarded.

> Jive has been in the process of evolution from the early years following World War I. The Prohibition Era, the Gangster Period, the Age of Hardboiled, Quick-shooting Heroes, and their seductive molls contributed to it. So did the decade known as the Great Depression. All this led inevitably to the Age of the Jitterbug, a spasmodic era

with a background of World War II and swing music contributing to its use and popularity (Burley, 1944, p. 63).

But most important, jive is a rebellious and different way of speaking.

Jive is language in motion. It supplies the answer to the hunger for the unusual, the exotic and the picturesque in speech. It is a medium of escape, a safety valve for people pressed against the wall for centuries, deprived of the advantages of complete social economic, moral and intellectual freedom. It is an inarticulate protest of a people given half a loaf of bread and then dared to eat it; a people continually fooled and bewildered by the mirage of a better and fuller life. Jive is a defense mechanism, a method of deriving pleasure from something the uninitiated cannot understand. It is the same means of escape that brought into being the spirituals as sung by American slaves; the blues songs of protest that bubble in the breasts of black men and women believed by their fellow white countrymen to have been born to be menials, to be wards of a nation, even though they are tagged with a whimsical designation as belonging to the body politic. Jive provides a medium of expression universal in its appeal. Its terms have quality, sturdiness, rhythm and descriptive impact. It is language made vivid, vital and dynamic (Burley, 1944, p. 11).

Conrad (1944) thinks that the origin of jive probably goes back into the very bowels of the Negro-American experience. As early as slavery times when Negroes had to sing, speak, and think in a sort of code.

We know that the Negro's music grew up out of his revolutionary experience, that his spirituals reflected his struggle, his "escape to the North." Jive talk may have been originally a kind of "pig Latin" that the slaves talked with each other, a code—when they were in the presence of whites. Take the word "ofay."[k] Ninety million white Americans right now probably don't know that that means "a white," but Negroes know it. Negroes needed to have a word like that in their language, needed to create it in self-defense (p. 6).

He also writes that the jive is another of the Negro Americans contributions to the United States. It began to evolve when white America forced a new and foreign language on African slaves.

Slowly, over the generations, Negro America, living by and large in

[k]"Ofay: a white person (from the pig Latin for foe)." Mezzrow, M. *Really the blues,* New York: A Signet Book, 1964, p. 308.

its own segregated world, with its own thoughts, found its own way of expression, found its own way of handling English, as it had to find its own way in handling many other aspects of a white, hostile world. Jive is one of the end-results (Conrad, 1944, p. 5).

According to Pound (1937) many of the words used by Negroes[1] were survivals of words used by 17th and 18th century Englishmen who settled here.

Ruth Banks (1938) differentiates in the use of what she calls idioms of the present-day American Negro. She feels that some of the idioms are found in the swing magazines and easily adopted for general use, while another group of words are used almost exclusively by urban Negroes. She also points out that many of the words are "common English words" that are given new meaning. And, where the words are adequate and clever they remain. Also, the expressions are often quickly discarded, which prevents the average white American from learning the special inflection of the voice needed to pronounce these words effectively.

Shelly (1945) calls the vocabulary "Jive Talk" and writes that the language was picked up from the whites and was embellished with racy and rich idioms by the Negro who traveled to Harlem from Africa. He also feels that the jive is incomprehensible to all but those who are "hep."

Boulware (1947) published *Jive and Slang of Students in Negro Colleges* and calls the language both slang and jive. Although Boulware is not too sure where the word jive originated, he feels that the word made its appearance with swing music. And just as jazz became swing, so has slang become jive.

"Colored English" or "Spoken Soul" is what Claude Brown (1968) calls the vocabulary. He claims that its roots are over three hundred years old. Starting with slavery and aided by malapropisms, colloquialisms, fractured and battered grammar, and quite a bit of creativity, the sound of soul or Colored English evolved. He points out further that spoken soul is less a language and more a sound.

> It generally possesses a pronounced lyrical quality which is frequently incompatible to any music other than that ceaseless and relentlessly driving rhythm that flows from poignantly spent lives. Spoken soul has a way of coming out metered without the intention of the speaker to invoke it. There are specific phonetic traits. To the

[1]In Pound's article, the word Negro is sometimes spelled with a small n. I am not sure whether this was intentional or whether it was sloppy proofreading. He also writes that "darkies are people that of necessity keep to themselves and maintain old ways (p. 232)." the uninformed reader may not know that the word Negro was not always capitalized. Actually, it was on March 7, 1930, that the *New York Times* announced that it would hereafter capitalize the word Negro. Furthermore, it was not until three years later that the *Style Manual of the Government Printing Office* followed suit with the capitalization (Mencken, 1944). Interestingly, today many black authors spell Negro with a small n.

soulless ear the vast majority of these sounds are dismissed as incorrect usage of the English language and, not infrequently, as speech impediments. To those so blessed as to have had bestowed upon them at birth the lifetime gift of soul, these are the most communicative and meaningful sounds ever to fall upon human ears (p. 88).

Brown also differentiates between soul and slang. Whereas slang lends itself to conventional English, soul does not. When Negroes do adopt words from the white vocabulary, they become "soul words" and take on a different meaning. The concept of words with double meanings is discussed further in this chapter and may be related to the double meanings in many blues songs.[m]

Schechter (1970) refers to the lexicon as soul vocabulary or vernacular that Negroes have invented for themselves. The syntax and vocabulary have moved from "slave riddles to blues slang to jive and into the current Soul vernacular (p. 159)." He feels that today's soul vocabulary is more open, more humorous, has more irony, and is more socially aware than past Negro expressions and is reflective of today's blacks openly seeking identity and full equality.

According to Daniel (1970), survival for blacks meant their developing a private and secret patois, or private public language with which they could communicate privately. Schiffman (1971) writes that the Negroes' language originated with the code or patois that slaves created to keep their white masters ignorant of their discussions.

Grier and Cobbs (1968) use the term patois to refer to the jive and hip language that has developed. They suggest that the language served an adaptive function in slavery days and today. It was and is "used as a secret language to communicate the hostility of blacks for whites, and great delight is taken by blacks when whites are confounded by the language (p. 125)."

Mez Mezzrow (1964), a blue eyed Jewish jazz musician, reported on hearing the jive language in its early stages on the South Side of Chicago. It was a different language; different from the traditional language of the Southern Negro. The hipster's jive language was a knitting together of "tight secret society . . . which resents and nourishes its resentment, and is readying to strike back (p. 191)." The jive was not an escape valve or a defense mechanism of the traditional southern Negro, ". . . it's a kind of drilling academy too, preparing for future battles (p. 191)."

Three recently published dictionaries of black lexicon are entitled *Black Jargon in White America* (Claerbaut, 1972), *Dictionary of Afro-American Slang* (Major, 1970), and *Black Language* (Andrews & Owens, 1973). Mencken (1963) writes that the "queer jargon called *jive* (p. 739)" emerged in the early

[m]For an article on the double meaning of Negro blues see Johnson (1927-28).

'40s and was a mixture of Harlem's Negro slang, the drug addicts' and pettier sort of criminals' argot, plus some additions from the theatrical gossip columns and the high school campus. At its inception jive also appeared to be in use by jazz musicians. Furthermore, though jive varies from city to city, "it manifests a surprising uniformity for an idiom that is almost exclusively spoken, not written (p. 745)."

Wentworth and Flexner (1960, p. xvii) in their *Dictionary of American Slang*, report that though some jive terms originated outside of Harlem, the peak of jive popularity was around 1935.

Gold (1964), in his *A Jazz Lexicon*, writes that the language of the jazz world is a fusing of the languages of the jazz musician and the Negro people.

> So we get a people in rebellion against a dominant majority, but forced to rebel secretly, to sublimate, as the psychologist would put it—to express themselves culturally through the medium of jazz, and linguistically through a code, a jargon. But as the music developed from New Orleans marches and early Dixieland through the blues-and-rhythm cycle and the swing era on into bop and modern, or progressive, jazz, an immense change took place in the life of the Negro. He became more urbanized and the life of the streets peppered his language, and so filtered into jazz parlance, which to this day is highly interrelated with Negro life. Always close (though hardly by choice) to the most squalid aspects of big-city life, the Negro assimilated the jargon of the rackets—dope peddling, prostitution, larceny, gambling—and the more interesting of these terms spilled over into jazz lingo. Then, too, the high frequency of Negro impressment into Southern chain gangs was another, unhappy source of Negro slang, much as it was a source of Negro work songs and folk songs.
>
> The totality of his experience in America stamped the Negro with a psychology demanding not only a unique and rebellious music, but a unique and rebellious way of speaking (p. xiv).

JIVE LEXICON AND COMMUNICATION

Discipline appears to be the overriding problem in inner city schools. However, like everything else, educators have attacked this problem too from a very unrealistic direction.

The hip urban streetcorner youngster appears to be causing most of the discipline problems in inner city schools. There also appears to be agreement that solving teacher-student communication problems would go a long way toward solving discipline problems. Therefore, common sense would suggest that improving teacher communication with these youngsters is paramount to solving inner city discipline problems.

We know that the urban, hip, streetcorner youngster is usually an aggressive, physical hustler, wise in the ways of street survival. He knows how to "run a game," to "signify," to "woof," to "loud talk," to "shuck and jive," and to "sound." He knows how to do all of these and more; he knows how to "run a game" to get what he desires from people. One of the most important parts of his game is his verbal ability, reports of lower class black youngsters being nonverbal to the contrary. Additionally, Lerman's (1966, p. 42; 1967) study of black and Puerto Rican youth argot reinforced the findings of linguists that "people who share modes of verbal communication are likely to share participation in a social and cultural community as well."

Indeed, the inner city teacher should begin to think of his streetcorner student's talking and acting as a performance with his audience his fellow students. If teachers will accept this concept, they will be on their way to understanding and coping with their streetcorner student's behavior.

Abrahams (1972, p. 29) pointed out, "There is an integral relationship between the speaking system and the social structure of any community," and that "each speaker has in his repertoire, different codes which arise in response to different situations." The reader must remember that school is included in the streetcorner youngster's social structure too.

In the black streetcorner community, the good streetcorner performer is respected whether his performance is verbal or otherwise. Additionally, the performance is judged in relationship to the performer's ability to achieve audience participation "and how well the utilization of these high affect actions is capable of producing the desired result for the performance" (p. 31). Usually, verbal performance contains a good deal of kinesic and verbal interaction with the audience. These performances or encounters contain a good deal more verbal repartee than do usual middle class verbal encounters.

In addition, these verbal encounters are more stylized and related to ceremonial procedures. Most importantly for discipline, this repartee is often verbally aggressive and related to machisimo in reputation and identity. Furthermore, verbally aggressive repartee is not a phenomenon of lower class black male behavior. The need to express one's masculinity, to act "tough," is, at other times, also expressed through language and physical interaction by men of all lower classes (Miller, 1958). In particular, Gans (1962) reports on the verbally aggressive behavior of lower class Italians in Roxbury in Boston, in the mid '50s.

Hopefully, the reader is beginning to relate what is being written to a classroom communication scene. If the student respects the good and forceful speaker and the verbal interaction considered a performance, the teacher must know how to relate on this dramatic and verbal level to gain his student's respect. Middle class teachers unfamiliar with lower class language style are too often overcome and their teacher role impaired or destroyed because of their ignorance of the verbal requirements.

This statement by Abrahams (1972, p. 31) describes what is going on in our inner city classrooms, a reality that is understood by too few teachers.

Because of the focus on talk—as performance, a feeling develops that the talker is potentially 'on' all of the time—that is, verbal behavior will be judged as if it were a performance and the speaker judged as if he were on stage. This means that virtually any conversation may turn into a routine or something else equally dramatic. But being "on" like this also means that, to a certain extent, the entire expectation pattern of the performance is invoked, including the special relationship between the performer and the audience.

One of the most important tools in the streetcorner performer's arsenal is the use of "strong words and hyperbolic expressions." And, according to Abrahams (1972, p. 32)

The most obvious of these is the use of slang and colloquialisms, in-group terms which self-consciously show the speaker to be in verbal control, and by extension, in control of the social environment. Slang is more characteristic of urban BE (Black English) because of the heightened importance of peer-grouping in the *hip* city environment.

There is a style and technique in the use of black lexicon in relation to high affect with the audience. These generally fall into three categories (Abrahams, 1972, pp. 32-33).

1. Words with double meanings. Often the second nonstandard meaning is in no way related to the standard meaning. Most often, as mentioned earlier, students use Standard English words with sexual connotations to upset their teachers—especially female teachers.
2. Discussing the behavior of others while emphasizing their nicknames rather than their given names.
3. Words used to describe those items that are considered important to maintain one's prestige and style with the "in" group—the reference points of a culture. These would include black lexicon for such items and activities as cars, clothing, girls and sexual intercourse, parts of the body, alcoholic beverages, drugs, entertainment, and parties.

The argument has now been made that the inner city streetcorner youngster is verbal, that often when he talks he is putting on a performance for his teacher and fellow students with some manipulative objective in mind. Often, this manipulative verbal behavior creates discipline problems. Additionally, his black lexicon is extremely important in peer identification and communication. The next step, therefore, is to look at some of the psychosocial and affective implications of language in general and black lexicon in particular, specifically as they relate to the inner city school.

PSYCHOSOCIAL IMPLICATIONS

The right language at the proper time can serve as a socializer, a relaxing agent, and a positive catalyst to enhance communication. Conversely, the wrong language or the improper time, or the improper interpretation of language can cause communication problems.

For everyone—not only blacks—their native or more familiar language is an important part of them; to deny their language is to deny them. Familiar language often has the ability to relax and put someone at ease. This phenomenon is observable with white ethnic and religious groups as well as with blacks. Realities 49 and 50 are two examples where language was used as a relaxer to enhance communication. Reality 49 is taken from the literature, and Reality 50 is the report of a personal experience.

REALITY 49

"I am there, once again at my office at Franklin. I see the careworn face of a little Puerto Rican woman, aged beyond her years from the poverty and hard work in the fields of her native island. She has come to see me on some matter relating to her son.

"Señora," I say to her in Spanish, 'sit down. Make yourself comfortable and we will talk about Miguel and his future.'

"And to the boy, also in Spanish, 'You sit down over there and do not interrupt us while I talk to your mother.'

"The only language of education is the language which people can understand—no matter where it originates. To this simple Puerto Rican woman I have suddenly become more than the principal of an English-speaking high school. I am a human being who understands and is trying to help her. In the eyes of the boy I have given respect and status to his parent. The process of education has been translated into human terms (D'Agostino, 1970, pp. XII-XIII)."

I observed Reality 50 while with a friend who was an assistant principal in a Harlem junior high school serving a black and Puerto Rican student population. The reactions of those described in Reality 50 are similar to those reported above.

REALITY 50

As we were leaving school one afternoon, an elderly Puerto Rican gentleman approached us and addressed us in a halting Spanish and English. His face reflected discomfort and distress.

My friend, who happened to be a Sephardic Jew responded easily and openly, in Spanish. The man's face broke out into a smile as he burst forth speaking in Spanish. His problem solved, the man left smiling. It was a warm, beautiful happening.

It is unfortunate that school personnel too often are rigidly bound and limited by their concept of correct Standard English. In the reality of the life outside the school, however, the proper language is the language that brings people together and succeeds in accomplishing an objective.

Politicians are notorious for winning votes by eating lox and bagels and wearing a yarmulke, by eating pizza, lasagna, or manicotti at an Italian block party, or speaking in the language of any group they are trying to win over. Narvaez (1970) provided an example of what is so common and accepted in big city politics.

REALITY 51

"Kumt arois un zugt sholom aleichem tzu eyer nexten Senator fun de stut fun New York," blares a loudspeaker atop a car in the Borough Park section of Brooklyn.

Inside the car Isaac Steinheim, a campaign worker for Leonard Silverman, the local Democratic candidate for the Assembly, ex- horted passers-by in "New York Yiddish" to come and meet Representative Richard L. Ottinger, the party's candidate for the Senate.

Mr. Ottinger, accompanied by Representative Hugh L. Carey and Mr. Silverman, walked along 13th Avenue in the predominately Jewish and Democratic area and was greeted enthusiastically (p. 49).

As the Director of the Mildred Goetz Day Camp of the Henry Kaufmann Campgrounds, I participated in the filming of a portion of a TV fundraising commercial for the Federation of Jewish Philanthropies of New York City. The filming took place at the campgrounds alongside our lake. The movie was to point up a senior citizen day camp program as one of the many programs supported by Federation. The short film centered on singer Steve Lawrence speaking with a number of senior citizens.

REALITY 52

As the lighting and cue cards arrangements were worked out, the senior citizens sat uncomfortably nervous; they were obviously ill at ease. Suddenly, by what appeared to be intuition, Steve Lawrence spoke two words in Yiddish (I do not remember what they were). It was a different ball game. The senior citizens smiled with pleased surprise *"E' is a Yiddish boychical?"*[n]

[n]"Is he a Jewish boy?"

They almost had to be restrained from petting him to death. Filming was then completed with ease.

A few years ago I participated as a guest lecturer in a preservice education program for teacher aides in a large city. My topic was classroom communication. The majority of the approximately 60 aides were black. Their reaction to my presentation was similar to the aforementioned incidents.

REALITY 53

The aides sat stiffly, stonefaced, staring at me. After a brief introduction, I gave out *Foster's Jive Lexicon Analogy Test* and *A Lexicon of Words with Standard and Non-Standard Meanings.*

As the aides picked up these items and began to read, the room appeared to come alive. They started to laugh, move in their seats, and talk. I could hear murmurings in dialect. The jive test was familiar to most of the aides, hence they related to it.

The white assistant director of the program rushed over to me, a broad grin on his face, and said, "This is the first time these aides have smiled and relaxed since the program began."

When the workshop session was over, many of the black aides approached me, shook hands, and stayed to talk awhile.

The aides' response reminded me of something I read in Jane Phillips's (1969) *Mojo Hand.* Miss Phillips depicts a society tea covered by photographers from the local black newspaper. The photographers have left and the ladies sit about like "china dolls . . . dressed in all the grotesque finery at their disposal" listening to classical music. Someone hunts through the stack of records, finds an old 78 blues recording, slips it onto the record player, and it begins to scratch forth its sounds.

REALITY 54

"I want to know if your jelly roll's fresh, or is it stale, I want to know if your jelly roll's fresh or is it stale? Well, woman, I'm going to buy me some jelly roll if I have to go to jail."

Almost immediately she heard shouts and shrieks from the other room.

" . . . Oh, yeah, get to it! . . . Laura, woman, how long since your husband's seen you jelly roll?"

"Gertrude, don't you ask me questions like that. Eh, how long since your husband's seen you?"

Eunice went back downstairs. Everyone had relaxed. Some of the women were unbuckling their stockings, others were loosening the belts around their waists. Someone had gotten out brandy and was pouring it into the tea cups.

"Give some to the debs," someone said, "show them what this society really is."

Eunice sat down. The record ground on and on, and it was then that she knew that she had to go find the source of herself, this music that moved her and the others, however much they tried to deny it (pp. 32-33).

During the summer of 1972, Sister Elizabeth Ann Donnelly took a graduate course with me. As a course project she administered my Jive Test to a hospital employee population of 95—42 blacks and 53 whites.[o] Though the black subjects scored higher than did the whites,[p] what is important were the aftereffects vis-à-vis the improved communication with the subjects after the test was administered. This conclusion to Sister Donnelly's paper is worth reporting.

In this large hospital where I resided this summer very often I would meet the personnel in passing. Before meeting the people to whom I gave the test, when I passed them in the corridors there was a slight nod or such. After I had given the test I noted a sort of transformation, especially among the black persons. They would always call to me and had something to say as I passed them. It seemed as though just this effort to get to know them better and their manner of communicating meant something to them. Their reaction was really a study in itself.[q]

Another interesting outcome of language differences was reported by Lantz (1958). He reported that blacks were in some cases more acceptable to white miners because they spoke English as compared with the foreign language of the immigrants. Because the miners could not understand the foreign languages, they were fearful and suspicious of the foreigners. The wife of a miner had this to say.

You couldn't understand the language of the foreigners. Why, I would just as soon live alongside a nigger family as some of these foreigners. I think that the niggers are whiter than the foreigners are because at least they speak your own language. Why, if you lived next door to a foreigner, they would be plotting to kill you and you

[o]The test population consisted of five categories of workers: (1) 17 Manpower students working toward Nurses' Aide certification, (2) 17 Manpower students working toward Practical Nurses certification, (3) 31 had completed Practical Nurses training, (4) 20 were Registered Nurses; and (5) 10 were Registered Nurses with B.S. degrees.

[p]Blacks performed significantly better than did whites in 99 out of 100 cases.

[q]Sister E.A. Donnelly, The inner-city school: teacher testing by pupils, July 31, 1972; an unpublished paper for course TED-518, Teaching In Inner-City Schools.

wouldn't even know it. At least you can understand the nigger's language (p. 47).

Claude Brown (1965) wrote about the Negro male's choice of the words "man" and "baby" as vicarious expressions of manliness and vehicle for comradery and blackness. He also reflected on the importance of certain words to communicate feeling.

The first time I heard the expression "baby" used by one cat to address another was up at Warwick in 1951. . . . The term had a hip ring to it, a real colored ring. The first time I heard it, I knew right away I had to start using it. It was like saying "Man, look at me. I've got masculinity to spare." It was saying at the same time to the world, "I'm one of the hippest cats, one of the most uninhibited cats on the scene." . . . If you could say it, this meant that you really had to be sure of yourself, sure of your masculinity. . . .

The real hip thing about the "baby" term was that it was something that only colored cats could say the way it was supposed to be said. I'd heard gray boys trying it, but they couldn't really do it. Only colored cats could give it the meaning that we all knew it had without ever mentioning it—the meaning of black masculinity (pp. 164-165).

I think everybody said it real loud because they liked the way it sounded. It was always, "Hey, baby. How you doin,' baby?" in every phrase of the Negro hip life. As a matter of fact, I went to a Negro lawyer's office once, and he said, "Hey, baby. How you doin'?" I really felt at ease, really felt that we had something in common. I imagine there were many people in Harlem who didn't feel they had too much in common with the Negro professionals, the doctors, and lawyers and dentists and ministers. I know I didn't. But to hear one of these people greet you with the street thing, the "Hey, baby"—and he knew how to say it—you felt as though you had something strong in common (pp. 165-166).

Though the debate continues as to whether school personnel even should learn or speak Black English, or in some cases whether it even exists, some workers have reported positive results from its use.

Berkowitz and Rothman (1960) have written that on some occasions the emotionally disturbed child expects his teacher to operate on his perceptual and emotional level. At this time, teachers may ". . . indulge in colloquial speech patterns, meeting the child with his own language and responding and participating with enthusiasm in the child's activities (p. 124)." Crawford, Malamud, and Dumpson (1950) reported that the New York City Youth Board workers became accepted by the language of the gangs. McQuown (1954) suggested that it is imperative that the teacher comprehend and respect lower class speech if he wants to gain the confidence of lower class children. Cohn (1959) holds that the teacher who "is unhampered by moralistic and snobbish attitudes, can help children overcome their ambivalence toward language expression (p. 435)." Narvaez (1969, p. 49), in writing about the activities of the Preventive Enforcement Patrol (P.E.P.), a special squad of Black and Puerto Rican policemen in Harlem, reported police officers rapping with the people and kids in their own language. Fantini and Weinstein (1968) suggest making "contact" with the disadvantaged child through his language.

One of the most important yet little known studies supporting the importance of black lexicon as a mode of communication for the urban black streetcorner youngster, came out of the New York State Training School for Boys at Warwick, New York. An attempt was made at Warwick to gather information relative to attitudinal changes toward the Training School that appeared to take place when new boys were placed into the main program. The first phase of the study concerned depth interviews with fifteen Training School youngsters. The findings were interesting.

> The response to two of the interview questions, "What do new boys learn about the Training School from other boys in the Orientation Program?" and "What do new boys learn about the Training School from boys in the Regular Program?" led to the second phase of the pilot study—*A psycholinguistic analysis of the subculture language.*
>
> Most of the boys interviewed said that the first thing they learned from other inmates was how to talk at State School. When asked for examples of this language, they gave such terms as "boody," "boppin'," "capped," "chickee-boy," "lap," "slop drop," and similar linguistic confabulations. From listening to tape recordings of these interviews, it became increasingly evident that a further exploration should be made of this language from the psychological and motivational point of view (Trent, 1954-1957, p. 41).

Despite the substantiation of the importance of jive lexicon as a medium of communication in urban male streetcorner peer groups as well as for teacher-student communication, there is very little available on the subject to help school personnel.

Dillard (1972), in what is probably the outstanding book ever published on Black English, referred to jive lexicon as "ethnic slang" and reported that there are only a few cases of research on vocabulary studies. Dillard suggested, however, that "Black English like any language deserves a dictionary of its own (p. 242)." He also wrote, however, that "bored amusement" has been the attitude of linguists toward popular treatments of slang.

In the main, linguists have concentrated on studies dealing with phonology and syntax in their investigations and research of Black English. Studying phonology and syntax may be important for reading materials and certainly an accepted scholarly endeavor in its own right. However, *in the primary area of communication in general, and of classroom communication in particular since it so vitally influences the affective domain and teaching and learning, this author argues that lexicon is of equal if not primary importance as an area of study.*

Indeed, black males scored highest in my Jive studies and are the group with whom the schools are having the greatest discipline problems. And remember, in crisis situations, just when communication is necessary for resolution of differences, the principals often revert to their more familiar and secure language code.

It may be that lexicon has been ignored because those whites doing the research in Black English: (1) have only had superficial relationships with blacks beyond those being studied; (2) have not been able to put the blacks with whom they have worked at ease; hence the blacks have been guarded; (3) have conducted most of their research in the primary grades where the youngsters may not have picked up very much of the streetcorner jive as yet; or (4) may be unfamiliar with the jive lexicon or its existence, or in some cases, the nonstandard definitions. Therefore, the lexicon is not recognized by the researchers and goes unreported and uninvestigated. Also quite possibly, the researchers may never have taught inner city black secondary youngsters where they would have had to deal with the real problems of face to face student-teacher communication.

There is a tremendous need for inner city educators to become familiar with and understand the jive lexicon of their students for reasons ranging from better communication to curriculum improvement and relatedness. However, to assist educators in their quest for this knowledge, we have very little to offer. Instead, in most cases, we are still arguing over whether the jive lexicon exists, or whether such tools as Western Electric's *The Dialect of the Black American* are great, or even relevant.[r] This author is of the former opinion.

CONCLUSION

If middle class educators are to improve communication with the black, disadvantaged student, they must accept his language. By accepting his language, school personnel will take a step toward accepting him. It is argued that school personnel's knowledge of and judicious use of the black lower class disadvantaged urban child's lexicon can play an important role in solving school communication problems that interfere with teaching and learning.

This chapter should not be considered as arguing against black disadvantaged children's being taught Standard English. Rather, it should be considered as demonstrating the importance of the school's unconditionally

---

[r]*The Dialect of the Black American*, a Community Relations presentation of Western Electric, available through local Western Electric business offices.

accepting the child and his language as the first step toward helping this youngster accept the school.

Unquestionably, the wrong person speaking in dialect can be interpreted as being paternalistic or insulting. However, this should not be used as an argument to ignore black dialect for in-school communication or curriculum. Neither should it be considered as arguing to replace Standard English with Black English. There is not any one solution to this problem because there is not any one question.

Just as school personnel should develop their teaching style based on their personality, so should school personnel judiciously use or not use Black English. Some teachers can use it positively and others cannot. In some situations the use of black dialect would be proper while in others it would not be proper. However, without a question, all inner city school personnel should know and understand Black English—particularly the jive lexicon.

In addition, educators should be aware of the role of their language and their student's language in school communication. When there is too great a difference, problems may arise.

> *Language of teachers (is) too remote from the child's developmental level*, or from the native tongue ordinarily used on his social plane. If that is the case, the child feels out of place, not really wanted, or even looked down upon, and begins to show signs of social-outcast reactions and protest (Sheviakiv & Redl, 1951, p. 46).

Finally, Negro slaves have not been credited with having contributed many words to the American vocabulary from their various African dialects (DeVere, 1872; Lloyd & Warfel, 1956; Mencken, 1963; Pyles, 1952, & Shuy, 1967). However, for the next few decades as the descendants of slaves continue to fight their way into American life, words from their lexicon may well equal or surpass the contributions already made by the American Indian and other ethnic and immigrant groups. Actually, the process has already started.

The attached glossary of words with double meanings is provided to give school personnel and others some examples. The double meaning lexicon is not all inclusive; it is a foundation onto which the interested can build. These words come from the New York City and Buffalo areas primarily.

GLOSSARY

These words, with their non-standard definitions, are just a few from the many this author has collected.

Word	Definition
apple, the big apple	New York City
attitude	to get mad without a good reason

bad	good
balling	sexual intercourse; having a good time, or partying
basting	making a derogatory or ridiculing remark about someone
bat	a job, an ugly girl
bear	an ugly girl
breeze	to leave
buns	buttocks
bush	to allow your hair to grow naturally
cakes	buttocks
cheeks	buttocks
click	a gang, a club
crib	house, home, apartment
crying buddy	best friend
cut	to remain out of sight or to be unobtrusive
deal	to fight
deep	nice, smart, used as a superlative to describe almost anything
dig	to understand
dike	a lesbian
dip	a party, a dance
dog, dag, dog it	shucks, darn
dozens	a method of verbally insulting, degrading, and/or vilifying someone's female relatives with lewd and obscene remarks that usually degrades or negatively reflect upon the masculinity of someone present.
ease	to leave
five	see "skin"
fly	nice, pretty, high fashion
forget you	used to disguise "fuck you"
fox	a pretty girl
fronts	clothes
fur	a woman
game	a line of talk given someone
grease (greeze)	to eat
grind	a slow sensual dance
grit	to eat
hawk	a cold wind, a powerful person
heart	courage
heifer	a prostitute, a loose woman
hoe, ho	whore
ice	to stab or knife someone
jeff	a white

Jew	the boss
joey	a white
johnson	penis
joke	penis
jones	penis, a job
knit	a Banlon or imported Italian knit shirt
knot	a person's head
lamb	a fearful person, someone who does not know what is going on
lame	a person who is "out of it"
lid	hat
lizard	lizard shoes
loud	to make fun of someone, to yell at someone
man, the	the police, the boss, whites
nose	to have someone's attention, to have someone under your control
nut	to act crazy
off	to kill, destroy, or beat up
oscar	penis
people	your friends, your gang
pig	last year's Cadillac
private	penis
process	straightened hair
rags	clothing
rank	to insult someone
rap, rapping	talking, giving a girl a smooth line
scab	an ugly girl
shades	sun glasses
short	an automobile
sides	records
silks	a silk suit
skin	slapping each other's palms
slave	a job
smack	sexual intercourse
snack	penis
solid	good, all right
split	to leave
static	to give someone trouble
stone	the best, outstanding, very good
suction	to give someone a hard time
swift	good
swipe	penis
tack	a person who does not know what's going on

taste	whiskey, wine
T.C.B.	take care of business
threads	clothes
tight	best of friends
tip	a girl, to leave
together	good, to be dressed well
train	when two or more males have sexual intercourse with one girl
trim	a girl, sexual intercourse, vagina
turf	territory, neighborhood
turk	territory, neighborhood
vines	clothing
waste	to beat someone up, to kill
weak	something that is phony, out of fashion
wheels	a car
wolf, wolf'n, woof woofin, wolf ticket	can mean anything from making fun of someone to challenging someone to a fight, a powerful person
work	to fight, to dance with fervor

NOTES TO CHAPTER 4

Aarons, A.C. (Ed.) Black dialect issue. *The Florida FL Reporter* 10(1 & 2), 1972.

Abrahams, R.D. "Talking my talk": Black English and social segmentation in black communities. *The Florida FL Reporter* 10(1 & 2): 29-38, 58, 1972.

Andrews, M. and Owens, P.T. *Black Language*. Los Angeles, Calif: Seymour-Smith, 1973.

The anguish of blacks in blue. *Time*, November 23, 1970, pp. 13-14.

Bagdikian, B.J. *In the Midst of Plenty: The Poor in America*. Boston: Beacon Press, 1965.

Banks, R. Idioms of the present-day American Negro. *American Speech* 13: 313-314, 1938.

Baraka, I.A. and Fundi. *In Our Terribleness*. New York: Bobbs-Merrill, 1970.

Berkowitz, P.H. and Rothman, E.P. *The Disturbed Child*. New York: New York University Press, 1960.

Bernstein, B.A. Some sociological determinants of perception—an inquiry into subcultural difference. *The British Journal of Sociology* 9: 159-174, 1958.

Bessie Smith the World's Greatest Blues Singer, Columbia GP 33.

Bonham, F. *Cool Cat*. New York: E.P. Dutton, 1971.

Borders, W. Cool welfare militant: Dr. George Alvin Wiley. *New York Times*, May 27, 1969, p. 32.

Botkin, B.A. *A Treasury of American Folklore.* New York: Crown, 1944.

Boulware, M.H. *Jive and Slang of Students in Negro Colleges.* Hampton, Va.: Marcus H. Boulware, 1947.

Brewer, J.M. "Hidden language": ghetto children know what they're talking about. *New York Times Magazine*, December 25, 1966, pp. 32, 34-35.

Brown, C. *Manchild in the Promised Land.* New York: Macmillan, 1965.

Brown, C. The language of soul. *Esquire* 69(4): 88, 160, 162, 1968.

Brown, C. *The Life and Loves of Mr. Jiveass Nigger.* New York: Farrar, Straus & Giroux, 1969.

Bullins, E. Clara's ole man. *Five Plays by Ed Bullins.* New York: Bobbs-Merrill, 1968.

Bullins, E. Goin'a Buffalo. In W. Couch (Ed.), *New Black Playwrites.* New York: Avon Books, 1971.

Bunky & Jake, L.A.M.F., Mercury Stereo SR 61199.

Burley, D. *Dan Burley's Handbook of Jive.* New York: Jive Potentials, 1944.

Button bit builds bank balance. *Star Journal*, November 3, 1965, p. 6.

Cady, S. Stoked surfers thrill hodads at Gilgo Beach's title meet. *New York Times*, September 11, 1966, p. 65.

Cain, G. *Blueschild Baby.* New York: McGraw-Hill, 1970.

Calitri, C.J. The nature and values of culturally different youth. In A. Jewett (Ed.), *Improving English Skills of Culturally Different Youth in Large Cities.* Washington, D.C.: U.S. Government Printing Office, No. OE3-0012 (Bulletin 1964).

Claerbout, D. *Black Jargon in White America.* Grand Rapids, Mich.: William B. Eerdmans, 1972.

Cleaver, E. *Soul on Ice.* New York: Ramparts (McGraw-Hill), 1968.

Clemmer, D. *The Prison Community.* Boston: Christopher Publication House, 1940.

Cohn, W. On language of lower-class children. *School Review* 57: 435-440, 1959.

Conrad, E. Foreword. In D. Burley, *Dan Burley's Handbook of Jive.* New York: Jive Potentials, 1944.

Cooke, B.G. Nonverbal communication among Afro-Americans: an initial classification. In T. Kochman (Ed.), *Rappin' and Stylin' Out.* Chicago: University of Illinois Press, 1972.

Cooper, M. *Black Star.* New York: Bernard Geis Associates, 1969.

Couch, W. (Ed.), *New Black Playwrites.* New York: Avon Books, 1971.

Crawford, P.L. and Malamud, D.I. *Working with Teenage Gangs: A Report on the Central Harlem Street Club Project.* New York: Astoria Press, 1950.

D'Agostino, G., with Covello, L. *The Heart Is the Teacher: The Teacher in the Urban Community.* Totowa, N.J.: Littlefield, Adams, 1970.

Daniel, J.L. Black folk and speech education. *Speech Teacher* 19: 123-129, 1970.

D'Evelyn, K. *Meeting Children's Emotional Needs.* Englewood Cliffs, N.J.: Prentice-Hall, 1957.

DeVere, M.S. *Americanisms: The English of the New World.* New York: Charles Scribner, 1872.

Dillard, J.L. *Black English.* New York: Random House, 1972.

Edwards, W.J. *Twenty-Five Years in the Black Belt.* Boston: 1918. Cited by E.F. Frazier, *The Negro Family in the United States* (Rev. & Abr. Ed.). Chicago: The University of Chicago Press, 1966, p. 11.

Evans B. and Evans, C. *A Dictionary of Contemporary American Usage.* New York: Random House, 1957.

Fantini, M.D. and Weinstein, G. *The Disadvantaged–Challenge to Education.* New York: Harper & Row, 1968.

Fickett, J.G. *Aspects of Morphemics, Syntax, and Semology of an Inner-City Dialect (Mexican).* West Rush, New York: Meadowood Publications, 1970.

Fight against subway graffiti progresses from frying pan to fire. *New York Times,* January 26, 1973, p. 39.

Finn, J.D. Patterns in children's language. *School Review* 57: 108-127, 1969.

The Florida FL Reporter 10(1 & 2): entire issue, 1972.

Foster, H.L. A pilot study of the cant of the disadvantaged, socially maladjusted, secondary school child. *Urban Education* 2: 99-114, 1966.

Foster, H.L. The inner-city teacher and violence: suggestions for action research. *Phi Delta Kappan* 50(3): 172-175, 1968.

Foster, H.L. A pilot study of the cant of the Negro disadvantaged student in four secondary schools for the socially maladjusted and emotionally disturbed. *C.E.C. Selected Convention Papers: 1967.* Washington, D.C.: The Council for Exceptional Children, 1968.

Foster, H.L. *Dialect–lexicon and listening comprehension.* Doctoral dissertation, Columbia University, Teachers College, 1969.

Foster, H.L. *Dialect–lexicon and listening comprehension.* Doctoral dissertation, Columbia University, Teachers College. Ann Arbor, Mich.: University Microfilms, No. 70-13,770; Annual Index - June, 1971, Vol. VI, No. 6, June 1971, p. 152, ERIC Index # ED 048 265.

Foster, H.L. *Foster's Jive Lexicon Analogy Test, Series I.* Williamsville, New York: Herbert L. Foster, 1970.

Foster, H.L. *Foster's Jive Lexicon Analogies Test: Series IIA.* Williamsville, New York: Herbert L. Foster, 1972.

Frazier, E.F. *The Negro Family in the United States* (Rev. & Abr. Ed.). Chicago: Phoenix Books (The University of Chicago Press), 1966.

Gans, H. *The Urban Villagers: Group & Clans in the Life of Italian-Americans.* New York: The Free Press of Glencoe, 1962.

Glossary of terms used in space flight. *New York Times,* March 4, 1969, p. 15.

Gold, R.S. *A Jazz Lexicon.* New York: Alfred A. Knopf, 1964.

Goldberg, M.L. Adapting teacher style to pupil differences: teachers for disadvantaged children. *Merril-Palmer Quarterly* 10: 161-178, 1964.

Goldstein, R. This thing has gotten completely out of hand. *New York Magazine,* March 26, 1973, pp. 34-39.

The graffiti "hit" parade. *New York Magazine,* March 26, 1973, pp. 32-33.

Grier, W.H. and Cobbs, P.M. *Black Rage.* New York: Basic Books, 1968.

Guitar, M.A. Not for finks. *New York Times Magazine*, November 24, 1963, pp. 50, 52, 54.

Haley, A. *The Autobiography of Malcolm X*. New York: Grove Press, 1966.

Harrington, M. *The Other America*. Baltimore: Penguin Books, 1965.

Harrison, P.C. Tabernacle. In W. Couch (Ed.), *New Black Playwrites*. New York: Avon Books, 1971.

Heard, N.C. *Howard Street*. New York: Dial Press, 1968.

Heffron, P.B. Our American slang. *Elementary English* 34: 429-434, 465, 1963.

Henderson, S.E. "Survival motion" a study of the black writer and the black revolution in America. In M. Cook and S.E. Henderson (Eds.), *The militant black writer in Africa and the United States*. Madison, Wisc.: The University of Wisconsin Press, 1969.

Hibbert, C. *The Roots of Evil*. Boston: Little, Brown, 1963.

Holt, G.S. "Inversion" in black communication. In T. Kochman (Ed.), *Rappin' and Stylin' Out*. Chicago: University of Illinois Press, 1972.

Hughes, L. and Bontemps, A. *The Book of Negro Folklore*. New York: Dodd, Mead, 1966.

Jackman, M.E. Flowers for the trashman. In L. Jones and L. Neal (Eds.), *Black Fire: An Anthology of Afro-American Writing*. New York: William Morrow, 1970.

Johnson, G.B. Double meaning in the popular Negro blues. *Journal of Abnormal Social Psychology* 22(1): 12-20, 1927.

The Joint Commission on Mental Health of Children. *Crisis in Child Mental Health: Challenge for the 1970's*. New York: Harper & Row, 1969.

Jones, L. *The Baptism and The Toilet*. New York: Grove Press, 1963 & 1966.

Jones, L. The Toilet. *Kulchur III* (Spring) 9: 25-29, 1963.

Jones, L. and Neal, L. (Eds.). *Black Fire: An Anthology of Afro-American Writing*. New York: William Morrow, 1970.

Just, W. Captain blue pencil obliterates a "poisonous" Saigon comic book: no heroes or villains—only fools. *The Washington Post*, August 2, 1966, pp. 1, 11.

Keller, S. *The American Lower-Class Family: A Survey of Selected Facts and Their Implications*. New York: State of New York, Division for Youth, 1965.

Kelly, W.M. If you're woke you dig it. *New York Times*, May 20, 1962, pp. 45, 53.

Killens, J.O. *The Cotillion; Or, One Good Bull is Half the Herd*. New York: Pocket Books, 1972.

Knebel, F. *Trespass*. New York: Doubleday, 1969.

Kohl, H. *Golden Boy as Anthony Cool*. New York: Dial Press, 1972.

Kohl, H. and Hinton, J. Names, graffiti, and culture. *The Urban Review* 3(5): 24-37, 1969.

Lantz, H.R. *People of Coal Town*. New York: Columbia University Press, 1958.

Lerman, P. *Issues in subcultural delinquency*. Doctor of Social Welfare Dissertation, New York, School of Social Work, Columbia University, 1966. Ann Arbor, Mich.: University Microfilms, 67-799,3131A.

Lerman, P. Argot, symbolic deviance and subcultural delinquency. *American Sociological Review* 32: 209-224, 1967.

Liebow, R. *Tally's Corner*. Boston: Little Brown, 1966.

Lindsay signs bill to combat graffiti. *New York Times*, October 29, 1972, p. 79.

Lloyd, D.J. and Warfel, H.R. *American English in Its Cultural Setting*. New York: Alfred A. Knopf, 1956.

Major, C. *Dictionary of Afro-American Slang*. New York: International Publishers, 1970.

Malamud, B. *The Tenants*. New York: Farrar, Straus & Giroux, 1971.

Marckwardt, A.H. *American English*. New York: Oxford University Press, 1958.

Maurer, D.W. *A Correlation of the Technical Argot of Pick-Pockets with Their Behavior Patterns*. New Haven: College & University Press, 1964.

McDowell, T. Notes on Negro dialect in the American novel to 1921. *American Speech* 5: 291-296, 1930.

McNeil, E.B. Personal hostility and internal aggression. *Journal of Conflict Resolution* 5: 279-290, 1971.

McQuown, N. Language-learning from an anthropological point of view. *Elementary School Journal* 54: 402-408, 1954.

Mencken, H.L. Designations for colored folk. *American Speech* 19: 161-174, 1944.

Mencken, H.L. *The American Language: An Inquiry into the Development of English in the United States* (Abr. Ed.). R.I. McDavid, Jr. (Ed.). New York: Alfred A. Knopf, 1963.

Mezzrow, M. and Wolfe, B. *Really the Blues*. New York: Signet Books, 1964.

Miller, W.B. Lower-class culture as a generating milieu of gang delinquency. *Journal of Social Issues* 14(3): 5-19, 1958.

Morgolis, R.J. The two nations at Wesleyan University. *New York Times Magazine*, January 18, 1970, pp. 9, 49, 54, 60-62, 64.

Narvaez, A.R. New police patrol a hit in the slums. *New York Times*, November 19, 1969, p. 49.

Narvaez, A.R. Democrat visits Brooklyn. *New York Times*, October 29, 1970, p. 49.

National Commission on the Causes and Prevention of Violence. Commission statement on violent crime: homicide, assault, rape, robbery. Washington, D.C.: National Commission on the Causes and Prevention of Violence, 1969.

Nelson, L.E. Language has personality. *The Clearing House* 38: 543-547, 1964.

New York City Youth Board News Release. Street jargon has a flavor all its own, October 16, 1964 (mimeo).

No landlord–tenants run slum tenement. *Herald Tribune*, July 1, 1972, p. 3.

O'Grady, T. Cager was on unfamiliar court. *Buffalo Evening News*, August 29, 1969, p. 31.

Oliver, P. *The Story of the Blues*. Philadelphia: Chilton, 1969.

The Panthers and the law. *Newsweek*, February 23, 1970, pp. 26-29.

Parks, G. Whip of black power. *Life*, May 19, 1967, pp. 76A, 76B, 77-78, 80, 82.

Peebles, M.V. *Ain't supposed to die a natural death: tunes from blackness*, Almo Music Corporation, A&M Records, Advantage Sound Studios, N.Y.–SP 3510.

Pharr, R.D. *The Book of numbers*. New York: Doubleday, 1969.

Phillips, J. *Mojo Hand*. New York: Pocket Books, 1969.

Pound, L. Survivals in Negro vocabulary. *American Speech* 12: 231-232, 1937.

Prail, F.J. Subway graffiti here called epidemic. *New York Times*, February 11, 1972.

Pyles, T. *Words and Ways of American English*. New York: Random House, 1952.

Redl, F. The concept of life space interview. *American Journal of Orthopsychiatry* 29: 1-18, 1959.

Redl, F. Strategy and techniques of the life space interview. In R. Newman and M.M. Keith (eds.), *The School-Centered Life Space Interview*. Washington, D.C.: Washington School of Psychiatry, 1964.

Reed, I. *Mumbo Jumbo*. Garden City, N.Y.: Doubleday, 1972.

Roberts, H.E. *The Third Ear: A Black Glossary*. Chicago, Ill.: The English Language Institute of America , 1971.

Roberts, S.V. My whole family said, "Leon, you is lazy." *New York Times*, March 26, 1967, p. D 17.

Rowe, M.B. Science and soul. *The Urban Review* 4(2): 31, 1969.

Salisbury, H.A. *The Shook-Up Generation*. New York: Harper & Brothers, 1958.

Sapir, E. *Culture, Language and Personality*. Berkeley, California: University of California Press, 1966.

Schechter, W. *The History of Negro Humor in America*. New York: Fleet Press, 1970.

Schiffman, J. *Uptown: The Story of Harlem's Appolo Theater*. New York: Cowles, 1971.

Sebastian, J. Negro slang in Lincoln University. *American Speech* 9: 290, 1934.

Selby, H. Jr. *Last Exit to Brooklyn*. New York: Grove Press, 1965.

Shelly, L. (Ed.). *Hepcats Jive Talk Dictionary*. Derby, Conn.: T.W.O. Charles, 1945.

Sheviakov, G.V. and Redl, F. *Discipline for Today's Children* (Rev. Ed. by S.K. Richardson). Washington, D.C.: N.E.A., Association of Supervisors and Curriculum Development, 1964.

Shirey, D.L. Semi-retired graffiti scrawlers paint mural at C.C.N.Y. 133. *New York Times*, December 8, 1972, p. 49.

Shuy, R.W. *Discovering American Dialects*. Champaign, Ill.: National Council of Teachers of English, 1967.

Slim, I. *Trick Baby*. Los Angeles, Calif.: Holloway House, 1967.

Stein, V. (Ed.). *The Random House Dictionary of the English Language: The Unabridged Edition*. New York: Random House, 1966.

Stevens, S. *Way Uptown in Another World*. New York: G.P. Putnam's Sons, 1971.

Stewart, J.T. Announcements. In L. Jones and L. Neal (Eds.), *Black Fire: An Anthology of Afro-American Writing*. New York: William Morrow, 1970.

Stiff antigraffiti measure passes council committee. *New York Times*, September 16, 1972, p. 41.

Stocker, D.S. The ghetto child can relate to the graffiti fence. *Phi Delta Kappan* 52(7): 456, 1971.

"Taki 183" spawns pen pals. *New York Times*, July 21, 1971, p. 31.

Temple, T.R. A program for overcoming the handicap of dialect. *The New Republic* 165(12): 11-14, 1967.

Thomas, P. *Down These Mean Streets.* New York: Alfred A. Knopf, 1967.

Thompson, H.S. *Hell's Angels: The Terrible Saga of the Outlaw Motorcycle Gangs.* New York: Balantine Books, 1967.

Trent, R.B. *An Exploratory Study of the Inmate Social Organization: Volume Five.* Warwick, N.Y.: Warwick Child Welfare Services Project, New York State Training School for Boys, 1954-1957.

Tshombe talks in tribal tongue after injection. *Buffalo Evening News*, October 6, 1967, pp. 1-2.

Vetter, H.J. *Language Behavior and Communication: An Introduction.* Itasca, Ill.: F.E. Peacock, 1969.

Wambaugh, J. *The New Centurions.* Boston: Little, Brown, 1970.

Ware, C.F. *Greenwich Village 1920-1930.* New York: Harper Colophon Books, 1965.

Welburn, R. In our terribleness: reviving soul in Newark, N.J. *New York Times Book Review*, February 14, 1971, pp. 10-11.

Wentworth, H. and Flexner, S.B. *Dictionary of American Slang.* New York: Thomas Y. Crowell, 1960.

White, J. Toward a black psychology. *Ebony* 25(11): 45, 48-50, 52, 1970.

Williams, F. (Ed.). *Language and Poverty: Perspectives on a Theme.* Chicago: Markham, 1970.

Wolfe, T. *The Electric Kool-Aid Acid Test.* New York: Bantam Books, 1969.

Wolfe, T. *Radical Chic & Mau-Mauing the Flak Catchers.* New York: Farrar, Straus & Giroux, 1970.

Yurick, S. *The Warriors.* New York: Pyramid Books, 1966.

Yurick, S. *The Bag.* New York: Trident Press, 1968.

Chapter Five

Ribbin', Jivin' and Playin' the Dozens: Classroom Contests

Found most often in bars or in pool halls in urban areas, or outside a crossroads store in the plantation country with a bunch of fellows, or late evenings on the stoops of down-home shacks, men with prodigious memories swap tales, songs, and ballads.

—Langston Hughes, *The Book of Negro Humor*

". . . those young brothers came out of this woofing, diddy-boping and raising hell period. They had won this confrontation. They had met "the man" and found out that when you start being controlled by fear, then the people you were once afraid of are afraid of you."

H. Rap Brown, *Die Nigger Die!*

"If your sneakers slip and slide,
get the ones with the stars on the sides."

—Heard in a Brooklyn, New York high school

"If you signify, you qualify."

Streetcorner philosophy

In Chapters One and Two, it was suggested that one of the reasons we were not educating more urban lower class black youngsters was that urban educators were playing the game of teaching and learning by the wrong rules. The formal organizational rules of the urban teachers and administrators are not working. The rules actually running the schools are the informal rules set by the students which evolve from lower class urban black male streetcorner behavior and life style.

Three concerns of streetcorner behavior were also suggested. In brief, these include: (1) the rules, regulations, and conditions of streetcorner ritual coping and survival techniques; (2) the additional behavior involved in black streetcorner life style—some of which were language, running a game, aggression, the put down or put on, and the importance of style and a flare for drama; and (3) the difference between the student's concept of a teacher's role in discipline as compared with the teacher's concept of his own role.

Additionally, four categories of student behavior were suggested as operating within inner city classrooms. Of the youngsters in these categories, the streetcorner youngster was described most often using streetcorner coping and survival techniques—sometimes adapted for classroom use—in testing his teachers.

In Chapter Three it was pointed out that many inner city black youngsters are very verbal and that often they will run a streetcorner game to get what they want. Indeed, very often when the streetcorner youngster runs his game, he is putting on a performance for his classmates first and his teacher second, with some objective in mind. Sometimes the streetcorner youngster runs his game against the teacher with the students as his audience. At other times, he gets his student audience to join him in his disruptive tactics.

From the teacher's point of view, however, the incident usually is not considered a game but disruptive behavior—sometimes terrifyingly disruptive. Because the teacher may be unhip and square middle class, he has no idea that the game is being run; all he experiences is the interference, the disruption, a horrible personal hurt and a sense of personal inadequacy. He often calls his students impertinent and disrespectful. Sometimes he interprets the rhetoric and verbal repartee as a threat of imminent violence.

He usually has no idea that a testing game is being run in his classroom. In a rare case, the middle class teacher, while still maintaining his middle class ideals and feelings is "down with the action" and so quickly parries the attempt at manipulation and gets on with the lesson.

Such a knowledgeable teacher is able to minimize and control the streetcorner youngster's surface behavior so that he (1) does not become a disruptive influence, (2) does not have to be reported to the "office" for punitive disciplinary purposes, and (3) is not abused physically or verbally.

Unquestionably, testing games are played in both inner city and suburban schools. However, in suburbia the games have much less of an effect on discipline. The suburban youngster's stronger ego provides a longer fuse so that usually he does not act out angrily against the person taunting him. Additionally, suburban youngsters and their parents would not countenance continually disrupted classrooms. Their desire for the grades required for college entrance is reality, not fantasy. Also, because the suburban teacher's life style is

closer to the life style of his students, he is not as fearful of his students.[a]
Furthermore, both black and white middle class youngsters play testing games
with their parents as part of their maturational development and growth. For
lower class black streetcorner youngsters, however, testing their ability to run a
game and to hustle or manipulate their teachers helps them develop what their
environment has taught them are streetcorner social and economic survival skills.

White (1970) reinforces this and points out that many disadvantaged
youngsters have developed survival skills and a mental toughness that he feels
makes them "in many ways superior" to their white suburban counterparts.
Indeed, black inner city youngsters know how to deal effectively with building
superintendents, pimps, corner grocers, bill collectors—as well as with death and
sickness. They also are psychologically original and clever in their ability to
"jive" school personnel, juvenile authorities, and welfare workers. These youngsters realize early in life that they exist in an often hostile and complicated
world. What they have mastered, although they probably cannot verbalize it, is
the sense of the basic human condition that existential psychologists write
about: "that in this life, pain and struggle are unavoidable and that a complete
sense of one's identity can only be achieved by both recognizing and directly
confronting an unkind and alien existence (p. 45)."

Although these testing games used by inner city youngsters are
sometimes modifications of black lower-class male streetcorner survival and
coping techniques, reporting suggests that almost all lower class urban male
groups, not just blacks, play verbally and physically aggressive streetcorner
games.

Gans (1962), for example, reported on the life style of lower class
Italian teenagers and young adults in the Roxbury section of Boston where there
was lively competition for status, respect, and power. The residents' "action
seeking" behavior consisted of ongoing encounters intended to show skillfulness
and superiority of one person over the other. Their encounters took the form of
continuous verbal and physical duels and card games. The Italian West Enders
expressed their verbal strength and skills by denigrating the achievements and
characteristics of others by teasing, bragging, wisecracking, and insulting others
(pp. 81-82).

In another study of black and white, early, middle, and late
adolescent males and females living in "slum districts," Miller (1958) found that
"in the syndrome of capacities related to 'smartness' is a dominant emphasis in
lower class culture on ingenious aggressive repartee (p. 10)." He found this skill
practiced and learned within the context of streetcorner group life. Often the
repartee took two forms: the semiritualized razzing, kidding, ranking, and
teasing, and the more highly ritualized, mutual insults interchange of the

---

[a]Chapter Six contains comparative points of view by white suburban youths
and black streetcorner youngsters. There is a tremendous difference in the way each group is
willing to test a teacher and how far each will go.

"dozens." Although he found the dozens practiced on its most advanced level by black adults, he found "less polished variants" played by male and female lower class whites.

It must be reemphasized that for lower class black urban street-corner men, rhetoric, repartee, and gamesmanship are survival and coping techniques in the aggressive, hustling, verbal world of the streetcorner. These almost ritualized games are, in a sense, attempts at coping with and surviving economic and social racism, and to some extent are a way of getting even or beating "the system."

On the streetcorner, verbal ability is rated as highly as is physical strength. Most often, when men gather, a boasting or teasing encounter takes place. Verbal contest participation is an important part of peer relationships. Starting a verbal attack is "mounting" or getting above an opponent. To lose a verbal battle is to become feminized. Strength and masculinity are shown by boasting or "putting down" an adversary or a group of adversaries. Abrahams's (1970, p. 56) reporting emphasizes the manliness involved in a verbal encounter. "Being bested in a verbal battle in front of a group of men has immense potential repercussions because of the terror of disapproval, of being proved ineffectual and therefore effeminate in the eyes of peers (p. 56)." Furthermore, the ritual battle of words is accepted and rated as a means of masculine release from anxiety.

Abrahams (1972) also writes that "Through the dozens or some other verbal context, one establishes his place, his reputation in male street society—especially during the swinging years (p. 36)." The importance of the verbal repartee was also reinforced recently by a black high school student who told me, "Look, Dr. Foster, when I ease to Jefferson Avenue,[b] it's the con and conversation that's *important—nothing else.*"

To help the reader differentiate between these verbal contests or ritualized coping and survival techniques as played out in the classroom, the three broad categories of "ribbin'," "jivin'," and "playin' the dozens" will be used.

The reader should be aware, however, that the name given a verbal contest in one city, or even a section of the same city may be different from designated names used elsewhere. The age group or sex of those involved in the verbal encounter may determine the supposed sophistication or lack of sophistication of the repartee. There also may be some difference between the way the game is played on the streetcorner as compared with the classroom. What is important though, is that: (1) we not get hung up in a purist argument over what the proper designation for the game is, (2) that the reader begin to understand that these verbal games exist and should begin to recognize them, (3) that urban

[b]Jefferson Avenue is the main street of the black community of Buffalo, New York.

educators begin to develop nonpunitive techniques for coping with the games, (4) that urban educators learn how to use these games as indicators of a student's academic potential, and (5) that urban educators should study possible use of these games for their teaching and learning potential.[c]

RIBBIN'

The term ribbin' or ribbing is used in Buffalo to describe the verbal game of taunting, denigrating, or making fun of someone, e.g., people, their clothing, parts of their body (particularly their genitals, or matters related to sexual intercourse). Recently, a black Buffalo junior high school student told me that her friends use the term dippin' to refer to "gettin' into personal things." A junior high school youngster once told me that "you laugh on someone when you rib on them." In a Yonkers, New York, junior high school my informants used the term chopping. In Pottsville, Pennsylvania, the term is sounding. In Oklahoma it is called medlin'. In a Brooklyn, New York, secondary school the terms ranking and sounding are still used. A Buffalo, New York, junior high school student's response to what ribbing is fairly well sums up its meaning. "She is talkin' about you—but she is only playing. Sometimes she be ribbin' good, and I can't take it. And, I'll fight her. But sometimes I can take her ribbin'." In the primarily white northern suburbs of Buffalo, New York, the game, played with less intensity and less often, is referred to as mocking out.

The rules governing the number of participants in a ribbin' game are flexible. Ribbin' may be directed against any number of persons; for example:

1. One youngster ribbin' another youngster.
2. Two or more youngsters ribbin' one or more youngsters.
3. One or more youngsters ribbin' a teacher or teachers.
4. When an unknowing teacher or administrator tries to intercede and break up a student ribbin' session, the students may join and turn to rib the teacher or administrator.
5. A student who is being humiliated in a ribbin' game with another student or group of students may turn on a teacher or student he feels is verbally or physically weaker and start ribbin' that person. This is a diversionary tactic to take the pressure off of himself while keeping the game going.

[c]In the "600" schools, I have worked with supposed nonreaders who could recite stories about Shine in his Great Titanic adventures and also go for more hours with various versions of the Signifyin' Monkey. For two versions of Signifying Monkey see Oscar Brown, Jr.'s "Sin & Soul," Columbia CL 1577 and Rudy Ray Moore's *The Second Rudy Ray Moore Album*, Kent Comedian Series KST-002. For the Titanic see Rudy Ray Moore's *The Rudy Ray Moore Album*—Eat Out More Often, A Comedian, Inc., Enterprise, COM S 1104.

For additional information on The Great Titanic and the Signifying Monkey see Abrahams.

6. A student may be so humiliated by another in a ribbin' encounter that she may lose her temper and attack the other student physically.
7. Similarly, a teacher may try her ability in a ribbin' contest with a student only to be bested by the student, whereupon, she may report the youngster for "insulting" her. This is a negative move for the teacher. What she is doing is asking others to help her solve a discipline problem that she created herself.
8. A teacher may be in a ribbin' contest with a student when other students join in ribbin' the student. The teacher must be careful to make sure that the encounter does not become too humiliating for the student.

A separate Reality will not be used to describe each example of ribbing. Instead, Reality 55 will be used as an example for ribs related to clothing. Reality 56 will illustrate ribs related to sex. Reality 57 will demonstrate ribs related to parts of the body where there do not appear to be any sexual overtones or implications. Additional examples will be provided with each Reality.

Most often, regardless of what is being used as a vehicle for the rib, the two important aspects of the encounter are: (1) the student is most likely vying for control of the class; and (2) he is playing to his fellow students to assist him in disrupting the class. If this student is also dominating the class physically, the teacher may have additional problems that go beyond merely ribbing.

There are two additional side effects of the ribbing, or for that matter any of the verbal repartee, that give ego satisfaction to the winner or winners—even if the winning is fantasy. The first is related to the ego support the youngster receives when his ribbing has thrown the teacher off balance. This happens because the teacher's life style usually has not prepared him for this type of encounter; it certainly was never discussed in teacher training. Wolfe (1970) describes the feeling experienced when blacks see whites off balance, reeling and fearful.

> It wasn't just that you registered your protest and showed the white man that you meant business and weakened his resolve to keep up the walls of oppression. . . . There was something sweet that happened right there on the spot. You made the white man quake. You brought *fear* into his face.
>
> . . . And now, when you got him up close and growled, this all-powerful superior animal turned out to be terrified. You could read it in his face. He had the same fear in his face as some good-doing boy who just moved onto the block and is hiding behind his mama . . . while the bad dudes on the block size him up.
>
> . . . It not only stood to bring you certain practical gains. . . . It also energized your batteries. It recharged your masculinity. You no longer had to play it cool. . . . Mau-mauing brought you respect in its cash forms: namely, fear and envy (pp. 119-120).

The second side effect is the whole additional ego support game that transpires as the students discuss, fantasize, and relive the humiliation of their teacher. Wolfe (1970) writes about this feeling after the confrontation.

> . . . the aces all leave, and they're thinking . . . We've done it again. We've mau-maued the goddamn white man, scared him until he's singing a duet with his sphincter, and the people sure do have power. Did you see the look on his face? Did you see the sucker trembling? Did you see the sucker trying to lick his lips? He was *scared*, man! That's the last time that sucker is gonna try. . . . He's gonna go home to his house in Diamond Heights and he's gonna say, "Honey, fix me a drink! Those mother-fuckers were ready to kill me!" . . . And then later on you think about it and you say, "What really happened that day? Well, another flak catcher lost his manhood, that's what happened." . . . did you see the *look* on his face? That sucker—(pp. 118-119).

REALITY 55

The class was seated waiting for the period-ending bell. Suddenly, there was yelling from the back of the room, and two boys started fighting.

The teacher broke up the fight and asked what had happened?

One of the boys, still whining, said, "He say I be clean 'cause it mother's day."

The teacher looked puzzled. "So what," he said, "is that a reason to start a fight?"

Later, one of the other youngsters explained that mother's day is the day the welfare check arrives—usually on the first or 15th of the month. The intent of this rib was to say that the youngster was on welfare and is dressed well only because his mother's check arrived.

Sometimes the wording may be slightly different although the intent is the same. The wording may be changed to "You look clean, it must be the first of the month," "You look clean, it must be the fifteenth of the month," or just pointing or looking at a youngster's clothing and saying, "It must be mother's day." This can be done to any piece of clothing or possession.

Taunting someone about clothing and welfare is typical and common. Being on welfare is a touchy subject and has all sorts of negative feeling for inner city secondary school youngsters. Clothing is also the area that many of the middle class undergraduates with whom I work, the teachers to whom I lecture, and the teachers who take my courses do not understand.[d] To some of the middle class, who have so much in material goods, clothing means little. To the disadvantaged youngster who does not have money, the correct clothing

---

[d]In Chapter Six I discuss my rules concerning the dress of students who wish to come into my undergraduate program.

becomes important and a visible status symbol that he strives for, and that he respects and envies others for. Remember, it is the pimp or hustler with his expensive clothing who is respected by the ghetto adolescent.

When money began coming into ghetto youngster's hands via the poverty and work study programs of the Johnson administration, the first purchases made often were clothing, as has been attested to by many observers working or living in the ghetto at the time.

Some of the specific ribbing about clothing includes such negative terms as "Pacific Oceans," "floods," and "high waters." A youngster makes fun of someone's pants by teasing him about the length of the trousers. This may take the form of referring to someone's pants as Pacific Oceans, floods, or high waters. This may be done in many ways with the same idea in mind. The implication is that the pants are too short for the youngster's height. Therefore, he could walk in the Pacific Ocean, walk through a flood, or walk through high water without getting his trousers wet.

I can remember a similar taunt when I was a kid. We used to say something like "Why don't you have a party and bring your pants down to meet your feet."

Two *ribs* related to welfare are G W's and S A's. Referring to someone's clothing as either G W's or S A's refers to the youngster as being poor or on welfare—G W's referring to Good Will and S A's referring to Salvation Army. Or, as a junior high school youngster stated, "They tryin' to say they got cheap clothes. He got them in a rummage sale." Or even saying, "I saw George down at Goodwill the other day."

In addition to the aforementioned ribbing, clothing in general is target for ribs. Someone saying, "You got your brother's shirt on," may start a fight. Someone's socks, shoes, jacket, any article of clothing may be the target of ribbing.

The style of clothing being worn is particularly important. A youngster wearing low instead of high socks may inspire ribs such as: "Hey, you got your ankle breakers on" or "Where did you get the ankle breakers?" In this case the youngster was being chided about his short socks. The implication was that if he got wet, the socks would shrink and break his ankles.

Another rib concerning clothing is related to the color of a youngster's socks. A youngster walks into the room wearing red socks; whereupon someone yells out, "Did somebody cut you?" The class bursts into laughter. "I know you burnin' " might be said to a youngster wearing heavy pants on a warm day. Heavy pants worn on a warm day are known as a burner.

A female student may have a run in her stockings and will be ribbed about it. Or, someone may rib on another student's shoes for not having high platform soles and heels. Female students are often ribbed for supposedly wearing their brother's clothes.

Teachers are also fair game for ribbing. Ghetto youngsters delight in ribbing teachers, particularly about their clothing. If the teachers' clothing is out of style, student ribbing may be carried on in front of them or behind their backs. Youngsters usually know, for example, how many suits, sport coats, dresses, skirts, or shoes teachers may own or wear to school. Sometimes, they even bet about what a teacher will wear. It is common to hear, "Shit, she wore that raggedy dress twice this week already."

Indeed, some students will actually keep score of how often a teacher wears a certain dress or suit. I have observed students rib a teacher from her shoes to her hair style. The ribbing was so heavy on one teacher, he had all his suits and sport coats recut to conform to style. What a teacher wears has a good deal to do with how she relates to students, particularly if the teacher is young and active.

As a part of a New Teacher program with the Buffalo schools[e] a coed panel made up of some of the tougher discipline problems in the Buffalo schools discussed the ribbing of a teacher. The following was transcribed from the panel discussion.

> "Like, we used to rib on one teacher . . . and he [the teacher] would turn red and everything, and we used to get on his clothes, and his hair, and everything, and I think one time he got on somebody in our room. He got on pretty strong.
>
> "And, you know, we felt kind of bad. We didn't think he had it in him, and we kind of cooled off for then. Then, we started up again. And then he got on another one of us so we sort of cooled again.
>
> "It din't help him. He got mad, ran out of the room. We was talking about something he had on. He ran out of the room, got Mr. _____ , and everything. I don't know, I like them better, rather like them better if they, if they, get us back—we sort of shut up a little while."

Sneakers are another extremely important area related to prestige and as such are excellent targets for ribbing. A student may be walking the hall and say to another student, "I see you got your brogans on." This seemingly innocent remark may result in anything from laughter, to an argument, to a fight. The word brogans is used to ridicule someone's old, worn out, or not so popular brand of sneakers or shoes. "Brogans," "cousins," "liberty specials," and "buddies" are words used in some schools.

One student ribbing another about his sneakers may say, "I see you got your slip-and-slides on." The implication here is that the tread on this person's sneakers are worn causing a person to slip and slide. As one student told me, "You can stand on the gym floor and slide all over the place."

[e]See Chapter Seven for a description of the New Teacher and Teacher Aide program.

When I asked two students why two girls had fought when someone used the word buddies, one's response was:

"Something about sneakers. Like, um, somebody got on some old raggedy sneakers, say Diana, for instance. And, you could talk about their sneakers and they might not like it. Because, you know, they spent their own hard earned money for it, and they get mad. You know, and they don't like you doin' it so they'll fight you about it."

You sometimes get the feeling that these youngsters cannot really explain why they respond to ribbing by fighting. Or even why the insults have such an effect on them. Sometimes it seems as though some unwritten code of honor says they must fight, and so they do.

For many years, low cut white Cons were the sneakers to wear (at least in the Northeast).[f] Adidas sneakers are now coming into favor and appear to be challenging Cons for popularity. Inner city youngsters who cannot afford Adidas, purchase less expensive imitations at discount houses. On their own or with the help of understanding teachers, they draw the requisite number of black stripes on their less expensive sneakers making them look like Adidas.

An incident that happened to me a number of years ago will give you an example of the importance of the "right" sneakers. One day, when I opened my clothes locker to get something, a number of high school students were with me.

When the locker was open, one of the fellows looked inside and yelled, "Mr. Foster, those two pair of Cons yours?"

"Yeah!" was my response.

For about two weeks, I was big man in the school. My reputation blossomed because the students spread the word that I owned and used two pair of Cons, low cut and white. A number of students came to my room and asked whether it was true that I really owned two pair of Cons?

Flaste (1973) discusses with some Sands Junior High School (in Brooklyn, New York) eighth-graders their preference for sneakers, such as Keds, Cons, Gold Seal, and Pumas (they are out for these youngsters because they cost $20). According to Sands teacher Toni Jo Scott, "Keds and Cons are the one material possession that separates the in-group students from the outcasts (p. 38)." I have always found, though, that if you know your way around you can usually find some store that is selling seconds where you can get a "better" sneaker for a cut price.

---

[f]Cons are a shortening for Converse sneakers. A number of years ago Cons were *the* sneaker. Another sneaker manufacturer attempted to immitate them by placing the same blue strip across the back heel of the sneaker just as Cons had. The manufacturer, however, did not place the Cons blue star on the patch. Cons are also referred to as All Stars.

When we were kids, my brothers and I wore Hood sneakers when Keds were the "in" sneakers. Though we do not remember any ribbing about them, we felt that somehow we were not "in." Also, roller skates had to be a certain kind. As we recall, Union Hardware were the "in" skates and we had Winchesters.

Interestingly, in the above article, "taunting" about a student's wearing a less popular sneaker is mentioned. To some extent, the impact of the taunting is mentioned. The word used for the ribbing or taunting is "reject."

A youngster is asked what he would do if his mother brought him a pair of "rejects." His response is that he would "throw them out the window (p. 38)." Style is important. "If a boy does wear 'rejects' to school, he's going to be teased (p. 38)."

Someone offered a "taunt" that some of the youngsters sing:

"Rejects.
They make your feet feel
    fine.
Rejects.
They cost a dollar ninety-
    nine (p. 38)."

A recent visitor from California informed me that in some schools you can recognize gang members by their sneakers. One gang may wear Tigers, another Cons, another Pumas, and still another Adidas.

Have you forgotten your feelings, as a kid, of power and speed when you put on a new pair of the "right" brand of sneakers? If you have, read about the sneakers that could make you run as fast as a deer, "could jump you over trees and rivers and houses. And if you wanted, they could jump you over fences and sidewalks and dogs (Bradbury, p. 15)" in Ray Bradbury's (1959, p. 14-18) *Dandelion Wine.*

Not just any sneakers though, but a pair of "Royal Crown Cream—Sponge Para Litefoot Tennis Shoes: LIKE MENTHOL ON YOUR FEET (p. 16)." Douglas Spaulding asks Mr. Sanderson how can he sell his sneakers unless he "can rave about them and how you going to rave about them unless you know them (p. 17)."

"Feel those shoes, Mr. Sanderson, *feel* how fast they'd take me? All those springs inside? Feel all the running inside? Feel how they kind of grab hold and can't let you alone and don't like you just *standing* there? Feel how quick I'd be doing the things you'd rather not bother with? You stay in the nice cool store while I'm jumping all around town! But it's not me really, it's the shoes. They're going like mad down alleys, cutting corners, and back! There they go!" . . .
Mr. Sanderson stood amazed with the rush of words. When the words got going the flow carried him; he began to sink deep in the shoes, to flex his toes, limber his arches, test his ankles. He rocked softly, secretly, back and forth in a small breeze from the open door. The tennis shoes silently hushed themselves deep in the carpet, sank as in a jungle grass, in loam and resilient clay. He gave one solemn bounce of his heels in the yeasty dough, in the yielding and welcoming earth. Emotions hurried over his face as if many colored

lights had been switched on and off. His mouth hung slightly open. Slowly he gentled and rocked himself to a halt, and the boy's voice faded and they stood there looking at each other in a tremendous and natural silence (pp. 17-18).

Another area for ribbing is related to aspects of sex. This includes the use of standard vocabulary words with a second meaning, usually a sexual meaning. Most often, as discussed in Chapter Four, these second meanings are unknown to the teacher. These ribbing techniques are used most effectively against female students and female teachers.

In Realities 27 and 28, examples were provided of how female teachers are ribbed by students using the word trim. Another word that is used often, and was also mentioned earlier, is the word ho, which is short for whore. There are a number of clever derivations in the use of the ho for ribbing on students and teachers. Reality 56 is one example.

REALITY 56

The 5th period was just ending. A new young female teacher was having a rough 5th period. Her students were lined up waiting for the bell when one of the girls walked up to her and asked loudly, "Mrs. Elderson, are you a garden tool?"

Mrs. Elderson, beaten and harried, asked, "What do you mean? What kind of a question is that?"

Her students began to laugh just as the bell rang. They kept laughing and jostling one another as they ran from the room.

The sixth period for Mrs. Elderson was unassigned. So, she pulled the curtains down, locked the door, sat down at the desk, and just cried.

So many new teachers in inner-city schools take such an emotional beating that many do just sit down and cry. And, many wish they could—men included.

Although these youngsters did not tell Mrs. Elderson what a garden tool was, instinctively she knew that something was amiss-that she was being made the butt of another prank. A garden tool is a hoe. And a *hoe* (ho) is short for a whore.

There are also occasions when a male or female student will ask a teacher, "Are you a virgin?" in a loud clear voice for all students to hear. This form of ribbing is done most often to young new female teachers.

Another rib related to whore is where the students take a piece of paper at least 8½ x 11 and hand print ƎOH on it. The paper is then tacked or pasted somewhere near the teacher. This rib is one that teachers don't catch too easily. The idea is to turn over the paper so that ƎOH becomes hoe—again a form of whore.

A favorite rib is for a number of the youngsters to get together and plan to hum "Hi ho, hi ho." The students will come into the room, sit down, and start humming. If the teacher walks close to someone who is humming, he will stop and others farther away will pick it up. Sometimes the humming will go up and down the rows. When this has happened, I have observed teachers running up and down the rows trying to find a portable radio.

I was standing outside a classroom one afternoon when I heard a commotion coming from inside. When I saw the teacher later, I asked what had happened. She told me that she was yelling at her students because they were always asking to leave the room when one of her bigger students had come up to her and said, "Give me a pass for the third period. I want to go ho hunting."

Male and female students often play this next rib usually on female teachers. A student will approach the teacher and say, "What you need is a jones." Or, sometimes, "What you need is a johnson." Both words have the same meaning—a penis. Sometimes the connotation is a black penis. Those who saw *Putney Swope* may recall one of the actresses informing one of the males, "I'm gonna soften your johnson."

A female graduate student who is teaching told me this story. She was in her junior high school class when one of her students approached her and said, "What you need is a jones." She shook the youngster up when she responded with, "I know, I got one and he is great." Of course, the youngster's objective of ribbing the teacher backfired as the class laughed at him.

Another form of ribbing is to use graffiti to get at someone, or to get a number of youngsters at one another. This is accomplished by leaving some graffiti somewhere in or around the school.

I came across a graffitied bulletin board in a guidance office that was combination of ribbing and signifying.[g] Under the graffiti "Hoes of Buffalo sign here" were five names. This was a ploy to get the youngsters mad at each other. What usually happens in such an incident is for someone, probably the graffitti writer, to go to each of the girls and say, "Did you see what _____ wrote about you?"

In discussing this ribbing through graffiti with a number of female students, their response was, "No one would do that. It was done by someone who was agitatin'. It look like somebody try to be smart. Like, it wouldn't be nobody who will sign their name up there. Who wrote that sign somebody's name up there as if to say they wrote it up there."

While discussing ribbing techniques with a coed group of junior high school students someone mentioned the word trim and it set-off the following very rapid verbal exchange.

Female student: "Somebody always askin for some trim and haven't even got anything."

[g]H. Rap Brown (1969) presents his version of signifying: "Signifying is more humane. Instead of coming down on somebody's mother, you come down on them (p. 27)." "Signifying allowed you a choice—you could either make a cat feel good or bad. If you had just destroyed someone or if they were just down already, signifying could help them over. Signifying was also a way of expressing your own feelings (p. 29)."

Male student: "Your hole ain't no bigger than a pin hole."

Female student: "You a story."

The exchange ended as quickly as it started, and we went off to another subject. Such an exchange can perplex a teacher as to his role. Too often, the teacher will keep the discussion hot and going by interceding. Usually, if the teacher can get the students moving to another subject or to get them to return to the subject they were discussing before the outbreak, without belaboring the incident, he is better off.

The last group of ribbing games to be described is related to parts of the body with no apparent sexual overtones or implications. Also some of the ribbing that appears is related to nicknames. Reality 57 provides an example of name-calling.

REALITY 57

The bell had sounded and the students were changing classes. Suddenly, there was yelling and fighting at the end of the second floor. About fifteen youngsters were involved.

After the teachers and administrators broke up the fighting and had control, they brought those fighting to the main office. Upon calming everyone down, they managed to find out what had happened. One of the boys had called a girl a "pumpkin head" as he passed her in the hall. This young lady was in a bad mood, was twice the size of the young man, and promptly started to pummel him, whereupon a number of their friends took sides and got involved.

Inner city youngsters are masters of the art of making up nicknames for one another. Sometimes, of course, the names demean. However, whether the nicknames demean or not they are usually accurate and descriptive.

Sometimes the nicknames are personalized; for example, "block head," "cabbage," "toad," and "big head." Sometimes the names are generalized for a school. For example, in one school any youngster called a "piranha" is insulted in the highest order and is usually compelled to fight back physically. Of course, how students react to these ribs usually depends upon how they feel on that day or at that moment, and how many other students are around to witness the actions. And also, of course, which teacher or administrator happens to be nearby.

In a school I have visited, a ribbing comment such as "your comb is all green and junk," could start a fight. In this school the word green used in reference to clothing, or some other possession, appears to be an insult. Such expressions as "You look like some burnt pussy," and "Oh! you ain't shit," also usually elicit violent reactions.

Someone may have a permanent or temporary physical deformity that becomes fair game for ribbing. A female secondary school student told me this story about her thyroid problem. "He may have a problem and they get on your problem. When I was in third grade my throat had a thyroid gland and it kept gettin' big. It ain't big no more and this boy started ribbin' and makin' fun of it and I started fightin' him."

Youngsters may be ribbed about an operation, protruding or missing teeth, a face or body blemish, height, and weight. A girl with short hair may rib a girl with a "bush" by saying, I got more hair than you," etc.

Parts of the body are also the objects of ribbing. A young man may start by saying, "My arms are better than your legs." And, the other youngster may come back with "Those raggedy things arms?" Sometimes, even the way a youngster walks is a source for ribbing.

One of the most devastating ribs a teacher can experience is to be feeling great about finally beginning to relate to students and teach them, when one youngster you thought you were getting through to says, "Shit, man, get away from me, your breath stinks!" The teacher's response will be one of upset and embarrassment; whereas if he recognizes this as a rib, he will be able to empathize better with the youngsters who are always the butt of ribs themselves.

JIVIN'

A number of the verbal coping and survival techniques which black urban males have developed and refined in order to manipulate, persuade, and hustle others to survive will be discussed under "jivin'.[h] Those to be discussed are "shuckin' " and "jivin'," "woofing," and signifying."

The versions of these verbal techniques used in school may be less sophisticated than adult streetcorner usage, and may be used differently when with friends as compared with an authority figure such as a policeman or a teacher. Jivin' behavior may also differ when a male is confronting a male teacher as compared with a female teacher or with one of his "people" as compared with a girl whose "nose" he wants. Further differences in usage may also depend upon age and sex, section of the country, or even section of a particular city. But what is important is how streetcorner youngsters play out their games in school, not what the games are called.

The manipulative jivin' games usually work because of the fantasies blacks and whites have of one another. White fantasies alternate between blacks being hedonistic, aggressive, gorilla studs or shufflin' children requiring his help. The black streetcorner youngster knows the fantasies whites have about him and fulfills these role expectations to manipulate him. If all else fails, he can always switch from the cat role to the gorilla, bogarding role, because he may feel most whites are faggots and fear him.

Shuckin' and Jivin'

Some of the coping and survival techniques are defensive mechanisms blacks started developing during slavery days and have perfected in order

[h]The following books are suggested for those wishing to investigate this area in more detail: Brown, and Kochman.

to cope with overt and covert racism. One of the techniques is called shuckin' and jivin', or shuckin' or jivin', and possibly other names depending upon location.

John Dotson (1972) mentions shuckin' and jivin' as part of the recent arguments over black exploitation films. Many middle class blacks and whites attack movies such as *Shaft* and *Super Fly* for reasons from "creating a poor black image" to providing a "fantasy black stud image" that, to some extent, misses the essence of the movies.

> There is more to enjoy in the new black movies than just the superspade stuff. There is a special humor that some of the pictures impart. Harry Belafonte's shucking and jiving in "Buck and the Preacher" was a particularly telling portrayal. When in trouble with the white folks, he grinned and preached for that was his protective shield, but when he was with Buck he became a sly, crafty gunslinger (p. 82).

Schuckin' and jivin' is a verbal and physical technique some blacks use to avoid difficulty, to accommodate some authority figure, and, in the extreme, to save a life or to save oneself from being beaten physically or psychologically. Gestures, facial expressions, speech pronunciation, and body poses are all used to provide the authority figure with the appearance deemed acceptable and subserviant to placate him. Shuckin' and jivin' also often requires an ability to control and conceal one's true emotions.

Eldridge Cleaver (1968, p. 168) provides an example of shuckin' and jivin':

> Then one day, we were out driving and I ran through a red light just a little too late and this motorcycle cop pulled me over.
> "Say, Boy," he said to me, "are you color-blind?" I didn't want a ticket so I decided to talk him out of it. I went into my act, gave him a big smile and explained to him that I was awfully sorry, that I thought that I could make it but that my old car was too slow. He talked real bad to me, took me on a long trip about how important it was that I obeyed the laws and regulation and how else can a society be controlled and administered without obedience to the law. I said a bunch of Yes Sir's and he told me to run along and be a good boy (p. 168)."

I once witnessed a middle-aged, prim, proper, and very bigoted white female teacher drag a black female high school student to the assistant principal and demand that the assistant principal "Make her tell me her name."

REALITY 58

The teacher marched into the office with her hand holding the student's arm tightly.

"Make her tell me her name," she spat out at the black assistant principal as she released the girl's arm.

The student gave her name in a Southern accent.

The teacher was not hearing her. "Make her tell me her name," she yelled.

Again, the student gave her name in a Southern accent.

"_____ , tell her your name," said the assistant principal in a soft voice.

The student slouched, and in a trembling voice once again repeated her name. This time, however, in a hesitating voice minus the Southern accent.

"Thank you," the teacher said curtly as she turned on her heel and walked away. The student burst in tears.

The teacher had continued her psychological brutality until the youngster had acquiesced to the teacher's concept of how a black female student should talk. When she gave her name for the first time in the office, I was easily able to understand her. The teacher was using the youngster's dialect as an additional way of showing her racist feelings.

Many streetcorner youngsters have developed an amazing sense for determining the shuckin' and jivin' behavior that school personnel want and expect from them. Kochman (1969) also notes this ability in nonschool settings. "They [those who are shuckin' and jivin'] became competent actors. Many developed keen perception of what affected, motivated, appeased or satisfied the authority figures with whom they came into contact (p. 29)."

For many blacks, shuckin' and jivin' is a survival technique to avoid and stay out of trouble. It is also used to escape suspension or punishment for misconduct when caught. In fact, it is also used to escape being caught. Reality 59 provides an example of a youngster shuckin' and jivin' his way out of a misconduct charge. Reality 60 depicts a youngster shuckin' and jivin' his way out of being caught.

REALITY 59

A sixth grade female teacher was walking in the hall. One of her male students approached her and asked, "You wanna grind?" (The grind is a slow sensual dance. The couple dancing barely move anything but their pelvises in a grinding motion.)

The teacher ignored the question and walked on. The question, however, bothered her. Instinctively she knew there was something wrong about it and she reported the young man and the question to her assistant principal.

The assistant principal called the youngster to his office. When questioned about the incident, the youngster went into his shuckin' act.

He explained that he guessed he had not spoken too clearly because what he said was, "Would you wanna grind a carrot with me?"

The assistant principal let the young man go with a warning to speak more clearly and wrote a note of explanation to the teacher. Of course, if we attach the double meaning of penis to carrot, the youngster had really jived them both.

REALITY 60

There were about ten minutes left in the last period of a ninth grade history class. A youngster was playing around and had the class in stitches. He had managed to involve a number of his fellow students in his disruptive pranks. The teacher, in desperation, called for assistance on the intercom.

The disruptive youngster ran out of the classroom seconds before the assistant principal arrived; they almost collided. The youngster walked the assistant principal away from the door as he began to shuck and jive.

"Boy, am I glad you got here," he said in a hesitating almost whining voice. I was about to go and get you to help Mrs. Frank. There are some crazy cats in there who are trying to get me in trouble again. They won't let her teach," he added as the bell rang.

"OK, if I go?" he asked weakly but quickly, "I got to go and pick up my kid sister."

"Yes, I guess so," the assistant principal responded, getting out of the way of running students.

By the next morning, the assistant principal had forgotten that he had even been called to the room.

Reality 61 concerns a nonschool incident of shuckin' and jivin' that parallels Reality 60 but this time with a tragic result. As reported in the *New York Times* (Fraser, 1973, p. 24) a man allegedly "tricked" police officers into shooting and killing a transit patrolman.

REALITY 61

It started on the platform of the Hunts Point station of the IRT in New York City. An off-duty transit patrolman in civilian clothing allegedly saw a black man named Richardson carrying a gun in the waistband of his trousers. The patrolman, after identifying himself, ordered Mr. Richardson to lean against the wall. Mr. Richardson appearing to comply, supposedly pulled out a .32 caliber hand gun, shot the patrolman in the shoulder, and ran for an exit with the wounded patrolman pursuing and shooting at him.

As Richardson rushed from the subway, he was met by a number of police officers hurrying to investigate the commotion. Richardson called to them that there was "a crazy man with a gun" shooting at him. The police seeing the oncoming out-of-uniform patrolman brandishing his gun instantly reacted hitting him six times with gunfire. The patrolman died four hours later in the hospital. This time, however, the shuckin' and jivin' helped no one. Mr. Richardson was indicted by a grand jury on seven counts: felony murder, manslaughter, attempted murder, escape, possession of a weapon, reckless endangerment, and possession of stolen property—a correction officer's badge.

Andrews and Owens (1973, p. 93) define *Shuck* as "Worthless, no good rappin. Usually followed by jive. 'Why don't you quit *SHUCKIN* and jivin.' " Their definition holds in particular for school youngsters shuckin' and jivin' one another. H. Rap Brown (1969, p. 24-25) gives an example of shuckin' and jivin' a friend.

> "We went and got some 'pluck' (wine) and I told him I was in college. He asked what I wanted to be. I told him rich. He looked up at the ceiling and paused for a minute before he said, 'You know, I've never given any thought to what I want to become.' I told him he should think about it, but I knew I was shuckin' and jivin'. Hell, hardly any of us ever thought about what we wanted to become. What was the future? That was something white folks had. We just lived from day to day, expecting whatever life put on us and dealing with it the best we knew how when it came. I had accepted the big lie of a Black man succeeding (pp. 24-25)."

John O. Killens (1973, p. 193) mentions shucking and jiving in *The Cotillion: or One Good Bull is Half the Herd.*

Woofin'

Another survival technique streetcorner youngsters often use to test a teacher's mettle is "woofin'," How a teacher reacts to a heavy *woof* may determine his tenure in a classroom. Andrews and Owens (1973, p. 106) define wolf (pronounced woof) as "A vicious verbal attack, similar to signifying except that it's not as intellectually cunning as signifying. Also there are three people directly involved in signifying, two in woofing." Their definition[i] is reasonably accurate. However, it must be remembered that in most cases, school youngsters challenging a teacher or classmate are also playing to their audience. Therefore,

---

[i]Other definitions: *Woofing,* n., aimless talk, as a dog barks on a moonlight night; (Hurston, 1942), a *woofer,* n., applied to one who talks constantly, loudly, and in a convincing manner, but who says very little; (Sebastian, 1934), *woof,* n., to talk much and loudly and yet say little of consequence; (Sebastian, 1934); *wuffin',* when some little boy picks on a big boy orally (Buffalo, N.Y., 1970); *wolf,* v., to make fun of someone (Foster, 1966); *wolf,* v. N.Y.C. Youth Board, 1964); *wolf,* a male who chases women; (Burley, 1944); "The whole thing is that if you can woof and woof hard enough and long enough and be willing to back it up, few people will push you (Brown, 1969, p. 81)." "I turned around and started wolfing at the guy, and he just strolled off (Alcindor, 1969, p. 36)."

although two are involved in the verbal aspects of woofing, the audience that may be affected by the outcome may also determine the outcome by their presence and reactions to the woofing encounter. Woofing is another jivin' or manipulative technique. Earlier, Shelly (1945, p. 50) described *woofin* as "to tell an improbable yarn," and classified as G.I. jive.

Youngsters may woof on one another or they may woof on a teacher. And, as noted in Chapter Four, to accept a challenge to a fight is to accept a Wolf Ticket. In one case, however, a Wolf Ticket was used to stop a fight.

REALITY 62

While still teaching graphic arts in the "600" schools, I gave a friend who was an assistant principal in a Harlem junior high school a number of Wolf Tickets that my students had printed.

Some time later he told me of an incident in which two male students had been fighting. No matter what he did verbally, they would not stop. Then, remembering the Wolf Tickets he handed one to each of the protagonists. The fight stopped immediately and soon the whole class was clamoring for a Wolf Ticket. Interest in the tickets superseded interest in the fight.

Just as with many of the other terms we are discussing, usage and definition differ in different regions and social groups. In some areas, signifying and playing the dozens may be called woofing by certain age groups. Or, as described by H. Rap Brown (1969, p. 58), the act of loud, threatening talk can be called *woofing* while what you are using as a tool for *woofing* may be the dozens. "He just stood there and woofed at the police, talking about their mamas and shit like that. You know a blood. Play the Dozens in a minute."

Sometimes, "loud mouthing" or "loud talking," "sounding," "screaming on someone," or even "bogarding" are synonyms for woofing.

For the middle class teacher, woofin' can be a terrifying experience; or it can be a false perception of reality. The white teacher's fantasies and feelings about blacks and her perceptions concerning black militancy can affect her response to a youngster woofin' on her. For example, if she perceives an Afro or dashiki as evidence of a militant antiwhite attitude she may feel threatened physically if the youngster *woofin'* her is wearing a dashiki.

Brown points out that to woof well you always have to be on the offensive. "I knew damned well they wasn't gon' let a nigger get the drop on the sheriff and then let him go, but you got to stay on the offensive all the time. 'What you mean I'm under arrest? for what, goddammit?' I was woofing like a champ."

Woofin' has also come to some institutions of higher learning. In some ways, many colleges and universities are beginning to resemble inner city schools or urban schools receiving bussed-in ghetto students. White university faculty, administrators, and students have as many problems relating to street-corner youngsters as do most inner city school personnel and middle class students.

One of the differences is that the academicians had the option of actually doing some good; however, they too fumbled the ball. Instead of bringing into the universities those urban lower class black youngsters with the middle class skills and behavior required to succeed and to relate to the middle class students, most institutions recruited and are still bringing in I-hate-whitey "ghetto blacks." Most of these youngsters, even with tutoring, have not and will not succeed in the university.

Like streetcorner action, they hustle the university for subsistence until, periodically, someone catches on or they lose interest and leave for a better hustle. Whether university people are acting out of guilt, ignorance, incompetence, or fear, is debatable. Sadly, some of the blacks administering these programs are into the hustle too; they are playing the white game even to hustling both blacks and whites.

Woofin' is used differently in our universities from the way it is used in inner city schools. In the schools, woofin' disrupts the teaching and learning process. In the colleges, it is used usually for personal or group gain. In some rare cases, woofin' has actually been used to procure an undergraduate degree in mostly independent study. Black streetcorner students woof on faculty, secre-taries, white student government leaders, and their adult advisors, frightening them into providing funds either improperly or by skirting established student government procedures. Assuredly, some of the woofin' has been precipitated by whites trying to hustle blacks out of goods and materials promised or rightfully theirs. Interestingly, white males frequently fear woofin' more than do white females. It is a rare white college student, college staff member, or administrator who is capable of standing up to woofin'. (This was particularly true on college campuses during the upheavals of a few years ago, particularly at Cornell University.)

Reality 63 reports how an undergraduate female student government officer stood up to woofin' with the result that the black students involved backed off and tried a hustle instead. In Reality 64, woofin' was successful.[j]

REALITY 63

As a monthly student government meeting was called to order, seven black male students, five dressed all in black, walked into the meeting room with two tape

---

[j]Although this is a book about inner city secondary schools, I'm annoyed with many of my fellow professors telling public school people how to get their shops in order without looking at their own shops. For example, has anyone heard a university professor who called for accountability for public school teachers call for accountability for himself and his fellow professors?

recorders and sat down. As a female student officer began giving a report, one of the blacks started woofin'.

"Why hasn't the Black Athletic Association been recognized as a club? We haven't heard a fuckin' thing on our application. What the hell is going on?"

Simultaneously, two of the black students walked to the student government officer's desk and held up their recording microphones. A third black student opened a pad and began taking notes.

The female officer responded, "Club recognitions have been backed up. Yours will be taken up in its turn as we get to it."

A black student interrupted her, "Wait a second, we want to know why it hasn't come up."

"Just wait, just listen. I'll tell you . . . . " She tried, but was interrupted again.

"We're not saying its because people are prejudiced. We're not mentioning anything like that. We just find it strange that our club is the only one that hasn't had any word about recognition," one of the black students yelled out.

The student officer picked up a handful of forms and objected, "Look at these fifteen forms from other clubs. They haven't any word either because of the change in administration and the state of the files."

At this point, a white male student in the audience jumped up and made a motion "that we rush recognition of the Black Athletic Association ahead of the other clubs."

Before a second could be made, the female officer shouted back. "No, I won't do it. Ten club applications were received before theirs. We will work according to the clubs that came in first and when we get to theirs we will vote on it. I will never put any club before another club. Either it will be run fairly or not at all."

The motion was not seconded, and the meeting adjourned soon afterwards. After the meeting, the black students approached the female officer and pointed out that they didn't want to give anyone a hassle. "Take your time. When we get it, we get it," they said.

Their woofin' had not worked. Now the black students decided to try to run a game on the student officer.

Two days later, several of the black students came to her office for a meeting. They discussed the $5,000 they owed student government which had to be paid back before they could receive this year's budget. Indeed, she informed them that they would not receive recognition as a club until the money was paid back.

They told her that they had a contract with local businessmen to get the $5,000. When they received recognition, the businessmen would help them pay the money back.

She informed them that recognition could not be given until they presented proof that they would repay the $5,000. They told her the business-men would not give them the $5,000 until they received recognition as a club. They added that they needed the recognition by following Wednesday or the businessmen would withdraw their offer. She relented a bit. If they could get letters of intent from the businessmen, she would get them a letter of recognition.

That Friday their Association received provisional recognition with the understanding that letters of intent had to be in by Monday for them to receive official recognition by Wednesday, at which time they would get their budget.

Although they received the letter, they never followed through to get their $5,000. A few months later, however, one of the students saw the officer and told her that the matter with the businessmen was still pending.

Where woofin' in Reality 63 failed, woofin' in Reality 64 succeeded, possibly because it was more intense. During the college upheavals of the late '60s and early '70s, white college students learned how to intimidate college personnel by throwing a few FUCK words at them. Black ghetto college students, however, are masters of the art and more adept at using FUCK as part of their verbal repertoire. Hence, their woofin' puts language, appearance, and physicalness together to intimidate the college community. (In looking at the nation, the Black Panther woofin' had the nation, and the FBI intimidated.)

Reality 64

It was mid afternoon and a few students were lazing around in the student government office. Suddenly eight black students burst into the office shouting and cursing.

"Where the fuck is our twelve hundred dollars? We were promised the fucking' money by the last administration. We need the fuckin' money to get to a fuckin' lecture down south. We need the fuckin' money for travel, motels, food, and fees. We are sick of bein' pushed around, we ain't leavin' this fuckin' office 'till we git our money."

The secretary hesitatingly told them she would try to check the record to find out about the money if they would just please wait a minute.

One of the black students continued his woofin', "I want my fuckin' money now. I want my fuckin' money so I can get the fuck out of here. Shit, I gotta make reservations."

"I won't talk to you until you learn how to talk right," the secretary screamed as she scurried around looking for the records.

"Get the fuck over here and give me my fuckin' money," the student yelled as he moved toward her waving his hands.

The secretary fled crying into the inner office where an advisor and student treasurer were talking. They tried to calm her amidst the continued woofin'.

"I want my fucking money," yelled the same black student who had followed into the office.

The other black students pushed into the office. The adult advisor told them,

"You guys should keep your own records as a check on student government 'cause things could go wrong in our files. At least you guys would have some proof of what occurred."

"You fulla shit you white mutha fucka'," yelled one of the other students.

"You are a black bastard and get the hell out of my office 'till you can conduct yourself halfway decently," shouted the adult advisor.

The woofin' continued a bit, and the black students eventually received the money, the student officers saying that they had to provide the funds to fulfill the commitment of the prior officers. To the best of my knowledge, there was neither any record of the promise of funds found in any minutes nor was a check made with previous year's officers.

Whether these students had attempted to get the money earlier through a more middle class approach, or whether this was their first attempt, I don't know. What I do know is that the woofin' worked.

The woofin' observed in use most often in public schools takes the form of the youngster making a face and yelling at the teacher. The woofer may also move his body in a menacing way to make his woof more threatening and intimidating.

He may woof for anything from a pass to leave school early to gaining control of the class by frightening the teacher. Or, he may woof on the teacher to get another sandwich at lunch, or to get into class without a pass when late.

I observed a woofin' contest in a junior high school where many students roamed the halls refusing to go to class during a minor uprising. In one room, however, most of the students were in class and giving their new inexperienced teacher a rough time. An experienced teacher from another school happened to be there and he entered the room to help when he saw the teacher having problems.

As he spoke with the students, one of the bigger boys jumped up from his seat and woofed the visiting teacher with "I'm gonna punch you," as he started walking toward him.

The teacher looked at the youngster, laughed loudly, and said, "You gonna punch me?"

The youngster stopped in his tracks, looked at his fellow students who were now laughing, and started laughing himself. As he returned to his seat, he said, "Naw, I was only kidding."

The teacher talked with the class for about twenty minutes about what was going on and then left.

Reality 65 describes a teacher using a "soft" woof on five junior high school inner city youngsters and getting away with it.

REALITY 65

A teacher was walking down the hall when he noticed a commotion near an auditorium door. Walking to the door, he found five boys giving Mr. Rice, the guidance teacher, a hard time. Mr. Rice was not in trouble but was having a problem extricating himself from the conversation with the students.

"What's the matter, Mr. Rice? Can I help," he asked.

"These guys won't go away. I have to work with the kids inside on a play and these guys are trying to come in," responded Mr. Rice.

"Oh heck," said the teacher. There are only onnne-twoo-threee-fourrr-fivvve of them. Five, that's light stuff. You go inside, and I'll take care of them."

The students looked from Mr. Rice to the teacher.

Two of them said, "Shoot."

They all turned and walked away. Mr. Rice and the teacher laughed. The teacher left, Mr. Rice closed the door, and started his rehearsal.

Sometimes, youngsters will work together to run a woofin' game. This can happen if a youngster wants his class disrupted because he did not do his homework, he does not want to take a test, he does not like the teacher, or for almost any other reason. Woofin' can also be planned when a youngster comes to a teacher's classroom door and woofs until the teacher loses his composure and chases the student while the class spills out into the hall to watch the action. In one case where I observed this, I actually had to physically restrain the teacher and push him back into his classroom while telling him that I would get the youngster.

Signifying

A good deal of signifying goes on in inner city schools. It usually starts when one youngster approaches another and says something like, "You know what Russell said about you?" The fellow signifying keeps at the other until he provokes him to go after Russell, who may not have said anything at all.

Sometimes, inner city youngsters will signify one teacher against another, student against teacher, teacher against student, and administrator against teacher or vice versa.

Although there does not appear to be consensus as to exactly what signifying is, there is agreement that it does exist as a technique that differs from shuckin' and jivin' and other forms of provocation or put down. Signifying has been defined by a number of writers. Andrews and Owens (1973, p. 95), write that *signifying* is to tease someone, or to provoke someone into anger. "The signifier creates a myth about someone and tells him a third person started it." They suggest signifying is successful "When the signifier convinces the chump he is working on, that what he is saying is true and that it gets him angered to wrath."

Signifying, according to H. Rap Brown, (1969, p. 29) is one of the many forms of "what the white folks call verbal skills. We learned how to throw them words together." He writes that the person signifying has an option of either making someone feel good or bad. If someone was down, signifying could also make him feel better.

Signifying was also a way of expressing your feelings:

"Man, I can't win for losing
If it wasn't for bad luck, I wouldn't
    have no luck at all. . . .
I'm living on the welfare and things is
    stormy
They borrowing their shit from the Salvation
    Army. . . ."

Signifying is also telling tales or stories or "throwing the bull" or what in Yiddish is called "fonfering."[k] Brown feels that real signifying is best when,

> . . . brothers are exchanging tales, I used to hang out in the bars just to hear the old men "talking shit." By the time I was nine, I could talk Shine and the Titanic, Signifying Monkey, three different ways, and Piss-Pot-Peet, for two hours without stopping (p. 30).[l]

Ed Bullins, one of the most prolific black playwrights in America, who grew up on the streets of North Philadelphia, also has a concept of *signifying*. Anderson (1973), interviewed Bullins and discussed a press release that appeared to be motivated by the recent black exploitation films. He then writes that, "There is a lot of what Bullins would call 'signifying' in that release. It contains digs at real people but the names have been changed to protect the guilty (p. 76)."

Abrahams (1970, 1970a), who has been prolific in his reporting of black verbal behavior, suggests that to signify is "to imply, goad, beg, boast by indirect verbal or gestural means (1970, p. 264)." Further, signifying is a device

___

[k]In Rosten's *The Joys of Yiddish* (1968, p. 119), "fonfering" and a "fonfer" is defined as "to nasalize . . . a double talker . . . , a shady, petty deceiver . . . , and a specialist in hot air, baloney–a trumpeter of hollow promises (p. 119)."

[l]For additional information see footnote c, above.

linking the dozens to childhood behavior (p. 51), and it can have any number of meanings. In the Signifying Monkey toast it "refers to the trickster's ability to talk with great innuendo, to carp, cajole, needle, and lie (p. 52)."

In still other cases it can mean the ability to talk around a topic without ever coming to the point. Signifying can also refer to talking with eyes and hands and innumerable gestures and expressions. It can also be used to refer to making fun of a situation or a person. Indeed, telling stories about neighbors to stir up a fight is also signifying, as is ridiculing a police officer by imitating his actions behind his back (p. 52).

According to Kochman, (1969, p. 32) when *signifying* is used to shame, embarrass, frustrate, or to downgrade someone, a direct signifying taunt is used. Furthermore, when the object of signifying is direct action, the signifying is subtle, deceptive, indirect, and counts on the gullibility or naiveté of the recipient for its success.

> . . . the signifier reports or repeats what someone else has said about the listener; the "report" is couched in plausible language and hostility. There is also the implication that if the listener fails to do anything about it—what has to be "done" is usually quite clear—his status will be seriously compromised (Kochman, p. 32).

Mitchell-Kernan (1972) agrees that signifying is usually a verbal dueling tactic that is an end in itself, and that the discussion most often reported relates to that concept of signifying. She points out that signifying "also refers to a way of encoding messages or meanings which involves, in most cases, an element of indirection (p. 315)." Although Mitchell-Kernan could not obtain a consensus from blacks in defining signifying, she reports "most informants felt that some element of indirection was critical to signifying (p. 316)."

Her further reporting suggests the black concept of signifying includes basically a "folk notion" and that dictionary reporting of vocabulary are not always adequate for interpreting messages or meanings. The real understanding of a word may go further than the reported interpretations. Left-handed methods may be used to make a complimentary remark. The context in which a word is used may determine its actual definition. What is assumed to be informative may actually be designed as persuasive. Tone of voice and facial expressions also are used to interpret true meaning. While meaning is narrowed by situational contexts, knowledge of the personal background of a speaker may show a different interpretation. Indeed, "expectations based on role or status criteria enter into the sorting process. In fact, we seem to process all manner of information against a background of assumptions and expectations (p. 317)."

To this point, she holds that indirection or metaphorical reference is one of the defining characteristics of signifying. Abrahams (1970, pp. 66-67) also mentions indirection. "The name 'signifying' shows the monkey to be a trickster, signifying being the language of trickery, that set of words or gestures achieving Hamlet's 'direction through indirection' and used often, especially among the young, to humiliate an adversary." Through this indirection appears to be a function of style, it may also serve the function of being diplomatic or euphemistic (p. 326).

> Indirection means here that the correct (referential) interpretation or signification of the utterance cannot be arrived at by a consideration of the dictionary meaning of the lexical items involved and the syntactic rules for their combination alone. The apparent significance of the message differs from its real significance. The apparent meaning of the sentence "signifies" its actual meaning (p. 326).

The real meaning of "indirection" grows from the decoding of the participants' shared cultural knowledge and operates on two levels. First, the participants must understand that signifying is taking place and "that the dictionary—syntactical meaning of the utterance is to be ignored (p. 326)." Second, "this shared knowledge must be employed in the reinterpretation of the utterance (pp. 326-327)." Additionally, the artistry of the speaker is judged by his cleverness in directing all involved in the shared cultural knowledge.

Mezzrow (1964, p. 310) reports that to signify is to "hint, put on an act, make a gesture." He writes about the Harlem scene when bootlegging and the numbers were flourishing.[m] The hip Harlem Negroes did not "take" to the rackets' leaders and their trigger and muscle men. Instead, just as today on the streetcorner, they respected the man who could make out by his wits. Mezzrow describes a signifying scene in Big John's bar in Harlem, when about five of Dutch Schultz's torpedoes swaggered in and ordered drinks for the house.

> One of them ankled over to the juke box to play some records. As soon as the music started, one of the guys in our crowd yelled real loud, looking straight at this guy, "Man, that's a *killer!*" He could have been talking about the music, but everybody in that room knew different. Right quick another cat spoke up real loud, saying, "That's *murder* man, really murder," and his eyes were signifying too. All these gunmen began to shift from foot to foot, fixing their ties and scratching their noses, faces red and Adam's apples jumping. Before we knew it they had gulped their drinks and beat it out the door, saying good-bye to the bartender with their hats way down over their eye brows and their eyes gunning the ground. That's what Harlem thought of the white underworld (p. 197).

[m]Milton "Mezz" Mezzrow was a white Jewish clarinetist who was very much a Titan on the jazz scene in the '30s and '40s. With Bernard Wolfe, he wrote *Really the Blues*, his autobiography. His obit was printed in the *New York Times*, August 9, 1972, p. 34.

As with the other verbal techniques, signifying may be played with more or less sophistication depending upon the age of the participants, their sex, the section of the country they are from, or even whether they are in a junior or a senior high school. Additionally, signifying may also be called woofin', sounding, screaming, or other names.

In school, it appears that signifying is often combined with the dozens or with ribbing. Since the dozens is in the next and final area to be discussed, only a few examples will be provided here.

Typically, in signifying by using the dozens, one youngster may come up to another and say, "George, he say you' mother is a ho," or "Larry, he be saying some nasty things about your sister Dolores." Or someone may come up to a female student and say, "Harold telling everyone you pulled a train last night." Some may approach a male student and imply something about his manliness by saying, "Jim told me you punked out last night, he say you laid in the cut while your people went down on the Chaplains." (To lay in the cut could be to stay on the corner or in your house while the other members of the gang fought.)

Signifying in school can also revolve around athletics in general or a particular team. For example, if someone did something foolish in a game, he may be signified about it. Girls are also the objects of much signifying by male students. The signifying may relate to a girl's looks or whether she was having sexual relations or allegedly having them with her boy friend or others.

Assuming that none of the story descriptions are true, the youngster signifying is attempting to goad into fighting the youngster to whom he is telling the story or perhaps trying to break up a friendship with the youngster he claims is spreading the story. Sometimes, a signifying story may get to someone third hand.

In the basic toast or story of the Signifying Money, the monkey uses childish devices to goad the lion into fighting the elephant. The ensuing dialogue is typical of the verbal art of signifying. Just as happens so often in school, without any obvious provocation, the monkey starts his signifying to getting the lion and elephant into a fight.

"Deep down in the jungle where the coconuts grow
Lived the signifyingest motherfucker that the world ever know.
He said to the lion one bright sunny day
It's a big bad burly motherfucker coming your way.
I'm going off in the jungle and stay out of sight.
Cause when you two meet its going to be a hell of a fight.
But if ya'll two fight, I know you can win."

Above we see the monkey getting the lion upset and annoyed. He then starts his signifying, which is similar to the examples provided of school signifying.

"He said you mama was a slut like a dog in a pack
Running around the street with a mattress on her back."

The monkey plays the dozens with those two lines and then gets
onto the other members of the lion's family.

"He talked about your daddy and put your sister on the shelf
He said your sister had the illness and your daddy got
   the claps . . .
He said he fucked your baby sister and poked your baby niece
And when he sees your little brother he's going to ask him
   for a piece
He said your sister sold pussy and sucked dicks for cash . . .
He even talked about your grandma and I told him she was dead
Long cow-pussy bitch, that's all he said. . . ."

After the lion and the elephant fought, the lion "crawled off to the
jungle more dead than alive. . . . And that's when the monkey started his
signifying jive." The monkey then tells the lion how his strong rap got him to
fight the elephant.

"I set it up and you fell into my trap
And I copped your dumb butt with my bad-ass rap."

The monkey's signifying gets him so excited he falls out of the tree
and,

"Like a bolt of lightening and a streak of white heat
The lion was on his ass with all four feet."

The monkey must now extricate himself. He does this by calling for
sympathy by copping a plea and then challenging the lion's pride in manliness.

"The monkey looked up with tears in his eyes
And said please Mr. Lion I apologize.
The lion said ain't no use in apologizing
I'm going to put an end to your signifying.
The lion grabbed the monkey by his bullet shaped head.
And said I'm going to beat your little ass till you're damn
   near dead.
The monkey said if you jump back like a gentlemen should
I'll kick you big ass all over the woods.
If you just let get my dick out of the sand

I'll fight you like a natural man.
The lion jumped back and squared off for a fight
And the monkey hit the tree and jumped clean out of sight . . .
He said you're so motherfucking dumb you make me sick.
But if you think you're bad and you want to bend
I'll turn you over to my elephant friend."

In this story, the monkey lived to continue his signifying. In other versions, the monkey is killed.

Most interested inner city school personnel appear to have problems differentiating between ribbing and signifying; at least as far as school is concerned. Reality 66 describes what most teachers felt was signifying. Their reasoning was that an "inside" definition was used to make fun of someone. Everyone else knew about the "inside" definition except for the teacher involved or the person being taunted. This is somewhat akin to earlier explanations.

REALITY 66

Mr. Shaw was in his room preparing a test. Three boys walking the hall stopped in to chat. As they were leaving, after talking for a few minutes, one of them pointed to the teacher's socks and said,

"Hey, Mr. Shaw, those are nice ankle huggers you got on."

Mr. Shaw smiled, looked down at his socks, and said, "Yes, I like them. I just bought them."

Once outside his room, they gave one another five and ran down the hall, laughing.

At lunch, Mr. Shaw commented to some of the teachers, "I must finally be making it. Some of the kids complimented me on my socks. One of them called my socks 'ankle huggers.' "

Two of the teachers almost choked on their food as they tried holding back their laughter. A third teacher explained to Mr. Shaw that he was really being ridiculed because the expression "ankle huggers" refers to low socks, and low socks are out of style for men, only being worn by lames (a chump, a stupid person).

The guidance counselor who told me the story reasoned that signifying took place because the students knew what ankle huggers were and the teacher did not.

One final example of what some felt was signifying and not ribbing. This must be qualified in that this was the adult's concept, not the student's. This example of signifying was played on a student by a teacher. The teacher said to one of his students, "Where do you do your shopping—at the G. & R. Store?"

Those nearby, and to whom the teacher had winked, began laughing and jostling one another. G. & R. means Grab and Run.

The Dozens

From personal observations, playing the dozens in inner city schools probably causes more school fights and disruptions than does any other activity. Cohen (1935, p. 161) in reporting on what appears to be lower class Negro behavior, describes the dozens as a prolific source of stabbings and shootings. Clemmer (1940, p. 9) writes that in prison, *playing the dozens* "has caused more fights among prisoners than any other cause." *The dozens* is also evident everywhere in black literature.

The dozens and playing the dozens has also been referred to as sounding, signifying, crackin' on the kitchen folks, going in the kitchen, getting down on the crib, ribbin', gettin' on the kitchen folks, "playing (Abrahams, 1962, p. 209)," mamma talk, soundin' on the moms, getting on moms, "joaning (Dollard, 1939, p. 15)," putting a man on the wheel, and giving a man the spoke (Berdie, 1947, p. 12) and by many more names. However, most school youngsters probably refer to the game as talkin' about moms.

My first experience in being put in the dozens is described in Reality 67. The experience was educational and enlightening since neither my religious nor cultural background had either exposed or prepared me for the game.[n] Consequently, my initial reaction to a student putting me in the dozens disgusted my students. They were annoyed with me. My response, or more accurately, my lack of response, went against every concept they had of how a man should react when he is put in the dozens.

I had observed students playing the dozens with one another for a long time, although I did not understand its ritualistic and cultural ramifications. One of the first times I tried breaking up a bout of the dozens between two boys, it happened that they had the same mother but different fathers. No matter what they said or how they tried to explain their actions to me, I could not understand their talking about their mother the way they did.

Grier and Cobbs (1971, p. 9) somewhat similarly raised the question of what white members of the armed forces must have experienced during World War II when they were exposed to the dozens for the first time. "It is a pity that the reactions of the young white soldiers when first exposed to the dozens were not recorded, for surely that must have been the purest example of 'cultural shock.' "

Again, this reinforces the point that what is important is how your students feel you should react to an incident, not how you feel you should react. *Most often, streetcorner youngsters respect the teacher who can best them at their games without losing his dignity and without coming down too hard on them.*

---

[n]I have since observed some black and white male teachers who grew up playing the dozen react, violently to being put in the dozens by their students.

REALITY 67

I was in my room with about ten high school students when two of them began verbally abusing one another. As they became louder, I told them to cut it out. Instead of stopping, the fellow who was being bested began to direct his feelings toward me.

"I fucked your mamma last night Mr. Foster," he said.

"Oh, cut the crap out," I said.

Since they left one another alone, I tried getting everyone back to work, thinking everything was straightened out; but not in my students' opinions. They seemed to be taken aback and could not quite understand my lack of concern and anger over what had been said about my mother. They came at me verbally.

"You afraid of him?"

"Shit, hit him man!"

"Go upside his knot."

"Why you let him say that about you moms?—shit."

And so on.

Slowly, I realized that I was doing something wrong; I had better do something right and fast. I was not, somehow, following an unwritten code of action and honor that they were privy to. Then, luckily, I began to catch on.

"Why should I be mad? I said, "He can't be talkin' about my mother 'cause I know my mother. At least I know who my mother is."

As I said these last words, I looked at the youngster who had put me in the dozens and started chuckling. The other students laughingly pointed at him.

"He ranked you out," one of them said laughingly.

Still another said, "Oh, sound."

While two others gave one another some skin.

He sulked off to his seat, and we got back to work. I knew I had done something right when one of the students put his hand out for some dap and returned it after I had given him some skin.

The dozens has been described as a ritualized game or survival technique used to: (a) express aggressive feelings; (2) develop verbal skills; (3) cut a boy free from matriarchal control; and (4) teach youths how to control their feelings and tempers. There is also evidence of a clean and a dirty dozens.

Although there are usually two participants in the dozens, at times more play or participate. Often, the participants also play to the audience. Although the dozens is usually played by boys, girls also play. Actually, "some of the best Dozens players were girls (Brown, 1969, p. 27)."

Sometimes, the dozens may be a game of amusement where two or more exchange obscene references and rhymes to see who can creatively best the other. They may be alone or have a large audience. At other times the dozens may become vicious, with someone being beaten, stabbed, shot, or killed as a result of what is said.

The dozens sometimes takes the form of rhymed couplets while at other times insults, taunts, and curses are circumventive or to the point. These usually consist of references to alleged adulterous or incestuous activities of the opponent's mother, grandmothers, daughters, sisters, wife, or other female relatives. At other times, statements are made concerning the cowardice, homosexuality, stupidity, or inferiority of the participants and their families. Sometimes, a bystander may be brought into the game by one of the participants; usually by the one who is being bested.

The three lengthiest investigations of the *dozens* are by John Dollard (1939), R. Berdie (1947), and Roger Abrahams (1970). In Dollard's study entitled "The Dozens: Dialect of Insult," he reported on the dozens in a number of Southern and Northern large and small cities where his informants included adolescent and adult groups which crossed social class lines. He reported that the dozens appears to be played very widely among Negro Americans and exists in all social classes within the "Negro caste."

The dozens follows a "pattern of interactive insult," and is guided by rules that are well recognized and which govern and permit emotional expression. He found the dozens played by boys and girls, adolescents, and adults. The forbidden notions of the dozens are often expressed by adolescents through rhymes. For some, the only purpose of the game appears to be to amuse onlookers and participants. While the game may be described as an aspect of aggressive play, at other times fighting displaces the game aspect. The group's response to the sallies and rhymes of the players is crucial; "with group response comes the possibility or reward for effective slanders and feelings of shame and humiliation if one is bested (p. 4)."

The joking appears to take as its theme those aspects that our social order condemn the most in other contexts. Accusations are made about the opponent's committing incest with his sister or mother, passive homosexuality is inferred, cowardice is suggested, taboos related to cleanliness are said to have been broken, and personal defects such as inferiority, stupidity, or crossed eyes are played upon. The mentioning of dead relations, however, appears to be taboo (p. 5).

In his Southern big city study Dollard found that lower class youngsters most commonly used sex themes. Very often the dozens was used to exploit a youngster's weak point such as a father in jail or a sister with an illegitimate child. Often, a fight was the only recourse to a noneffective comeback.

Dollard found Southern big city middle class adolescents playing basically the same type of dozens as did big city lower class boys. Though middle class boys had a "slight tendency" to supress vulgar expressions, class status dozens such as "Your mammy is a nigger (p. 10)" had a particularly stinging effect. In some cases it appeared as though the players would quiet down but for the ridicule of the observers. Additionally, when an out-group member pursued the dozens with an in-group person, a fight usually ensued. In some cases, he found that the dozens was played by middle class boys to break the monotony of a dull party.

Dollard noted that Southern big city lower class adults depended "on directly improvised insults and curses, and seem to be altogether more crude and direct in the expressions (p. 14)." Their jives appeared to be related to homosexual practices and the promiscuity of a protagonist's mother or sister.

In a small Southern city he found the dozens characterized primarily by obscene references and rhymes. The upper and middle class adolescents appeared to play the dozens for amusement and considered fighting over them as foolish. However, lower class verbal dozens bouts usually ended in fights.

In a Northern big city Dollard found the middle and upper class boys played by using items related to cowardice, stupidity, and various types of inferiority. Often the offended person expressed a sense of loss of "personal honor," which was perceived as insult resulting in fist fights and broken friendships. The lower class boys more often used sexual themes for the dozens.

Berdie (1947) while working with black and white prisoners in a Navy Disciplinary Barracks, asked over 100 whites and 100 Negroes whether they had ever heard of playing the dozens or knew its meaning.[o] None of the whites expressed any knowledge of the dozens while more than 90 percent of the blacks had heard of the term and could give some inkling of its meaning. The only whites who had some knowledge of the term were mental health professionals working with blacks.

Berdie described the dozens as a "formalized expression of aggression (p. 120)," where one or more persons attempts to arouse another to the point where he will initiate fighting. The dozens is played by combatants exchanging insults to the approval and encouragement of observers. The exchange becomes "progressively nastier and more pornographic, until they eventually include every member of the participants' families and every act of animal and man (p. 120)."

One of the participants, most often the subject, usually reaches his saturation point and goes after this tormentor using fists, a knife, or an improvised weapon. When this happens, the tormentor, sometimes joined by the observers, often physically injures the subject.

In addition to the one-on-one dozens, Berdie reported the game being played as a sort of round robin with insults passed around from person to person, each trying to insult all the others. A small riot is the usual end to this game. He further reports the dozens played with "rhymes and limericks," that had almost "traditional respectability," while some were improvised during the encounter.

Sometimes the dozens was played as entertainment to relieve boredom. The group appeared to give social approval to the initiator of the game if he could manipulate the subject into losing his composure.

---

[o]The men were divided equally between the North and the South.

The individual who strikes the first physical blow carries the stigma, the first person struck has the glory of defending his honor. The tormenter, who bears the responsibility for the conflict, is thus saved the disgrace of starting the fight, and the subject is responsible in the eyes of his mates because of his inability to "take it" (p. 121).P

According to Abrahams (1962), the substance and form of lore reflects the special problems and values of a group and those within it. Hence, studying the dozens provides insight into the "cultural imperatives" of the lower class black. Abrahams reported on his two years of research with blacks in a South Philadelphia neighborhood and additional observations in Texas.

He suggested that the dozens is an institutionalized mechanism lower class black youngsters use in searching for masculine identity. The dozens represents the point in his life where "he casts off a woman's world for a man's and begins to develop the tools by which he is to implement his new found position, as a member of a gang existence (p. 215)."

The dozens functions as a verbal game, training lower class black youths for their changing world and the verbal needs of adulthood. Indeed, the dozens is a verbal contest that plays a significant role in the psychological and linguistic development of the players.

When boys play the dozens, according to Abrahams, the protagonist verbally insults someone from another's family, and those observing and waiting for the vilifications goad the combatants on. The insulted youngster must then reply in kind concerning a member of the protagonist's family. The reply must be clever enough to defend his honor and hence his family. Throughout this bantering, the onlookers continue goading the two. At this point in the dozens, Abrahams reports that boredom or some other subject or interest usually takes over. He reported that fighting is "fairly rare."

When dozens players are just entering puberty, the emphasis is on reversing the roles of the mother and the father in the rhymes.

"I hear you mother plays third base for the Phillies."

"Your mother is a bricklayer, and stronger than your father (p. 210)."

As youngsters grow and become more sexually aware, the puns, rhymes, and vilifications of the mother begin to take on sexual meanings; the contests become more heated. Abrahams (p. 20) provides an example of two fourteen- and fifteen-year-old boys playing the dozens.

In a joking conversation, someone mentions the name of the boy's mother. Someone in the group replies with "Yeah, Constance was real good to me last Thursday."

PThis concept and others of the dozens *must* be understood to provide school personnel with insight and understanding into some of their school discipline problems.

Constance's son must then respond. " 'I hear Virginia (the other's mother) lost her titty in a poker game.' "

The other youngster may then respond with " 'Least my mother ain't no cake; everybody get a piece.' "

The other youngster has to do better and may come back with,

"I hate to talk about your mother,
She's a good old soul.
She's got a ten-ton p---y
And a rubber a--h--e.
She got hair on her p---y
That sweep the floor.
She got knobs on her titties
That open the door (p. 48)."

The retorts continue as each tries to outdo the other. As boys grow, their verbal dexterity expands to where innuendo and subtlety replace the obvious rhymes and puns.

Abrahams' research indicated that playing the dozens appears to wane as an institution between the ages of sixteen and twenty-six. However, the game lingers and is not forgotten. He also points out that when the dozens is played under "very tense and restrictive conditions of regimentation for which the young Negro is not completely suited," it usually leads to a fight (p. 211).[q] Additionally, when the dozens is played by adult males in a poolroom or bar, "it usually ends in battle (p. 211)."

He also reported that signals are provided in the dozens by pitch and stress of voice and sometimes syntax. The language used when "playing is different from the contestants' everyday language. Additionally, Abrahams also reported that the insults used by young adolescents in particular are directed against or toward certain things and these are rather rigidly constructed. Adult male players, on the other hand, only fleetingly refer to the family and not usually against any specific aspect of life. However, most often all playing concerns sexual matters.

Abrahams (1970) also reported a "clean dozens" and a "dirty dozens." He found that in the clean dozens, the insults are mostly personal with only some directed at mothers. In the *dirty dozens*, the slur is almost always about the other's mother, and these usually take the form of "illicit sexual activity, usually with the speaker (p. 40)."

In addition to the above three studies, there is some additional reporting on the *dozens*. White (1970, p. 52) writes that the dozens is part of the

[q]An argument could be presented that this reporting holds for the school too. In this case, Abrahams was referring to the armed forces.

black's oral tradition, and is a game of "One-ups-man-ship, where clever remarks about mamas, grandmamas, and aunties of the players are exchanged." Furthermore, gestures, voice changes, and body motions accompany these idioms and words. Playing the dozens, according to Johnson (1971, p. 180) is a "very special kind of bantering." When playing the dozens, the mother or other female members of the family are spoken about in a derogatory way. This is usually done cleverly in an insulting or humorous way. Though males play the dozens primarily, girls also play the game.

Hurston (1942) defined playing the dozens as "low-rating the ancestors of your opponent (p. 96)," and *mammy* as "a term of insult never used in any other way by Negroes (p. 95)." The ghetto youngster, according to Hannerz (1970), gains information about his sex role from street peers of his same age or only slightly older. A good deal of the verbal and joking contests such as the dozens and the "more or less obscene songs" of ghetto males, helps free them from depending upon mothers or mother figures while also educating them to somewhat antagonistic and exploitive feelings towards women (p. 177). Furthermore, "standing up for one's family" is one of the expectations of the *dozens.*

David Schulz (1969) over a three and one-half year period studied 108 persons from ten families who at one time lived in large public housing projects. He reported the "custom of 'playing the dozens,' " as part of the masculine struggle against female domination (p. 67). His subjects reported the dozens as a predominately male game also played by some girls. Whereas boys usually begin to play at about age eleven, girls begin to play at about age eleven and one-half. The dozens also functions as a sexual "primer," acquainting children with details of sexuality before they are usually aware of them.

Schechter (1970) reports that the dozens, although usually begun in jest, often ends in murder or violence. The dozens, he contends, is characteristic of low income blacks and may be a way to pass time or a form of social entertainment. The game consists of competitive banter to see who can put down or completely insult the other. The banter may concern an opponent's potency, status, his wife or sweetheart's virtue, his odor, shade of skin, heterosexuality, or cleanliness. Often, knives appear when the game reaches mother talk.

The dozens, according to Grier and Cobbs (1971, pp. 3, 9), is a "degrading, humiliating custom of mutual vilification" that is an integral part of the black boys growing up from ten through late adolescence. Additionally, they wrote that the dozens consists of ritualized rhymed obscenities concerning the speaker and often his mother in gross sexual acts. It is inappropriate, however, to put anyone in the dozens unless it is established that he plays.

They reported that the crowd is a crucial part of the game as they scorn the inept and reward the witty. The players try to make each "rhyming riposte funnier than the last (p. 4)" as the onlookers make known their favorite with tumult and laughter. Sometimes, the apparent loser may drag someone from the crowd in the game with a remark such as "If you grin, you're in (p. 5)." If a player loses his composure and fights, he loses face.

They also pointed out the psychological aspects of the dozens as a puberty ritual leading to manhood and "a way traveled by all black boys (p. 5)." The ritual of the dozens requires black boys to put aside a mother's special sanctification. The natural inclination to defend a mother's honor must be suppressed as young black males move to their world of men where love of mother "is perverted in the medium of wit (p. 5)." Black males know that while freeing themselves through the dozens they also betray their mothers.

Participating in the dozens affects a boy's pride. The dozens also educates and instructs black males in how to use self-control and wit in response to a verbal attack. Grier and Cobbs also suggest that in persisting so long, the dozens has won out over other rituals.

> It has persisted because it meets a group need, accomplishes certain work, and does it all in a universal language. It takes the medium of childhood sexuality and the intense passionate involvements within the family and with this as a requirement of manhood. It consists that he understand that humiliation may be the texture of his life, but states also that manhood can transcend such onslaught.
>
> No doubt the most instructive aspect of boys' response to the dozens is the reaction of healthy youngsters, the grace and balance developed under this vicious pressure (p. 10).

According to Paul Oliver (1960), the laid-off, the unemployed, and the temporarily idle black has a good deal of free time. So, when he has fished, hunted, cut the wood, repaired the tools, etc., "he joins his fellows to tell 'lies,' 'put in the Dozens,' sing the blues. Or gamble . . . (p. 176)." He writes that the dozens is "on the fringe of the blues." Youths often play the dozens to "work off their excesses of spirits in harmless and cheerfully pornographic blues singing competition (p. 152)." Furthermore, the dozens

> developed as a folk game in the late nineteenth century. A number of persons would gather and endeavour to exceed each other in the insults that they invented with a view of goading someone present to eventual wrath. In the process many obscene and scandalous inferences as to the ancestry of the individuals concerned would be made. Sometimes the anger of persons who had received unfair treatment or who were the victims of racial prejudice would be so dissipated, but at other times the 'Dozens' were sung with intent to hurt and to provoke (p. 151).

According to H. Rap Brown (1969), young "bloods" are educated in the streets not in school. He did not learn how to talk "from reading about Dick and Jane going to the zoo and all that simple shit." He too learned how to talk in the street (pp. 25-26). Though his teachers tested his vocabulary weekly and gave him arithmetic to exercise his mind, "Hell, we exercised our minds by playing the Dozens.

> I fucked your mama
> Till she went blind
> Her breath smells bad,
> But she sure can grind. . . .

And the teacher expected me to sit up in class and study poetry after I could run down shit like that. If anybody needed to study poetry, she needed to study mine. We played the Dozens for recreation, like white folks play Scrabble (p. 26).

Brown also pointed out that the dozens is a "mean game" where you attempt to completely destroy someone with words. It's another way in which blacks fight each other. He also reinforced the important role of the observing crowd which signals the winner by their reaction to what is said. Often, "40 to 50 dudes" would observe the playing. The real objective of the dozens was to get someone so mad that he would fight or cry. The game could be played for hours, and some girls were the best dozens players.

Some additional definitions of the *dozens* include "A contest to see which young brother can remember or make up the greatest number of obscene, rhymed couplets reflecting on the opponent's parents. Sometimes called 'signifying' or 'momma talk' (Dove, 1968, p. 38)." Hughes and Bontemps (1966, p. 483) defined the *dozens* as "humorous but vulgar references to someone else's mother." Brewer (1966, p. 32) wrote that in the dozens, "Children try to outdo each other in trading insults and deprecating each other's family." According to Merwin (1960, p. 295) the dozens is a "stylized and derogatory verbal assault on the parent or parental surrogate of the victim in which the victim's mother is the chief target." Sebastian (1934, p. 289) reported that when Lincoln University students played the dozens they spoke "slanderously on one's (or another's) parents." Clemmer (1940, p. 9) reports that the dozens in a prison community is "the commonest way a convict has of using profanity. . . . anything of the vilest and worst that can be said about anyone's people (immediate family). Instead of cursing one directly, they talk about the mother, sister, wife, or sweetheart of the other." Mezzrow (1964, p. 304) defines the dirty dozens as an "elaborate game in which participants insult each other's ancestors."

The Dozens in Literature
In 1969, a play *The Dozens* opened at the Booth Theater in New York City. The play did not last long, and Leonard Harris (1969), WCBS-TV Arts Editor, signified the play on the Eleven O'clock Report by saying, "But *The*

Dozens, as played at the Booth, turns out to be a dull and pointless game."
Richard Watts, Jr., in reviewing *The Dozens* for the *New York Post*, wrote that
"The meaning of the play's title is rather unclear to me, although I gather it has
something to do with a game of insults played in Harlem (1969, p. 63)."

When Clive Barnes (1971, p. 27) reviewed J.E. Franklin's *Black Girl*,
he wrote.

> There is a game in the ghetto called "The Dozens" where people
> pile insult upon insult on one another, not only with good humor,
> but also with a purely esthetic appreciation for the insults thus piled.
> It seems to me that an understanding of this is essential to the white
> understanding of black dramatic writing. There is both an exagger-
> ation and also a wryness that flavors the black playwright.

To name but two movies, the dozens was acted-out in *M*A*S*H*
during the football game. It was almost played in *Cotton Comes to Harlem*. In
one scene two New York City policemen are sitting in a car when one of them,
Raymond St. Jacques, starts the dozens only to be stopped by Godfrey
Cambridge's response "I don't play that game." At times the dozens in a mild
form can also be observed being played on TV's "Sanford and Son."

Gordon Parks (1967) and Claude Brown (1965) in their autobiogra-
phies wrote about the pressure of maintaining your manhood by having to fight
when put in the dozens. Parks described his run-in with the dozens in a Civilian
Conservation Corps (CCC) camp.[r]

> Tate became enraged and called me a dirty son-of-a-bitch when I
> beat him in a checkers game. I ignored him at first but then he "put
> me in the dozens," or, to put it simply, he cursed me in the name of
> my mother. For this, unless you were a coward, you fought (p. 128).

Brown recounted how he forced someone to fight him by putting
him in the dozens.

> We wouldn't have had that fight if I hadn't said something about
> his mother. He had to fight after that, because a guy who won't fight
> when somebody talks about his mother is the worst kind of punk
> (p. 61).

Hurston (1942) in early "Harlemese" jive, describes two down cats
playing the dozens in a style that is rarely used today. Additionally, the cats can

---

[r]The Civilian Conservation Corps was a federal agency organized as part of the
New Deal in 1933, and formally organized by Congress in 1937. Its function was to provide
training and employment for unemployed young men in such public conservation work as
building dams, planting trees, and fighting fires. When the CCC was abolished in 1942, more
than 2,000,000 men had served.

be observed trying to outdo one another as they proceed from banter to almost fighting and then back to giving some skin.

"Sweet Back, you fixing to talk out of place."
Jelly stiffened.
"If you trying to jump salty, Jelly, that's your mammy."
"Don't play in de family, Sweet Back. I don't play de dozens. I don told you."
"Who playing de dozens? You trying to get you hips up on your shoulders 'cause I said you was with a beat broad. One of them lam blacks."
"Who? Me? Long as you been knowing me, Sweet Back, you ain't never seen me with nothing but pe-olas. I can get any frail eel I wants to. . . . I recon I'll have to make you hep. I had to leave from down south 'cause Miss Anne used to worry me so bad to go with me. . . . Man, I don't deal in no coal. . . . If they's white, they's right! If they's yellow, they's mellow! If they's brown, they can stick around. But if they come black, they better git way back!" . . .
"Aw, man, you trying to show your grandma how to milk ducks. Best you can do is to confidence some kitchen-mechanic out of a dime or two. Me, I knocks de pad with them cack-broads up on Sugar Hill, and fills 'em full of melody. Man, I'm quick death and easy judgment. Youse just a home-byoy, Jelly, don't try to follow me."
"Me follow *you*! Man, I come on like the Gang Busters, and go off like the March of Time! If dat ain't so, God is gone to Jersey City and you know He wouldn't be messing 'round a place like that." . . .
"Jelly, de wind may blow and de door may slam; dat what you shooting ain't worth a damn!"
Jelly slammed his hand in his bosom as if to draw a gun. Sweet Back did the same.
"If you wants to fight, Sweet Back, the favor is in me."
"I was deep-thinking, then Jelly. It's a good thing I ain't short-tempered. 'T'aint nothing to you, no how. You ain't hit me yet."
Both burst into a laugh and changed from fighting to lounging poses.
"Don't get to yaller on me, Jelly, you liable to get hurt some day."
"You over-sports your hand your ownself. Too blamed astorperious. I just don't pay you no mind. Lay de skin on me (pp. 88-90)!"

Playing the dozens is almost a reflex action for blacks. In Heard's (1968) *Howard Street* a drunk reacts to what he has overheard as a challenge to him via the dozens.

The bum lying on the floor woke up again. "Whatcha say, kid?"
Jimmy realized that he'd spoken aloud, but he repeated it automatically to the wino. "I said, 'How the hell was we to know it was his mother?' " But he'd said it softly, almost to himself.

"Whatcha talkin' about, kid. You talkin' about my dead mother? I don't play the dozens, kid. Don't talk about my mother. I'll kill ya right now (p. 78)."

The dozens has also appeared in books written by whites. Bernard Malamud (1971) in *The Tenants*, writes about the conflict between a Jewish and a black author. Lesser, the Jewish author, is sleeping with a black woman while Bill (the black author) is having an affair with Lesser's white girl friend. Lesser attends a party of mostly blacks and is put in the dozens. However, he does not appear to understand the game and only half-heartedly plays.

One of the blacks at the party taps his finger against Lesser's chest and tells him, "We have a game we got we call the dozens. Like the brothers play it no ofay has that gift or that wit, and since whitey ain't worth but half a black I'm gon play you the half-dozens (p. 132)."

Lesser is informed that the dozens is a game of "naked words, . . . and the one who bleeds, or flips, or cries mama, he's the loser and we shit on him. Do you dig (p. 132)?"

As the game gets underway, Lesser is told that if he is going to fuck black he has to face blacks. Furthermore, they probably should "off the shmuck," anyway. Bill informs Lesser that he is not going to be too hard on him to start with; he will not "work on your mama and sister, which is the way we do it, but come right to the tough-shit funk of it. . . ." Lesser is told to do better than Bill on that one but stands mute.

Lesser finally comes back with a good one and the blacks laugh. They appreciated a good comeback, regardless of the author. The game ends as Bill comes down heavy on Lesser, and Lesser throws in the towel. The observers also get bored by Lesser's poor showing.

The next day, Bill tries to explain to Lesser that his use of the dozens as a form of verbal aggression saved him from physical aggression.

> "Sam wanted the brothers to beat up on you and crack your nuts for putting the meat to his bitch, but I got you in the game so they could see you get your shame that way and not want your real red blood (p. 137)."

A number of reports, books, and articles evolved from the Watts riots. Only one, Robert Conot's (1967) *River of Blood, Years of Darkness*, appears to accurately report on the verbal discourse of the combatants. Conot describes some blacks coming down hard with the dozens on a white police officer.

> Few women ever go into the park, and it was strictly a masculine crowd that formed a semicircle around the car.
> "Hey man," a youth called to the white officer. "I saw your mother the other day!" The crowd laughed, knowing what was

coming. "She come down here wanting to know what a real man could do, and I give her the best fuck she ever had."

"That's right, man," another called out, grinning. "She even give me a blow job for six bits (p. 231)."

Another white author, Joseph Wambaugh (1970) also reported on the *dozens* in his book *The New Centurions*.

"Shut your mouth," said Serge.
"*Chinga tu madre!*" said the boy.
"I should have killed you."
"*Tu madre!*" . . .
"*Tu madre,*" the boy repeated, and the fury crept over Serge again. It wasn't the same in Spanish, he thought. It was so much filthier, almost unbearable, that this gutter animal would dare to mention her like that. . . .
"You don't like that, do you, gringo?" said the boy, baring his white teeth in the darkness. "You understand some Spanish, huh? You don't like me talking about your moth . . . (p. 121)."

Ed Bullins (1973) in his *The Reluctant Rapist*, Ralph Ellison (1947) in his *The Invisible Man*, LeRoi Jones (1963) in his play *The Toilet*, Louise Meriwether (1970) in her *Daddy Was a Number Runner*, Richard Wright (1963) in his *Lawd Today*, and John A. Williams (1967) in his *The Man Who Cried I Am*, all have some of their characters using the dozens.

Bullins (1973) wrote about Jess and Chuck walking to Jess's home. They walked together and Jess "lied and laughed with Chuck, finding out what he could about Chuck so he could use it later for some put-down or the dozens game (p. 131)."

Ralph Ellison's (1947) use of the *dozens* would probably get by all but those who are familiar with its usage: "From your ma-" I started and caught myself in time. "From the committee," I said (p. 400).

Earlier in his book, however, he actually mentions the dozens: "I looked at him, feeling a quick dislike and thinking, half in amusement, I don't play the dozens. And how's *your* old lady today (p. 211)."

The Toilet by LeRoi Jones vividly portrays the language and raw life of the streetcorner played out in a high school boy's toilet. The dozens is played often in the play.

Ora talks about "your momma's house," and Love responds with "At least I got one (p. 26)." Ora's retort to the accusation that he gets his kicks out of rubbing up against half dead white boys is, "I'd rub up against your momma too."

To which Love responds with, "Ora, you mad cause you don't have a momma of you own to rub up against."

Ora comes back with "Fuck you, you boney head sonofabitch. As long as I can rub against your momma . . . or your fatha' . . . I'm doin' alright (p. 33)."

Louise Meriwether (1970) wrote that "I had to curse some though to stay friends with Suki, but I didn't play the dozens, that mother stuff, . . . (p. 28)." John Williams (1967), in addition to using jive lexicon in his novels, has his characters play the dozens too.

> *"Your mamma's a nigger."*
>
> *"Oops! The dozens, is it? I made you salty. eh? Now you slip me in the dozens, just like that? I told you, you was a nigger."*
>
> *"Your mother's a nigger."*
>
> *"Hee, Hee, well, your mother don't wear no drawers. How could she, when she was giving birth to you—my son. Ha! So you know your mother don't wear no drawers. How's that? Youse a mother-fuckin' mutherfucker, Oedipus Rex! Thas how come you knows so much."*
>
> *"I know so much because I'm you daddy (p. 188)."*

Richard Wright also used jive lexicon in his stories. In *Lawd Today* (1963, pp. 79-81), for example, his characters went from ribbing to signifying and ended up playing the dozens; all for recreation.

The bout is conceived when Jake noticed and became annoyed with Al's new shirt and smug composure. Jake wanted to shake Al's composure and take it for himself. He started his agitating by asking Al where he stole his shirt? Wright then goes beyond just putting words into his characters' mouths. He also keeps the reader informed as to what is transpiring. He writes that Bob and Slim, who were listening silently, hoped that Al and Jake would get into the dozens. Wright then has Jake explain what Al was doing by having Jake tell Al to cut out his signifying. Finally, Al and Jake get into the dozens. Jake escalates the signifying to the dozens by telling Al ". . . Colonel James was sucking on your ma's tits."

> Al came back slowly, to make sure that none of his words would be missed. ". . . when . . . Colonel James was sucking at ma's tits . . . your . . . baby brother . . . (was) . . . watching with slobber in his mouth. . . ."
>
> As a comeback, Jake looked out of the window rather nonchalantly, crossed his legs, and responded with, ". . . grandma was . . . in the privy crying 'cause she couldn't find the corncob. . . ."
>
> Al, not to be outdone, narrowed his eyes and retaliated with, " 'When . . . grandma was crying for the corncob, your . . . aunt Lucy was . . . back of the barn with . . . Colonel James' old man, . . . she was saying . . .: Yyyyou kknow . . . Mmmister Cccolonel . . . I jjjust ddin't llike to sssell . . . my ssstuff . . . I jjjust lloves to gggive . . . iit away. . . . (pp. 79-81)' "

The point made earlier about how the contestants are also playing to their audience, is also shown by Wright. Throughout the contest, Slim's and Bob's reactions as onlookers are reported. They held their stomachs while rolling on the sofa; stomped their feet as they groaned; howled and screamed holding one another; and they beat their fists on the floor.

Finally, Al gave Jake the crusher.

> "When my greatgreatgreatgreat grandma who was a Zulu queen got through eating . . . chitterlings, she wanted to build a sewer-ditch to take away her crap, so she went out and saw your . . . greatgreatgreatgreat*great* grandma sleeping . . . with her old mouth open. She didn't need to build no sewerditch. . . ."

Jake tried hard to think of a return. No matter how he bit his lips or screwed up his eyes, he could not think of a return. His mind was a complete blank. Al's latest image was too much for him. "Then they all laughed so that they felt weak in the joints of their bones."

The dozens can also be found in poetry by blacks. Harrison's Hamm tried to hip Adam by putting him in the dozens.

> Hamm: . . . In the jungle your only duty is to survive, man. Ask your mama bout that.
> Adam: Don't be talkin 'bout my mama.
> Hamm (derisively): I wouldn't talk 'bout your mama. Wouldn't let anybody else talk 'bout your mama. Your mama is all right with me Adam. In fact, she'll be my horse if she never wins a race.
> Adam: I don't play that shit, Hamm (pp. 98-99)."

Another example of the dozens can be found in the works of John O. Killens (1972, pp. 26-27).

> "Go on Mother," Bad Mouth said, good-naturedly. "Go sell your papers on another corner." . . .
> "I ain't your mother," the old lady repeated, shouting even louder this time. "If your mother hadda brung you up right, I wouldn't have to be putting your backside down this late in life." . . .
> "Grandma putting old Bad Mouth in the natural dozens—damn!"
> "Blow, grandma! Blow, baby!"
> "Old Bad Mouth do not play the two-time sixes! (pp. 26-27)."

Oliver (1969, p. 80) wrote about Speckled Red spending twenty years playing the Southern levee camps and the sawmills "leaving everywhere the memory of his riotous, obscene barrel house piano version of the Dirty Dozens." Eventually, Speckled Red was one of a number who cut records of the dirty dozens.[s] Even Melvin Van Peebles' play *Ain't Supposed to Die a Natural Death: Tunes from Blackness* contains the dozens.[t]

History of the Dozens

There does not appear to be any definitive work substantiating the origins of the dozens. There does, however, appear to be some evidence that similar forms, styles, or behaviors of the dozens have been developed independently in this country and around the world by many groups. Berdie (1947) suggested that the behavior involved in the *dozens* in the United States, or other versions, is characteristic of many groups. However, only one group appears to have labeled the game.

Joking relationships and insult contests have been reported among the Manus (Mead, 1934), the Tikopia (Firth, 1936), in the songs of the Aleutians (Weyer, 1932), in the "drum fights" of the Greenland Eskimos (Thomas, 1937), and are found in many groups throughout Africa and Europe (Huizinga, 1950).

The cultures of ancient Rome, Greece, Germany, as well as Colombian and Aribic tribes have reported similar outlets for frustration. The *munafra* was the Aribic version of the dozens. The Norse *jul feast* includes a "comparing of men." In the contest between Thor and Odin, celebrated as part of the Edda song, the *harbardslojad*, there are variations where a form of the dozens is played by two gods or royal kings (Schechter, 1970).

There is also reporting of African origins for the American dozens. Schechter (1970) reported verbal contests common among Ashanti natives, who sang *opo* verses. According to Johnson (1972) the calypso has origins in the West African insult songs and to the *mamaguy* of Trinidad, which is a game "quite similar to the 'dozens' of black America (p. 56)." Desai (1968) in reporting on the kinship system and tribal origins among the Gikuku, found that the worst a man can do to infuriate another man is to "mention his mother's name in an indecent way (p. 17)." Usually, this resulted in fighting to defend the mother's sacred name. Elton (1950) also ties the American dozens to the "joking relationship" particularly among the Dahomeans and the Ashanti of Africa. Jones (1963, p. 27) reported the dozens as a survival of the African songs of recrimination.

Further support for the African origins of American Negro dozens is presented by Hobel (1954, p. 240). He quotes a Dr. Manet Fowler as reporting that twenty-five years ago in Louisiana, "the taunt 'your mother!' was enough to start a good fight," among Negro boys. He also pointed out that Louisiana was one area where we know Ashanti slaves were brought.

Both with the Ashanti and the Trobriands, insults to the chief or his

---

[s]Speckled Red, *The Dirty Dozens*, Delmar DL 601.
[t]Melvin Van Peebles, *"The Dozens"* Aint Supposed to Die a Natural Death, Stereo, Side 2, A. & M. Records SP 3510.

court retinue were capital crimes. Whereas for ordinary men, "insults were private delicts," to insult a chief the same way meant you were deprecating his royal ancestors' character too. "To say, 'wo'ni' (your mother!), 'wo'se' (your father!), 'wo'nana' (your grandparent!) carried a freight of implications that was enough (p. 240)." Insults of a more explicit nature included "the origin of your mother's genitals." Though thumb-biting and nose-thumbing were unknown to the Ashanti, holding the thumbs upward with the fists close together could imply all of the above insults.[u]

Personal discussions with blacks around the country found many suggesting the dozens as a game that taught them to keep their tempers; many remembered just sitting around with other boys playing the dozens. Ossie Guffy was born in 1931 and grew up in the "world of lower middle class America." In *OSSIE: The Autobiography of a Black Woman* (1971), she described an incident that reinforces the concept of the dozens as a form of game which teaches control.

She and four other youngsters were playing when one of the boys gets hit and starts "doin' the dozens" instead of hitting back. Her grandfather overhears this and lectures and paddles them.

> "When I was coming up," Grandpa said, "I heard about that game, only I heard about it the way it used to be, and I heard how it started and why it started. It was a game slaves used to play, only they wasn't just playing for fun. They was playing to teach themselves and their sons how to stay alive. The whole idea was to learn to take whatever the master said to you without answering back or hitting him, 'cause that was the way a slave had to be, so's he could go on living. It maybe was a bad game, but it was necessary. It ain't necessary now (p. 48)."

Ossie's mother, however, does not find much wrong with the game as long as "maybe they shouldn't use bad words, . . . 'doin' the dozen'—there's nothing wrong with that game. My brothers used to play it back in Cincinnati and they always said it taught them to hold their temper (p. 50)." White (1970) also supports the historical explanation of the dozens being a game that has taught blacks "how to keep cool and think fast under pressure."

As for the term dozen, Schechter (1970) reports that the commonest theory for the origin of the term dozen derives from a "recurring insult whereas the opponent's mother was supposed to be one of the dozens of women available to the sexual whims of her master (p. 13)."

According to Dan Burley (1960), research has revealed that the

---

[u]Sometimes, if a teacher is attempting to really stop the dozens playing, just saying "she," "m," or holding your wrist, or even holding your elbow, could be considered as putting another boy in the dozens.

dozens originated with American "field slaves" who used it in place of physical assault on the "more favored 'house slaves' on Southern plantations."

> Knowing they would suffer the lash or be deprived of food if they harmed the often pampered house servants, the lowly cotton pickers, sugar-cane workers, and other laborers in the field vented their spleen on the hated uniformed black, brown, and yellow butlers, coachmen, lackeys, maids, and housekeepers by saying aloud all types of things about their parents and even their most remote ancestors. As this discomfort of the abused became known, the vilification steadily became more lewd, pointedly vulgar, and filthy.

Furthermore, Burley wrote that the dozens, just before World War II, moved into Negro Folklore on a level with the development of the Negro spiritual, the blues, and jazz. By 1917 the dozens were refined to "where one talked about another's parents in highly explosive rhythmic phrases." Indeed, today, " 'The Dozens' are universal among Negroes (p. 121)." Further reporting by Berdie (1947), Dollard (1939), Elton (1950a, b) and Abrahams (1970) contained similar and additional discussions concerning the history of the dozens.

The Dozens in School

If you discuss the dozens with secondary school youngsters, and in many cases adults too, they may not know the game as the dozens unless you describe it. Except for the more sophisticated and street-wise students, few know the game as the dozens. Furthermore, the new inner city teacher may not realize that he is being put in the dozens unless he is aware of the game and local street connotations, as per Reality 68.

REALITY 68

As a new male teacher was walking into the student's lunchroom, he was approached by a youngster with a sad look on his face. This took place as he came abreast of a table around which sat a number of ninth grade boys.

The youngster said, "Hey, your mother be on the corner of Franklin and Chipewa sometime?"

The teacher looked at the youngster and at his seated, leering friends, and got a queasy feeling in his stomach as he walked away quickly looking straight ahead at the other door without answering. The youngsters at the table started laughing.

Basically, the teacher was put in the dozens by the youngster calling his mother a prostitute. He did this by suggesting that "your mother be on the corner . . . sometime?" He added emphasis that she was a low class prostitute—a two dollar hooker—by implying that she worked the corner of Franklin and Chipewa, a corner of disrepute in the City of Buffalo.

Reality 69 is an example combining ribbing and half the dozens. I do not remember how it all turned out. What I do know is that it happened to a new, white male teacher in a junior high school.

REALITY 69

> Student: "You married?"
> Teacher: "Yeah."
> Student: "Do you have a naked picture of your wife?"
> Teacher "What! Are you kidding?"
> Student: "No. Do you want to buy one?"

Sometimes, youngsters walking in the halls may start with ribbing and end up with the dozens. Sometimes this type of incident can escalate into a real brawl. However, in most cases, if teachers would not interfere, these incidents would sputter out. If the teacher interfering and trying to break up what he perceives as a very threatening and dangerous situation is a weak teacher, the youngsters involved will join to take him on.

In such cases one of two things usually happens. Either the teacher will lose because he usually cannot compete verbally with them in their games, or he may report and discipline them for what was not really an incident of any consequence. Reality 70 is a typical situation.

REALITY 70

The first student is walking down the hall. He approaches another youngster.

> Second student: "Skinny."
> First student: "Owl eyes."
> Second student: "Say, you mamma what?"
> First student: "She had to—to feed you."
> First and second student both laugh and walk on.

Reality 71 is presented verbatum from the teacher's anecdotal report.

REALITY 71

"As I was walking into a fifth grade room to sub once, there was a big fight between two boys in the doorway. I asked what the problem was, and this is the answer I got:

"Joe said, 'He say he saw my mother at the gas station yesterday.' The inference was that Joe's mother *pumped* (fornicated). I asked Joe what his mother did; did she work? He told me that she worked at the hospital. I turned to the other boy involved and said, 'You must have made a mistake, Joe's mother works at the hospital and she was there yesterday. Now, you may both take your seats.'

"Somehow I got out of that situation fairly easily!"

The teacher who wrote Reality 71 is in her mid twenties, white and attractive. My reason for mentioning this will be discussed further in the next chapter. However, the point should be made here that you do not have to be a muscular male to teach successfully in an inner city school.

Recently I gave a talk in a Buffalo area suburban school district. I was a bit uncertain whether what I would have to say about the games inner city youngsters played on their teachers or on one another would be appropriate for this district, since I did not think this particular school district had many black youngsters or poor whites attending their schools. However, when the presentation was over, a number of teachers approached me and we talked about their experiences.

One male teacher was all smiles. He told me that he had only one black child in his class, and she happened to be very bright. However, she constantly disrupted his class and he was at a loss to know how to deal with her. Laughing, he said, "Now I know, she was playing the dozens on me. Everytime she said something the entire class broke up laughing," he added. Interestingly, the white students in the class knew the game and the teacher did not.

SOME ADDITIONAL GAMES

Although many of the streetcorner coping or survival techniques or games were covered in this chapter, there are a few more that should be investigated, for they too affect classroom teaching and learning. Two additional ones that will be mentioned briefly are "working game" and "putting someone on." Most of these games are used to manipulate others. Streetcorner youngsters are masters of these games. Sometimes they will work in consort to run a game on a teacher.

To "put someone on" or "hype" them is to lead a person into believing you are going along with them or what they have to say while subverting (hence rejecting) what they are trying to get across. Of course, the put-on fails if the other person becomes aware of the game. Wellman (1970) provides further insight in his article "Putting on the Youth Opportunity Center."

I have observed innumerable youngsters "working game" on teachers, including me. Sometimes they will do this to get money from the teacher without any intention of ever paying it back. Schulz (1969, pp. 80-82) in providing some examples of this said "they always had a ready reason for needing the money."

Inner city youngsters will run these games on one another as well as on their teachers. Sometimes, when one youngster realizes that another has run a game on him and will not return the money or a borrowed item, a violent confrontation results. I describe such an incident in the next chapter.

THE ROLE OF SCHOOL PERSONNEL IN
GAME PLAYING

The first suggestion for school personnel is that everyone in the school should become aware of the games and understand them. This is *not* "lowering yourself to their level." This is learning what is going on so that you can ameliorate rather than exacerbate a simple situation that could result in disorder and interfere with the teaching and learning.

Second, I suggested earlier that each teacher develop his or her own teaching style reflecting his or her personality. Similarly, if you can judiciously play the games and maintain order and teach—do so. Those who cannot, should not. I have observed some excellent and some poor teachers playing the games. I have also observed some outstanding teachers who will not have a thing to do with the games. I would question, though, whether these teachers really reached their students on an effective level.

One of the points that must still be remembered is that the streetcorner youngster respects you if you can achieve in the area that he deems important. Some school personnel, therefore, can play some of his games and gain his respect without losing their own ideals or standards as adults. (If you speak with white suburban youngsters, they usually like the teachers who are "different" or sometimes a "little crazy" but not to the point of where they try to be "one of the kids.")

Herbert Gans (1962) wrote about Jews and Protestants moving out of Roxbury in Boston and poor Italians moving in. Today, however, the Italians are gone, and Roxbury is populated by blacks. Many of the problems experienced by the Italians are similar to those being experienced by blacks today. "The caretakers and West Enders related to each other across a system of cultural and emotional barriers that prevented the development of satisfactory interaction (Gans, 1962, p. 155)." One of the problems that Gans reported is germane to this chapter and involves the unruly and destructive Italian adolescents and their settlement house workers: ". . . by their actions, they hoped to taunt the caretakers into giving up their middleclass standards, and into resorting to revenge (Gans, 1962, p. 156)." However, one staff member was able to relate to the teenagers fairly well because he could play their games without giving up his values.

Only one staff member was able to deal with the teenagers. This he did essentially by adopting peer group competitiveness. Able to return wisecracks or hostile taunts, he even invited them, thus giving the teenagers an opportunity to measure their skill against his. At the same time, he never surrendered his allegiance to the settlement house and did not cross to their side. While the teenagers did not always obey him, they did respect him, and were attracted to the relationship he offered. He respected them in turn, partially by not being afraid, and by not retreating either from them or from his values. . . . he was able to insist on limits to their hostility and destructiveness (p. 156).

Claude Brown (1965, p. 81) who certainly was a streetcorner youngster, verbalizes the reasons he and the other boys at Wiltwyck School for Boys liked a counselor named Nick. Relating Brown's appraisal, however, does not mean my acceptance of all his criteria for a good counselor.

In a couple of months, Nick was running Carver House. We were all part of his gang. He would never help us rob the kitchen and stuff like that, but he used to take us on hikes around Farmer Greene's apple orchard and look the other way sometimes. He . . . liked a lot of the things we liked. He would play the dozens, have rock fights, and curse us out. But I think we liked Nick mostly because he was fair to everybody. Nick never liked to see anybody get bullied, but he was always ready to see a fair fight. I liked the way Nick was always lying to us. Everybody knew he was lying most of the time, but we didn't care, because he used to tell such good lies. Nick didn't get excited real quick . . . Nick had sense. I was always getting into fights with Nick, since I knew I wouldn't lose too bad (p. 81). . . .

My own teaching style has always been to play the games judiciously. I guess this is because of my own high school experience and because I love to talk, and am physical, too. The high school I went to, The New York School of Printing, was integrated. Furthermore, my high school buddy, Joe Agnello, and I joined St. Peter Claver (a Catholic church which had a Catholic Youth Organization program for teenagers) in Brooklyn, so that we would have a place to run and work out. We were part of a mostly black group of fellow students who started a track team in our senior year. Most of the black students came from the area surrounding St. Peter Claver in Bedford-Stuyvesant in Brooklyn. As a result, I guess I grew up fearing neither blacks, nor the lower socioeconomic physicalness and life style.

I know many excellent teachers who used to and still do play the dozens with their students. One of them did an amazing thing one day. His students just would not stop getting on one another's mothers. No matter what the teacher did they kept at it. No real fights, just continuous digging at one another.

When his students returned from lunch, he called the roll. However, he did it differently than they had ever heard it before.

"Bertha"

"Gwendalyn"

"Gussy"

"Rosemary . . . etc."

His students did not say a word. He was calling the attendance by their mothers' first names. It was a low blow but it worked. His students did not play the dozens in his class again.

I discussed with some students how they felt about teachers who ribbed on them. Generally, their feelings were that it was all right if the teacher did not get mad when ribbed back. They told me about a teacher who sometimes ribbed on the boys by saying "yes, ma'm," or "yes, dear." "There a teacher down the hall, he rib on you for nuthin'. You rib on him, he rib you right back. You don't mess with him." I also know of teachers who allowed themselves to get into ribbing contests with their students. Then, when they were put down hard, they reported the students for cursing or ridiculing them.

There appears to be a standard retort for stopping ribbing, jiving, or playing the dozens in your classroom. To say, "I don't play that game." Or, "Don't play that game in my room," usually works. Of course, your students have to sense that you can back up your demand.

In this chapter, I have presented a discussion of the ribbing, jiving, dozens, and other games that streetcorner youngsters play in inner city classrooms. Actual examples were provided, along with my philosophy concerning game playing in inner city classrooms. So much of the inner city classroom disruption comes about when these games are played on unknowing teachers or played on the students in their classrooms.

Finally, we must remember that the middle classes generally take words, particularly insults, at their literal meaning, while in the ghetto, exaggeration and hyperbole are often part of the verbal repartee with their meanings related to eye and body movements, intonation, and a host of additional nuances that include the audience.

NOTES TO CHAPTER 5

Abrahams, R.D. Playing the dozens. *Journal of American Folklore* 75: 209-218, 1962.

Abrahams, R.D. *Deep Down in the Jungle.* Chicago: Aldine, 1970.

Abrahams, R.D. *Positively Black* Englewood Cliffs, N.J.: Prentice-Hall, 1970a.

Abrahams, R.D. "Talking my talk"—Black English and social segmentation in black communities. *The Florida FL Reporter* 10(1 & 2): 29-38, 58, 1972.

Alcindor, L. UCLA was a mistake. *Sports Illustrated* 31(18): 35-40, 45, 1969.

Anderson, J. Profiles. *The New Yorker*, June 16, 1973, pp. 40-44, 46, 48, 51-52, 54, 59, 61-62, 66, 68, 70, 72-79.

Andrews, M. and Owens, P.T. *Black Language*. West Los Angeles & Berkeley, Calif.: Seymour-Smith, 1973.

Barnes, C. Stage: the maturity of a 'black girl.' *New York Times*, June 18, 1971, p. 27.

Berdie, R.F. Playing the dozens. *Journal of Abnormal and Social Psychology* 42: 120-121, 1947.

Bradbury, R. *Dandelion Wine*. New York: Bantam (Pathfinder Editions), 1959.

Brewer, J.M. 'Hidden language'—ghetto children know what they're talking about. *New York Times Magazine*, December 5, 1966, pp. 32-35.

Brown, C. *Manchild in the Promised Land*. New York: Macmillan, 1965.

Brown, H.R. *Die Nigger Die!* New York: Dial Press, 1969.

Bullins, E. *The Reluctant Rapist*. New York: Harper & Row, 1973.

Burley, D. *Dan Burley's Handbook of Jive*. New York: Jive Potentials, 1944.

Burley, D. The "Dirty Dozen." *The Citizen Call*, July 30, 1960. Cited by L. Hughes (Ed.), *The Book of Negro Humor*. New York: Dodd, Mead, 1966.

Cleaver, E. *Soul on Ice*. New York: A Ramparts Book (McGraw-Hill) 1968.

Clemmer, D. *The Prison Community*. Boston: The Christopher Publication House, 1940.

Cohn, D.L. *God Shakes Creation*. New York: Harper & Row, 1935.

Conot, R. *Rivers of Blood, Years of Darkness*. New York: Bantam Books, 1967.

Couch, W. (Ed.) *New Black Playwrites*. New York: Avon Books, 1971.

Desai, R. *African Society and Culture*. New York: M.W. Lads, 1968.

Dollard, J. The dozens: dialect of insult. *American Imago* 1(1): 3-25, 1939.

Dotson, J. I want freedom to see the good and the bad. *Newsweek*, October 23, 1972, p. 82.

Dove, A. Soul story. *New York Times Magazine*, December 8, 1968, pp. 38-41.

Ellison, R. *Invisible Man*. New York: Signet Books, 1947.

Elton, W. Playing the dozens. *American Speech* 25: 148-149, 1950.

Elton, W. Playing the dozens. *American Speech* 25: 230-233, 1950.

Firth, R. *We, the Tikopia*. London: George Allen & Unwin, 1936.

Flaste, R. For eighth-graders, the sneaker is more than sum of its parts. *New York Times*, May 12, 1973, p. 38.

Foster, H.L. A pilot study of the cant of the disadvantaged, socially maladjusted, secondary school child. *Urban Education* 2: 99-114, 1966.

Fraser, C.G. Man accused of tricking police into shooting indicted in slaying. *New York Times*, July 19, 1973, p. 24.

Gans. H. *The Urban Villagers: Group & Clans in the Life of Italian-Americans*. New York: The Free Press of Glencoe, 1962.

Grier, W.H. and Cobbs, P.M. *The Jesus Bag*. New York: McGraw-Hill, 1971.

Guffy, O. *Ossie: The Autobiography of a Black Woman*. New York: W.W. Norton, 1971.

Hannerz, U. Another look at lower-class black culture. In L. Rainwater (Ed.), *Soul.* Chicago: Aldine, 1970.

Harris, L. WCBS-TV arts editor Leonard Harris reviews "the dozens," a new play, *WCBS-TV New Release* (mimeo), March 17, 1969.

Harrison, P.C. Tabernacle. In W. Couch (Ed.), *New Black Playwrites.* New York: Avon Books, 1971.

Heard, N.C. *Howard Street.* New York: Dial Press, 1968.

Hobel, E.A. *The Law of Primitive Man: A Study of Comparative Legal Dynamics.* Cambridge, Mass.: Harvard University Press, 1954.

Hughes, L. and Bontemps, A. *The Book of Negro Folklore.* New York: Dodd, Mead, 1966.

Huizinga, J. *Homo Ludens, a Study of the Play Element in Culture.* Boston: Beacon Press, 1950.

Hurston, Z.N. Story in Harlem slang. *The American Mercury* 55(223): 84-96, 1942.

Johnson, K.R. Teacher's attitude toward the nonstandard Negro dialect—let's change it. *Elementary English* 48: 176-184, 1971.

Johnson, T.A. Off to trinidad. *Black Enterprise* 2(10): 55-56, 84, 1972.

Jones, L. The toilet. *Kulchur III* 9: 25-29, 1963.

Jones, L. *Blues People.* New York: William Morrow, 1963.

Killens, J.L. *The Cotillion; Or One Good Bull is Half the Herd.* New York: Pocket Books, 1972.

Kilson, M. The black experience at Harvard. *New York Times Magazine,* September 2, 1973, pp. 13-14, 31-32, 34, 37.

Kochman, T. 'Rapping' in the black ghetto. *Trans-action* 6(4): 26-34, 1969.

Malamud, B. *The Tenants.* New York: Farrar, Straus & Giroux, 1971.

Mead, M. Kinship in the Admiralty Islands. *Anthropological Papers of the American Museum of Natural History* 34: 181-358, 1934.

Meriwether, L. *Daddy Was a Number Runner.* Englewood Cliffs, N.J.: Prentice-Hall, 1970.

Merwin, D.J. *Reaching the Fighting Gang.* New York: New York City Youth Board, 1960.

Mezzrow, M. and Wolfe, B. *Really the Blues.* New York: Signet Books, 1964.

Miller, W.B. Lower-class culture as a generating milieu of gang delinquency. *Journal of Social Issues* 14(3): 5-19, 1958.

Mitchell-Kernan, C. Signifying, loud-talking and marking. In T. Kochman (Ed.), *Rappin' and Stylin' Out: Communication in Black America.* Chicago: University of Illinois Press, 1972.

New York City Youth Board. *Reaching the Fighting Gang.* New York: New York City Youth Board, 1960.

Oliver, P. *The Meaning of the Blues.* Toronto, Ontario: Collier Books, 1960.

Oliver, P. *The Story of the Blues.* Philadelphia: Chilton, 1969.

Parks, G. *A Choice of Weapons.* New York: Berkley Medallion Books, 1967.

Rosten, L. *The Joys of Yiddish.* New York: McGraw-Hill, 1968.

Schechter, W. *The History of Negro Humor in America.* New York: Fleet Press, 1970.

Schulz, D.A. *Coming up Black: Patterns of Ghetto Socialization.* Englewood Cliffs, N.J.: Prentice-Hall, 1969.

Sebastian, H. Negro slang in Lincoln University. *American Speech* 9(4): 289-290, 1934.

Shelly, L. *Hepcats Jive Talk Dictionary.* Derby, Conn.: T.W.O. Charles, 1945.

Sowell, T. Radical chic is vicious. *Psychology Today* 6(9): 41-44, 1973.

Stein, J. *The Random House Dictionary of the English Language.* New York: Random House, 1966.

Thomas, W.I. *Primitive Behavior.* New York: McGraw-Hill, 1937.

Wambaugh, J. *The New Centurions.* Boston: Little, Brown, 1970.

Watts, R. Jr. American blacks in new Africa. *New York Post*, March 14, 1969, p. 62.

Wellman, D. Putting on the youth opportunity center. In L. Rainwater (Ed.), *Black Experience: Soul.* Chicago: Aldine, 1970.

Weyer, E.M. *The Eskimos.* New Haven: Yale University Press, 1932.

White, J. Toward a black psychology. *Ebony* 25(11): 45, 48-50, 52, 1970.

Williams, J.A. *The Man Who Cried I Am.* Boston: Little, Brown, 1967.

Wolfe, T. *Radical Chic & Mau-Mauing the Flak Catchers.* New York: Farrar Straus & Giroux, 1970.

Wright, R. *Lawd Today.* New York: Walker, 1963.

Chapter Six

Discipline

"MRS. Oliver, my homeroom teacher, didn't even bawl me out for being late as I slid into my seat. I was disappointed. Maybe she didn't like me anymore."

—Meriwether, *daddy was a number runner.*

Five points must be made. First, all the earlier chapters should be read before reading this one. Second, if I can generalize from the courses I have taught and the lectures and workshops I have given, teachers who have positive feelings, emotions, and attitudes about teaching in inner city schools and who have been frustrated by *teacher-room negativism* and by harried and frightened administrators, will gain strength from reading this book to go back and do battle again—with their fellow professionals, not with their students.

The third point is that there are innumerable lower class black youngsters who display middle class behavior and life style. I have not written about them but rather about the tough, lower class, streetcorner youngster whose testing games have been causing the inner city school problems that have prevented the middle class life styled youngsters from being educated. His testing games must be understood, if his disruptive influence is to be stopped. In so doing, we can educate him as well as the lower class youngster who has a middle class orientation.

The fourth point and possibly the most important is that inner city teachers must decide whether their role in classroom discipline is *passive* or *participatory.* Do teachers have a role in achieving discipline in their rooms or are their students expected to enter their rooms quietly, to be seated quietly, and quietly await their teacher's lessons? Or is getting students to be seated and quiet so that she may teach part of teacher responsibility?

To clarify the point. A teacher cannot teach unless there is a degree of discipline and order in the classroom. Since discipline and order are rarely

237

present in inner city classrooms due to lower class life style, the teacher has two choices. The first is the passive role, insisting that the students must discipline themselves for her.[a] The second is the participatory role, where the teacher actively brings about the discipline and order required for teaching and learning.

Once this passive-participatory teacher role in discipline is resolved, we can proceed to solving inner city school discipline problems. Of course, the related proposition, as noted in Chapter Two, of the inner city secondary school student's perception of his teacher's role in disciplining him may make the teacher's feelings about his role superfluous. I believe that the teacher *must* play an active participatory role in classroom discipline, not only because he or she is an adult, but because inner city students *expect* their teachers to make them behave. The teacher who does not accept this philosophy will not succeed in an inner city school.

In the State of New York, the State Education Department convened a number of committees to discuss the problems of disruptive students. Mr. Daniel Klepak, the newly appointed Director of the Office of Education Performance Review, reported that his letter survey of superintendents and school board members on the "crucial issues affecting the cost" of public education, revealed, among other things, "the high cost of attempting to teach unruly students (Clines, 1973, p. 22)."

The fifth point is that if you are looking for a blueprint for solving discipline problems you will be disappointed; the most I can do is give you some insights, ideas, and attitudes that may help you develop your own techniques and approaches based on your teaching style and personality.

For the past four years, the *Phi Delta Kappan* magazine and Gallup International (Gallup, 1973) have conducted national surveys of public attitudes toward education. All respondents were asked to cite the major problem confronting "the public schools in their community (p. 39)." Discipline has been reported as the most important problem over the past four years in the polls. Both laymen (22%) and professional educators (24%) agreed that discipline was their number one concern this past year (1973).

The points that will be presented will be different from those usually presented in most articles, chapters, and books dealing with discipline, particularly discipline in inner city schools. For some, they may suggest a new outlook and approach to the teacher's role in discipline in inner city schools. For some others, they will reignite positive dormant feelings and attitudes that have been squashed by fear and peer pressures.

THE NEW TEACHERS' FOUR-PHASE RITES OF PASSAGE

From a discipline point of view, most inner city secondary school teachers appear to experience part or all of a four-phase rites of passage, just as I did. The

---

[a]Very often, this teacher will take the point of view that "I did not become a teacher to become a cop."

four phases are: (1) friends, (2) rejection and chaos, (3) discipline, and (4) humanization.

The average new teacher enters the classroom with a positive, warm approach, and a middle class point of view that is almost naive because of his upbringing and teacher training. In his upbringing, discipline was probably verbal, reasonable, mild, and consistent. Relatively free and open verbal communication probably existed between him and his parents. He was reared in a relatively democratic atmosphere rather than through either laissez-faire or autocratic. His parents probably viewed themselves as reasonably competent adults, generally satisfied with themselves. His family life most often was warm, intimate, with a close relationship among himself, his brothers and sisters, and his two parents (Joint Commission, 1970, pp. 264-265). If his parents were divorced, the reasons probably involved their psychological and emotional interaction (Levinger, 1966). He expresses himself symbolically and conceptually.

The last time he was punched in the nose was in fifth or sixth grade or in junior high school. Once a week bowling and some sex is the total of his physical activity. Therefore, his physical activity is now mainly vicarious via TV or going to a hockey or football game or a movie.

He has been in a dependency role all his life. His parents administered to all his needs from birth through public school and college. He did, though, work some summers and part time in school.

Most undergraduate teacher education programs are too idealized and not pragmatic enough, and are directed and staffed by many who never taught school, or if they did teach, did not have too positive an experience. So the chances are, the new teacher's only contact with students and the classroom was his student teaching experience. He also probably lived in a white neighborhood and neither he nor his parents ever had any black friends.

He entered his new job with idealism, warm heartedly, and full of hope; he really wants to do a good job. He wants to like his students and he wants his students to like him. But something happens to him when his students do not react to him in an orderly fashion as friends.

Conversely, the typical streetcorner student has experienced a life which is characteristic of very poor families. Discipline has been inconsistent, harsh, and *physical*. Ridicule is used, punishment is based on whether his behavior bothered his parents. He was controlled largely physically and there was limited verbal communication within the family. There was little acceptance of him as an individual. He was most often reared through authoritarian methods. His mother usually ran the house, and when his father was home, he was primarily a punitive figure.

The streetcorner youngster's parents have a sense of defeat and a low self-esteem. If his family is large, his parents' behavior may have been narcissistic and impulsive. He yielded his independence early and abruptly; he has and still has an "excitement" orientation. Sex is viewed as an exploitive relationship. His aggression is alternatingly restricted and then encouraged (Joint Commission,

1970, pp. 264-265). If his parents are divorced, they probably viewed the "unstable physical actions of their partners" and financial problems as prime contributors to their discord (Levinger, 1966, p. 806). He expresses himself physically. His social structure and poverty tends to foster a life style that is characterized by poor impulse control, fundamental psychological depression, surrender to overwhelming odds, and hostility (Joint Commission, 1970, p. 266). This is an overview of poverty life styles that studies suggest very poor people adopt and which research indicates are not associated with children judged to be mentally healthy in our society. See, Joint Commission, 1970, pp. 264-265.

On the streetcorner, the student's behavior is typically imitative of his elders who "constantly work game, talk of sports and women, and get high (Schulz, 1969, p. 100)." There is a constant search for action, verbal taunting, and killing time. He must hustle or out-aggress the other guy all the time. Every day calls for another test of his machismo and toughness.

The new inner city teacher meets his students, some of whom exhibit streetcorner behavior. The teacher has obviously been raised differently from the student; each has his own life style with which he is secure. Each, as a result of living in a segregated community, has some fear of the other. Each also has fantasies and unrealistic expectations about the other, some conscious and some unconscious.

Because of the teacher's childhood, he does not have the need to be autocratic and to "boss" anyone around. He does not want to act the way the teachers he disliked acted. He enters the classroom with a passive (phase one) approach. He wants to be friends with his students, and he expects them to like him in return. He does not wish to be a disciplinarian.

Many of his streetcorner students, however, have a different expectation of their teacher, particularly if the teacher is a man. They want him to be tough enough to make them behave and to make them learn without being punitive or hurting them. They test him to see whether he possesses the machismo to control them. According to Cvaraceus and Miller (1964, pp. 68-69) the student's norm-violating behavior "reflects a syndrome crystallized around a strong dependency craving," and is a further test of school personnel's ability to satisfy their need for being controlled.

Strict control is highly valued among the lower classes. A close conceptual connection is made between nurturance and authority. The authority figure shows he cares when his control is firm. Therefore, according to Miller (1958, p. 13) frequent attempts are made to test the authority to see whether he can remain firm. The firmer the control the more caring is perceived, despite protests to the contrary.

Since "being controlled" is equated with "being cared for," attempts are frequently made to "test" the severity or strictness of superordinate authority to see if it remains firm. If intended or executed rebellion produces swift and firm punitive sanctions, the individual is reassured, at the same time that he is complaining bitterly at the injustice of being caught and punished. Some environmental milieux, having been tested in this fashion for the "firmness" of their coercive sanctions, are rejected, ostensibly for being too strict, actually for not being strict enough. This is frequently so in the case of "problematic" behavior by lower class youngsters in the public schools, which generally cannot command the coercive controls implicitly sought by the individual (p. 13).

Accordingly, the testing begins. In most cases, the new teacher does not know how to respond and he loses control. His class becomes chaotic and no one learns. When in desperation he asks a student what he should do, he is told he is too easy and he should "hit them—that's what they understand." This perplexes him because he feels his job is to teach, not to involve himself in discipline—and certainly not physically punitive discipline.

James Herndon (1968) describes his roll call with classes 9D and 7H. His description is clearly phase one.

> After roll call, I wasn't quite sure what to do. I had nothing in particular planned, but had counted on the class to give me a hint, to indicate in some way what it was they wanted or expected (pp. 33-34).
> 7H came charging and whooping up the stairs. . . . Later I came to recognize their particular cries coming up my way. . . . 7H dashed in, flung themselves out again. . . . They scattered from seat to seat, each trying to get as much free territory around him as possible, jumping up again as the area got overcrowded and ranging out to look for breathing space. . . . From these seats, wherever they were, they confronted me with urgent and shouted questions, each kid, from his claim of several empty desks, demanding my complete attention to him: Are you a strict teacher? You going to make us write? When do we get to go home? Where our books? Our pencils? Paper? (p. 36).
> At that moment there came a tremendous outcry from over by the door. I looked over and three or four kids were standing there, looking up at the door and yelling their heads off. Naturally the rest of the class soon began shouting insults at them, without any idea of what the trouble was. Everyone was standing up; calls of "water-melon-head!"[b] filled the room. The kids by the door wheeled and rushed up to me, furious and indignant. Vincent, who was one of them, was crying. What the hell? I began to yell in turn for everyone to shut up, which they soon did, not from the effect of my order

---

[b]This is an example of ribbing.

but out of a desire to find out what was the matter;... Alexandra began to threaten me with her mama. Roy, tempted beyond his own indignation, began to make remarks about the color and hair quality of Alexandra's mama.[c] It shows how upset Alexandra was; it was fatal to ever mention your mother at GW, which Alexandra of all kids knew quite well (p. 37).[d]

Phase two (rejection) begins as the teacher becomes fearful, humiliated, frustrated, and isolated, even though only a few of his students are testing him. Most are just looking on hoping that he can be adult enough to get some order so that they can learn; sometimes, though, they too join in the taunting and fun.

The result is that the teacher begins to feel ineffective and, therefore, inadequate as a teacher and as a human being. He begins to have doubts about his future as a teacher and to question his attitudes about blacks because they will not return his invitation to be friends. He may break his engagement or his marriage may become shaky. He may begin to lose or gain weight and go to his doctor for tranquilizers. In the morning when he gets up he gets a queasy feeling in his stomach. He may even break out in hives or suffer other physical symptoms of a psychosomatic nature.

Phase two may also include some soul searching. He may begin to question what he is doing wrong. If he is lucky, he will be in a school where other teachers or a supervisor offers help.

For some, phase two does not mean introspection and growth but rather scapegoating. The principal and the curriculum are blamed for being unsupportive and irrelevant. Some new teachers actually go so far as to justify what they are doing or not doing in the name of self-expression, democracy, and relatedness. Some give up and leave teaching. Others go on to suburban or other supposedly "easier" schools. Some go on to graduate school to become psychologists or guidance counselors. Some leave the real profession to write about their experiences, condemning the "system," and becoming self-certified professional critics, educational lecturers, and writers.

Of those who remain, a goodly number realize that something is wrong and begin to take an active participatory approach as they enter phase three—discipline. They become disciplinarians. They participate in gaining control of their classes. At this phase, some sensitive teachers begin to hate themselves for what they are doing in the name of discipline. (I tell new teachers

[c]This is ribbing and the dozens.

[d]Interestingly, all of my black students dislike this book because they felt Herndon was ineffective in achieving order in his class and giving his students direction. Most of my white students, however, think he is a great teacher who was hampered by the administration, the curriculum, and the "system."

that when they begin to hate themselves for their toughness, they are beginning to grow and make it as a teacher.)

During this phase, they start giving youngsters the grades they deserve instead of giving them a "break." They do not give so many second, third, or fourth chances. When speaking with parents, they become more honest. They also begin to solve their own discipline problems without sending students to the "office."

Unfortunately, out of every ten teachers who remain in inner city schools, seven or eight remain fixated at the discipline phase. They remain at this level—constantly on guard, never trusting, never expressing any positive feelings, and never relaxed. Their students are controlled and supposedly educated with worksheets, notes for copying, and other fruitless forms of "busy-work." The teacher remains ensconced at his desk throughout most of the period.

Phase four is humanization. Few teachers, perhaps two or three per cent, achieve this level. The phase four classroom has a relaxed atmosphere where feelings are expressed. The students have run their testing games and have learned their teacher's limits. Learning takes place in this positive, structured, yet relaxed atmosphere. Students move about the room knowing that no one will steal from them, that no one will pick on them, that no one will steal their clothing from the closet, and that their teacher is fair and will answer their questions. He respects them and they respect him. Their teacher is in charge and in control; and they can now relax.

Each of the phases that the new teacher experiences may last a different period for each teacher. Each teacher may approach and achieve each phase slightly differently.

THE NATURAL INNER CITY TEACHER

The first major comprehensive study of teacher relationships with students in the United States was reported by Fred W. Hart in 1934. Since then, innumerable studies have been published, all reporting similar "good" teacher qualities of: (1) fairness, (2) strictness, (3) ability to maintain discipline, (4) high standards, (5) knowledge of subject, (6) friendliness, (7) sense of humor, and (8) an ability to teach. During the past years, almost everyone who has written about teaching in inner city schools has also suggested lists of "good" qualities required for inner city teachers.

The eight qualities listed above apply to the professional whom I refer to as the "natural" inner city teacher. However, I will discuss this teacher relative to personality, curriculum, and discipline; a few more attributes will be added to the eight listed above, although some of these may merely reflect an aspect of or more of the above qualities. In this section I will discuss briefly those attributes that appear to particularly stand out as common among natural inner-city teachers.

Personality

My "natural" teacher, who may be male or female, is structured, organized, and possesses great inner strength. This person has warmth and really likes both children and adults. He has a sense of humor and is secure and capable of applying his personal standards pragmatically in the classroom. He has great physical energy and understands and is happy with his physical being. Many inner city children are extremely physical and relate well to teachers who are also physical. His physicalness comes across through the way he walks, talks, relates to his students and others, and the way he calmly straightens out disruptions without displaying panic or fear because he does not fear his students physically.

(Despite their protests to the contrary, too many teachers are fearful of their students. The teacher's fear causes the fearful child to act-out even more.)

Because this teacher is at home with his physical being, he is capable of getting close to his students physically without provoking them sexually. This is also because he has dignity and demands to be treated in kind.

Many male teachers relate physically to male students through playful roughhousing where some form of physical body contact is made. Where middle class children are fondled by their parents, particularly in early childhood, the lower class child is treated more harshly by his parents in early childhood. However, the lower class child still craves the fondling he missed. Therefore, he invites and enjoys this nonpunitive physicalness from many of the male teachers he likes.

Often the fearful teacher or administrator is horrified by this teacher-student physicality. Indeed, inner city principals and supervisors often express this fear with such edicts as "Never touch a child under any circumstances." Interestingly, when I discuss this topic with university students and teachers, many who are pacifists and many who are not secure with their own bodies accuse me of wanting to beat children. No matter how often I stress my opposition to corporal punishment, they are unable to separate the idea of hitting a child from warm physical fondling and occasional roughhousing.

The natural teacher is also introspective. His introspection, however, does not prevent him from making decisions and acting. He knows that if he is sleepy or has had a fight with his wife or girl friend, he may not relate too well to his students that day. He knows that how he perceives a situation may determine what the situation comes to. My natural teacher who is a female, is aware that, say, birth control pills may affect her personality. Furthermore, she knows that her personality may be affected by her menstrual cycle, by medications, and by her physical and emotional state at any given moment.

To be introspective is to know that how you feel on any day may affect how you relate to your students on that day. The introspective, self-aware teacher is aware of this and adjusts his relationships with his students accordingly.

The natural teacher practices what he preaches. By respecting the principal's rules, he gets his students to understand and respect his rules. He teaches by example, and by providing a model for emulation.

He dresses stylishly but does not try to dress like his students. She dresses stylishly and tastefully, being careful not to dress seductively or provocatively.

The natural teacher knows that black inner city children can learn. He or she is capable of accepting student aggression and looking through the aggression to find its cause.

Unquestionably, nonracist teachers are desired as inner city teachers. However, they are not necessary. Many black students have been hurt educationally and emotionally by supposedly nonracist white teachers who did not demand that their students produce educationally. Similarly, middle class black teachers have also hurt many black youngsters because they could not relate to their students' lower class life style. Some black teachers, on the other hand, have also hurt black students because their students' "middle classness" clashed with the teacher's concept and feelings of black militancy. Therefore, what is needed are teachers who will insist their students learn rather than loving them to death or being more interested in the political concept of blackness.

Finally, my natural teacher is "down with the action" in the school and neighborhood—i.e., he or she knows her students' peer references.

Sample Peer Reference List[e]

1. Girls in the city have their fashion fads just as suburban girls do. In suburbia, the style is a T-shirt and worn-out blue jeans (with hem turned out, naturally). In the city, the style is usually hot pants (or a short skirt), a pair of tights, knee socks, and multicolored wool socks all worn at once. The reason for all the socks is to take up some of the slack in their boys' sneakers (usually too big; their brother's), which are neatly monogrammed with all their friends' names. On top of all of this, if you really want to be cool, you wear your coat, never taking it off, even in 90° heat.[f]

2. The new style in hairdos, besides the common bush or Afro, is "cornrowing." The hair is neatly placed into braids, starting at the hairline and all

[e]This list was prepared for me two years ago by one of my graduate students, Mrs. Claudia Collins, who was also teaching in an inner city junior high school.

[f]Mrs. Collins now informs me that parts of No. 1 are outdated. The current trend is sloppy, or overly-long belled jeans and saddle shoes outside the city, and ankle-length, peg-legged jeans and platform shoes in the city (at least around New York, New Jersey, and Connecticut).

Illustration 6-1.

interlocking to the nape of the neck. A girl also might braid her hair in a perfect spiral around her head. These are from Africa (After, 1973, p. 14).

3. To be hip you carry an Afro "pick" around with you to "pick" out your bush while you're sitting in class; then you can stick the pick into your bush for safekeeping until the next class.

4. City kids, or underprivileged kids, who can't afford expensive Adidas track or gym shoes like the suburban kids, wear cheap imitations of Adidas that can be had at any downtown shoe store. If they can't buy these, they draw black stripes on their tennis shoes to make them look like Adidas.

Another aspect of inner city peer culture are the medallions youngsters are now wearing in school. One side of the medallion has a zodiac sign and on the other side there is a picture of a couple copulating.[g] Few educators know how to deal with this. In a suburban school district outside Buffalo, some of the black students who have moved into the area recently from Buffalo are wearing them in school. The staff is terrified of even talking to their students about them.

[g]Would a student's right to wear this come under New York State Education Department regulations that students may wear anything as long as it neither interferes with instruction nor health and safety?

Curriculum

Teachers and university professors sometimes claim that the irrelevant curriculum is at fault for deadening classrooms when, in fact, the classroom is deadened by ineffective teaching. I recall one teacher who taught a different academic subject each term. Every time he had problems in his class he would walk into the hall and observe another teacher doing a great job teaching another subject. Instead of realizing that *he* was the problem and not the curriculum, he badgered the principal into allowing him to teach the other subject the following term. Needless to say, he had the same trouble. Or, should we say his students had the same trouble. The greatest curriculum taught by an uninterested teacher will still turn students off.

Because my good teacher loves the subject she teaches, her enthusiasm, excitement, and command of the subject ignites and motivates her students into enjoying the subject. She does not complain about out-of-date materials. If the materials are inappropriate or inadequate she spends a good deal of her own time making relevant ditto masters. She also teaches reading regardless of her subject. Instead of complaining about where her students are, she individualizes her instruction wherever possible.

Discipline

The natural teacher has the ability to make her classroom safe and secure so that all students can relax and learn. Her class is disciplined because her students know she is in charge. It means that somehow, by the way she walks, talks, reacts to a crisis situation, and arranges her room, she lets her students know that she respects them and does not fear them. They know that she can handle the toughest youngster in the class if necessary. She rarely raises her voice. She listens to her students. Her intuition and instinct are correct; therefore, she acts instinctively.[h] She contacts her students' parents early, not waiting for trouble. She also contacts parents to compliment them on their children's positive accomplishments.

There is something about her that made some of her students fear her at first. The fear, however, has grown to respect. She moved her class from being disciplined to being disciplined and humanized. Students move about doing group or individual work. They talk quietly without interfering with others. Because the class is safe and secure they know that no one will steal their coat from the closet, no one will attempt to steal their money, and no one will

---

[h]The importance of teachers acting instinctively should be emphasized as part of undergraduate and graduate teacher education. Too often, a teacher's positive instincts get mired into inactivity and mediocrity by peer and supervisory pressures. O'Donnell, Powers, and McCarthy (1970, p. 210) in writing *Johnny, We Hardly Knew Ye*, point out how "once again, in deciding to accept the invitation from the Houston ministers, Kennedy had instinctively done the right thing against the advice of all of his advisors."

destroy their school work, clothing, or possessions. Though students do not sit with their hands clasped on the desk, there is no question that she is in control.

PSYCHING, ACTING CRAZY, AND REPUTATION

This section relates to three concepts that are not usually discussed in relation to discipline, or even teaching. The first concept concerns the teacher psyching himself as well as his students. The second concept relates to students respecting the teacher who is slightly "crazy." The third concept refers to a teacher earning a reputation as a teacher who is tough and not fearful.

Reality 72 provides an example of how as a new teacher, I sometimes used to psych myself. Reality 73 and 74 provide additional examples of psyching. Reality 75 is a teacher's report of how he earned his reputation.

REALITY 72

As a new "600" school teacher, after taking a verbal and emotional beating from my students for about two weeks, I knew I had to do something if I was going to last as a teacher. When this would happen, I would fall back on my psyching routine.

On Monday, I put on my "manly" outfit consisting of a short-sleeved shirt, a bow tie, and my corduroy sport coat. Wearing this combination somehow psyched me to feel like a MAN. The second part of my psyching routine consisted of waiting in the hall until my class was in the room, and then facing into a little alcove near the door of my shop, clenching my fists, shutting my eyes, and saying to myself something like,

"I am a man. I will not take this from a bunch of kids. Who the hell do they think they are even to try to do this to me. I am a man—I'm twenty-three years old—I'm a veteran—I will not take any more of their crap. I'll show them."

Thus psyched, I adjusted my jacket and tie, and walked into the room. The psyching affected me so that when I walked into the room, somehow by the way I walked and carried myself, I created an atmosphere. My students sensed that there was something about me today that told them, "Do not mess around with this guy today." I guess I psyched myself into overcoming my middle class "nice-guy" approach and they could feel it.

Reality 73 provides another example of psyching. This time, however, it was a student teacher who had to do the psyching.

REALITY 73

I was speaking with one of our female student teachers recently and teasing her about all the rings she was wearing on her fingers. My position was that her generation of students had attacked mine and earlier generations for being materialistic. However, she and her female peers seemed to be wearing a ring on almost every finger. By my standards, this is crass materialism which makes her generation hypocrites.

She finally interrupted me and said, "No, that's not why I wear rings. I had difficulty separating my role of a student in the university from that of a teacher. So, by putting the rings on, psychologically I was putting myself into a different state of mind. Normally, I don't walk around with rings on. The rings were part of my past when I used to dress up a lot. I started wearing the rings when I started student teaching."

In her case, wearing the rings helped her establish a line of demarcation between her university role and her new role of student teacher. Even though the rings were associated with an earlier and younger period in her life, the rings also helped her convey an attitude of confidence. In her case, it may have been that her four years at the university were without constraint. Therefore, by her wearing the rings, she brought herself back to the earlier constraints of her high school days.

I have observed and participated in many forms of psyching. Psyching is particularly effective when the student you are trying to psych is big with a mile-long record of teacher and student assaults and continual disruption. Sometimes he can be psyched out to behave and listen to you without having to go to a physical confrontation.

At one of the high schools where I taught, we had a supposedly rough student who at two hundred and thirty pounds was no slouch. He played Sunday sandlot football and a number of us teachers used to go and watch him play and then discuss the game with him. Some of us also showed him pictures of us playing football at an earlier time. We also participated in some schoolyard touch football games with him. Our interest in him also gave him some self-respect and helped in psyching him to where he was rarely in trouble in our school.

I know of some cases where some of the male teachers would go to the gym to play basketball with students they were trying to psych. Smilingly, they would go in for a layup and knock the youngster down. They would then go over to him still smiling and brush off his clothes, while commenting something like, "Sorry, but once I get going I can't stop."

Other teachers have been observed just going to the gym to play so that their students would see them playing. Another teacher I knew used to "accidentally" bump or brush against the youngster he was trying to psych in the hall and almost knock him down. Another teacher I knew had a dramatic routine he worked out with some of the bigger students that he used occasionally when new students entered his room. Reality 74 describes this.

One point must be made here before going further. In this psyching, the teachers were conveying to these students, on terms *they* could understand, that physically they were not fearful. This approach is often effective with a particularly physical streetcorner youngster. He has to "feel physically" that you are not fearful of him. Also, the teacher using this type of psyching has to be sure of the youngster's emotional stability on the day he is acting physical. If it is the wrong day, such actions could cause a fight. This approach should not in any way be considered corporal punishment or a punitive approach. Actually, this approach alleviates the desire to use corporal punishment while recognizing that the youngster respects physical prowess.

REALITY 74

A teacher had worked out this routine in advance with four students prior to the class. Three of the students entered the class and sat around close to the new students. About ten minutes into the class, the fourth student came in late.

The teacher approached him at the door and wanted to know why he was late.

His response was, "Man, I had to go."

Thereupon, the teacher would grab him by the shirt front and begin to make believe that he was slamming him against the door. Each time he would push him against the door, he would kick the bottom of the door with his foot.

Throughout this routine the youngster being pushed against the door would be screaming for mercy while promising never to come to class late again.

Meanwhile, the three other accomplices would be helping with the psych job by suggesting to the new students.

"Man, that teacher is crazy. He don't take shit from anyone."

"That teacher is a black belt."

"Jiiiim, that mutha nearly killed me two weeks ago."

As the new students took all this in, the teacher removed his hands from the student, and the student slid down the door to the floor settling in a heap.

The teacher would walk toward his desk saying, "Don't anybody help him." As he nears his desk, the student would get up and walk toward his seat calling out, "Ok, my word, I'll never be in late again."

For further effect, the teacher would walk around the room and stop by the desks of the new students.

These physical techniques worked for the teachers involved. The teachers were not sadists. They taught their students well and developed techniques based upon their personalities and the life styles of their students. All were teaching in very rough schools. Before anyone condemns these psyching techniques, he should spend some time teaching in a tough inner city secondary school.

Although psyching is rarely, if ever, discussed educationally, it surrounds us in the real world. The classic example of a psych job was carried out by the old hustler Bobby Riggs on Margaret Court.

He saved his best efforts for weakening his rival. Riggs reminded Court of the pressure of carrying the banner of liberated women everywhere; he also referred ominously to her alleged history of folding in tense situations. Margaret had no such history, but Riggs is such a consummate con man that he soon had many people—perhaps including Margaret—believing him. Then he climaxed his psych job by arriving for the Mother's Day match with a bouquet of a dozen red roses and presented them to his foe at center court.

. . . Margaret never did regain her composure. . . . She succumbed with all the docility of Riggs' kind of woman (The Hustler, 1973, p. 77).

(Of course, Billy Jean King eventually outpsyched Riggs and beat him badly.)

Those who watched the 1968 Olympics in Mexico will remember how Richard Fosburg of the United States used his "Fosburg Flop" to win the high jump. When asked why he was rocking back and forth at the starting line, he responded that he was psyching himself.

Although psyching is spoken of most often in sports, Golda Meir, former Prime Minister of Israel, allegedly tried to psych out the Pope on her visit to the Vatican in 1973. She was reported to have said that she looked the Pope in the eyes and refused to take her eyes from his.

Boxers at weigh-ins usually attempt to psych one another.

Kingston, Jamaica, Jan. 22—Joe Frazier and George Foreman met eyeball-to-eyeball today in the most momentous confrontation since Golda Meir's confrontation with Pope Paul VI. It was only the weigh-in for their fistfight for the heavyweight championship of the world . . . but they traded glares so freighted with menace that the temperature around them dropped 20 degrees (Smith, 1973, p. 33).

Muhammed Ali is well known for his physical and verbal psyching. The United States swimmers had a "Psych Room" at poolside during the 1972 Olympics at Munich (Axtheim, p. 67). Jay Meisler, a schoolboy high jumper, eats sandwiches and sodas between jumps that help him get rid of butterflies and "They also psych me up and give me strength. I usually offer some to the other guys, but they get mad. It probably psychs them out (Meisler's, 1973, p. S 4)." At a wrestling match in California, the Southern California College coach entered a female wrestler in the match. The coach did this in the hope that the other team would default. "She said she had hoped her opponent would back off. 'At first, she psyched me out,' Peryer admitted. 'I wondered if she knew karate or something' (Girl, 1973, p. 24)." And more than chess buffs remember the way America's Bobby Fischer psyched out Russia's Boris Spassky.

Psyching in inner city schools, then, is where the teacher psychs himself—that is, puts himself in a certain frame of mind so that he can deal with the realities of his teaching assignment. For middle class teachers, most often, the psyching function helps them overcome their middle class, nonphysical, open personality to where they can, hopefully, fearlessly deal with the reality of some of their students' streetcorner life style. If the teacher has to psych himself every day, however, he probably does not belong in an inner city school because one cannot survive having to continually psych oneself to walk into a classroom.

Acting Dramatic or Crazy

An area sometimes discussed in the educational literature is the importance of teachers acting dramatically as a strategy for motivating students, particularly the noninterested or hard to motivate youngster. A form of this drama for inner city teachers could be referred to as "acting crazy." In line with my hypothesis that contact can be made with the streetcorner youngster through his own frame of reference, Claude Brown writes about acting crazy as part of streetcorner life.

> The bad nigger thing really had me going. I remember Johnny saying that the only thing a bad nigger was scared of was living too long. This just meant that if you were going to be respected in Harlem, you had to be a bad nigger; and if you were going to be a bad nigger, you had to be ready to die. I wasn't ready to do any of that stuff. But I had to. I had to act crazy (p. 122).
> ... I thought they were all jive. The way I saw it, those niggers weren't so crazy. They were just acting like they were crazy. And they'd only act like that with cats who didn't know any better. Now I knew that if I was to breeze and they came after me, one of us would get hurt—me or whoever it was. But I just couldn't get too scared of them. I'd seen cats like that just about all my life (p. 138).

Additionally, there is reporting of how acting crazy supposedly affects athletic opponents. Al Feuerbach (Munich, 1972, p. 54) in preparing for the Olympic trials, grew a bushy head of hair and a mustache because "you've got to make people believe you're crazy. Nobody can beat a crazy man." Also in the Olympic tryouts, Brian Oldfield acted in a way that earned him the name of the "Wild Man." He accomplished this by puffing on a cigarette between tosses of the shot and "competing in a blue fish-net shirt and a brief, flowered bathing suit (Munich, 1972, p. 54)."

Shep Messing, who is probably the outstanding United States soccer goalie, also believes that "you've got to be daring and a little crazy to play goalie

(Yannis, 1972, p. 105)." During the first qualifying round of Olympic play, the United States drew three games with El Salvador, and each team was given five penalty shots. The United States players made all five.

> When El Salvador converted its first two penalty shots, Messing took matters into his own hands to end what appeared an interminable match.
> All he did was go slightly berserk. "Nothing was planned," he said, "it was really quite spontaneous."
> "Just as the El Salvador player was to take the third kick, I ripped off my shirt and started screaming obscenities in English. I actually left the goal and went out and slapped the guy on the back to encourage him not to miss." Messing said. "Well, the guy was so confused he made the worst penalty kick I have ever seen (p. 105)."

Although the streetcorner youngster is not technically the teacher's "opponent," he often acts that way as he contests the teacher for control of the class. Actually, though the teacher may not consider the streetcorner youngster his opponent, the youngster does indeed consider the teacher his opponent, as he does all authority. Therefore, very often the teacher who acts in a dramatic, "crazy" way not only throws off the streetcorner youngster's game of attempting to manipulate the class to his own ends, but may also win over the other students to his side. *Indeed, the teacher can only control the class when he controls the streetcorner youngster.* And remember, the teacher can only teach in a class where he has control and a degree of order.

Acting crazy as a teaching style is not for all. I would emphasize again that each teacher must develop a teaching style based upon his own personality. Acting crazy may work for some and may not work for others. In my observations of teachers concerning the crazy style, I have found that those who succeed at this style are usually outgoing, good humored, and extroverted.

The crazy teacher may be male or female. She may jive or woof on her students and enjoy going a bout of ribbing with them.

"She was a crazy teacher. She rib on you for nothing. You rib on her, she rib you right back" may be heard about this teacher.

Though this teacher plays these games, she controls her class. She separates play from work. Her students are taught that play must stop when work starts. Actually, her acting crazy provides a break in the monotony of the school day. Often, this teacher is told laughingly. "You ought to see the principal—you are crazy." Or, "The next time I see the counselor, I am going to tell her to give you an appointment because you are sick."

Some incidents for which my high school students called me crazy involved two of the reference points of the streetcorner—talking, and physical prowess. I often played a verbal game.

My class would be seated around a large work table. After taking the attendance, I would pick up my *New York Times*, open it and read.

"Wow, did you guys see this?"

"John Frank was picked up by the police outside of the A & P on 125th Street for stealing a lolly pop from a baby in a baby carriage."

The class would laugh and howl, and I would note who was laughing the loudest.

"José Rodriquez," I would make believe I was reading, "was arrested for knocking over a Boy Scout who was helping an 80-year-old lady across the street. According to the arresting officers, José was running after having stolen twenty-five cents from the poor box at the church around the corner."

I would go on for awhile and then we would get to work, all laughed out and relaxed.

Another crazy act I pulled one day was to pick up one of the boys and hang him by his coat on the top of the classroom door. Seeing the surprised look on his face as he hung there had us all laughing and rolling on the floor. Even he began to laugh.[i] Sometimes I would jump up on my desk or the work table in the midst of an impassioned presentation. I would get the good feeling when one of the students would say, "Come on, stop playing, I want to work."

In discussing the "crazy" teacher with white suburban youngsters, I found they like the crazy teacher too.

Reputation

One of the signs that a teacher has completed his rites of passage is the reputation he earns with students. If the teacher has cleared his rites of passage positively, his reputation talks about his toughness and "don't mess with him." If the passage has met with disaster, his reputation may be "Oh, he's a faggot, he's afraid of everyone." Similarly, female teachers also gain reputations. Their positive reputation is very much like the male's: "You can't run no games on her." If her passage was a disaster, boys may report her reputation as, "Shit, you sit up front you always see up her dress."

An interesting aspect of reputation building has to do with whether the students feel positively towards a teacher. If they do, minor incidents can be drawn all out of proportion in the teacher's favor. For example, after the gang fight described in Reality 19, I gained an exaggerated reputation. Some of the stories reported me beating up at least eight of the attacking gang. When questioned, I denied the story of inflicting a beating to the other gang. However, my students considered my denial a manifestation of my modesty. Of course, there are also the teachers who exaggerate incidents in an attempt at building their reputations on false foundations.

[i]For an excellent example of humor easing a tense situation, see Gene Hackman and Al Pacino in the movie *Scarecrow*.

Reality 75 is a new white teacher's description of an incident between a male student and female student where the teacher intervened and earned an outstanding reputation in a tough secondary school. The situation described is not as untypical as it may appear to be.

REALITY 75

"One morning . . . while separating two students who were fighting in the halls during the change of classes, I was hit from behind with a sneaker. As I was restraining someone at the time, I could do little but look at who did it. It was somebody I didn't know or even recognize, and he was trying to agitate more trouble with shouts about the 'mother-fucking honkies.'

"I *asked* him to let her go. I was totally ignored. Then I moved closer and *told* him to let her go. This was met by a surprised look and a half-dozen obscenities and threats. He didn't let go and the girl continued to scream in pain. I then intervened by grabbing a pressure point on his wrist and forcing him to release the girl.

"By now, a number of students had gathered, as well as three neighboring teachers. The young man was now in a rage. . . . He threatened to kill me and then launched into an incredible racist tirade.

"He turned to put his sneakers down in preparation for a physical confrontation. I stood there silently listening and thinking that this guy must be deranged. I remained calm and cool, totally unmoved and showing no emotional reaction to his threats. The fact that I expressed no fear seemed to enrage him even more. Remember, we were now before twenty students who were just waiting to see how each of us moved and what we said.

"We stood face to face for at least a minute. Each threat or curse was met by a very matter-of-fact verbal response from me as I stood nonchalantly, with folded arms (with a sense of boredom and overconfidence).

"This attitude enabled me to remain detached enough to control my actions consciously. I was ignorant of the fact that he had a 6-inch straight razor in the hand he held behind his back. The students *were* aware of this and were amazed by my "courage." I was expecting that I might have to defend myself, but had no idea he had a weapon.

"One of the other teachers approached cautiously and suggested I return to my classroom as I was the object of his rage. I felt it best to let the other faculty present handle the situation. My very presence was enough to escalate the situation further. . . .

"It was only later that I learned about the razor. Kids came up to me all day asking if I was scared, and what would I have done if . . . ?

"This incident was the beginning of my particular school reputation. It was based essentially on fantasy, exaggeration, overstatement, and an unintentional situation in which my ignorance of circumstances enabled me to continue surviving.

"I was told later by some informed colleagues that this kid was known . . . , and had a record of slashing people. He was at one time under psychiatric care. This fellow later pulled the razor on two teachers at the end of the corridor. Both teachers filed charges but were told by the police warrant officer that the young man could only be charged with harrassment, and possibly trespassing as he wasn't even a student at (that school). No court action has yet been taken. We were told that there would be a suspended sentence at worst if he was convicted at all, since there was no blood and nobody was actually hit."

DISCIPLINE AND SOME GUT ISSUES

We have not solved the problem of discipline in inner city schools because we have not been willing to come to grips and discuss openly some gut issues. The remainder of this chapter will discuss these issues as they are related to discipline.

These issues include: (1) controlling those streetcorner youngsters who use real negative aggression and violence to test their teachers; (2) the interventionist model for training personnel to be able to cope with this real violence and aggression; (3) the differentiation between corporal punishment and physical restraint; and (4) teacher-student sexuality and discipline.

A Statement Concerning School Discipline

There are two questions here. First, is the teacher's role in discipline participatory or is it passive? The second is, considering the middle class origins of most teachers and the inadequacies of teacher education programs, how much can we expect from new teachers in disciplining the really rough aggressive acting-out inner city youngster?

Every time city teachers get together, someone will say, "But I didn't become a teacher to be a cop."—that is, if you allow them to talk openly and honestly. But how should the statement be taken? Should it be considered as a cry of despair by someone who should not really be an inner city teacher? Was it made by someone who was really trying but just could not deal with one or two really tough streetcorner youngsters in his classroom? Was it made by a successful teacher who was describing what he perceived as a big part of his role and was bothered morally and philosophically? Or was it a little of each?

Accepting that all children test their teachers and always have,[j] the teacher must be capable of controlling the class and providing a healthy, relaxed

---

[j]Being able to control a class of students has always been a problem. In a history of Niagara County, New York in 1821, the following was reported.

atmosphere where learning can take place. Therefore, the teacher's role in discipline must be participatory. The reality is that some youngsters in each class are ready to test their teacher's ability to control them and to make them learn. Hence, the teacher who looks at his role in discipline as passive—"My job is to teach, not to get them seated and quiet"—does not belong in the inner city school but in a school where the students' backgrounds have prepared them for school learning. This person could teach if black inner city youngsters would not test him the way they do. Who is at fault? The children for testing as they do, the teacher who just *wants to teach*, or the political system that produced them both? Would not more black youngsters learn if the teacher were allowed to teach in a classroom that was orderly?

Suppose we rid our schools of those who do not look upon their teaching role in discipline as participatory. How much of the aggressive, physical, sometimes frightening testing can we honestly expect the teacher to cope with even though he accepts his role in discipline as participatory?

I have been tested by these games and have observed others being tested similarly. The testing in many cases goes beyond what could properly be considered reasonable. Some of the testing of teachers that I have observed violates the teacher's civil rights as well as being in violation of Article Five of the United Nations Universal Declaration of Human Rights: "No one shall be subjected to torture or to cruel, inhuman, degrading treatment or punishment."

I have observed male and female, black and white teachers in uncontrolled crying because of the inhuman and frightening testing they were subjected to. In most cases these were idealistic new teachers desiring to do a good job. They neither abused anyone racially nor did they hit anyone. They were tested with aggressive, physical, and frightening streetcorner games because they happened to be teachers in inner city schools.

I suppose unless you have been exposed to the testing you cannot understand the depth of the feelings you experience. One streetcorner youngster told me, "I walk up to the teacher and tell him to 'get out of the way.' If he moved, I got him."

Another streetcorner youngster told me, "I walk into the class late so I can put on my act. I usually run off at the jib" (jive talk for mouth).

In one of my graduate classes, a number of inner-city and suburban high school youngsters were invited to talk with my students. The high school

---

In those days the question was not, "Has the teacher a good education?" but "Is he stout? Has he good government?" It was frequent practice in some districts to smoke out the entire school or to "bar out" the teacher. Frequently there was a conspiracy among the large boys to whip the teacher and break up the school. Their attempts in this direction were successful for several years, and then, when the district had won a bad name and come to be shunned by the generality of pedagogues, a stranger with well-developed governing powers would happen along, open a school and speedily reduce the belligerent, "big boys" to a condition of subjection and prompt if not cheerful obedience, thus setting the ball of education rolling on (p. 97).

students were all on varsity teams. The ghetto youngsters were in one room and the suburban youngsters in another room. Neither group heard the other. My students heard both.

The contrast between the groups' feelings about testing teachers was predictable. Each group spoke of their testing teachers in a style that was commensurate with their social class life style. Each was at opposite ends of the continuum.

The suburban youngsters talked about the importance of good grades, getting into good colleges, and not getting into trouble in school. They also talked about nonphysical ways of "getting away with things" only up to a point. Their outlook was realistic and always came back to getting to college and then a good job. Some of their suggestions included:

1. How to "brown" the teacher. (To *brown* or *brown-nose*, is to curry favor from a teacher.)
2. "You see how much you can get away with."
3. "You don't push the teacher—then you find out what you can get away with."
4. "Never threaten a teacher. You can get thrown out of school if you do."

The inner city youngsters, on the other hand, in a tone that was always physically aggressive, always talked about "running something," and "You can't let someone take your stuff. You have to fight for all you got." Their approach to life reflected their black frame of reference for fame and fortune via either a "super star" or political role. In referring to teachers, they pointed out that "some of them have a natural fear of you. You bluff them hard and you can do anything." Their tactics included:

1. "Don't take no shit from anyone."
2. "If any teacher gives off the impression that he's afraid, I'll put the pressure on him and I'll keep on putting the pressure on him 'till I get him."
3. "Me and him have a stare-down all day."
4. "You can tell how a teacher looks nervous. He will fiddle with his pencil; look down and say 'ah,' 'ah,' 'ah'; he will have a nervous smile; he will say 'I'll have your respect'; a quick nervous look around the room; you keep looking at the teacher—you move when he moves."
5. "Loud talk the teacher. Murphy and psych him out with double talk. If it is a woman teacher, sweet talk her."
6. "Tell the teacher to meet you in the gym or the parking lot. You tell him he better be able to back up his talk."
7. "Keep after the teacher that you want this and you want that."

8. "Like a murphy, you psych him into doing what you want."
9. "Nod out[k] in class. When the teacher comes up to you, come up mad."

In spite of the physical and aggressive bravado with which they test their teachers, at the end of their talk the students added, "Some better teachers would be a whole lot better." Hence, we see the inner city student's real desire for teachers who are capable of overcoming their actions to control them and make them learn.

Accordingly, we see their dilemma and the dilemma they cause in attempts to discipline them. On one hand there is the need for the endless testing and proving of machismo, the never-ending drive to prove superior manhood. And, where the teacher is white, there appears to be an additional racial feeling added to the machismo drive. This feeling of black over white is akin to the writings of many black authors proclaiming that all white males are *fags* and all black males fearless studs. Where the teacher is black, the faggot feelings appear to be applied to the black teacher being tested because he appears to be playing the white "nonmasculine" role of a teacher.

These youngsters do not seem to understand how self-destructive their behavior is. They do not realize how their behavior is preventing them and their fellow students from receiving an education. They seem to be playing out a street-ordained role over which they have no control.

At the same time, however, they long to be controlled by the use of tactics and emotions that are important to them and which they understand. They yearn for someone who can stand up to them, physically and emotionally. And, as far as they are concerned, it does not have to be in a nonpunitive way. I will argue though that it should and *can* be in a nonpunitive way.

One reason that this streetcorner youngster's physically aggressive approach to testing teachers is so effective, is the difference between his lifelong exposure to real physical aggression and violence as compared with his teacher's contact with violence that is usually vicarious.

Hunter Thompson (1967) writing about the Hell's Angels of California, pointed out the phychological and emotional edge the Angels held over most middle class men because of the difference in experiences that each has had. He described a relationship that is analogous to the streetcorner youngster's experience with aggression and violence as compared with his teacher's experiences.

There is not a Hell's Angel riding who hasn't made the emergency-ward scene, and one of the natural results is that their fear of

[k]To nod out in class is to feign sleep or tiredness. Nod comes from the drug term.

accidents is well tempered by a cavalier kind of disdain for physical injury. Outsiders may call it madness or other, more esoteric names . . . but the Angels inhabit a world in which violence is as common as spilled beer, and they live with it as easily as ski bums live with the risk of broken legs. This casual acceptance of blood-letting is a key to the terror they inspire in the squares. Even a small, inept street-fighter has a tremendous advantage over the middle-class American, who hasn't had a fight since puberty. It is a simple matter of accumulated experience, of having been hit or stomped often enough to forget the ugly panic that nice people associate with a serious fight. A man who has had his nose smashed three times in brawls will risk it again with hardly a thought (p. 128).

It is pointless to "blame" ghetto streetcorner youngsters and their families or their teachers for the ongoing lack of discipline in inner city schools. The condition must be accepted as it is, without wasting time, energy, and emotions looking to assign guilt or responsibility. Instead, we should begin to work to solve the problem. It is possible that merely getting this reality into the open for discussion could start a new move toward solutions. We have not been able to solve anything to date because we have not recognized the true problem. Or, perhaps maybe we have not wanted to admit what the problem really has been.

It seems to me that the first order of business is to recognize that there are a number of lower class, black, male, streetcorner youngsters who test their teachers with a great deal of aggressive and violent behavior. Furthermore, because staff cannot cope with this behavior, the resulting disruption prevents more black school children from learning. This is the problem as it exists in many of our inner city schools.

The second order of business is for educators to stop being so squeamish about aggression and the positive feelings many teachers have about it. Once we have accomplished this, too, the problems of aggression and violence can be further identified and examined and strategies developed for ameliora-tion. We must also realize that we may have to develop nonpunitive physical restraint techniques to control the behavior of acting-out streetcorner young-sters. *And, that there is a difference between corporal punishment and physical restraint.*

I feel certain that if educators would talk honestly about these realities, without guilt, more teachers would find they possess the ability to cope with the aggression of their streetcorner students. Finally, we have to develop specialists—I call them *Interventionists*[1]—who can cope with real aggressive or violent behavior.

[1]The Interventionist concept was first presented at the 49th Annual Inter-national Convention of the Council for Exceptional Children, Miami Beach, Florida, April 1971. A version of the presentation was also published as: "To reduce violence: the Interventionist Teacher and Aide," *Phi Delta Kappan* 53: 59-62, 1971.

The Interventionist

From the discussion of discipline, two points should be recalled. First, there are some youngsters who test their teachers with a good deal of aggression and violence. Second, for various reasons, there are not enough teachers who can cope with this student aggression and violence.

Moreover, even when we have succeeded in educating more teachers to cope with their acting-out youngsters, we would still need specialists to resolve or prevent some of the major disruptive problems created by the acting-out students, particularly those who are emotionally disturbed. The Interventionist is just such a professional model.

Each day brings additional reports of uncontrolled aggresssion and violence in our public schools which interrupts instruction, thereby depriving innumerable youngsters of their right to an education. According to Owen B. Kiernan (1970) "The disruption of education in our high schools is no longer novel or rare. It is current, it is widespread, and it is serious (p. v)."

Unquestionably, some of the disruptive behavior is caused by classroom and school processes. However, reporting also suggests that some of the aggressive and violent behavior exhibited in our schools by a minority of youngsters is of an extraterritorial nature and originates with outside-of-school fears, conflicts, and frustrations such as poverty, broken homes, racism, and emotional problems.

School personnel vary in their ability to cope with this behavior, just as the amount and type of disruptive behavior varies from school to school and area to area. Some school administrators and teachers already have the ability to deal with this behavior; consequently, in some schools the negative effects of aggression and violence are minimized.

Educators appear to respond with either of three traditionally punitive alternatives to these problems. The first response is the increasing cry for the return to "corporal punishment," more school suspensions, in-school detentions, and expulsions. The second approach is to ignore all preliminary signs of impending disorder in the hope that the problem will dissipate. The third response, usually after the disruption and violence has erupted, is to call the police.

The police presence, however, often creates additional problems. Their presence may not only provoke further disorder, but also—and more important—regardless of how unsafe and unmanageable the school situation that required police, the students' and often, the community's esteem for the school staff deteriorates when the police arrive. It is analogous to the inept teacher who had to call for outside help to discipline and motivate his class. Any respect students had for this teacher dwindles every time the outside authority arrives.

In the present school setting, except in the case of the most calamitous emergencies, adoption of unimaginative and traditional control devices seems to produce perverse and contraproductive results. Tensions and violence tend to be increased rather than reduced; basic constitutional rights, involving both substantive and procedural "due process," tend to be violated, thereby increasing the feeling of all too many young people that they are victims of authoritarian whim, not subjects of the equitable law that in civics classes they are asked to reverence (Bailey, 1970, p. 33).

As a consequence, and because we just do not have enough personnel who can cope with either aggression and violence or lower class physicalness, it is imperative that we develop new staff and techniques to prevent and cope with this negative aggression and violence that has been interfering with instruction.

Innumerable urban schools have some form of security officers. In some cases, the security officers wear uniforms while in others they wear blazers. However, most of these positions appear to be based upon a police oriented security guard model and their supervision and direction appears to come from former police officers.

To offset this trend, educators must develop an educational professional—the Interventionist and Interventionist aide—based on an educational model. It is imperative that this personnel model be developed from an educational model rather than from a police oriented model. However, the Interventionist must be capable of intervening to prevent or contain school-centered acts of violence by students and sometimes by nonstudents.

We have the beginning of such an educational model in special education and in many inner city schools. The Interventionist is a more contemporary educator and paraprofessional developed from Morse's Crisis Teacher's role (Morse, 1965; 1962). Although there is sparse literature that deals with educators; coping with and preventing real violence (Foster, 1964; 1968a; 1968b; 1969a; 1969b), there are many years of unreported expertise and experience developed by those working with aggressive acting-out youngsters.

The meager reporting appears to have come about because too many in leadership positions in special education and education in general have either been unaware of or have refused to face the reality of violence in our schools. Whether this results from political or psychological reasoning, or for other reasons is an area ripe for speculation and research.

The subject of violence has been denied and hidden, with the result that many teachers and administrators have developed feelings of guilt and despair over their inability to teach effectively, and millions of children have been denied an education as a result of classroom disruptions. And, because the problem persists and is not recognized, we have not been able to work toward its resolution. I must emphasize that the Interventionists' education and responsibilities will emphasize early intervention and resolution of problems before they escalate into crisis.

I developed the Interventionist concept from sixteen years of almost daily personal experience with aggression and violence in the New York City "600" day and institutional schools, as well as a short period with the Junior Guidance Classes Program. During my last two years with the "600" schools, I acted in the role of an Interventionist and helped eradicate corporal punishment as a mode of behavior modification. Today, in that particular "600" school, through the Interventionist philosophy the level of negative aggression and violence has been lowered significantly, if not erased. Additionally, a course at the State University of New York at Buffalo was conducted to prepare professionals to work with aggressive and violent youngsters and helped develop further the Interventionist concept (Foster, 1970). (See Chapter Seven for a description of the course.)

The Interventionist's responsibility would include:

1. Getting to know staff and students.
2. Becoming sensitive to the early warning signals of impending overt aggressive behavior.
3. Calming and talking with children on the verge of losing control or who have lost control and are interfering with instruction or becoming a physical threat to themselves, a teacher, or a peer.
4. Replacing police in the halls and/or, making their presence unnecessary.
5. Developing reciprocal communication links with all community groups.

The emphasis will be on intervention and resolution of problems and returning the youngster to class and preventing any interruption of instruction.

The education of the Interventionists involves expertise in the two broad areas: (1) verbal, nonverbal, and psychological intervention, and management concepts, techniques and philosophy; and (2) nonpunitive physical intervention techniques. The Interventionist's education will emphasize amelioration and resolution through verbal and psychological intervention techniques rather than through physical intervention.

Intervention teachers and Intervention aides should operate in integrated teams of two or three. The teams should be integrated as to sex, and reflect the ethnic or racial background in the school's student population. Interventionists will carry neither sidearms nor clubs and they should be in civilian dress.

The responsibilities and expectations of the Interventionist will depend upon each school situation. Requirements for those working in the inner city public school will differ from those who are institutionally based or those working in a day school for the emotionally disturbed. Interventionists should be teachers or guidance counselors.

Verbal, Nonverbal, and Psychological Intervention, and Management Concepts, Techniques, and Philosophy. In working with others, the Interventionist's feelings, emotions, and attitudes will play an important role in the way he relates to each situation. Therefore, the first step in educating the Interventionist to work with others is to help him recognize and understand his own emotions, feelings, and attitudes.

The Interventionist's education will include discussions and readings on student problems and incidents, worker introspection, and the emotional aspects of his role in working with normal, disruptive, and aggressive students. An overview of the professional literature related to counseling, emotionally disturbed and socially maladjusted students, and life space interviewing will also be included. Particular emphasis will be placed upon historical and contemporary examples of how one man's or woman's action either calmed or exacerbated a particularly volatile situation. Additionally, the history of American violence will be studied as related to ethnic, religious, political, economic, racial, radical and antiradical violence, as well as violence in the name of law, order, and morality. Role playing will be used to discuss and discover the many behaviors that can be used in preventing, managing, and mediating crisis situations. Also emphasized will be the legal and civil rights and responsibilities of all concerned, perpetrators, victims, and mediators.

In addition, the Interventionist will be educated to differentiate between ghetto rhetoric and a real threat, as well as becoming conversant in black dialect or any of the nonstandard dialects spoken by the ethnic, religious, or racial minorities found in his school.

The Interventionist will be well versed in first aid techniques. He will also be educated to "sniff out" the pot smoker and to differentiate between the alcoholic high, drug high, and acid high. He will also be educated to counsel and refer students on any of a myriad of problems. Some Interventionists should be certified teachers, for the need may arise for the Interventionist to remain with the class while the teacher leaves to work with the disruptive child.

The history of the contributions to America of the religious, ethnic, and racial minorities also will be included in their education of the Interventionist. Particular emphasis will be placed upon the life style of the group in the assigned school.

Nonpunitive Physical Intervention Techniques. It must be realized that no matter how expertly the Interventionist deals with an acting-out student, the youngster may continue to demonstrate behavior that will have to be contained physically. For example, the need may arise to remove a student physically to protect another child, to prevent "contagion," (the spreading of the negative behavior), or for his own safety. Therefore, the Interventionist will have to be educated in nonpunitive physical intervention techniques and philosophy. It must be emphasized that the Interventionist will use physical intervention techniques only as a last resort.

Much of what is perceived as threatening and illegitimate violence is nothing more than the testing of the teacher's or Interventionist's ability to control and set limits. Therefore, the Interventionist will also be educated to differentiate between actual out of control behavior and lower class, norm violating behavior that is not really violent or threatening, though often perceived as such by the ill-trained.

Another important objective in the use of nonpunitive physical intervention techniques is to lower the level of violence by reducing the youngster's anxiety and need to retaliate. When a youngster loses control of his surface behavior, he often seeks controls from an outside source. However, when the outside physical controls are punitive, most often the child's anxiety and aggression is escalated even though the surface behavior may be controlled momentarily because of the fear of further physically punitive retaliation.

When the Interventionist nonpunitively holds the child, he demonstrates a number of concepts and feelings to the child. First, because of the Interventionist's willingness to "get physical" with the child, he demonstrates that he is not afraid of the child. Second, by getting physical, the Interventionist demonstrates that he is stronger than the child; hence he is strong enough physically to help the child control his impulses. Third, the Interventionist has also demonstrated that because he is stronger than the child physically, he could have hurt him but has chosen not to. Elliot Shapiro (Hentoff, 1970) in describing an incident with a youngster gives an example of the feelings that are transmitted when a warm adult is willing to become "physical" with a youngster.

> A few weeks later, he challenged me to box him. He had to reassure himself that physically I *could* take care of him. That way, if I were going to help him, my help would be worthwhile by his criteria. In other words, was I "soft" only because I was helpless? You know, the man who lived with the "mother" who took care of John before she died was very cruel, but John missed his beatings in a way because he felt a man as strong as that could give him some kind of security. So he came into my office, I closed the door, and we boxed for about three minutes. Mostly I outfeinted him, although occasionally I'd hit him lightly on the face. He was really trying, but he was quite pleased that he lost, because now he felt I could take care of him (Hentoff, 1967, p. 23).

Another important point is that the disadvantaged youngster equates the worker's willingness to use nonpunitive physical force with caring and warmth and he perceives fear as prejudice. Also, the way the Interventionist copes with the out of control student may be an important factor in helping the youngster himself to cope with his own anxieties.

The Interventionist's willingness to become physical can also help the child who has been forced into a fight to save face. This youngster may be too fearful to stop because he is afraid of his peers who forced or manipulated him into the fight. Here the youngster can use the Interventionist's superior physical strength as a legitimate excuse for stopping the fight until his own controls are sufficient for him to withstand the verbal and physical onslaughts and manipulations of his peers.

Often I have observed anxious, supposedly out of control youngsters go directly to the Interventionist or worker they knew was not afraid to control them physically. Conversely, this reporter suggests when the professional shows fear, he may provoke an already frightened youngster to act-out further.

Interventionists must be educated in the following "last resort" nonpunitive physical intervention techniques:

1. Methods and techniques of separating students who have lost control and who may be fighting.
2. The use of minimal nonpunitive physical force for disarming students or unauthorized visitors who may be threatening or attacking others with weapons.
3. Physical nonpunitive restraint of students or unauthorized visitors who are physically attacking someone, "ripping off" school equipment, "trashing," attempting to burn or blow up a building, or otherwise interfering with instruction or threatening a student or worker with physical harm.

. The Interventionist's confidence in his physical capabilities, secured through the mastery of techniques, will provide him with the following psychological set which will help him to resolve potential crisis situations:

1. Removal of the fear of physical injury.
2. The ability to retain composure in a confrontation or violently physical situation.
3. The knowledge that if the situation gets out of hand, he can handle it physically.

The student who has underdeveloped control of his behavior gains strength to control his behavior from: (1) the inner strength of the worker; and (2) if necessary, the willingness of the worker to restrain him physically. In most cases of disruption, the disorderly student usually gives innumerable warning signals that can be read by the well trained worker to ameliorate or prevent the impending situation.

The emphasis should be on positive intervention and management that prevents an incident from deteriorating into crisis. However, in some cases, no matter how expertly the Interventionist tries, a student may still demonstrate behavior that will have to be contained.

Ongoing Staff Communication

When the Interventionist is introduced into the school, a certain amount of time must be expected to elapse while the professional staff tests to see whether the Interventionist will really provide the assistance he has been billed to provide. The Interventionist will probably have to work hard to substantiate his worth before he is accepted.

To increase the proficiency and acceptance of Interventionists, it is imperative that ongoing communication be scheduled between the Interventionists and the staff to resolve issues that may arise. This articulation would, hopefully, overcome the tendency of the professional staff and the Interventionist to develop inaccurate expectancies of each other's roles. A deep trust and respect for one another's roles must be developed between the professional staff and the Interventionists.

Mutual trust is particularly important in relation to the removal and returning of children to class or to school. For example, the teacher must have faith in the Interventionist's decision that the child is calm enough to be returned to class. Similarly, the Interventionist must trust that the teacher seeks his aid because he needs it.

Teachers and Interventionists must also become used to the nuances of one another's professional styles so that they may use these verbal and nonverbal signals to resolve potentially volatile situations.

In-Service Education

The Aide. The aide should have on-the-job or released time career ladder opportunities to enable him to advance toward a college degree or teacher certification, if he so desires. Summer stipends should also be available to the aide so that he may take college course work.

Physical Aspects. The Interventionist should keep in a high state of physical condition. His mastery of nonpunitive physical intervention techniques should be ongoing.

Affective Aspects. Educational programs should be developed to effect positive changes in the feelings, emotions, and attitudes of the Interventionists. For example, much discussion in the literature has centered upon teacher understanding of student aggression. However, there appears to be little literature related to helping teachers cope with their own aggressive feelings which may build up after hours of working with aggressive and violent children.

Included in the continued in-service program, therefore, must be a system to help the Interventionist understand and release his pent-up emotions and feelings of aggression in a positive way. One such system is the discussion groups described in Chapter Seven as part of the New Teacher Project.

Help-Seeking System

Many systems have been suggested for use in securing the assistance of the Interventionist. These systems have run the gamut from sending a child for help to the use of a buzzer or light system activated by a key or push button.

The system I would suggest would provide each teacher with a small transmitter with its own frequency. These transmitters would be small enough to be hooked onto a belt, hung around the neck or placed in a pocket. Because of the size of the transmitter, the teacher could carry it on his person and actuate the transmitter which could activate a buzzer and light on a monitor panel.[m]

Parent Understanding of Interventionist Role

Upon intake of students, the role of the Interventionist must be explained to parents, *particularly the Interventionist's last resort nonpunitive physical restraining role.*

The question no longer appears to be whether we need such professionals in our schools. A distorted model of the Interventionist is already in many urban schools. The question seems to be whether those who are now there should be allowed to continue to follow a police security model.

In the main, it appears that the majority of administrators have opted for the passive role in discipline and security. They have negated their legal responsibilities and have turned the job over to police oriented security programs. Hence, most of our schools are following a security instead of an educational-Interventionist approach.

The foregoing should not be taken as derogatory of many competent and concerned men and women who have transcended the police model to perform excellent intervention work.

A prerequisite for receiving an Interventionist team would be for the school to organize a problem solving program and procedure that would include staff, students, parents, and community representatives.

CORPORAL PUNISHMENT VS. PHYSICAL RESTRAINT

The concept of corporal punishment probably has been argued since there have been schools. However, the reason that the anticorporal punishment arguments

---

[m]A system named Silent Communication Alarm System Network (SCAN) designed by NORCON Electronics Inc., 1257 Utica Avenue, Brooklyn, New York 11203, is now operating in a number of schools.

and court actions appear to have lacked success, when compared with some of our humanitarian advances in other areas, is that most of those arguing against its use appear to have done so in isolation from the reality of school conditions. Very often, corporal punishment is a teacher's last resort in response to a continuing and intensely frustrating condition.

There are also differences in viewpoint between the suburbs and the inner city in relation to the corporal punishment discussion. Inner city parents seem less concerned about corporal punishment than they are of illegal suspensions, improper labeling of students, the covert racist ploys that some educators use knowingly or unknowingly on black youngsters,[n] as well as the assigning of acting-out or handicapped youngsters to home instruction because of a lack of alternative, but often legally mandated, facilities.

Some of the inner city school conditions that must be considered within the context of the anticorporal punishment position include the following:

1. There are students who lose control of their behavior and act out in a negatively aggressive and violent way against their fellow students and teachers and thereby interfere with instruction and endanger the health and safety of students, school personnel, and themselves.
2. Many lower class students court aggression and violence and have been conditioned for physical and autocratic discipline.
3. There are some aggressive and violent students who lose control of their behavior and must sometimes be stopped and controlled physically.
4. Few alternatives to corporal punishment have been available to educators when a student has refused a reasonable request for compliance with school rules.
5. Very few placement alternatives such as the assistance of special teacher or resource rooms are available to help the emotionally and physically handicapped, or the child with learning disabilities.
6. The teacher is usually completely on his or her own with little or no support from anyone.

Throughout this and earlier chapters, many of these six considerations have been discussed. Therefore, this discussion will deal with the difference between corporal punishment and physically intervening by restraining the child who has lost control of his behavior.

Because there are these youngsters in our schools who lose control of their behavior, we must develop methods and techniques, and a guiding philosophy for nonpunitive physical intervention and restraining techniques and

[n]I am unalterably opposed to corporal punishment as well as to the covert racist or inhuman ploys. I am on the Board of Directors of the National Committee to Abolish Corporal Punishment in Schools, which grew from a meeting of the American Civil Liberties Union and the American Orthopsychiatric Association (Maeroff, 1972).

responses to overt negative aggression and violence in place of corporal punishment. This is philosophy that is sorely lacking, not only with school personnel but with law enforcement authorities. American educators and others appear to lack understanding of the need to develop nonpunitive intervention techniques. Most Americans, it often appears, would rather use a gun than Mace to stop someone.

For those who feel queasy about touching or becoming physical with a school-age youngster, the National Commission on the Causes and Prevention of Violence (1969) suggested that there is "legitimate" as well as "illegitimate" violence within the "context of a particular human society or cultural tradition (p. 3)." Additionally,

> All societies must draw moral and legal distinctions between legitimate and illegitimate violence. One traditional and vital function of social order, of the state and its laws, has been to determine in particular cases when violence is legitimate (as in self-defense, discipline of children, . . .) when it is illegitimate (as in violent crime, . . .) (p. 2).
>
> There is, therefore, no universal agreement of a definition of the term "violence" which makes it mean something that is always to be condemned. For purposes of commencing our study, we have defined "violence" simply as the threat or use of force that results, or is intended to result, in the injury or forcible restraint or intimidation of persons, or the destruction or forcible seizure of property.
>
> There is no implicit value judgment in this definition. The maintenance of law and order falls within it, for a policeman may find it necessary in the course of duty to threaten or use force, even to injure or kill an individual. Wars are included within this definition, as in some punishment of children. It also includes police brutality, . . . and the physical abuse of a child.
>
> This definition has important implications for our understanding of the causes and prevention of the illegitimate violence that our society condemns. For example, it helps us to recognize that illegitimate violence, like most deviant behavior, is on a continuum with and dynamically similar to legitimate violence. The parent who spanks a child may be engaging in legitimate violence, but for the parent to break the child's arm would be illegitimate violence.
>
> A neutral definition of violence also helps us to recognize that some minimum level of illegitimate violence is to be expected in a free and rapidly changing industrial society. Maintaining a system of law enforcement capable of eliminating all illegitimate individual and group violence might so increase the level of legitimate violence that the harm to other values would be intolerable. . . .
>
> The elimination of all violence in a free society is impossible. But the better control of illegitimate violence in our democratic society

is an urgent imperative, and one within our means to accomplish (p. 3).

With that in mind, one of the important points that must be understood is that when a student acts in a violent way against others, some form of counter violence or force may have to be used to contain or stop his actions. However, the amount and type of so-called violence or force that must be used is what is important. The concept of physically controlling a child has implicit in its approach that one use only as much force as is necessary to physically restrain the youngster. Meting out punishment is not the role of the professional. Additionally, as noted earlier in this chapter in relation to the Interventionist concept, the youngster being restrained physically does not, then, have the need to "get even."

To establish further the difference between physical restraint and corporal punishment, the following definitions are suggested.

1. Physical restraint is intended to be used solely to stop the action of the child.
2. Physical restraint does not intend the force exerted to restrain to be experienced as a punishment, while corporal punishment intends pain to be experienced as a penalty or punishment.
3. Physical restraint is applied only during the performance of the negative act by the child while corporal punishment may be administered during the performance of the act or after it has been completed.
4. When corporal punishment is used during the negative act, its function is both physical restraint and punishment. When applied after the act, it serves only the function of punishment. The important point is that where corporal punishment is administered during the act, physical restraint could have been used instead to stop the child's negative action.[o]

The use of physical restraint on a child does not preclude additional punishment if indicated. However, the additional punishment should be reasonably nonphysical and not carried out in the heat of confrontation.

Finally, it seems illogical and hypocritical for educators to preach the need for nonviolent resolution to problems while in the same breath calling for the retention of corporal punishment. Educators must realize that when they practice corporal punishment, a value is attached to the use of physical force to achieve goals, and this action becomes a model of negative aggression and violent behavior which could and often does lead to imitation by school children. There

[o]These points were presented in a slightly different form in a paper "Corporal Punishment and Physical Restraint: There is a Difference," presented by Ms. Adrienne James, Executive Director, Operation Friendship, Detroit, Michigan at the 48th Annual International Convention of the Council for Exceptional Children, Chicago, Illinois, April 23, 1970. Printed with the permission of Ms. James.

is already a good deal of evidence that finds physically aggressive children coming from homes where they were disciplined physically and aggressively. If educators do not play a role in stopping the circular action of negative aggressive behavior, who will?

Furthermore, when a teacher uses corporal punishment, he foolishly allows his board of education to place him in this position by their not providing him with a nonpunitive alternative to controlling a child's negative behavior. Indeed, teachers should remember this point as discipline increasingly becomes an element in negotiations between teachers and school boards.

Teacher-Student Sexuality and Discipline

The phenomenon of teacher-student sexuality exists in all schools— inner city, suburban, and rural. As Greenberg (1968, p. 178) noted, "Adults of varying experience and children in varying stages of psychosexual development encounter each other within the school, and inevitably many feelings are aroused." Additionally, as Gilder (1973, p. 42) pointed out, "sex is the life force and cohesive impulse of a people, and their very character will be deeply affected by how sexuality is sublimated and expressed, denied or attained." Generally, the expression of sexuality between students and teachers is handled in a mature, nondisruptuve way. However, when sexuality is based on widely differing life styles and conflicting expectations and racial fantasies, and when it arouses strong conscious and unconscious sexual feelings, it can play a role in discipline.

Teacher-student sexual feelings may cause problems in all schools. However, their effect is exacerbated when the relationship is between adults and youngsters of different socioeconomic life styles and color, the situation which exists in so many inner city schools.

In inner city schools, these aroused sexual feelings may lead to the suspension of black male students. They may also be the cause of the volatility of black female students—particularly in the junior high school. This section will discuss the relationship between student-teacher sexuality and discipline problems in inner city schools. The discussion will not be all-inclusive; rather, it will be a beginning that others, hopefully, will add to with further discussion and investigation.

Reality 76 describes a physical attack on a young white female teacher by a black fifteen-year-old male student. After the incident, the student was suspended and then sent to a special school for maladjusted boys. The description will show the incident was a frightening experience for the young teacher and for the young male student as well.

REALITY 76

The class was seated waiting for the period to start. The teacher was at the door supervising the changing of classes.

A male student about fifteen years of age grabbed the teacher's arms as he entered the room. He pushed her toward the desk, while turning the lights off. He then bent the teacher's back over the desk and he placed himself between her legs.

"You my woman. Everyone knows it," he said as he leaned over her holding her arms down on the desk beside her head.

The teacher in a frightened voice cried out, "No, I'm not. You are too young."

After a few more words, the youngster released the teacher and ran from the room.

If a sexual attack was intended, it never took place as the youngster never opened his pants. If a physical attack was the objective, he did not succeed in this either as he only held the teacher's wrists tightly. Actually, the incident was the culmination of the white teacher's inappropriate, and possibly unknowing, sexually provocative behavior.

The teacher was in her early twenties, about five feet four inches tall, slightly built, and frail in appearance. Her classroom discipline and organization was poor. Her students did pretty much as they chose. Her guiding philosophy was to play the role of the forlorn woman and have her students discipline themselves for her; a completely passive role in discipline.

She wore short skirts and often sat on her desk when talking to the class. Older boys were known to pinch her backside when walking in the hall. In the main, she did nothing to discourage this student behavior.

In her relations with the student who attacked her, she had permitted a certain degree of intimacy. She often remained after school alone with him in her room. On many occasions, he helped her on with her coat and she allowed him to look through the pictures in her wallet when alone with him.

After the incident, the youth's mother reported that she knew her son was uncommonly interested in the teacher. For the past few weeks he was dressing specially for her and talked about her incessantly at home. The mother, although worried and uneasy about her son's behavior at home, did nothing. Had the teacher been more mature and aware of her own sexuality and the historical problems associated with black male and white female relations, the incident need not have taken place.

Unfortunately, the actions of the youngster and the teacher in Reality 76 may be more typical than we wish to admit. There are three reasons for these teacher-student problems: (1) the historical perspective of our sexual customs, (2) the differences in the way lower class and middle class life experience educates and conditions us to cope with sexuality, and (3) the male and female black and white relationships that are affected by the historical racist fantasies related to black and white male and female sexuality.

Johnson and Johnson (1968) report that our attitudes, laws, and moral standards are an outgrowth of the Jewish patterns of the Old Testament.

In the Old Testament, sex, although regarded highly, was subjected to strict regulation and was considered to be primarily for propagation. An additional influence on our sexual standards resulted from the highly negative attitude toward women that the early Christian fathers added to Jewish sexual regulations, which they adopted almost totally into the body of Christian sexual morality. Today, our official legal structure and sexual morality is based upon the Judeo-Christian sexual tradition that was brought in intensified form to America by our seventeenth century Puritan fathers, who added a "highly regulatory and antisexual pattern (p. 86)." Innumerable threads of these three factors affect the relationships of white male and female school personnel with black secondary school students.

In light of the above, and despite all the supposed social changes that relate to our patterns of sexual attitudes and behavior, the female is still very sensuous, easily arousing the male sexually. Because of past conditioning, the male possesses no such power to equally arouse the average female by his merely being in close proximity. Even if the female is aroused, she does not possess the anatomy to embarrass her.[p] And, as Kate Millett (1970, p. 116) has informed us,

> All the best scientific evidence today unmistakably tends toward the conclusion that the female possesses, biologically and inherently, a far greater capacity for sexuality than the male, both as to frequency of coitus, and as to frequency of orgasm.

To which we can add Gilder's (1973, p. 42) point that,

> Males are the more sexual outsiders and inferior. A far smaller portion of their lives is devoted to specifically sexual activity. Their own distinctively sexual experience is limited to erection and ejaculation; their primary sexual drive leads only toward copulation. Beside the socially indispensable and psychologically crucial experience of motherhood, men are irredeemably subordinate.

To add to these inherent advantages, the middle class woman begins to develop her female sexual patterns, practicing even more and various forms of

[p]It is common for middle class adolescent males to wear a "jock" over underwear or to wear a number of pairs of underwear to a dance or party so that his dancing partner will not feel his erection. Hence, his embarrassment reinforces his conditioning to withdraw, to repress, or sublimate his sexual feelings. Furthermore, the one real ego-building power he imagined he held over females, the power to impregnate, has been taken from him too, with foams, coils, pills, and diaphragms. Through legalized abortion and birth control, the female now has complete control over procreation.

An additional male depressant derives from the anatomical and biological aspects of male and female sexuality. Accepting that both are entitled to sexual satisfaction, we again find an unevenness in early sexual experience and conditioning. The adolescent male's quick climax and resulting loss of erection, often leaves his partner frustrated and him with feelings of inferiority. Hence, these early experiences also lead him to repress, to be ashamed of, and to sublimate his sexuality.

sexual display, adding to her innate sexuality—particularly that artful display of her body.q

Actually, supposedly for the first time in the history of this country, we are beginning to hear reports of impotence on the part of young men in their early twenties. Impotence reports used to be heard from men in their forties and fifties. The point is that many females are very sensual. Furthermore, our middle class sexual mores permit, and even expect, a certain amount of provocative activity by attractive girls. When they use this sexuality with middle class males, the middle class males are expected to withdraw, suppress, or sublimate their sexuality. This then is the behavior middle class males and females have become conditioned to when they come to teach in an inner city school.

On the other hand, in poverty and ghetto life styles, sex and sexuality in language and actions are treated with greater openness and acceptance. Poussaint (1972) reports that blacks have, in particular, a unique cultural and social experience.

> From Africa, blacks brought with them an unperverted attitude toward sex and procreation. Though erotic outlets were regulated by the customs and mores of many different sub-groups, chastity was not necessarily a virtue and appropriate premarital relations were not frowned upon. Sex was considered an important and pleasurable part of life (p. 91).

Lower class males and females, particularly males, are not conditioned to sublimate or repress their sexuality; in fact, the lower class life style conditions for a more open sexuality.

Although the sex studies performed in the United States have ignored blacks, one recent study dealing with "Sexuality, Contraception, and Pregnancy Among Young Unwed Females in the United States" by Zelnik and Kantner (1970), had a total population of 4,611 aged 15 through 19, of whom 1,479 were black females. Although they dealt with "simple demographic controls, such as age and race," and refrained from using controls related to socioeconomic status, undoubtedly some of the differences they found in sexual behavior between blacks and whites can partially be accounted for "in terms of differences in socioeconomic factors."

qTo walk on a liberal university campus during the warm months is to be continually stimulated with bra-less sexuality of women. When this is discussed with females, they insist that this is only a male problem; it is not their fault that males are affected this way. For that matter, even with a bra, little is left to the imagination. Indeed, this fall, returning students and faculty described the beaches they visited where women bathed topless.

It seems to me that many men and young men must be repressing or fantasizing their sexual feelings when viewing either of the above scenes; to look and not touch can be a frustrating emotional experience. To argue that it is society that has conditioned the male to become so easily excited and that he will just have to learn not to become excited, is absurd.

They found pronounced differences between blacks and whites. Blacks, for example, had intercourse at a significantly earlier age than whites, and proportionately more of them had intercourse. Their data reported that by age eighteen, 80.8 percent of the black females have had intercourse while only 40.4 percent of the whites have had intercourse. By age sixteen, 46.4 percent of the black females have had intercourse as compared with only 17.5 percent of the white females. Interestingly, the study also found that although more black females have had intercourse, the white nonvirgins are more promiscuous and have sex more frequently. This suggests that black nonvirgins are more loyal to their lovers while white female nonvirgins are less loyal to their lovers. Hence, the black female may attach more feeling to her loving.

This may suggest an explanation for the volatility of black female students, particularly in the junior high school. For example, even in all white schools, we find female students jealous of attractive female teachers and female student teachers. It appears that the female students apparently see new young female teachers as threatening rivals for their boy friends.

The same feelings may be going on in inner city schools intensified by the racial fantasies and socioeconomic differences between students and teachers. In the white middle class school the behavior of the white female teacher is familiar to both students and teachers. In the inner city school, the white female, as both the forbidden fruit and the white queen, is acting in her middle class flirtatious-sexually provocative way toward their black female students' boy friends (to whom they are more loyal than are white girls to their white boy friends) in a way that they see as unfair competition. Sensing or assuming this interaction between the white female teacher and their boy friends, the black female students may react by being in a constant state of sexual jealousy, which may explain the volatileness.

The experiences of the black and white workers in the Southern civil rights movement also reflected the black females' feelings of being threatened by the black male-white female relationships.

> Black girls were sometimes frantically jealous of the white girls and in a state of panic because they feared that they would lose their boy friends to white girls. The black girls were usually the most insistent in demanding that whites be put out of the movement and were the strongest supporters of exclusive black consciousness programs (Poissaint, 1972, p. 10).

> Negro women tend to have a generalized, deep-seated resentment toward white women because of society's superior valuation of 'white standards of beauty.' . . . They see white female civil rights workers as competitors for their Negro men; and since the Negro man has been brainwashed for centuries with 'sacred white woman-hood,' many of the Negro girls see these white girls as unfair competition (Poussaint, 1966, p. 403).

Additionally, though black males in the Mississippi civil rights project were concerned over white men's racist exploitation of black women, they were not as threatened as were black women over the black male-white female relationships.

My contention about the negative effects of some white female teachers' flirtatious actions is further supported by the evidence gathered by Dr. Alvin Poussaint (1972) in interviews and personal participation with black and white workers during the Mississippi voter registration drive of the summer of 1966. Many of the actions of white female middle class civil rights workers are parallel to the actions of some white middle class teachers in inner city schools. Indeed, Poussaint reports that the black power philosophy which came to the forefront in the summer of 1966, "in part reflected the already-existing strong anti-'white civil rights workers' sentiments among black participants in the movement (p. 7)," much of this was precipitated by the actions of the white workers, particularly the females.

This antagonism came about for a number of reasons. Many of the white volunteers possessed "certain psychological attitudes of racial superiority which were often subconscious, which blacks sarcastically referred to as the 'White African Queen Complex' in the female and the 'Tarzan Complex' in the male (p. 8)." Many of the white workers exhibited deep psychological problems. Not only did they use the movement to try to work out their problems, but they used the black communities as a setting to express their rebellious and antisocial behavior. In an attempt to show how "free" they felt they were about working with blacks, many of the white workers flouted the social and moral standards of the black and white communities they were working in with "unorthodox behavior." An unkempt style of dress was one of the more common manifestations of this pathology. (This is discussed further in the next chapter.) The local inhabitants who could not go North after the summer looked on this behavior as "thinly veiled white racism" and disrespect toward the black community.

Many of the white workers exhibited a pathological guilt need that caused them to court dangerous and painful situations that often led to jail or the sought-after badge of the bruises from beatings. That this behavior involved not only their safety but that of their black coworkers and the black community, often seemed to be of secondary concern.

Very often, the crisis in black-white worker relationships centered around sociosexual conflicts, as well as the need to suffer.

> For instance, a white girl, wishing to display her newfound sense of racial brotherhood, might reach out and affectionately take the hand of a black male worker in front of a Mississippi Highway Patrolman or local white toughs, or worse still, both. In Mississippi, this might well be considered a suicidal gesture on the part of the girl. However, it could also be a homicidal gesture subconsciously directed at the male, who, under the circumstances, might easily be

lynched or beaten up. Similarly, a black fellow might get beaten up by local officials while the white girl escaped with an epithet, if they were apprehended riding in a car together (p. 10).

In addition to the aforementioned, the black male and white female relationships greatly preoccupied the black males' time. They were very much aware that their relationships with white women broke the most sacred of Southern taboos. Because of this

.... in nearly all social situations with white women, they were plagued by ambivalence as well as by a mixture of feelings of fear, hate, suspicion, and adoration. In fact, so much energy was expended by both black men and women on discussing white girls that there were many days when no project work was accomplished. The problem was further exacerbated by the sometimes deliberately flirtatious behavior of white girls. Even some of the "black national-ist" types continued a vigorous pursuit of the white volunteers (Poussaint, 1972, p. 11).

In turn, some of the white girls appeared overly preoccupied with how frequently they were propositioned.

Many of these white female workers, as well as teachers in inner city schools, experienced situations that were often physically dangerous as well as psychologically nervewracking. Most often, the white workers found "them-selves at the center of an emotionally shattering cross fire of racial tensions, fears, and hatreds that have been nurtured for centuries (Poussaint, 1966, p. 401)."

Some of the white girls were insightful and mature enough to handle the cross-currents and problems and were able to be productive and function. Most, however, despite their good intentions and strengths, were not able to cope with tensions of their frustrations and personal fantasies concerning their missionary role in civil rights. Often they were blamed for problems which any of the projects were experiencing; they became scapegoats. At times they became the targets of vulgar and lewd accusations. Often, no matter what a white girl's personal relations were, she was "accused by both white and black Southerners of having perverse sexual interest in Negro men (Poussaint, 1966, p. 406)."

Although white males appear not to have created the sociosexual problems that the white females and black males created during the voter registration programs, their historical role in perpetuating sexual myths about blacks set the tense atmosphere for the problems.

The English who settled America brought with them set social attitudes, sexual mores, as well as "certain more or less definite ideas about African sexuality (Jordan, 1968, p. 136)." Englishmen associated lecherousness and sexuality with "heathen, savage, beast-like men," which they considered Negroes to be (p. 33). Their association of potent sexuality with Africans and warm climates predated any real English contact with Africa. Virtually all those living on the continent were convinced by the literature of Europe that Africans were venerous and lustful (p. 33). One report by a Spanish Moroccan Moor who converted to Christianity wrote in 1526, that Negroes, in addition to other beastial qualities, "have great swarms of Harlots among them; whereupon a man may easily conjecture their manner of living (p. 34)." Additional reporting described Negro men with "large Propagators (p. 34)."

Although there were regional styles in racial intermixture, miscegenation was extensive in all the English colonies. In the American colonies, and even now, typical sexual liaisons involved white men and black women. However, the combination of white women and black men was "far more common than is generally supposed (Jordan, 1968, p. 138)."

In some colonies—the West Indian colonies, for example, and to some extent in South Carolina—the miscegenation practices were more inflexible than in others. White women neither married nor slept with black men, while white men customarily took black women as mistresses. As black slaves assumed a greater work role, the white female appeared to become more protected and more of an ornament. She could "withdraw from the world or to create an unreal one of her own (p. 148)." A tense biracial atmosphere was created where

> ... she was made to feel that sensual involvement with the opposite sex burned bright and hot with unquenchable passion and at the same time that any such involvement was utterly repulsive. Accordingly, ... she approached her prospective legitimate sexual partners as if she were picking up a live coal in one hand and a dead rat in the other (p. 149).

Jordan (1968, p. 150) also points out that the colonial American and English cultures and experiences were male dominated. Hence, the specifically masculine modes of behavior and thought that shaped the psychological needs of men to a considerable extent set the sexually oriented beliefs of the black that still hold in America today.

The colonial male considered the black woman especially passionate. Though the white woman's experience to some extent inhibited her sexual expression, the different situation the Negro woman found herself in encouraged it.

> For by calling the Negro woman passionate they were offering the best possible justification for their own passions. Not only did the Negro woman's warmth constitute a logical explanation for the white man's infidelity, but, much more important, it helped shift responsibility from himself to her. If she was *that* lascivious—well, a

man could scarcely be blamed for succumbing against overwhelming odds (p. 151).

The concept that the black male was rather promiscuous, lusty, and virile gave the white man a more potentially explosive and complex problem to deal with. Consequently, the English colonists in America appeared to add a half-conscious and interesting corollary that is still a part of today's fantasies and fears. He believed that all blacks lusted for white women. Of course there probably was some basis for this feeling as a black male's sexual intercourse with a white woman would have some symbolic gesture of retribution against white men (as indicated by Cleaver, 1968, p. 14). However,

> No matter how firmly based in fact, . . . the image of the sexually aggressive Negro was rooted even more firmly in deep strata of irrationality. For it is apparent that white men projected their own desires onto Negroes: their own passion for Negro women was not fully acceptable to society or the self and hence not readily admissible. Sexual desires could be effectively denied and the accompanying anxiety and guilt in some measure assuaged, however, by imputing them to others. It is not we, but others, who are guilty. It is not we who lust, but they. Not only this, but white men anxious over their own sexual inadequacy were touched by a racking fear and jealousy. Perhaps the Negro better performed his nocturnal offices than the white man. Perhaps, indeed, the white man's woman really wanted the Negro more than she wanted him (Jordan, 1958, pp. 151-152).

The white man's fear of the black's supposed superior sexuality had led to early laws calling for the castration of Negroes for crimes (Jordan, 1968). Additionally, many black men have been "publicly castrated and lynched for supposedly raping white women (Poussaint, 1972, p. 114)."

These fantasies and fears that grew from our racism have conditioned many black and white Americans to act in ways based on their unconscious feelings related to black and white sexuality. Many of these actions can be observed being played out in the inner city classroom by teachers and students.

A black youngster growing up in the ghetto may attach to his white teacher the image of a clean and wholesome middle class America; she may become his feminine ideal. And, depending upon her maturity, he may be helped or hurt. On the other hand, she may become the object of a black student's pent-up aggression and hate. To do something negatively to her may serve as a source of revenge for his pent-up rage. To some black males, to seduce or rape as many white women as possible is to sexually and symbolically restore their manhood. To Eldridge Cleaver (1968, p. 14), for example, rape was his "insurrectionary act."

I became a rapist. To refine my technique and *modus operandi*, I started out by practicing on black girls in the ghetto—in the black ghetto where dark and vicious deeds appear not as abberations or deviations from the norm, but as part of the sufficiency of the Evil of a day—and when I considered myself smooth enough, I crossed the tracks and sought out white prey. I did this consciously, deliberately, willfully, methodically—though looking back I see that I was in a frantic, wild, and completely abandoned frame of mind. . . .

Rape was an insurrectionary act. It delighted me that I was defying and trampling upon the white man's law, upon his system of values, and that I was defiling his women—and this point, I believe, was the most satisfying to me because I was very resentful over the historical fact of how the white man used the black woman. I felt I was getting revenge. From the site of an act of rape, consternation spreads outwardly in concentric circles. I wanted to send waves of consternation through the white race.

Philip Roth (1967) in *Portnoy's Complaint* also expressed a need to get even, to get revenge. However, because he was white and Jewish and had experienced a different life style, his revenge was not violent. Nevertheless, his revenge was also through a sexual outlet. For him, to seduce (not rape) a WASP; to make love to an "aristocratic Yankee beauty whose forebears arrived on these shores in the seventeenth century: a phenomenon known as Hating Your Goy and Eating One Too (p. 233)," was enough.

"What I'm saying, Doctor, is that I don't seem to stick my dick up these girls, as much as I stick it up their backgrounds—as though through fucking I will discover America. *Conquer* America—maybe that's more like it (p. 235)."

. . . Sally Maulsby was just something nice a son once did for his dad. A little vengeance on Mr. Lindabury for all those nights and Sundays Jack Portnoy spent collecting down in the colored district. A little bonus extracted from Boston & Northwestern, for all those years of service, and exploitation (pp. 240-241)."

James Baldwin (1963, p. 151) also writes of the relationships between sex and violence in the experience of black men. His words graphically describe the depth of the black man's feelings.

In most of the novels written by Negroes until today (with the exception of Chester Hime's *If He Hollers Let Him Go*) there is a great space where sex ought to be; and what usually fills this space is violence. . . .

This violence, . . . is gratuitous and compulsive . . . because the root of the violence is never examined. The root is rage. It is the rage, almost literally the howl, of a man who is being castrated. . . . . [T]here is probably no greater (or misleading) body of sexual myths in the world today than those which have proliferated around the figure of the American Negro. This means that he is penalized for the guilty imagination of the white people who invest him with their hates and longings, and is the principal target of their sexual paranoia.

An awareness of this background should give us some insight into the nature of the discipline problems evolving from white and black teacher-student relations. Too often, female teachers, knowingly or unknowingly, act in sexually provocative ways. Sometimes, also, youngsters behave negatively against female teachers without being sexually provoked. At times black male students may say something to a white teacher that may be only a test of her ability to control him and set limits without sexual connotations. At other times, his actions may actually reflect a reaction to her overt sexuality, or they may grow out of his own fantasies, or racism, or a combination of both.

Some white female teachers' conscious or unconscious sexually provocative actions that have been observed run the gamut from acting in an excessively flirtatious way, to placing or pressing one's breasts on the desk or against a male student's arm or body while helping him with his work, and include wearing a sheer or see-through blouse or tight sweater, with or without a bra; wearing an overly tight skirt, dress, slacks, or pants suit; or sitting in front of the class with an excessively short skirt that exposes her underpants when she bends over or reaches up to write on the board.

Depending upon his control, a lower class black male student may react to sexual provocation in many ways indicative of his makeup. However, his reaction to sexual stimulation and provocation is usually more direct than that of the middle class male student. The lower class black male usually *acts*, while the middle class white or black male usually sublimates or represses his response. Reality 76 was but one example.

A reading of report slips by white female teachers concerning black male students showed incidents in which students grabbed the teacher, threatened the teacher, stood in the door blocking her way, cursed, punched, took the teacher's keys, or pinched her. Others reported "rubbing against me, touching my dress, or touching me." Additional reports included, "He ran his hand down my backside." "He ran his hand down my arm," and "He ran his hand through my hair."

Most of these reports described reasonably controlled black male student reactions to white female teachers. Part of the reason for the reaction of the youngster described in Reality 76 was that the provocation obviously was of greater duration. Although he had more control to start with, even he had reached his saturation point.

Often, the white middle class female teacher is unable to differentiate between a threat, a proposal, and teasing. Usually she can differentiate and handle this from someone who is white and middle class; and, possibly from someone who is black and middle class. She has not, however, been educated to deal with aggressive sexual behavior from someone who is black, male, and lower class.

In the next few Realities, the black male student's actions toward white female staff are described. Whether they acted in response to the female teacher's conscious or unconscious sexual provocation is uncertain. However, the students apparently interpreted the teacher's style or specific actions in a way that suggested to the student that he try his testing game. Or he may have believed all the racist fantasies he has learned. Consequently black male students most often test new female teachers in a sexual way while testing a male teacher physically.

REALITY 77

The new teacher was attempting to teach a history lesson when one of her black male students said,

"You look very pretty."

She blushed and said, "Thank you," as the class laughed.

Whereupon, he said, "I would like to take you to bed. Don't worry; I will know what to do."

Her blushing turned to tears and she ran from the room.

REALITY 78

The class had just ended. One of the boys remained to talk with the teacher.

"Are you going to the prom?" he asked.

"I'm thinking about it," she responded.

"Good, leave your husband home. We can go over to my place after the prom is over," he said, as he put his hand on her hand.

REALITY 79

The young teacher was attempting to get order so that she could start her lesson. As she approached the back of the room where a number of boys stood together, one of them mumbled, "I'm gonna fuck you."

REALITY 80

The assistant principal was in his office on the second floor when he received a call from the secretary.

"Please, come quickly," she screamed.

He ran down the two flights to the office and found her alone and looking frightened.

"What happened?" he asked.

Hesitatingly, she reported. "You know that tall boy that was reported to you yesterday? He came in here, stood in front of my desk, and opened his pants. Then he tucked in his shirt. After he tucked in his shirt, he closed his pants, zippered them up, put his belt back, and then left. It took him a long time to do it. He did it to me twice. I saw him standing outside waiting for the office to be empty."

The assistant principal thought for a few minutes and said, "Take this telephone book and put it over here on this front table. Then, if he comes in again, ask him to please hand you the book after he finishes tucking in his shirt. Or, if you want, tell him in no uncertain terms to get out of the office if he has to fix his shirt."

"I can't. You talk to him."

The assistant principal agreed and left to look for the youngster. After hunting through the school, he found the youngster in his class. He asked him to please step outside to talk.

"Hey, what the heck are you trying to do to the secretary downstairs," he asked.

"Oh man, nothin'," the youth answered.

"Look, you have that woman so scared, the next time you pull that pants business on her, she is going to panic and go out of the window. Then I'll get you on homicide—so cut it out. You proved your point. She is afraid of you."

His face broke into a smile and chuckled. He put his hand out for some skin, and said, "Ok, no more."

He never did it again. Actually, his behavior improved after the incident and he was eventually graduated from the school.

Some additional examples include the following. A young, short female teacher in a tight, short dress had a habit of turning her back to the students and reaching up to write on the top of the board. When the class left the room, she stood in the doorway with her back against the door jamb. Consequently, the students had to be careful not to brush against her as they left. Once, one of the male students looked into her eyes as he was passing and said, "You got some fine legs."

The teacher did not know what had precipitated the comment and was completely confused by it.

In another incident, a black male high school student terrified a new art teacher when she was alone in her classroom. He entered, took a tray of paper clips from her desk and sat down on a chair directly in front of her. He stared at her as he slowly sank into his chair moving his legs out straight in front and apart. He then took one clip at a time and started to make a clip chain. The teacher sat looking at him transfixed and frightened, and not saying a word. The mood was broken when an older experienced teacher entered the room and chased him out.

As soon as he was out of the room, the teacher burst into tears. Whether the teacher's sexual fantasies about black males, or males in general, frightened her, we do not know.

Unquestionably, some male teachers and aides also flaunt their sexuality. However, the flaunting of their sexuality does not appear to cause as many problems as does the female teacher's flaunting of her sexuality. Male teachers and aides can be extremely flirtatious and sexually arouse some female students by wearing tight pants, wearing an open shirt exposing their chests, or wearing a see-through shirt without an undershirt.

They can also arouse or annoy a female student by touching her more often than is necessary, by staring at her breasts or her legs, or by teasing. They can embarrass, arouse, or annoy her to the point where she may become disruptive. Additionally, a male teacher who is very repressed sexually may cause problems for a female student who expresses a good deal of openness and sexuality.

More aggressive female students have been known to proposition young male teachers. Such questions as "Are you a virgin?" "Are you good in bed?" or "How would you like to go to bed with me?" are often asked of new young male and female teachers by male and female students. However, what is important here is that, most often, the male teacher who makes advances, either on his own or in response to a female student's actions, or provokes a female student may be suspended or fired. Indeed, when there is a sexually motivated problem between a white female student and a black male teacher, the black teacher is always "guilty."

Some white female teachers know that they are both the forbidden fruit and prize, and will consciously or unconsciously tease young black male students. Most assuredly, however, this teacher will usually break out of her fantasizing of being threatened and dominated by a stronger being, and the male student will be disciplined in no uncertain terms. Because of her conditioning, she expected that he was supposed to look but not touch. Taking all this into consideration, the relations between black male students and white female teachers appear to be more precarious and dangerous to the black student than are the relationships between white male teachers and black female students.

When white male teachers flirt with black female students, they are not violating the dogmas of the dominant white society. It appears that some of the liaisons do end in bed where, presumably, each works harder at satisfying the other sexually in fulfilling America's sexual mythology.[r] In reality, however, in

---

[r]My personal feelings must be pointed out here. It is wrong for any teacher to have an affair with a student, period.

most cases, the sexual achievements of both remain the expression of their racist fantasies about one another.

What is important is that the black female student (who may even be more experienced sexually than her white teacher) will not be disciplined for "attacking" or "attempting to rape" her teacher. She is not sent to a school for disruptive or delinquent girls as a result of the affair. Hopefully, the liaison was not brutal and no emotional scars were left. In addition, although data is not available, it appears as though more male teachers than female teachers marry their students.

Stated another way, because black male-white female teacher relationships are more against our society's mores, the black male student's actions more often lead to his being punished through suspension or other disciplinary action. On the other hand, black female students are rarely punished for involvement with white male teachers, even where the flirtations result in actual intercourse.

It must also be noted that black female teachers are increasingly having the same problems with black male students as do the white female teachers. One reason for this phenomenon may be that larger numbers of blacks are moving into the middle classes. Consequently, more black middle class females are becoming teachers.

The problem related to black and white male and female sexuality between teachers and students also exists among teachers. Occasionally, white female teachers have discipline problems that stem from their being emotionally upset by a black teacher's trying to seduce them. Sometimes, when all else fails, the black male teacher will run the game of calling the white female teacher a racist in hopes of working on her guilt and immaturity. At other times, white female teachers have upset a school because of their zeal in chasing black faculty. Of course, I am sure there have been cases of white male teachers reporting black female students for putting aside their advances.

"Faggot" is probably one of the most often used words in an inner city school. This usage is, to some extent, probably related to the lower class involvement with machismo. Consequently, the overtly homosexual or lesbian teacher may also have discipline problems resulting from students taunting them. Unquestionably, these problems related to male and female sexuality take place in suburban, urban, and rural schools too. However, the problems are exacerbated in inner city and urban schools because of skin color and social class life style differences.

In this discussion of teacher student sexuality, the female and male teachers who acted in a sexually seductive way acted immaturely and should not have been teaching in the inner city in the first place. Some of these immature female teachers have been conditioned to use their sexuality as a tool to achieve their wishes. However, what worked with their fathers, husbands, and middle class boys will not work with lower class boys.

Some who act this way may be the affection-starved daughters of successful middle class parents. Still others may be the children of the *noveau* liberated or "swinger" parents who have not taught them how to control or withdraw their sensory sexual impulses. Of course, mixed in with all of this is a combination of white guilt and conscious and unconscious fantasies about black men as sexual and lustful studs, as well as just plain honest male-female sexuality.

It must be emphasized that although I stressed female teacher sexually provocative behavior, I am not suggesting that only female teachers act in a sexually provocative way. The actions of some white female teachers have been emphasized because in our school culture, particularly in inner city schools, the black male has been judged the aggressor and the white female teacher the helpless victim. Consequently, in most of the sexually provoked school incidents, it is the *male* teacher who is forced to resign or is fired and it is the *male* student who is suspended or expelled.[s] Hence, the "plantation mentality" is still being played out in our inner city schools. If school leaders can break their plantation mentality to a single standard based on equal rights in assignments, advancement, and responsibilities, then we can have a single standard for evaluating these incidents and assigning the blame squarely where it belongs in each incident.

Finally, in addition to those problems mentioned, as well as those problems stemming from overt teacher-student sexuality in the classroom, another phenomenon that may lead to discipline problems is the increasing fear of crime by those who live in the suburbs where many inner city teachers live. According to Greenhouse (1972), fear of crime in the suburbs is growing faster than actual crime in the suburbs. In a study in Baltimore in 1968, it was found that suburbanites were five times more likely to be fearful of crime than were those living in the slums. In actuality, however, the suburbanites were ". . . five times less likely to become victims of crimes than the slum residents (p. 12)."

The white suburbanite's excessive fear of crime may well be a contributing factor in inner city school problems. The teacher coming from a suburban environment to a slum school sees in the inner city child's testing of him a justification for the fear that he (the teacher) brings with him. His insecure behavior toward his students may provoke an already fearful student to act out or withdraw even more. Hence, the senselessness continues.

SUMMARY

As noted in the introduction to this chapter, those who hoped for a prescription for discipline have not found it here. Instead my impressions and feelings,

[s]The notable exception somewhat related to this rule has been the suspension or school-discharge of the pregnant student. Although many districts have organized special programs for pregnant students, few allow them to attend regular co-ed classes.

sometimes broad and sometimes pinpointed, were presented. Many of the areas considered in this discussion of discipline are atypical to the usual discussion of discipline, just as this book is different from most books in this field.

While in some cases I was definitive in my feelings, in other cases the problems are unresolved. Although I am against corporal punishment and have explained my philosophy about physical punishment, I have not completely resolved the problem as it concerns the physical testing of teachers by the really tough, physical, aggressive acting-out streetcorner youngster. What continually frustrates me are the seemingly implacable laws of street machismo. I have witnessed some outstanding teacher-student relationships which grew from a physically violent encounter between a tough male student and a tough male teacher. It is as though, as men, they *had* to test one another physically before they could offer one another respect and friendship. The feelings, I guess, are somehow related to the machismo of physical combat that some men have the need to subject themselves to; somehow, the physical encounter was necessary for them.

On the other hand, I have observed both petite young and elderly women succeed in disciplining classes that the toughest males could not control. Somehow these female teachers conveyed to their students, without hurting them emotionally or physically, that they were mature adults who demanded to be treated as such.

What we need in inner city schools are *secure and mature* men and women who have feelings for their students and who respect them as well as empathizing with their problems, who love the subject they teach, who are at home with their physicality, and who are both good talkers and good listeners. Not only must they believe in their students' ability to learn, but they must not let their feelings of empathy get in their way of demanding learning and standards from their students.

Once the successful teacher gets beyond the first testing period, physical size, sex, or color is unimportant. Of these secure and mature teachers, male and female, each has to develop a teaching style based on his or her personality that is also compatible with the students' life style and expectations.

NOTES TO CHAPTER SIX

After the Afro. *Newsweek*, February 26, 1973, p. 44.

Anderson, D. 'I'm so psyched, I'm ruined.' *The New York Times*, February 18, 1973, p. S 4.

Axthelm, P. The Olympics: new faces of '72. *Newsweek*, September 11, 1972, pp. 64, 65-71.

Bailey, S.K. *Disruption in Urban Public Secondary Schools.* Washington, D.C.: National Association of Secondary School Principals, 1970.

Baldwin, J. *Nobody Knows My Name.* New York: Dell, 1963.

Brown, C. *Manchild in the Promised Land.* New York: Macmillan, 1965.

Cleaver, E. *Soul on Ice.* New York: McGraw-Hill, 1968.

Clines, F.X. New state education reviewer to study 2 slum-area schools. *New York Times,* July 19, 1973, p. 22.

Cvaraceus, W.C. and Miller, W.B. *Delinquent Behavior: Culture and the Individual.* Washington, D.C.: National Education Association, 1964.

1821 history of Niagara County, N.Y. with illustrations descriptive of its scenery, private residences, public bulidings, fine blocks, and important manufactories, and portraits of old pioneers and prominent residents. New York: Sanford & Co., 1878.

Foster, H.L. Teaching industrial arts to the emotionally disturbed student. *Industrial Arts and Vocational Education* 53(1): 22-23, 1964.

Foster, H.L. A pilot study of the cant of the socially maladjusted, disadvantaged, secondary school child. *Urban Education* 2: 99-114, 1966.

Foster, H.L. The inner-city teacher and violence: suggestions for action research. *Phi Delta Kappan* 50(3): 172-175, 1968; *Research in Education,* April 1969, Vol. IV, #4, p. 100. ERIC index #ED 024 631.

Foster, H. The Inner-City School: Violence, Fear, and Failure. *Innovations in Educating Emotionally Disturbed Children and Youth: Proceedings of the Fourth Annual Conference of the Association of New York State Educators of the Emotionally Disturbed.* Hawthorne, New York: Association of New York State Educators of the Emotionally Disturbed, 1969.

Foster, H.L. Some suggestions for action research. *New York State Journal of Health, Physical Education and Recreation* 21(1): 21-32, 1968.

Foster, H.L. The inner-city school: a different drumbeat. *University Review* 2(2): 29-32, 1969.

Foster, H.L. The intervention teacher and aide: contemporary educators for resolving and preventing school disruption and violence. *Exceptional Children Conference Papers: Diagnostic and Resource Teaching; Research in Education,* November, 1971, Vol. 6, No. 11, p. 6. ERIC index #ED 052 401.

Foster, H.L. To reduce violence: Interventionist teacher and aide. *Phi Delta Kappan* 53(1): 59-62, 1971.

Gallup, G.H. Fifth annual Gallup poll of public attitudes toward education. *Phi Delta Kappan* 55(1): 38-51, 1973.

Gilder, G. The suicide of the sexes. *Harpers* 247(1478): 42-45, 49-50, 52-54, 1973.

Girl loses toehold on breaking college wrestling sex barrier. *The New York Times,* February 17, 1973, p. 24.

Greenberg, H.M. *Teaching with Feeling.* New York: Pegaus, 1969.

Greenhouse, I. Violent crimes rise in suburbs. *New York Times,* October 9, 1972, pp. 1, 12.

Hart, F.W. *Teachers and Teaching.* New York: Macmillan, 1934.

Hentoff, N. *Our Children Are Dying.* New York: Viking, 1967.

Herndon, J. *The Way It Spozed to Be.* New York: Simon and Schuster, 1968.

The hustler. *Newsweek*, May 28, 1973, p. 77.

James, A. Corporal punishment and physical intervention: there is a difference. Paper presented at the 48th Annual International Council for Exceptional Children Convention, Chicago, Illinois, April 23, 1970.

Johnson, W.R. and Johnson, J.A. *Human Sexual Behavior and Sex Education: Perspectives and Problems* (2nd Ed.). Philadelphia: Lea & Febiger, 1968.

The Joint Commission on Mental Health of Children. *Crisis in Child Mental Health: Challenge for the 1970's.* New York: Harper & Row, 1970.

Jordan, W.D. *White Over Black: American Attitudes Toward the Negro, 1550-1812.* Chapel Hill, N.C.: North Carolina Press, 1968.

Kiernan, O.B. Foreword. In S.K. Bailey, *Disruption in Urban Public Secondary Schools.* Washington, D.C.: National Association of Secondary School Principals, 1970.

Levinger, G. Sources of marital dissatisfaction among applicants for divorce. *American Journal of Ortho-psychiatry* 36: 803-807, 1966.

Maeroff, G.I. Drive is on to ban corporal punishment in U.S. Schools. *New York Times*, May 8, 1972, p. 37.

McMahon, H.G. *Chautaqua County: A History.* Buffalo, N.Y.: Henry Stewart, 1964.

Meggyesy, D. *Out of Their League.* Berkeley, Calif.: Ramparts Press, 1970.

Meisler's lunch aids jumping. *The New York Times*, February 18, 1973, p. S 4.

Miller, W.B. Lower class culture as a generating milieu of gang delinquency. *The Journal of Social Issues* 14(3): 5-19, 1958.

Millett, K. *Sexual Politics.* New York: Doubleday, 1970.

Milner, C.A. and Milner, R.B. *Black Players: The Secret World of Black Pimps.* New York: Bantam Books, 1973.

Morse, W.C. The crisis teacher, public school provision for the disturbed pupil. *The University of Michigan School of Education Bulletin*, April 1962, pp. 101-104.

Morse, W.C. The crisis teacher. In N.J. Long, et al. (Eds.), *Conflict in the Classroom: The Education of Emotionally Disturbed Children.* Belmont, Calif.: Wadsworth, 1965.

Munich, here we come. *Newsweek*, July 24, 1972, p. 54.

The National Commission on the Causes and Prevention of Violence. *Progress Report of the National Commission on the Causes and Prevention of Violence to President Lyndon B. Johnson.* Washington, D.C.: U.S. Government Printing Office, 1969, 0-331-948.

O'Donnell, K.P., Powers, D.F., with McCarthy, J. *Johnny, We Hardly Knew Ye.* Boston: Little, Brown, 1970.

Poussaint, A.F. The stress of the white female worker in the civil rights movement in the South. *American Journal of Psychiatry* 123: 401-407, 1966.

Poussaint, A.F. *Why Blacks Kill Blacks.* New York: Emerson Hall, 1972. (See Chap. 7.)

Poussaint, A.F. Sex and the black male. *Ebony* 27(10); 114-118, 120, 1972.

Reitman, A., Follmann, J., and Ladd, E.T. *Corporal Punishment in the Public Schools: The Use of Force in Controlling Student Behavior.* New York: American Civil Liberties Union, 1972.

Roth, P. *Portnoy's Complaint.* New York: Random House, 1967.

Schulz, D.A. *Coming Up Black.* Englewood Cliffs, N.J.: Prentice-Hall, 1969.

Smith, R. Frazier, Foreman see eye-to-eye on scales. *The New York Times,* January 23, 1973, p. 33.

Thompson, H.S. *Hell's Angels.* New York: Ballantine Books, 1967.

Wineman, D., James, A. et al. *Corporal Punishment in the Public Schools.* Detroit: Metropolitan Detroit Branch, American Civil Liberties Union of Michigan, 1967 Mimeo.

Yannis, A. Goalie says it helps to be crazy. *New York Times,* August 6, 1972, p. 10 S.

Zelnick, M. and Kantner, J.F. *Sexuality, Contraception and Pregnancy Among Young Unwed Females in the United States.* For the Commission on Population Growth and the American Future, Contract No. HD05255, National Institute of Child Mental Health and Human Development, U.S. Department of H.E.W.

Chapter Seven

Summing Up

"Go back to Mississippi, go back to Alabama, go back to South Carolina, go back to Georgia, go back to Louisiana, go back to the slums and ghettos of our northern cities, knowing that somehow this situation can and will be changed. Let us not wallow in the valley of despair. . . .

"This is our hope . . . with this faith we will be able to transform the jangling discords of our nation into a beautiful symphony of brotherhood. . . . And if America is to be a great nation, this must become true. So let freedom ring . . . from every village and every hamlet, from every state and every city . . . to speed up that day when all God's children, black . . . and white . . . , Jews and Gentiles, Protestants and Catholics, will be able to join hands and sing in the words of the old Negro spiritual, 'Free at last! Free at last' Thank God Almighty, we are free at last!' "
—Reverend Martin Luther King, Jr. at the Lincoln Memorial, the March on Washington for Jobs and Freedom, August 28, 1963

In the main, despite the energy and money that has been expended to change our inner city schools during the past two decades, the lot of the average teacher and student has not changed very much. In addition to the earlier noted reasons for this lack of movement, there are two other reasons. The first is that the research and creativity centered on the "big picture" and ignored the educational footsoldier—the classroom teacher, and the many and varied tasks and problems that he has to deal with daily. The second is that the schools cannot advance people if their society does not allow them to advance. Schools only reflect their community and can do only what the community allows them to do.

Despite the curriculum changes, the modern buildings, the modular or bell-less school day, the new math and social studies, contracts, computerized

293

materials, and individual prescriptions, the teacher still has to be able to relate to his students to use these aids. This is precisely what so little of our educational research and writing has dealt with: the nakedness and inadequacy the middle class teacher feels when he or she tries to relate to lower class students. What of the basics of the classroom; the feelings, emotions, and attitudes of the affective domain; the insecurities and feelings involved when the teacher, particularly the new teacher, tries to achieve some order so that she can fulfill a real desire and a main goal, which is to teach?

We must remember that teaching and learning cannot take place in a chaotic atmosphere. The insecure teacher passes on only one thing to his students—his insecurities.[a]

The last chapter of most books about inner city schools usually deals with either of two concerns. One group of books, written by self-styled inner city teaching experts who taught for one or two years, ends by discussing why the author was fired or "could not take it" any more. Usually, the system, the curriculum, or the administration and teachers are blamed for their leaving. Never, no never, do they find fault with themselves for being poor inner city teachers. Always, someone else caused their problems.

The other group of books about teaching in inner city schools consists of collections of papers and articles collated by professors of higher education who usually conclude these books with something like "we are getting closer to a solution but we still have a long way to go." Or, "we have to do a better job of communicating with black disadvantaged children." Or, "we have to improve the preparation of teachers." The suggestions are usually philosophical rather than concrete, without any suggestions of "how to."

This last chapter, like the other chapters of this book, breaks with tradition. Just as earlier chapters discussed reality situations and how to cope with them, this chapter discusses some of the ideas and successful programs with which I have been involved. There are also some additional suggestions for educational or political action. This chapter will, hopefully, provide public school and university people with additional ideas to solve their problems. The layman too will be given something to think about. Pragmatic implementation is stressed—not mere philosophy.

Most of these ideas and programs have not been reported in the literature because those of us who were involved have worked at what we were doing rather than having concerned ourselves with writing and publicizing. We were, and are, teachers first and authors second.

One of the projects to be reported, the New Teacher and Teacher Aide project, as far as we know, set a national record by retaining all the teachers who started in the project, with the exception of a few teachers who

[a]Recently, I was watching a TV program concerning dressage narrated by Haywood Hale Broun. He pointed out a similarity where the rider must be calm before he can make his horse calm (and thus able to perform the demanding feats required).

left for nonteaching reasons.[b] This was a cooperative project with the Buffalo Public Schools and the University of Buffalo, to help new secondary teachers of the disadvantaged over their first year's teaching hurdles.

Also to be discussed and described will be the undergraduate teacher education program that I direct. Outdoor education, or as it is now beginning to be called, outdoor pursuits, and its usage in all my programs and courses will also be described.

UNDERGRADUATE TEACHER EDUCATION

There is universal agreement that there is a need for more realistic teacher education programs. Our Office of Teacher Education, Faculty of Educational Studies, the State University of New York at Buffalo, has some outstanding teacher education center programs located in public schools. These centers could show the way to other schools of higher learning. Quietly, with meager budgets and no P.R. announcements, we have been doing what other schools dream about. It is in these public schools that all or almost all of our students' classroom and practicum education work is performed. Each of our centers is run a little differently from the others, with the personalities and philosophies of each staff giving direction to the center. The Woodlawn Teacher Education Center, which I direct, is designed to prepare undergraduates for teaching positions in inner city schools and will be described.[c]

The Woodlawn Center program is housed at Woodlawn Junior High School in the City of Buffalo. The school has an all-black student population and is located in the so-called inner city area of Buffalo. Historically, the school lists broken promises somewhat similar to I.S. 201 in New York City's Harlem. For various reasons, the school was never integrated and now has an all-black student population. I assumed the directorship of the Teacher Education Center at Woodlawn in September of 1967.[d]

The outstanding aspect of the program is the involvement of the Woodlawn professional staff. Three of the Woodlawn staff, presently Domenic Mettica, Judson Price, and Michael Romance, are given instructor's rank at the University, and we plan and teach the course work and organize our students' practicum experiences. Many additional Woodlawn personnel help in working with our students and student teachers in their practicum and student teaching

[b]We had 65 teachers in each of two years.

[c]A new dimension was added to the Center about two years ago when we instituted a graduate course. I have conducted the course since then for any of Woodlawn's interested faculty.

[d]The Woodlawn Center was organized by Professor H. Warren Button in September, 1965, as the Woodlawn Cooperative Teacher Education Center, an outgrowth of the Teacher Education Project of the Research Council of the Great Cities School Improvement Program 1964-65.

experiences, by coming into our classes to talk with our students, as well as talking and helping our students whenever they are at Woodlawn.

After assuming responsibility for the program and organizing two additional centers in the Buffalo Schools, I began a series of meetings with the principals (or their representatives) of the schools housing our Centers to discuss the Center programs. After a number of meetings, we agreed to a "Statement of Understanding."

Basically, the Statement set forth our feelings of the role and responsibility of the school and the university. One of the important points agreed to was that if a university student became involved, in any way, in a problem with a Woodlawn student or teacher, our student would leave the program, regardless of his or her involvement in the problem, if the school authorities so requested. This agreement has provided a solid foundation and safety valve preventing problems. (To date, none of our students has been asked to leave.)

The next things I did were to integrate our staff of Woodlawn personnel, and to set a dress code for our university students when at the Center. Many of our students had been arriving at Woodlawn in a dirty and unkempt state of dress and exhibiting poor personal hygiene. Interestingly, the Woodlawn students and many of the Woodlawn staff wanted to know who these "filthy hippies" were who were coming to Woodlawn to work with them.

Consequently, we set a dress code for the Woodlawn Center students. However, when a few of them began to ingore and flaunt the rule, we put it into writing as a prerequisite for the course and it still stands today. This one move has paid tremendous dividends by gaining respect for our students and acceptance by the Woodlawn staff and students. Since we use a contract system with our university students, they must agree to the following.

> *Dress Prerequisite*
> *All students must be neat, clean, and well groomed everytime they are at Woodlawn Junior High School or on similar visits as class members.* For the males—at least a shirt and tie, pants cleaned and pressed, and shoes shined. For the females—dresses, skirts, and, in some cases, pant suits or slacks. Discretion and good judgment should be used in relation to wearing or not wearing a bra. If this prerequisite provides a financial burden, students are requested to speak with the staff.
>
> A student's willingness to accept these rules is a prerequisite for this course as these rules are enforced rigidly. Noncompliance will result in a student's being dropped from the course. In addition, no smoking when at Woodlawn Junior High School.

Of course, we explained to our students the reason for the rule. Usually, after discussion, our students are satisfied and accept the rule. First, we explain that by dressing well you show respect for your students and what they respect. During the days of campus riots, many students felt they could relate better to black youngsters by wearing jeans and being quite unkempt and, in many cases, downright dirty. They were really taken aback when we explained that such a feeling was racist because it suggested that all blacks dress poorly and are dirty.

They had no idea that the general feeling within the black community was rather conservative. Indeed, they could never imagine black parents being annoyed with their children's Afro as might white parents be annoyed by their children's long hair. They had no idea that black parents and children had feelings of how a teacher should dress and behave.

Interestingly, a number of our students who had long hair that they considered "au naturel" were really rocked back on their feet when black students called them faggots.[e] They really could not understand why the black students treated them so disrespectfully because they (the university students) really felt they had compassion for "the plight of their people." All these students eventually left the program; they were confusing their middle class rebelliousness and insecurities with the racist problems faced by blacks.

It is interesting to note that Alvin Poussaint (1972) reported behavior similar to the above among many of the white workers who went South to work in the voter registration drives.

> There were some whites who, anxious to show off how "free" they felt around blacks, flouted the moral and social standards of the black community with their unorthodox behavior. One of the more common manifestations of this pathology was the attempt by many whites to get "soulful" and "earthy" affecting an unkempt style of dressing. Such individuals wore filthy clothes, refused to use deodorant, and rarely combed their hair because their warped conceptions of black people were that blacks were this way. None would have been willing to admit that such practices were racist because they conformed to the white-held stereotype of black people. It was as if these whites believed "anything goes in the black community."
> . . . Soon, local people viewed this behavior as a manifestation of disrespect for the black community and of thinly veiled white racism (pp. 9-10)."

Another point we make in our Center concerning dress is that inner city youngsters respect the good dresser. They feel that the teacher is middle class, has money, and therefore should spend his money on stylish clothes. They feel that the good dresser who is neat and clean respects himself and, therefore, respects them.

[e]The black male who has his hair in corn row style is surprised to be called a faggot in Africa. In Africa only the females wear their hair so styled.

Recently I was discussing the importance of dress with a group when one of the participants added emphasis to my point. He explained that he was a group worker and was leading group discussions with convicts at Attica State Prison. He explained how after a few months of meetings with the prisoners, they attacked him verbally. They wanted to know why a man with a college degree who was making good money dressed so sloppily and out of style. To the prisoners, clothing and style were important. Also, from observations of inner city students, I would estimate that most of the money earned by secondary school students while working in various Job Corps programs in schools and municipal agencies during the Johnson administration was spent on clothing.

The importance of dress also came up in a conversation with a friend who was involved in a program that sent university law students to work with prisoners. His students were having a problem of relating to the prisoners. The first question I raised concerned how his students were dressing when they visited their clients in jail. When his response did not include shirts, ties, and suits, I suggested a change. According to the prisoner's values, a man respected himself when he dressed well; hence, if a man did not dress well, he did not respect himself. Consequently, if he did not respect himself, he was not considered by the prisoners as being able to help them. (How many middle class persons would have any respect for a poorly dressed lawyer?)

Inner city students are very conscious of their teacher's physicalness and dress; they will take particular note of what the teacher is wearing. I have observed them making bets on which of their teacher's three shirts or suits he will wear on a particular day; or which outfit their female teacher will wear. They will really rib on a teacher who is not dressed stylishly—either to his face or behind his back. This, however, should not be taken as suggesting that teachers dress as their students dress.

Two last points concerning dress. John T. Malloy (The Groomer, 1972) considers himself a "Wardrobe Engineer." He teaches dressing habits that, according to him, "enable salesmen to sell more insurance, trial lawyers to win more cases, and executives to exert more authority. Wardrobe engineering, Malloy says, 'is putting together the elements of psychology, fashion, sociology and art (p. 67).' "

He began to develop his grooming theory in the late 1950s while teaching in a Connecticut prep school. His observations suggested that student performance was affected by teacher's dress.

To help substantiate his theory, he planted an actor dressed in lower middle class style—greenish-blue suit, black shoes with large buckles, thick glasses, a white shirt, a gold expansion watch band, and a "chintzy" blue polyester tie—to act as a trainee in a New York City corporate office. Dressed this way, the actor was able to get only twelve out of fifty secretaries to go to the files for him.

By changing the actor's dress to upper middle class—an expensive blue suit, styled hair, silk polka-dot tie, beige shirt, and brown cordovan shoes—this actor succeeded in getting forty-two of fifty secretaries to work for him.

The last point concerning the importance of dress can be taken from Ulf Hannerz's (1969) inquiry into the Washington, D.C. ghetto culture and community. He reported that one of the characteristics of "ghetto-specific masculinity" was a concern for appearance, particularly for clothing. This was shown in three ways. One was the way a man dressed; the second was what he had in his closet; and the third was what a man's real concern for clothing was although he could not afford to purchase anything that was really expensive.

It is held important that colors match; ideally, one should not wear more than two colors. A man who ignores this rule too conspicuously, appearing in clothes of many bright colors not considered matching, may be branded a "bama"; the word is derived from "Alabama" and denotes an ignorant rustic. . . . There is also considerable awareness of prices and brands. A man in a boasting mood talks of his pairs of "forty-dollar shoes" and his "thirty-dollar hat," all of expensive brands of some renown—a renown of which ghetto men may be more aware than most people. As young ghetto males ransacked Washington stores during the violent days after the assassination of Martin Luther King, it was conspicuous that the downtown stores which particularly attracted their attention were the male fashion stores, and such establishments were also prominent among those raided on the ghetto main streets. . . .

Concern with clothing is not necessarily apparent in everyday dressing habits. Some men are conspicuously shabbily dressed and may actually seem less concerned with appearances than most mainstream-oriented men. . . . But once more we must remind ourselves that a concern is not always something with which one is completely successful. The lack of money certainly prevents many ghetto men from acquiring the wardrobe they desire, although a few prestige objects are usually within the range of real possibilities. Also, the men dress to fit the occasion. For hanging out at the street corner one can as well use an old army coat and dirty boots, leaving the expensive coat and the forty-dollar shoes at home in the closet as treasures which may be proudly displayed to a visitor and used on more special occasions (pp. 83-84).

INTAKE INTO THE PROGRAM

We do not use any unique intake procedure. All our University Center programs are advertised to all sophomore students through mailings and a required meeting. Those who choose Centers are interviewed by the various directors. In the case of the Woodlawn Center, we suggest students visit Woodlawn for a day or two to help make the decision to sign up or not.

We do, however, try to keep out those with obvious emotional problems, and those who want to work in inner city schools to "love poor black kids." We look for students who are emotionally secure, reasonably happy, good talkers, physical, and who are not burdened with white guilt. The program is presently made up of about 60 percent black and 40 percent white students.

THE PROGRAM

Almost universally, our black and white university students report they were frightened when they first entered Woodlawn. They were frightened by the students running in the halls or just by the students as they are. However, because of their involvement in the school, they soon lose their fear. They also soon become totally immersed in every aspect of the school.

Ideally, students enter the program in the lower half or fall semester of their junior year, starting a one-to-one-and-a-half year, four-course-and-practicum sequence. The four courses are:

1. TED 321—Educational Sociology—fall of the Junior Year—4 credit hours.
2. TED 418—Teaching in Inner City Schools—spring of the Junior Year—4 credit hours.
3. TED 425-426—Student Teaching—fall of the Senior Year—6 credit hours.
4. TED 419—Practicum in Mental Health, Methods & Techniques of Teaching—concurrent with student teaching during the educational semester (student teaching semester) of the Senior Year—2 credit hours.

TED 321 and TED 418 meet at Woodlawn Junior High School. The practicum experiences are either in the school or within its community. The first class meeting is held on the university campus to arrange for car pools, to explain the program to new students, and to provide maps and information about Woodlawn. The TED 419 class meets almost anywhere—on the university campus, at Woodlawn, or at someone's home.

At the first meeting of the course, each student is asked to list five of the areas he wants covered. These lists are combined and divided up for perusal by faculty and student committees. These committees quickly report back to the class and the semester's objectives are set.

However, even with these objectives in mind, we are still flexible. For example, recently, our students (the majority of whom are females), wanted to get more information from female teachers concerning such questions as: (1) how female teachers are tested; (2) how do you carry yourself; (3) how do you dress; (4) how do you handle sexuality, etc. Because our program is housed in a public school and we have excellent relations with the staff, at our next meeting we had four female teachers, black and white, carry on a dialog with our students.

Our flexibility within our structure provides our students with a reality model to emulate when they become teachers. Also on our first day at

Woodlawn, we ensure everyone's getting to know one another. As students enter the room, each is given a three-by-five card and asked to write his name and three adjectives about himself. The staff does this too. Next, we form an inner ring and an outer ring. Each ring walks around and we read one another's cards and try to communicate nonverbally. Students and faculty then pair off with someone they do not know and spend about fifteen minutes getting to know one another verbally. The pairs then form fours, and so on, until we get everyone to know everyone else. A dittoed sheet is then made up with everyone's (faculty's and students') name, address, and telephone number. These are distributed to all class members.

Students are then divided up among the faculty. They work with this faculty person throughout the program, sharing their feelings and observations, which are recorded in a log. Additionally, students are notified that staff are available around the clock in an emergency.

A sample contract is discussed and made final. As part of the contract, students are asked to list their expectations of the faculty. Arrangements are made for students to begin their practicum observations. All of this is accomplished by the second class meeting.

The overall objectives of the Woodlawn Teacher Education Center program follow.

1. To help each student develop his or her own teaching style and techniques that will be relevant to the urban disadvantaged child, his family, and community.
2. To help the student develop generalized techniques for preparing, structuring, and organizing the classroom and himself to meet the needs of this child so that discipline becomes secondary and teaching the primary function.
3. To prepare teachers so that they may be able to bridge the difference between their culture and life style and the child's culture and life style without the deleterious consequences of the "cultural shock."
4. To provide each student with a frame of reference that will infuse him or her with an awareness of the teacher's responsibility, as an agent of change, to relax, motivate, and educate.

Our students meet for two hours of class work and two hours or more of practicum experiences per week. Practicum experiences involve various aspects of the community life, tutoring students, working with teachers and students, and participating in school activities. Students have one year of practicum experience at Woodlawn prior to their student teaching.

An overnight outdoor education camping experience is required of all students. No tobacco, drugs, or alcoholic beverages are allowed on the outdoor education experience.

CONTRACTS

As noted, we use a contract system with our Center students. We are aware that our university students will teach the way they are taught. Some requirements apply to all students, while those students who chose to work for an A or B grade must complete additional work beyond that required for an S or U.

Students are presented with an open contract. After discussion, the contract is formalized and signed. A sample contract follows.(Fig. 7-1).

Another point that should be stressed is that our faculty will disagree, at times, in front of our students. Sometimes we do it purposely. Despite our overall agreement on philosophy and objectives, we have retained individual approaches and teaching styles. We agree that what works for one teacher may not work for another. And, we let our students know about this.

Such an approach makes at least two points for our students: (1) educators can have professional disagreements very openly and still respect and work with one another; (2) if the teacher is secure, he or she need not worry about differences of opinion or viewpoints opposing those of the teacher being expressed in the classroom. If our students experience a classroom atmosphere that is open, where all sides are presented and argued (even against our faculty), and see that respect for one another can continue despite the disagreements, then, hopefully, they will be able to teach in this accepting way when they become teachers.

Another point stressed is that the teacher's control of the classroom is not an end in itself but rather a means toward an end, that end or goal being the students' learning concepts and skills and developing their ability to reason and think. The teacher must be more than a disciplinarian. He must be prepared and know what he is going to teach, how he is going to teach it, and how he is going to measure his success. We also philosophize that structure, organization, and discipline are compatible with freedom and democracy. Indeed, students are looking to their teachers for realistic limits.

The evening group meetings referred to earlier are held at homes of our staff or students. These are the small group meetings on the contract and attendance is optional. At these meetings the topics discussed sometimes are open and varied while at other times we have a single, prepared topic.

One incident that occurred during a small group meeting stands out in my mind. We were meeting at the home of a black teacher. One white female student kept going upstairs to use the lavatory. Somehow, she and I got into a discussion later and she explained why she kept going upstairs.

She had never been in a black person's home before, and she just did not know that blacks could own a home like hers. The reason for her going upstairs so much was really to look over the house and furnishings. Interestingly, this young lady grew up in a middle class home in a completely white community. Academically, she was no slouch; however, her experiential back-

Figure 7-1. Sample Teaching Contract

STATE UNIVERSITY OF NEW YORK AT BUFFALO
Office of Teacher Education
319 Foster Hall

Course Contract — A

Name _____

Local Tel. No. _____ Home Tel. No. _____

Local Add. _____ Home Add. _____

_____ _____

Student No. _____ Soc. Sec. No. _____

Circle Correct Designation:

Class	TED 321	TED 418	4 Hours
	Spring	Fall	197_____

Faculty Advisor _____

I   *Teaching Team*

Dr. Herbert L. Foster, Mr. Domenic Mettica, Ms. Rose Nwako (student teacher supervisor), Mr. Judson Price, and Mr. Michael Romance.

II   *Class Meetings*

Class meetings are held on Wednesdays at Woodlawn Junior High School in Room 253 from 1:00 to 3:00 p.m. It is your responsibility to call our office to find out about a meeting, if you have missed the prior class meeting.

1. Sept. 5
2. Sept. 12
3. Sept. 19
4. Sept. 26*
5. Oct. 3
6. Oct. 10
7. Oct. 17
8. Oct. 24
9. Oct. 31
10. Nov. 7
11. Nov. 21
12. Nov. 28**
13. Dec. 5
14. Dec. 12

Dec. 13   — Instruction ends
Dec. 14–22   — Examination week

III   *Office Hours* — All by Appointment

All students are expected to meet with their advisors. Appointments must be made. *All staff members are available any time—day or night—in an emergency.*

IV   *Dress Prerequisite*

Your willingness to accept these rules is a prerequisite for this course as these rules will

or *S.*   *Date by which you must decide whether you want to work for a letter grade

**Any student with papers, practicum time, or other course requirements outstanding beyond this date may receive an incomplete grade. *An incomplete grade will be changed to an F grade if the outstanding work is not turned in within one month of the end of examination week unless a request for an extension is received and approved.*

be enforced rigidly. Non-compliance will result in your being dropped from the course.

You must be neat, clean, and well groomed every time you are at Woodlawn Junior High School or on similar visits as a class member. For the males—at least a shirt and tie, pants pressed and clean, and shoes shined. For the females—dresses, slacks or pantsuits. Use discretion and good judgment in relation to wearing or not wearing a bra.

If this dress prerequisite provides a financial burden for you, please speak with us. If you have any doubts about anything in this section, please ask advice.

V *Examinations and Student Growth*

No examinations will be given unless the students decide upon an examination. Everyone will be assigned to meet with a team member for ongoing discussion and consultation concerning each student's growth in each of the criteria areas.

VI *Course Evaluation*

Some form of written or oral evaluation of the course will be used. Student input will help determine the type of evaluation to be used.

VII *Grades & Grading Criteria*

A grade of *S* or *U* will be given for a minimum of acceptable work. A grade of *S* or *U* will be based upon:

1. *Class attendance and verbal participation*—30 hours—If you miss more than two classes, you will be in danger of receiving an incomplete or failing grade. If the class does not meet for 30 hours, the hours will be added to practicum experience hours. Also, no smoking in class at Woodlawn Junior High School.

2. *Practicum Experiences* (Contract 1)—Observations and experiences with students, with teachers, with work in the community, etc. A minimum of 31 hours is required. Additional hours are suggested.

   Mr. Romance will help direct you in your assignment. You are also required to sign in and out on all practicum experiences. Mr. Romance and the practicum sign-in sheet are located in Room 106.

Practicum Experiences: 31 hours

   a. Practicum Observation—Teaching, Administration, and Special Services—16 hours.

   b. Practicum Participation—Your subject area—15 hours.

   a. Practicum Observation—16 hours—These experiences should be reported in your log (Contract 2).

   A. Required—*Teaching*—Nine hours of observing various subject areas plus three hours in your major area—12 hours.

      1. Homeroom
      2. Art
      3. Business Subjects
      4. Homemaking
      5. Language Arts
      6. Mathematics
      7. Music
      8. Physical Education
      9. Science
      10. Social Studies
      11. Industrial Arts

    B.   Required—*Administration*—Two hours

       1. Principal
       2. Assistant Principal
       3. Chief Engineer
       4. Audio Visual
       5. Security
       6. Supplies
       7. Cafeteria

    C.   Required—*Pupil Personnel Services*—Two hours

       1. Attendance Teacher
       2. Guidance Counselor
       3. Home School Coordinator
       4. Nurse
       5. Psychologist
       6. Secretaries
       7. Visiting Teacher

  b.   Practicum Participation—15 hours

     Required

     Fifteen (15) hours are required in this area. The experiences must include at least:

       1. Take the attendance.
       2. Prepare a bulletin board.
       3. Construct a dittoed or mimeographed test, work sheet, or activity sheet that is approved by your cooperating teacher.
       4. Demonstrate the use of at least two pieces of audio-visual equipment.
       5. Familiarize yourself with all forms, passes, and referral slips.
       6. Design and grade a test under the supervision of your cooperating teacher.
       7. Familiarize yourself with a grade book.
       8. Teach small and large groups.

3. *A Log*—(Contract 2)—You will keep a log in which you will record your feelings, experiences, responses to class discussions and the literature, assignments, and your practicum experiences. The log will be shared with your faculty advisor.

4. *Small Group Meetings*—(Contract 3)—These are usually held in the evenings at someone's home. A minimum of six (6) hours are required.

5. *Paper*—(Contract 4)—One three-to-five-page paper is required. The paper should follow some recognized academically accepted standard of writing for term papers or dissertations. Papers must be double spaced. The paper is due by November 28th. Your paper should be based on any one of the following or all. Additionally, include in the paper whether the experiences of those you are writing about are in any way related to today's inner-city schools. Circle option chosen.

    a.   A book and/or a number of articles reporting on how earlier members of your religious, ethnic, social class, or cultural group first went to school in the United States.

    b.   Interview a parent, a friend, a relative, and/or a grandparent who may have been the first in his or her family to go to school in the United States.

    c.   A general paper about how earlier immigrants or the lower classes have fared in our schools.

    d.   A position paper to any of the above, or a position paper about an inner-city school problem and what you would do about it if you were in a decision-making role.

6. *Outdoor Education Experience*—One Day—(Contract 5)—Participation on a day outdoor education experience: no tobacco, no alcoholic beverages, and no drugs while on the outdoor education experience.

    Participation is also required on at least one of the planning committees for the outdoor education experience. An outdoor education fee is required.

7. *Additional criteria agreed to by the class*

8. *Grades of A and B will be based upon*:

    Numbers 1, 2, 3, 4, 5, and 7 above.

9. *For a Grade of A or B* (Contract 6)—An academically acceptable project of "Superior or a high distinction of competence."

10. *Outdoor Education Experience* (Contract 7)—Two-night overnight. Participation on a two-night overnight outdoor education experience. No smoking, no drinking of alcoholic beverages, and no drugs while on the outdoor education experience.

    Participation is also required on at least one of the planning committees for the outdoor education experience. An outdoor education fee is required.

VIII *Substitution Work* — (Contract 8)

Anyone who feels he or she could gain more from work equal to, but different from, the suggested requirements can secure a change.

IX *Papers*

Papers not picked up from Dr. Foster's secretary within one month of the end of examinations will be disposed of. If you provide a self-addressed envelope, your paper will be mailed.

X   *Expectation of Staff's Role*:

a. *To be available for student meetings.*

b. To start class on time.

c. (Students suggest others.)

I have read the course requirements and accept them. I understand that I am being placed on my honor to neither smoke nor drink, nor take any drugs while on the outdoor education experience. I also understand that breaking this personal honor may result in my receiving a failing grade or being dropped from the class.

Date Contract Was Accepted   _____

Student Signature   _____

Advisor's Signature   _____

Date Contract Was Completed   _____

Student Signature   _____

Advisor's Signature   _____

Grade   _____

Student Signature   _____

Advisor's Signature   _____

ground had not included any relationship with blacks—other than the women who cleaned her home.

Another affective approach that we use is to remember our students' birthdays with a cake and candles. It is interesting to observe the feelings of some of our supposedly sophisticated college students when they are confronted with a birthday cake of their own. Birthday cakes are also provided in my graduate courses, where one day even I was surprised by a student's reaction to a cake. When the class was over that evening, the young male teacher for whom we had the cake stayed after class to speak with me. He thanked me for the cake and informed me that it was the first birthday cake he had ever had in his life!

THE NEW TEACHER AND TEACHER AIDE PROJECT

Another problem faced by school personnel is helping or supporting new teachers over their first year of teaching. This problem is even more acute when discussed in terms of new secondary school teachers of disadvantaged youngsters. Depending upon rumor, stories, or whose data you are reading, the turnover rate for new secondary teachers of disadvanted students runs from 30 to 90 percent.

The response to this turnover problem has been everything from ignoring the problem to in-service and university-public school support programs. Most of the university-public school support programs, however, appear to have been organized for elementary teachers. New secondary teachers have been largely ignored.

The elementary and secondary university-school cooperative support programs have followed many forms. The programs have included in-service courses, curriculum improvement programs, and ventures such as a $450,000.00 project between the New York City Board of Education (Junior High School 57 in Brooklyn) and New York University with funds provided by the Ford Foundation and New York City.

Our New Teacher and Teacher Aide Project was a cooperative venture between the Office of Teacher Education, Faculty of Educational Studies, The State University of New York At Buffalo, and the Buffalo Public Schools with funds provided by New York State Urban Teacher Corps Office, the State Education Department.[f] The project was designed to help first-year secondary school teachers over their teaching hurdles. Built into the project was a program for teacher aides from the inner city areas of Buffalo, and in the second and final year of the project, we had a second-year teacher program. The total cost of the project for both years was $123,000—$57,000 the first year and $66,000 the second year.

[f]The official title of the project was Cooperative Program for Pre- and Post-Service Teacher Education and a Teacher Aide Project for Auxiliary Personnel Indigenous to the Inner-City Area, under contract # C-37075 and C-45609.

Staffing

The staffing followed a simple table of organization. Both university and Buffalo Board of Education teachers were involved. I headed the program through a half-time position as project director. Leo DeMarco took a leave from the Buffalo Public Schools to become program director of the New Teacher aspect of the project. He was also a graduate student at the University. Mr. Zubie Metcalf directed the Teacher Aide part of the program for the first year. The second year of the program, Mrs. Maggie Wright took a leave from the Buffalo Public Schools to head the Teacher Aide program. She, too, was a graduate student at the university.

During the second year of the project, we added a Second-Year Teacher Program. Mr. Harold Bass, a Buffalo school teacher, directed the program. The second-year teachers primarily performed work in developing curriculum related to their academic or special teaching areas. Their meetings were held after school.

A number of Buffalo school teachers also came into the program as part time co-group and discussion leaders. Under Professor Murray Levine, director of the Graduate Program Community-Clinical Psychology, we also brought in a number of clinical psychologists. Some were working in the field while others were advanced graduate students. Some also had some teaching experience. The staff was integrated as to sex and racial background, and members from minority backgrounds were in some leadership positions.

Program

There were some minor program changes between the first and second years of the project. The second year's New Teacher and Teacher Aide Project will be reported.

Intake

An announcement concerning our project was mailed to all first-year secondary teachers in the Buffalo schools. Participation in the project was optional. The qualifications consisted of: (1) being a first-year teacher, and (2) teaching disadvantaged secondary school students. All who met these qualifications were accepted. The criteria for the teacher aides included: (1) years of service as an aide; (2) other work experience; (3) whether they had taken prior college courses; and (4) a desire to become secondary school teachers.

University Credit

Teacher participants received three hours of graduate credit per semester. A teacher who participated for both years of the project could have received twelve hours of graduate credit. The aides received four hours of undergraduate credit per semester as part of the project. They also had the option of taking additional undergraduate work at no cost to them. Some of the aides carried a load of twelve hours.

Orientation
Our orientation ran in conjunction with the Buffalo schools' orientation and consisted of five afternoon sessions from 1 until 4:30 p.m. The Buffalo school people took the morning part of the orientation.

The first afternoon consisted of a registration and introduction session, and a student panel. For the panel we picked some of the "toughest" black and white boys and girls in the schools. They discussed how they tested their teachers. Needless to say, most of the new teachers refused to believe them. The students also expressed their feelings about good versus bad teachers, and then joined the rest of the orientation week as staff members.

The second day consisted of two panels, one of parents and the other of principals. Both parents and principals *told* the teachers what they expected of them. An interesting verbal scuffle broke out between the parents and the students who had been on the earlier panel. The parents turned out to be much more conservative concerning dress and behavior than were the students.

The panel for the third day consisted of a number of male and female second-year teachers who described their first year trials and tribulations. This was a particularly good panel and we had a good deal of questioning and discussion.

Teachers and aides visited their schools on the fourth day. Additionally, our staff was available for any private meetings with teachers of aides who had questions.

The last day of the orientation was spent at three activities. First, new teachers worked with our staff to plan their first week of school. The rest of the afternoon was spent in language desensitization and understanding.

My Jive Test, mentioned earlier, was given and we discussed communication in general and black dialect in particular. We next gave everyone a desensitization test.

Desensitization and Awareness
As noted in earlier chapters, inner city youngsters very effectively use many techniques to test their teachers. One of the more effective techniques is the use of so-called "dirty" words or actions that upset their teachers and thereby interfere with the teaching and learning. This testing can take many forms. Sometimes the testing is subtle, sometimes it is carried out very aggressively, and often there are psychosocial, psychosexual, or psycho-racial-sexual overtones. In Reality 81, Claude Brown (1965, p. 86) describes the way many of his friends attempted rather unsuccessfully, to test a new female counselor at Wiltwick.

REALITY 81

> Mrs. Meitner was not out of place in Affrey House. The first week she was there, she showed us a lot of judo and won a whole lot of friends. Guys tried to make her leave by walking past the stairs naked when they heard her coming down, but that didn't work. Mrs. Meitner would just stop whoever it was and make him stand there and talk to her. The cat who was naked would get embarrassed long before she did. After a while, people just stopped messing with Mrs. Meitner and faced the fact that she was there to stay.

If all teachers could handle situations as Mrs. Meitner did, there would be fewer problems in the schools. However, most new teachers do not possess her ability.

In an attempt to deal realistically with this problem, we designed a desensitization and awareness exercise to help our new teachers and teacher aides develop immediate and ongoing strategies for coping with these problems. We felt it was imperative that our participants: (1) not be upset by so-called "dirty" words; (2) know the "other" meaning, particularly the sexual meaning, of the jive, slang, or dirty words in their students' vocabulary; and (3) learn the words specially designed to hide their true meaning—i.e., "forget you" for "fuck you."

The usual college teacher preparation programs rarely discuss students' use of foul language. Where they do, most often only the environmental reasons behind the use of the language are considered enough. Sad experience, though, has taught us that this is not enough.

With the help of experienced inner city teachers and inner city students, foul words were collected. From these words, a master list of thirty words was promulgated. Some of these were:

1. Train—where two or more males follow one another in having sexual intercourse with one female. Synonym—a gang bang.
2. Fellatio—the oral stimulation of the penis, especially to orgasm.
3. Trim—sexual intercourse or vagina.
4. Twat—vagina.
5. Cunnilingus—the act, practice, or technique of orally stimulating the female genitalia.
6. Sixty-nine—simultaneous cunnilingus and fellatio.
7. Schmuck—the accepted meaning is a jerk or fool (a Yiddish word for penis).
8. Balling—to have sexual intercourse; used to refer to a party.
9. Johnson—a penis.

10. Knockers—breasts. It appears that since the advent of women's liberation, this word and other words for breasts have also taken on the meaning of the male's balls or scrotum.
11. Booty—buttocks or backside.

These words were categorized, five each, under: (1) penis, (2) vagina, (3) sexual intercourse, (4) oral sexual stimulation or satisfaction, and (5) other parts of the body. Five signs were painted noting these categories and hung in front of the room.

Despite our belief in what we were doing, and out of respect for the moral beliefs our participants may have had, we notified everyone that on the next day we would carry out an exercise that would involve the use of so-called dirty words. We suggested that those who felt they would be offended, would be excused for the afternoon. As it turned out, everyone did attend.

As the participants entered the room the next afternoon, they were seated five or six at a table and in co-ed groups. Each participant was given an IBM scoring sheet and pencil.

We thought of putting the words on the overhead. However, after discussion, we decided that it was imperative that the participants actually hear the words.[g] Therefore, the words were called off and each participant had to classify each word on his IBM sheet according to its category. Upon collecting the marked sheets, participants at each table discussed: (1) the answers, (2) what each word described, and (3) possible antonyms and synonyms for the five categories of words. After a suitable time span, participants at each table appointed one representative to stand and verbally assign one word to its category until all table representatives had turns and all the words were assigned categories.

Next, group members joined in a general discussion of such questions as: (1) Why do students use these words? (2) What is the students' and teachers' expectation of the other when the words are used in the classroom? (3) Should the teacher differentiate between a child cursing him, cursing a fellow student, or cursing during the heat of a good but emotional discussion or in a ball game? and (4) What do you say to a student who asks a question such as "Can masturbation hurt you?"

Additionally, actual examples of incidents were read for discussion. The feelings of all groups were then shared with everyone. Folders were provided holding articles related to teacher and/or student usage of sexually related words to provide our participants with real situations. We also provided copies of a number of newspapers such as *Screw*. With the exception of possibly three of

[g]According to an article in *Look* (Faber, 1969) Prof. Gerhard Neubeck desensitizes the students in his University of Minnesota "Human Sexual Behavior" course by having them say the words out loud.

those assembled, most of the new teachers and teachers aides appeared relieved and more relaxed that we had publicly discussed this subject.

I have developed and refined the desensitization and awareness experience and have included the session in all my courses. In addition, I often use it when conducting workshops. Such a program sets a tone for openness and honesty.

Course Work

Once past the orientation week, the Project's assistance to new teachers and teacher aides was provided through a number of resources. These included: (1) small group meetings, (2) topical presentations, (3) Saturday workshops, and (4) a crisis service.

Small Group Discussions

The teachers and aides were divided into eight groups. Four groups met on a Tuesday after school and four groups met on Wednesdays after school. The group meetings were held in two centrally located inner city schools. Groups were assigned to each school on individual preference, but small group assignments were made homogeneously as to sex and racial background. Teacher aides were assigned as evenly as possible to all groups.

The discussion groups were designed to meet several problems which arise with new teachers. First, school organization promotes the loneliness of the teaching profession. Teachers isolated from each other rarely have the opportunity to discuss their problems in teaching openly and frankly with each other. Consequently, many young teachers have difficulty in distinguishing between problems related to difficult situations and those related to personal attitudes and to emotions. Moreover, because most supervisors are also involved in evaluating them, most teachers are reluctant to go to their supervisor with problems. The game for the young teacher frequently is one of concealing and covering up mistakes rather than examining them in order to learn.

Second, help is usually made available only when the teacher can not handle a problem. In consequence, seeking help is an implicit admission of failure. The discussion groups built in the concept that problems are to be expected, and permitted consideration of alternatives at an early stage in the teacher's awareness of a problem.

Third, young teachers frequently have problems in knowing (1) how much responsibility to take for difficult emotional and social problems among children in their class; (2) how closely they can permit themselves to relate; (3) how to deal with discipline, especially as it relates to the teacher's own attitudes toward accepting and integrating the authority mold; (4) how to maintain an idealistic attitude when practical considerations force change; how to relate to older teachers, principals, and supervisors; and (5) how to develop confidence in their own judgment. Discussion groups permitted the airing of these very personal, very important issues in a way that usually is not provided in schools.

Fourth, teachers in inner city areas frequently suffer from "culture shock" and it is important to explore the feelings and attitudes teachers develop as they work in situations which are difficult and different. Discussion groups permitted an airing of such issues and often a clarification for the young teacher.

The first goal of discussion groups was to reduce the personal anxiety, tension, and strain which is inevitable in young teachers. A second goal was to help the young teacher deal with personal feelings and attitudes which may influence or interfere with problem solving in the classroom. The range of alternative solutions available to the teacher may be greater as a consequence of the discussions.

A third goal was to help children through working with the teacher. It was our feeling that many problems (though certainly not all) can best be helped in the natural setting, by teachers. In any event, even if outside help is available, the teacher is still faced with handling the child's problem daily. Intervention at the level of the classroom is critically important in dealing with the 10-to-30 percent of children, *defined by teachers*, as having adjustment or learning problems.

The discussions in each group were led by one faculty member who had experience in group therapy or sensitivity groups, an educator from the project staff of part time instructors, and the project director and codirector. The discussions were problem centered, dealt with the teachers' concerns, and focused on here and now group processes only when such processes interfered with the ongoing consideration of problems (e.g., silence related to unvoiced disagreements; monopolization of "air time"; critical or nonaccepting attitudes of group members toward each other that promote defensiveness, etc.).

The groups were not for sensitivity training nor did they assume psychopathology. They did assume that in any interaction with children, parents, or administration, the teacher's feelings and attitudes play an important role. The group did assume that the first year of teaching is in the nature of a normal developmental crisis, and that the resolution of that crisis shapes the teacher's professional self.

Each session was tape recorded, with participant permission. Individual leaders often played back tape recordings for self-evaluation of their roles and to discover points in the discussion that needed more emphasis or clarification at later sessions.

All co-leaders met weekly as a group with an outside leader, who acted as a consultant and facilitator in group process. We profited from this experience, which aided us in our relationship role with our own groups. Any problems confronting the leaders were brought out at these meetings and attempts made to resolve them. Project administrative business was also a part of these meetings.

An analysis of the tapes revealed that because of the open format of the small discussion groups, a large variety of issues were discussed, including: (1) problems with discipline; (2) dependency, anxiety, and sexuality in children; (3) problems in teachers' handling of their own feelings of hostility; (4) the sense of discouragement over working in a difficult situation; (5) racial feelings; (6) problems with the administrative hierarchy of the school; (7) problems in obtaining help of school psychologists and social workers; and (8) problems in relating to parents and older teachers.

From the tapes we felt that, for most of the participants, the sense of loneliness and isolation had been overcome. The most important index was the reluctance of the groups to disband as the program drew to a formal conclusion. In addition to the teachers, the group leaders reported feeling a sense of loss, as when one departs from a friend. In fact, three groups decided to continue on their own and met a number of times past the original 30 sessions.

The discussion sessions seemed to provide a forum for the catharsis of feeling, for consideration of issues important in the schools but rarely explicitly considered or confronted in any other forum, and for replenishment of psychic resources used up during the teacher's professional activities. Teachers literally used the term "feeling refreshed" after a session, or of getting "a little ray of hope" from the sessions. Several spoke of the relief from feelings of guilt and personal inadequacy they derived from learning that others were experiencing similar problems and perceptions. Virtually any time that these issues were broached during a discussion, an aura of "me too" comraderie emerged quickly and pervasively.

In a few instances, teachers were able to use the discussion sessions to work out specific teaching problems, or problems with specific children. Examples of specific problem solving, however, were fewer than we had anticipated. The discussion time was insufficient for detailed presentations of specific instances, and others in the group often found little interest in discussing specific problems with specific children and would rather confront the general issues involved—loneliness, interpersonal relationships, responsibility, children's emotions, discipline, etc.

In addition to dealing with issues germane to teachers generally, the discussion sessions were used by a few of those involved also in a more traditional therapeutic sense. This usually involved greater appreciation and acceptance of a teacher's own feeling, or insight into aspects of their personal involvement with children.

TOPICAL PRESENTATIONS

In the first year of this project a second course was taught along with the small group discussions. The course consisted of didactic instruction, with lectures, outside speakers, consultants, and small workshops in teaching methods for various subjects taught in the secondary school curriculum. In spite of the fact that the didactic instruction was felt to be meaningful, practical, and specific to classroom problems, the project as well as the participants' evaluations suggested it to be somewhat limited in reaching the participants. It appeared that not all the participants were benefiting from the presentations of any one meeting.

To reach a greater number of new teachers, yet retain the two-course content of the previous year; to help the clinical psychologists deal with public education problems unfamiliar to them; and as an outcome of faculty and student evaluations, a new format was developed. As noted, the weekly small group discussion vehicle was retained throughout the year, led by the clinical and educator co-leaders. Thus personality problems as well as specific classroom problems were dealt with within the group as each leader lent the expertise of his or her professional specialty in helping to resolve arising problems. The sessions remained for the most part as group counseling sessions without either leader dominating discussions with lectures or passing judgments as to right or wrong ways of behaving. Attempts were made to maintain a "group theory" concept as much as possible.

As a consequence of this new format with the loss of a second weekly meeting for didactic instruction, teaching method suggestions and formal presentation of curriculum topic areas were drastically reduced. To compensate for this loss, two workshops were held. One dealt with aggression and how to deal with it in school, while a second focused on the drug problem and its consequences upon public school youth. In addition, (1) experienced helping teachers and second-year teachers were employed or asked to act as advisors to those of our teachers who appeared to be experiencing some difficulties; and (2) meetings concerning teaching methods were held when needed.

To further compensate for the loss of a second weekly meeting, a series of topics were scheduled for presentation. Attendance was optional except for the ones concerning behavioral objectives. Thus it was hoped that those truly interested and concerned would benefit more from the material discussed. The topics were as follows:

1. Behavioral objectives
2. Report card grading
3. Questioning techniques
4. Pupil-teacher planning
5. Motivational techniques
6. Individualization of instruction

The above list constituted didactic instruction given during the early months of teaching, September through November. The experience of the first year of the program aided our decision in formulating the list containing the most important general problems faced by new teachers during these months.

For the remainder of the year, we focused upon individual problems brought out in the group sessions where many of the above topics reoccurred.

WORKSHOPS

Two all-day workshops were organized for the teachers and aides in two pressing areas, aggression and violence in school, and the drug problem. The workshops were also open to those not in our project.

Aggression and Violence in the Classroom

We were able to bring in Dr. Nicholas J. Long, then Director of Hillcrest Children's Mental Health Center, Washington, D.C. and Professor of Education at American University. He presented a provocative lecture, providing insights into the behavior of violent and aggressive youth. Suggested ways of dealing with these problem students were offered to the participants using individual human resources. The lecture was followed up by twelve small group discussions led by staff members.

Drug Abuse Among School Youth

A panel of experts in the mental health field presented factual information concerning the availability, dissemination, and behavioral aspects of drug abusers. Panel presentations were followed by ten small group meetings with panelists, former addicts and parents of addicts leading discussions. Follow-up questionnaires indicated much satisfaction with the informal gains made by the teachers. Most felt the workshop to be helpful in future discussion of the drug problem with their students.

CRISIS SERVICE

Teachers and aides participating in the project had the opportunity to call upon any staff member with any concerns, whether personal or professional, at any time of day or night. A total of eleven persons participated in individual conferences with staff members. Five of them felt compelled and comfortable enough to discuss personal problems that indirectly affected their teaching competence. At the discretion of the caller, the conversations were held either over the phone or in person.

A mimeographed list of all staff and participants' school and home addresses and telephone numbers was provided for everyone.

EVALUATION

We felt that the general objective—to help new teachers to face the problems encountered in their first year—was achieved with a great deal of success. Only two teachers in our program left the Buffalo School System during the program's operation in the 1970-71 school year. One teacher left because of emotional problems and a second moved to California to care for an ailing mother.

Weekly attendance was high and the intensity of discussions was lively in all groups. We were encouraged by the number of comments made by individual teachers who felt they were profiting from the openness of problems brought to the groups.

Pre and posttesting with the use of (1) FIRO-B Test measuring interpersonal needs, (2) Rokeach Dogmatism Scale, and (3) a newly constructed questionnaire dealing with inner city children, were administered to the project participants. Preliminary indications are that the group as a whole changed in their attitudes and feelings since the beginning of the program.

A questionnaire evaluation of the orientation was conducted. The data indicated that 90 percent of the participants felt they had gained helpful information and were encouraged in facing their new teaching positions. Because we profited from the first year's orientation program and participant comments, the orientation was felt to be a profitable one. There was a great deal more enthusiasm displayed by the participants and more discussion following panel presentations.

Two areas related to models for emulation which were neither part of the objectives nor formally evaluated but certainly had a positive effect on the participants were related to the facts that (1) our staff was racially integrated and functioned together well; and (2) our staff disagreed with one another in class in a nonthreatening and acceptable manner. This came about often in particular discussions of techniques of teaching, and it helped get across the idea of individual teaching styles and techniques and the possibility of not being threatened when someone disagrees with you in a classroom.

Many of the teachers informed us verbally that they would have left teaching were it not for our program. Some achieved greater acceptance of their feelings toward children, and some were able to feel more comfortable having obtained realistic expectations about what they might manage to accomplish with their students. In the main, our assessment was that most teachers received help in the form of support, but that significant gains beyond that remain problematical.

We found no adverse effect of the groups on any of the participants. For whatever reasons, listening to the tapes convinced us that the atmosphere of the groups was predominantly supportive. There was no attempt at psycho-dynamic interpretations, or analysis of personality structure or problems of individual members. The group leaders and members kept the discussions focused on situationally and role related feelings, not on the individual members.

One frequent consequence of the group meetings was the realization by teachers that many of the problems defied individual solution. While such a realization resulted in the relief of feelings of guilt and inadequacy, it may also have influenced some to leave the situation, having diagnosed it as an impossible one. A lone teacher struggling with feelings of inadequacy might conceivably be more inclined to persist in trying to master the classroom situation—trying thereby to discount the feelings of personal inadequacy.

In the early days of the program, many of the new teachers and aides informed us that the only teachers or aides they knew in their schools were the teachers or aides they met in our program.

The first year of the New Teacher Program had a total of 66 teachers enrolled. Of these, 59 teachers completed at least one semester of the program, while 52 teachers completed the entire program. The second year of the program included 70 teachers. Of these, 66 teachers completed all or one semester of the program, and 55 teachers completed the entire program.

None of the teachers who left the program left for classroom reasons. The reasons for leaving included: (1) an after school position, (2) called up to military service, (3) transferred to an elementary school, (4) could not carry the additional college hours, (5) the college regularly attended would not accept the University of Buffalo's credits, (6) moved to another section of the country, (7) pregnancy, (8) left the state to care for an ailing mother, (9) graduate course conflict, (10) illness, and (11) personal conflict within a discussion group.

When the state no longer funded the project, and neither the university nor the Board of Education could find the funds to continue, many teachers did leave their inner city schools. Interestingly, a number of female teachers left because their husbands did not want them teaching in inner city schools.

We had fifteen teacher aides in the first year of the program and 25 in the second year of the program. Many of these aides now have their college degrees and are teaching. One is actually heading a school's remedial reading program; still another group of the aides is enrolled in the university, continuing to work toward their undergraduate degrees.

By any method of evaluation, the project was a success. The organization of the project was simple and can easily be replicated by other districts and institutions of higher education. One word of caution, however: *the project was a success mainly because of the staff involved.* The same organizational structure could fail easily if the wrong staff is involved.

SCHOOLS AS REINFORCERS OF POSITIVE BEHAVIOR

While still teaching graphic arts in the New York City "600" schools, I designed a system for rewarding my students' positive behavior (Foster, 1966). Basically, the system consisted of my sending a congratulatory letter to the parents of elected shop officers if they performed satisfactorily at monthly elected jobs.

Interestingly, a number of my students complained that their mothers were hitting them when they received my letter. Strange. Can you figure out why? How about a hint. When you were going to school, did any teacher ever contact your parents when you did something good? Probably not. We educators have conditioned parents to understand that the only time we get in touch with them is when their offspring have broken a school rule or in some way have done something wrong.

The experiences of the parents of children in the "600" schools were even more negative in relation to the schools than were those of other parents. (These negative feelings came about from experiences with regular schools, not the "600" schools.) What had happened was that my students' mothers were so conditioned that the receipt of a letter from school automatically meant that their child had done something wrong and was in trouble again. Even those parents who could not read were able to recognize the school's return address. It took some time but we eventually straightened out this misunderstanding.

Later, when I became an administrator, I moved my letter reward system to a schoolwide program. Youngsters earned letters for anything from attendance to citizenship. Sometimes, I would call parents just to say "hello," or to ask about a sick child. Even here, I trained myself to say quickly, "Hello, this is Mr. Foster from P.S. 624. Please don't worry, your son is not in trouble."

It is really sad that so many educators are fearful of their students' parents. The parents of inner city youngsters take so much abuse from the "system" that if teachers and administrators could only allow parents to get their feelings off their chests without feeling threatened, we could turn around a good many of our inner city school problems.

EDUCATING STAFF TO COPE WITH AGGRESSIVE AND VIOLENT YOUNGSTERS

Empirical evidence has shown that teacher and administrator physical fear of inner city students, whether based upon racism or life style differences, contributes to inner city school negative aggression and violence. Stated differently, when the school faculty or staff member shows his fear of his students, his student often is provoked to act out even more.

This hypothesis stems from two realities of inner city school problems that are related to physicalness, aggression, and violence. The first is the middle class educator's fear of physicalness and aggressive streetcorner behavior. The second is that there are some severely disturbed and socially maladjusted youngsters who act out their pathology in an aggressive, physical, violent syndrome.[h] Hence one may be, to some extent, imagined or perceived

[h]The reader must be reminded again that there are also many middle class behaviored youngsters in inner city schools.

violence while the other may be exceedingly real. Unquestionably, these two considerations lead directly to school problems that, to date, we have not been able to cope with—the reason being that we have refused to admit that they exist until the aggression has exploded into overt violence; or where we have admitted it exists, we have refused to assume any responsibility for amelioration of the problem other than in a punitive way.

Unquestionably, the school is just one of many agencies affecting this child's behavior and really cannot be assigned all the blame for causing him to behave the way he does. However, schools can do more to cope with these realities. If we would admit openly that the problems exist, we would find many teachers and administrators who possess the ability to cope with them. Some educators can cope more easily with negative aggression and violence than can others. For the real violence, though, we can educate professionals I call Interventionists who will be able to cope with the real violence (see Chapter Six). We can also educate other staff to be able to cope with either imagined or real violence. I have been reasonably successful in accomplishing these objectives in a number of ways.

The first is to expose my undergraduate students, through the Woodlawn program described earlier in this chapter, to the streetcorner behavior this book has reported. The second is through my graduate courses and workshops where we discuss not the fantasy but the reality of streetcorner behavior and how it is played out in the school. The third way is through a course designed specifically to help professionals cope with aggression and violence. The fourth was to lead 24 University of Buffalo students through a winter Outward Bound experience (Foster et al., 1972).

The course specially designed to help professionals cope with violence will be discussed here while the Outward Bound experience will be discussed in the next section on outdoor education.

An article in *Today's Education* (Assaults, 1972) concerning assaults on teachers reported Dr. Patterson from the New York City schools suggesting that school staff be educated in security and self-defense so that they will be able to deal intelligently with hostile pupils and emergencies. The article then went on to report that

> At least one course in this area has already been presented. In 1969-70, Millard Fillmore College of the State University of New York at Buffalo offered a controversial, no credit workshop, Methods and Techniques of Working with Children in Conflict. Taught by Herbert L. Foster, associate professor of education, the course met for 12 weeks—six weeks of lecture and discussion and six of gym instruction in physical intervention techniques. The purpose of the workshop was to instruct participants in how to help youngsters control aggressive and out-of-control behavior and how

to become sensitive to a child's early warning signals of impending overt aggressive behavior (p. 71).[i]

In more detail, the course was organized through our Millard Fillmore school to enable a greater latitude of entry into the course. Course participants included teachers, psychiatric nurses, social workers, a bus driver, case workers, and youth board workers.

Course Title

The course was announced as "Methods and Techniques of Handling Children in Conflict." However, some discussion concerning the word "handling" ensued. To some, the word "handling" implied hitting, becoming physical, or becoming punitive with a child. Consequently, "working" was substituted for handling and the title of the course was changed to "Methods and Techniques of Working with Children in Conflict."

Course Rationale and Objectives

Because of all that has been written earlier in this book, and because some of our school children must be helped to control their aggressive and out-of-control behavior in order to work toward a positive prognosis, workers have to be educated to: (1) cope with their student's aggression, acting-out, and out-of-control surface behavior; and (2) become sensitive to and work with the child's early warning signals of impending overt aggressive behavior.

We hypothesized that when the worker showed fear, he could provoke an already frightened youngster to act-out further. Additionally, the child who has underdeveloped controls or lacks controls of his behavior gains strength to control his behavior from: (1) the inner strength of the worker, and (2) if necessary, the willingness of the worker to nonpunitively but physically restrain the child.

In many classroom incidents of aggressive and violent acting-out behavior by the student either against his peers, his teachers, school property, or that which interferes with instruction, the student gives innumerable warning signals or clues that, depending upon their reading by the worker, can either exacerbate or ameliorate the impending situation. Furthermore, most workers have strong feelings against intervening physically with a child's out-of-control behavior. Many feel they should never touch a child under any circumtances. It is also perfectly normal for an adult to fear an aggressive child.

It was felt that the way the teacher organizes his classroom—for example, seats or desks, bulletin boards, displays—affects the child behavior. The

[i]The course was described in a paper I presented, *Educating Personnel to Work with Out-of-Control, Agressive, and Violent Surface Behavior*, at the 48th Annual International Convention, Council for Exceptional Children, Chicago, Illinois, April 19-25, 1970.

way the teacher structures the classroom procedures also affects the way the child relates in the classroom.

Finally, in interacting with children, parents, and/or administrators, the teacher's feelings, emotions, and attitudes play an important role in the way he relates to each situation. Therefore, the first step to educating workers to deal with their students' classroom aggression was to recognize that the problem exists and to help the worker to recognize his own emotions, feelings, and attitudes.

Classroom Workshop Meetings

The workshop included discussions and readings on the management of classroom problems, teacher introspection, and the emotional aspects of the teacher's role in working with disruptive and aggressive children. Local, state, and national professional organizations and an overview of the professional literature were presented briefly. Teacher behaviors in preventing and mediating crisis situations and curriculum methods and techniques were included. Incidence, identification, and diagnosis of emotionally disturbed and socially maladjusted children were also discussed.

Probably the most helpful technique was the playing of tapes in which a worker described a behavior incident. Workshop participants then discussed the incident from all points of view. Helpful to these discussions were the strategies for mediating a child's surface behavior, as suggested in Redl and Wineman's (1957) *The Aggressive Child* and listed separately in Long and Newman's (1965) *The Teacher's Handling of Children in Conflict*.

We also discussed incidents that were brought in by workshop participants. The most instructive evening evolved around a presentation by a woman school bus driver.

The emphasis was on the worker's not panicking and the positive educational and psychological management that prevents and ameliorates crisis situations. More pointedly, the emphasis was to intervene educationally and psychologically, thereby preventing the situation from deteriorating into a crisis. However it was also discussed realistically that in some cases, no matter how hard and expertly the worker tries, a youngster may still demonstrate aggressive out-of-control behavior that would have to be contained and/or controlled physically by the worker. Or the need might arise to remove a child physically to prevent contagion or for his own safety. We strove to get the participants to understand their own attitudes, feelings, and emotions; to develop their own style; and to be themselves.

Physical Intervention Techniques

The learning and practice of techniques of nonpunitively intervening physically with a youngster's out-of-control aggressive surface behavior took place for the first semester in the Buffalo Police Department's gym. For the second semester, the instruction was moved to the university's gym. In both semesters, instruction was given by a Buffalo Police Desk Lieutenant expert in judo. The objective was not necessarily to master techniques of physical intervention; rather, the objective was to reduce the worker's fear of aggressive children by demonstrating the most that an out-of-control child could do to the worker physically. This, to some extent, was demonstrated by showing the workshop participants that they could fall, be knocked down, have a dress or suit torn, get punched, have a watch or glasses broken, and still live to tell the story.

Participants, however, practiced techniques such as:

1. How to break up fights.
2. How to fall.
3. How to disarm a child who may be attacking with a knife, scissors, or lead pipe.
4. How to use a "come along" to remove a child.
5. How to restrain a child.

Throughout these sessions the point was demonstrated and emphasized that the secure worker need not overuse force. As in the classroom meetings, it was argued that there is a difference between corporal punishment and nonpunitive physical intervention. Similarly, there is a difference between punitively and illegally overusing force as compared with the nonpunitive and legal use of physical intervention.

Another area emphasized was educating the worker to differentiate between out-of-control behavior and lower socioeconomic norm violating behavior that is too often perceived by the worker as threatening or illegitimate violence or behavior. Much of what is perceived as threatening and illegitimate violence is nothing more than lower class testing of the worker's ability to control and set limits. If nothing else, the course demonstrated to the participants that someone was concerned and willing to discuss the very real everyday problems they were facing.

Additionally, as the course progressed and the participants became more aware of the reasons for negative student behavior, they became more understanding and accepting of this behavior. Hence they became less threatened and were better able to cope with classroom behavior situations by intervening and defusing potentially explosive situations as well as learning when to ignore behavior.

The positive results and feelings from our course were further reinforced in a conversation with David A. Pratt, Coordinator of Drug and Alcoholism Services, Erie, Pennsylvania. A number of years ago, he was the only male worker in a residential psychiatric treatment center between the hours of 9:00 to 4:00 p.m. The youngsters in the facility were approximately six to fourteen years of age. Some of the twelve, thirteen, and fourteen-year-olds were aggressive "acting-outers" and sometimes bigger in stature than some of the nursing staff.

Frequently, he was called to "come to the rescue" of various female staff who were being challenged by one of the youngsters. Although this was usually a problem with the boys, occasionally one of the older girls would act-out physically too.

According to Mr. Pratt,

> This created a problem for the acting-out child, who, having no internal controls to rely on, saw the external controls as being unable to hold his hostile angry behavior once his feelings would break loose. This caused him to panic and act out even more. Secondly, it caused the entire group to feel insecure in that they could not rely on the adults to protect them. Thirdly, my constant intervening made it impossible for me to carry out various group activities in which I was engaged when I received the S.O.S. My departure would anger the children in my group.

Although this problem was discussed frequently at staff meetings, no useful means of intervening in the problem was suggested until another area agency hired someone who happened to possess "fantastic methods of breaking up fights, of moving children from place to place without hurting them, etc."

A six-session course was set up with this worker at which he discussed his philosophy, and various physical intervention techniques were demonstrated.

> He suggested that the staff practice on one another but to say nothing to the children, feeling that this would merely challenge them further. As the lessons progressed, you could see the nursing staff developing attitudinal change as they began to think they *could* handle the children by themselves. After the lessons were concluded, we did nothing different in terms of group structure, composition, program policies or anything else. It was "business" as usual. To the best of my recollection, following these lessons, I was not called again to intervene in a one-on-one confrontation of child with female staff. More males were added to the staff but they were not called upon either.[j]

In a second situation later, when he directed a residential children's center, a similar problem arose with a male and female staff member. He set up a

[j]Personal correspondence and discussion with David A. Pratt, ACSW, Coordinator of Drug and Alcoholism Services, Mental Health and Retardation Office, Erie, Pennsylvania.

similar course and observed similar results. Additional discussions with others around the country suggests similar results too.

Controversy Concerning the Course

Our course became controversial for at least two reasons. The first was the anxiety of so many concerning the physical handling of youngsters. The second was an unfortunate incident concerning publicity about the course in a local newspaper.

The real controversy started when a letter was sent from our University Information Services to a local paper inquiring as to whether they would be interested in a reporter's doing a feature story on the course. Supposedly, the person to whom the letter was sent was away at the time. Someone from the newspaper thereupon turned the letter of inquiry into an article and injected the words "Core-Area Pupils (UB, 1968, p. 17)."

The headline read "UB Will Prepare Teachers to Handle Core-Area Pupils." The article also stated: "For five of the twelve class periods, students will meet with a Buffalo Police Academy judo expert, who will teach them to handle children with weapons and to control a class without causing the child or teacher to lose face (p. 17)."

Things then began to happen. A black U.B. student presented a motion before our Student Polity that the course be discontinued. Complaints were made to our University Institutionalized Racism Committee, the Buffalo Human Relations Commission, and someone from the Black Teachers Association of Buffalo called us.

On our part, we tried unsuccessfully to get the newspaper to print a retraction or correction. However, Professor Murray Levine, Director of the Graduate Program Community-Clinical Psychology, who was helping with the classroom aspects of the course, and I wrote a letter to the editor of the paper and it was published.

> We wish to correct an error in the article, "UB Will Prepare Teachers to Handle Core-Area Pupils,". . . . The course . . . is designed to help teachers, nurses, social workers, child care workers and others to be more effective in their work with socially maladjusted children. The course is not, as reported, designed to prepare teachers "to handle core-area pupils."
>
> One of the manifestations of emotional disturbance is aggressive and out-of-control behavior, which sometimes requires the adult to restrain the child and prevent him from hurting himself or others.
>
> The teacher or other child care worker who is faced with the problem of controlling a disturbed child's outbursts routinely reports feelings of fear, guilt, and distress. The portion of the course which deals with physical intervention techniques is designed to help

the worker to deal with the situation effectively and without hurting the child.

The teacher's ability to mediate a child's crisis situation often is the key to whether or not the child progresses.

The course also focuses on the emotional aspects of the teacher's role in managing the classroom and suggests psychological techniques to help children with problems. Much of the discussion centers on the teacher's ability to understand his own emotional state in his relationship with children in conflict.

Although the course is focused on teachers working with emotionally disturbed and maladjusted children in the classroom, it is open to anyone working with children.

The group taking the course includes teachers from suburban areas, Canada, Buffalo, social workers, and psychiatric nurses (p. 20).

We proceeded with the course while responding in a number of ways to our critics. In addition to the above letter, we prepared a packet of photo copies of the newspaper clippings, the course description, course announcement, and bibliography. This package was sent to various people around the city of Buffalo whom we knew had expressed an interest or were involved in education. We also met with the University Committee on Institutionalized Racism and calmed their fears.

The young man who raised the issue in our student Polity came to see me. He was from Queens in New York City and other than his being black and my being white, we had much in common. His reintroduced motion in the Student Polity called for the course to be expanded to two semesters—one semester of emotional restraint and one semester of physical restraint.

The entire controversy eventually dissipated and we gave the course a second time. It should be pointed out that all of this transpired while our students were acting-out against the university. Actually, had some of our university faculty and administration taken our course, maybe we could have escaped many of the problems we had.

Two last points that should be mentioned. Many of the older women who took the course had problems with the physical aspects of the gym sessions. Many of them dropped out. If the course were given again, we would try to build in a more gradual approach to the physical aspects of the course.

OUTDOOR EDUCATION

If you are from the greater New York City area, you probably have heard of the Herring *maven*. Well, I am an outdoor education *maven*. (In Yiddish, a *maven* is a good judge of quality, an expert, someone who is really knowledgeable, a connoisseur.) I joined the Cub Scouts when I was nine and progressed through the Boy Scouts, Explorers, and Rover Scouts,[k] and am now a merit badge counselor. I guess the Boy Scouts prepared me for my professional life at least as much as did my formal education.[l] The Scouts also helped me develop a love for the out of doors. I really have fond memories of my Scouting days with Troop 249, particularly the Rover Crew Days.

While an undergraduate at New York University, I met my future wife, Anita, in the N.Y.U. Outdoor Club. Also as an undergraduate, I camped out frequently in the Bear Mountain Harriman State Park particularly the weekend before exams, relaxing.

I took my Masters at New York University in what was then called Camping Education and is now referred to as Outdoor Education or outdoor pursuits. In those days, we used to hike with knapsacks. Now most high school and university students own backpacks. They are generally used for carrying books and groceries. Occasionally, students do use them for camping and hiking.

I am not the only person involved in outdoor education in the United States. Innumerable people were involved long before I was, and there are many more involved now. In no sense have I cornered the outdoor education market—I just want to spread the gospel on how to learn, to grow, to motivate and have fun all at the same time.

There are many explanations for outdoor education. Probably the most often quoted is that of L.B. Sharp (1957), "That which can best be learned in the out of doors through direct experience, dealing with native materials and life situations, should there be learned." A contemporary definition could refer to any experience outside the school's formal classroom environment—that is, any experience outside the school building.

Typically, today, outdoor education starts in the school yard and through learning experiences moves in concentric circles from the school to the "country." That is what is being suggested for those living in urban areas. For me, I like to go right out to the country.

Educators in Connecticut like the idea of outdoor education, too (Davenport, Jr., 1973). A federally supported New England program in Teacher Education (NEPTE) was organized to increase teacher effectiveness. Robert Gillette, a thirty-five-year-old English teacher, was awarded $300,000 to be used over a three-year period for his project. The two major stipulations of the grant were that he receive $1,000 more in salary than his superintendent and that the award go to a classroom teacher.

He and two other teachers, Mrs. Patricia Clark, a science teacher, and Charles Hussey, a history teacher, organized Operation Turn On. The project consisted of a number of outdoor education trips that integrated the school's

[k]Rover Scouting was disbanded shortly after World War II. It was for those over eighteen years of age.
[l]I was lucky. I belonged to troop 249 of the Boro Park Y.M. & W.W.H.A. Our Scoutmaster, Abe Hershkowitz, recently retired from being Executive Director of the Y.

history. English, and science curriculum with challenging physical activity. Mr. Gillette started his program four years ago by taking youngsters who were turned off by school on biking and hiking trips.

In this section, I will describe some of my outdoor education experiences as: (1) a teacher in the "600" schools; (2) a camping coordinator and curriculum consultant in the New York City Junior Guidance Classes Program; (3) an administrator in the "600" schools; and now, (4) as a university professor. Of course, there were usually some school objections to what I wanted to do in the way of outdoor education; however, I kept at it and always managed to overcome the problems. This is important because too many teachers either give up after being told "no" once by a supervisor, ask when they should just do, or use any excuse for not doing.

The "600" Schools

While teaching in an afterschool project "Operation More,"[m] I organized Boy Scout Troop 888. As part of the troop activities, we did quite a bit of day hiking on Staten Island. As I recall, it was raining and snowing the day of our first trip. We went anyway because as Scouts we were "prepared." Some of the school personnel laughed at us; they referred to our trip as "Foster's Folly." Little did they know that the idea of going on a hike regardless of the weather was a challenge for some of the tough gang youngsters in our school. Harrison Salisbury (1958, p. 163), wrote about our troop in his book *The Shook-Up Generation*.

> There is a Boy Scout troop at Public School 613. At first Boy Scouts were regarded as sissies by the street boys who make up the school population. Only a few boys joined, just one with a uniform. They went on Saturday hikes and cookouts. No matter what the weather, no matter how cold, how snowy, how rainy, the Scouts went out. They began to build a "rep" as tough guys. Bopping youngsters, tough members of the Chaplains, the Bishops, the Stonekillers, admitted that Scouts were not "chicken" after all. A year later the troop had sixteen members. Most of them had uniforms. Some of the Bishops and Stonekillers had joined up.[n]

We related much of Scouting's outdoor experiences to our school curriculum. Many of the academic teachers worked with us in arranging for

[m]"Operation More," was the popular name for project No. 22-239 of the New York City Board of Education's Committee on Juvenile Delinquency.

[n]The accuracy of one point in Salisbury's comments points up a common fear. We never went on Saturday hikes. We always went on school time. Someone apparently told Salisbury that the trips were on Saturday in fear of revealing that we were going on school time. I wrote an article about my troop, "Scouting in the Blackboard Jungle." *Scouting Magazine*, 1961, 49(8), 6-7, 26. It was edited and printed as "Scouting," 87th Congress, *Congressional Record*, 108:A444, January 23, 1962.

Scouts to use their academic areas to relate pre and posttrip experiences. Often, a good deal of juggling of classroom assignments had to be arranged for us to leave for the day. Sometimes, extra youngsters had to be taken if we wanted to go because of sudden teacher absence.

After innumerable day trips, we wanted to go on an overnight. However, we had a problem in securing permission for an overnight on school days. When informed that because of "insurance" considerations, we could not go, I asked, "Who said so?" Each pointing of the finger was tracked down until permission was obtained. Too often, new teachers give up too quickly when told "no" by an administrator. Instead, they should figure out a way to pragmatically manipulate the system to the benefit of their students. However, where the administrator's philosophy is diametrically opposed to that of the teacher, my advice is for the teacher to transfer out of that school.

Aurie McCabe, director of the Operation More Project, and Bernie Charles, who was the Assistant Scoutmaster for a while, were great helps with the Troop. In addition to the Scouts, I organized a hiking club that hiked to historical spots throughout the City. From what I hear, some of my Scouts have done well. One is now a teacher of special education, four own thriving businesses in New York City, and one is a radiologist.

The Junior Guidance Classes Program and Outdoor Education[o]

The Junior Guidance Classes Program received a $700.00 grant from the Johanna M. Lindlof Camp Committee to experiment with an outdoor education program.[p] This grant continued the New York City Board of Education's tradition of relating outdoor education to the curriculum. The Lindlof Committee and the New York City Board of Education conducted two earlier school-camping experiments. The first was a three-week sleep-in camp experience for 62 children and their teachers in June, 1947, at Life Camps. The second was a three-day sleep-over school camping experience conducted by the All-Day Neighborhood Schools at Hudson Guild Farm, Netcong, New Jersey.

I was in the "600" schools and my transfer to the Junior Guidance Program to direct the experiment was finally approved three weeks before the first trip was set to go.

Seven Junior Guidance Classes from three schools in Manhattan were involved in the experiment. Four second through fifth grade closed register classes were from P.S. 68. Second, third, and fourth grade open register classes

[o]The Junior Guidance Classes Program is a New York City elementary school program for socially maladjusted and emotionally disturbed youngsters.

[p]In 1938, the Honorable Johanna M. Lindlof was presented with a $400.00 surplus from a dinner given in her honor by several professional and civic groups. Mrs. Lindlof donated this money to a Camp Fund for Public School Children, from which grew the Johanna M. Lindlof Camp Committee for Public School Children.

from P.S. 199 were also included.[q] Two of the classes had five school camping experiences while the other two had one experience each.

We used the Flora Haas Site of the Henry Kaufmann campgrounds on Staten Island for all of our school camping experiences, thanks to Monte Melamed, Executive Director of the Henry Kaufmann Campgrounds.[r] The Flora Haas Site was selected because of its proximity to Manhattan, the experience of the Executive Director, and the availability of the campgrounds on a year-round basis. Additionally, the Henry Kaufmann Campgrounds had pioneered in day camping programs for large numbers of city children.

Overall Planning

Though we structured our program, we remained flexible, adjusting the program as we progressed. A multidisciplinary team of teachers, guidance counselors, social worker, resource teacher, and camping coordinator met often prior to the first trip, and biweekly between trips.

Parent Involvement

Parent involvement in the school camping experiment was an extension of Junior Guidance philosophy. By involving the parents, their concerns about the camping experience were allayed, and they then were able to help their children with any of their trip related anxieties.

Slides of my Scouts showing black and white youngsters camping were shown to the parents providing examples of the campgrounds and outdoor activities. Refreshments were served at our meetings which helped relax everyone. The parents supported the program wholeheartedly.

Choice of Classes and Staff

Careful analysis was made of all Junior Guidance classes to determine which would participate. Plans for and development of the five trip experience were enhanced by the fact that

[q]The open register class consists of fifteen youngsters in need of emergency therapeutic help. These youngsters are extremely disruptive and cannot be maintained in a regular class. Each class covers two overlapping grades and serves the entire district. Closed register classes serve poorly functioning children showing a wide range of behavior and personality symptoms. A track consists of a two class unit, usually a second and third grade class. Ten to fifteen students are assigned to each starting class. Classes are single-graded, and divided equally between girls and boys and balanced between aggressive and withdrawn children of at least average intelligence. Efforts are usually made to limit the hyperactive and disruptive children to two or three. Though most of the students are from the host school, some come from schools within walking distance.

[r]I had directed the Mildred Goetz Day Camp of the Henry Kaufmann Campgrounds for many years and was familiar with the Flora Haas Site. The Flora Haas Site was also used for many of the Scout trips described earlier. The Henry Kaufmann Campgrounds is an agency of the Federation of Jewish Philanthropies of New York City.

1. Both classes were relatively stable, and the students appeared to possess a degree of readiness for this program.
2. The three teachers of these classes were very receptive to the idea of the school camping experience and they had had some prior camping experience.
3. P.S. 68's location lent itself to easy access to sites for preneighborhood trips as well as food stores.
4. All the youngsters were able to participate in the experience.
5. There was a good multidisciplinary team of an assistant principal, a guidance counselor, a community agency social worker, a resource assistant, and the teachers were already functioning in the school.
6. The principal, Harold Sklar, was an experienced camp director and was enthusiastic about the school camping experiment.

Staff Preparation

Staff preparation began by showing slides of the campgrounds followed by a site visit. The visit was also used to help us decide the best route for the bus to travel to the Staten Island Ferry so that students could observe the Hudson River and pier activities. Additional curriculum planning during this staff experience included investigating picnic and hiking areas and facilities, as well as noting possible trouble areas. The limits and routines for our students were defined primarily on this trip. Finally, the staff trip also provided us with a myriad of ideas and suggestions for integrating the school camping experiences with the school's curriculum.

Food

The students and teachers planned all lunches. Local food stores were canvassed to find the managers and employees who would welcome our students' food purchases. As part of their learning experience, students also learned about healthy meals. Newspapers were used in class to discuss prices and a price limit was set for each person per meal.

Consideration was given to lunch types. If we cooked, most of the day would be spent cooking. Therefore, if we wanted to do a good deal of hiking and exploring, lunches would be taken or a group assigned to do the cooking.

The Bus and Ferry

The bus driver was apprised of our students and program. He was introduced to our students as soon as they boarded the bus. He cooperated, becoming an additional teacher, eating and participating with us on most of our experiences. At one point he even tried to talk a pouting youngster into eating.

Arrangements were made with the City of New York Department of Marine and Aviation for priority boarding privileges on the Staten Island Ferry so that we would be at the front of the ferry. This provided us with a good view of the harbor and put us on the outside, in the open, as we did not want to be in the center of the enclosed ferry with the fumes, smells, and heat that permeate that area and which might possibly cause some sickness.

In case of bus sickness, teachers were provided with paper bags and a deodorant spray; none of these items were used. To guard further against bus sickness, we served orange drink and punch exclusively on the bus and the trip because we felt that milk mixed with excitement, heat, and student overheating could possibly cause some digestive problems.

On the bus, each class sat with its teacher. One problem did arise. On the first return trip, one youngster who had sat in an aisle seat on the way to the campgrounds, wanted to sit near a window. His demands became contagious and some arguments and fights ensued.

This problem was eliminated for all other trips by simply announcing on the next trip, "Whoever sits near a window on the trip to camp will change with his partner on the way home." The problem never came up again.

Curriculum Goals

The resource assistant, Judith Schmidt, and I worked with the teachers in developing curriculum goals and in providing materials and methods to achieve these goals. We met at least biweekly in school time and sometimes in the evenings. Three of the most significant objectives related to curriculum included: (1) increased socialization of our students; (2) increased academic learnings; and (3) sharpened sensory perception and increased appreciation.

According to the staff's observations and some of our pre and posttesting, the students appeared to have increased their abilities in all objective areas. Additionally, the staff gained an understanding of how meaningful a unified curriculum could be.

OUTDOOR EDUCATION WHILE AN ADMINISTRATOR IN THE "600" SCHOOLS

A big plus at the Francis Parkman High School (P.S. 624, Manhattan) was our principal, Jud Axelbank's, favoring and supporting our outdoor education ideas. Despite his support, though, we still had to work out a number of problems.

Transportation

We were able to get free passes for using the surface transportation facilities of the City. However, since we took 40 to 55 students, using surface or subway transportation was a problem. And, if we wanted to carry any equipment, this added to our problems.

Luckily, the buses used to transport handicapped youngsters became available for our use. We put these buses to excellent use about once a month, including the driver in everything we did. Drivers were happy to drive us because of the standards of behavior which had been agreed upon cooperatively with the youngsters prior to the trip and which were maintained throughout. We did have a part of the curriculum programmed for the bus trip and one of our teachers played a guitar, so we also did some singing.

Food

At first, food for the trips was a problem because all "600" students receive free lunches. The first problem was worked out by getting the district lunch supervisors to provide us with a sandwich or cookout lunch as needed. At first, the lunch people opposed our proposals. However, they accepted our suggestions when we agreed to give them at least two or three weeks' notice of the date and type of lunch we wanted. This also included their providing ice for the milk or juice.

Once we set the date and type of lunch we wanted, we had to take the lunch even if a sudden rain washed out the trip. We shared these rules with our students so that they would be aware of all ramifications. When working with disturbed youngsters, even a lunch change could cause a youngster to become unduly upset.

On one trip, we were all set to go but the lunches had not arrived. This resulted in our delaying the trip for almost two hours. We solved this problem for later trips by having one member of the faculty take his car. This person could wait if the food was late while we left with the bus. The car also could provide transportation if a member of the faculty or a student were hurt or became sick.

Another important point is that all the staff, other than the person driving the one car, had to ride on the bus with the students. I feel that the camping experience gets a more positive start when the teachers travel to the site with the youngsters, thus setting the tenor and informal relationships while maintaining a mutual respect.

Types of Trips

We went just about everywhere in New York City. We visited the Staten Island Zoo, which is reputed to have one of the best reptile collections in the country. We went to Staten Island very often because of the ferry ride and Staten Island's parks. This ride provided an interesting and leisurely trip through New York Harbor.

We visited most of the parks and beach fronts on Staten Island. We did everything from planning meals and cooking out, doing art, nature study, to various sports activities or just lying in the sun.

We also started a schoolwide field day at McCombs Dam Park, which is across the street from the Yankee Stadium. The field day included morning track and field events and a student versus faculty softball game in the afternoon.

Curriculum

Curriculum was involved on all trips. The amount of curriculum planned for any specific trip depended upon where we were going and our objectives.

For example, even on a trip where we played touch football, we also had staff and students doing art work, creative writing, or exploring on a nature walk. Also, some teachers always did prior and follow-up curriculum work in their classes. We also started a school newspaper that carried articles about our trips.

Another aspect related to curriculum that was very important was what we wore. We were always encouraging our students to dress appropriately for the social situation they were in. On our trips, students observed staff in dungarees and chinoes while seeing them in tie and suit in school. Seeing their teachers as ordinary people in an out-of-school environment helped the youngsters to relate to them on another level.

Student Anxieties

Attendance was low on our first trip. Investigation revealed that our students had anxieties about going places other than the school and their neighborhoods. This was interesting when considering the supposed toughness of some of our students who held leadership positions in fighting gangs. However, under their tough exterior were many anxieties.

Our staff discussed this problem and we resolved it. The first thing we did was to better prepare our students for the trips in a number of ways. Some of us went to visit the site of the trip, taking pictures and slides which were shown to our students in classes and in the auditorium programs. Maps also were provided to show exactly where we were going; some teachers began bringing our trips into their class discussions. Some of us also began to stop at our students' homes the morning of a trip to pick them up and bring them to school. Our efforts worked out well, and attendance on all trips soared.

The trips had a number of positive effects upon the school. They brought both teachers and students together informally, creating additional positive relationships. Rarely do teachers get the opportunity to relate to one another on an informal basis. Therefore, the relationships induced by the trips created stronger staff and student relationships on all levels. Obviously, therefore, the trips had a good deal to do with the lessening of problems in the school.

Two more points. Where teachers related the outdoor education experiences to their classroom curriculum, there was also added interest and the youngsters worked more willingly. The second point is that in many cases, students disciplined one another on the trips. In one case, one of the youngsters started smoking pot while we were seated around a campfire. The staff had not been aware of the boy's having this with him. Before we noticed, another student took the "joint" out of the other youngster's mouth and threw it into the fire, berating him with, "Hey man, don't mess up! We want to go on these trips."

OUTDOOR EDUCATION AND THE UNIVERSITY

In this section, outdoor education will be discussed in relation to the areas of (1) Outward Bound, (2) my courses, and (3) my students taking their students on outdoor education experiences.

Outward Bound

For a while, after I arrived at the University of Buffalo, I did more talking than doing about outdoor education. Then I participated in an experience that changed me back into a doer: three other faculty members and I took 24 University of Buffalo undergraduates on an Outward Bound experience.

The Outward Bound experience had a profound effect on me. It somehow provided me with the set and emotional frame of mind to do what I dreamed of doing, and as a result of Outward Bound, I began to implement instead of just dreaming and fantasizing.

As noted earlier in the book, for a long time I had held the belief that many inner city teachers feared their students' physical life style. Therefore, if I could somehow expose teachers to challenging physical experiences, possibly they would become more secure physically and emotionally, and thus less fearful of their students. Along with this idea, I had been reading about the program called Outward Bound.

Outward Bound was started in 1941 in Aberdovey, Wales, to "instill a spiritual tenacity and the will to survive in young British seamen torpedoed during World War II (Outward, p. 1)." The aims, as promulgated by Outward Bound founder and educator, Dr. Kurt Hahn, stand today to serve as a model to emulate for teachers (and others) anywhere, most specifically those working in difficult situations.

> The aim of education is to impel young people into value-forming experiences ... to insure the survival of these qualities: an enterprising curiosity; an undefeatable spirit; tenacity in pursuit; readiness for sensible self-denial; and above all, compassion (Outward, p. 1).

After World War II, an Outward Bound school was organized in Colorado. Today there are six Outward Bound schools throughout the United States. My belief was that Outward Bound could provide the vehicle to help

[5]National Outward Bound is located at 165 W. Putnam Ave., Greenwich, Conn. 06830. The Outward Bound Schools are: Colorado, Texas, North Carolina, Northwest, Hurricane Island, and Minnesota.

educate and prepare teachers for inner city school positions by increasing their self-awareness and self-confidence and thus helping them overcome their fears.

After preliminary correspondence and phone calls with National Outward Bound, and some soliciting of faculty support, a number of us met with Robert Lentz, then Educational Director of Outward Bound. From this meeting came a cooperative venture between Outward Bound and the University of Buffalo. We wanted to investigate whether or not Outward Bound would be relevant to the curricular goals of two ongoing teacher preparation programs—specifically, the inner city program and the Professional Health, Physical Education, and Recreation program.

One of the positive aspects of the University of Buffalo was the flexibility to experiment without any real constraints. To minimize interference with the students' ongoing academic programs, they were advised to take a lighter load. They could also register for up to eight hours of independent study. Each of the student participants was required to discuss the experience with his course professors to arrange for the making up of work missed while away from campus.

After medical examinations and briefing meetings everyone met at the Student Union at 7:00 a.m. Sunday, February 13, 1971 for the trip to the Outward Bound Center at Dartmouth College in Hanover, New Hampshire. Dr. Diane DeBacy, Dr. William Loockerman, Mr. Roy Bartoo, and I provided our cars for transportation. The temperature on that morning was five degrees above zero, a foot of snow had fallen, and blizzard conditions prevailed.

Driving conditions were extremely hazardous, particularly for the first six hours. Secondary roads had to be used until the open section of the New York State Thruway was reached at Rochester. After approximately twelve hours, we arrived at Hanover. Our staff drove to the home of Will Lange, who was then Center Director, to meet with him and Bob MacArthur, D-11 course director. We discussed the plans and were informed that high school students would also be on the expedition.

The next morning we arrived at Dartmouth Outward Bound Headquarters at 8:00 a.m. Everyone gathered in a lounge where introductions were made and participants divided into gangs (groups). Each gang went to its assigned room to wait for a call to pick up gear. Once gear was picked up and packed, gangs were driven four miles to the Appalachian trail for the three-mile hike to Harris Cabin. Snowshoes had to be used almost immediately as the snow, although packed in places, was about three feet deep.

As each gang arrived at Harris Cabin, they picked a spot in the surrounding wooded area and set up their two- and three-person tents. Gangs were assigned to such duties as loading the sledge at the road, pulling it to the cabin, and then unloading the food or wood pulled, digging latrines, and cooking. One student who did not come with us arrived later—he had driven off the road into a snowbank the morning of the thirteenth.

For the next few days, meals were served in Harris Cabin and gang members became acquainted through various group techniques. Gangs planned their first expedition as to food, route to be taken, and the distance to be traveled. The first gang left Harris Cabin on its expedition on the second day. Within a few days, all gangs had pulled out, thus launched on a most challenging and demanding experience.

For the remainder of the Outward Bound experience, gangs participated in rappelling (rope descent on a rock cliff), three-day individual solos, a final expedition, and returned to Harris Cabin for the final marathon run and the awarding of Outward Bound certificates. The sequence of the above experiences varied with each gang. On the last day of the experience, all gangs hiked from Harris Cabin to Dartmouth, turned in their gear, showered, ate, and boarded a bus for Buffalo.

The final marathon run of four and one-half miles on snowshoes was the crowning event for me. I took pictures at the start of the run and then started running. I came in thirty-fourth out of 60. The last three-quarters of a mile or so almost did me in; I was really dead. What saved me and helped me to finish was my reverting to my old Boy Scout pace—I ran 50 steps and walked 50 steps until I finished. Upon finishing, one of my students took my picture which I enlarged. When I feel down or low, I look at the picture and get up and keep going (Figure 7-2).

The data and personal comments indicate that the University of Buffalo-Dartmouth Outward Bound experience was successful in many areas. Many student and faculty participants experienced some emotional or personal involvement that has been reflected in his or her personal or professional life. For many of the students and faculty, Outward Bound provided the cognitive and affective arena for looking and reflecting on oneself and moving to some form of action, change, or even reinforcement.

One of the pre and posttests we gave our students was the Thurston Temperament Schedule. The results of this test found that the stability trait improved significantly. Stability is characterized by being calm in a crisis and difficult to disturb or distract. This data supported the rationale for this study and suggested that the Outward Bound experience provided an excellent growth and learning experience for undergraduates preparing for teaching positions in inner city schools or, possibly, for teachers already teaching in inner city schools. One of the reported needs for inner city schools is for teachers who can retain their equilibrium amidst typical unsettling inner city school conditions. Experience has shown that the teacher's ability to remain calm and in charge often prevents a minor incident from deteriorating into disorder or a negative learning experience.

Some of the student participants commented that for the first time since they had arrived at the university, as a direct result of this experience they had found some direction and feeling about their life's aspirations.

One of the most positive outcomes of the experience was the interpersonal relationships that developed. In the mutual help environment of Outward Bound, new, informal, but respectful faculty-student relationships developed that could not have been achieved through normal campus faculty-student interaction.

Student comments about the experience included,

"I hope I'm more optimistic about myself and other people. I think that I'll be able to react with people more effectively because I've learned more things about myself. . . ."

"I think it's one of the greatest experiences I've ever had. I really found there is no such word as can't. . . . You decide it. When you say that you can't climb a mountain. The only reason you can't is because you think that you can't. Not because you can't."

"You look straight up and you know you gotta go up there and you gotta hang onto the trees to get up this ledge. You know, you say at the bottom of the hill there is no way I can do it. Then half an hour later you are up there.

"On the way up you're mad and you're swearing and all that. But man, when you get up there you're feeling really great. And, every time when something like that would come up I would find myself, that I wouldn't be that stressed anymore. It would come a little bit easier. I could contain myself and put up with it more. And I found myself helping other people."

"He was absolutely terrified of heights. At first he said he wasn't gonna go over. He didn't want to climb up the hill to go over the ledge. Everybody had done it and I guess group pressure made him climb the hill. And, he got into the harness. He really had to be talked down.

"He would move out on the ledge a few feet. He would look up and smile, and he would crack a nervous joke. He came up and said, 'Pull me a little tighter. Hand on to the belay.' And, everyone was really pulling for him.

"I knew he was gonna do it. . . .

"As soon as he came down, I ran up and gave him a tremendous hug. He was just like this, you know, he just couldn't believe that he had done something like this. That was really a fine moment."

All these student reactions served to reinforce my original contention that this type of experience had a definite place in teacher education. Outward Bound provided me with the impetus to do all of the outdoor education activities I had thought about but had not done.

Outdoor Education and My Courses

After Outward Bound I began to implement my philosophy. As noted earlier in my undergraduate course description, if you take an undergraduate course with me you must go on an overnight outdoor education experience if you want to contract for a possible grade of A or B. If you want to contract for a grade of S or U, you must go on at least a one-day outdoor education experience. The same rule holds true for my graduate students.

We had food and equipment committees for my first course that had an overnight. Other than an evening campfire with a role-playing skit, we did little more than sit around, drink beer, swim, and fish a bit. Since then, we have gradually developed a real outdoor education curriculum for our trips. Also, wherever possible, the overnight experience is at the beginning of the semester rather than at the end. These changes have come about because I now know what I want to do and have become more directive rather than waiting for some group processes to jell. Also, we evaluate each outdoor education experience and make appropriate adjustments.

The first day a graduate class meets, we organize four committees. Everyone, including me, serves on at least one committee—food, equipment, transportation and site, and activities. The committees begin meeting immediately at other than class times.

We now involve ourselves in all aspects of curriculum. Although the experience is well planned, we still remain flexible for individual relaxing time. We all take turns cooking and cleaning up. We eat our meals together in one large group.

On our last trip this semester, we had only about fourteen students so we went food shopping together. We divided into groups and each group purchased ingredients for one meal, which they cooked and served. It worked so well, we intend to follow this procedure on future trips.

Somehow we usually round up enough tents, stoves, and equipment for our needs. From the outdoor education fee required for this course we are beginning to build up a store of some equipment. This equipment also becomes available to my graduate students who are teachers for use with their students. We also take innumerable black and white photographs and slides.

The reactions of my students to the outdoor education experience trips are varied. Last summer (1973), 42 students signed up for my Teaching in Inner City Schools course. Only three students, one of whom was pregnant, dropped the course because of the outdoor education requirement. The overwhelming majority of students, many of whom are skeptical at first, finish the course with positive feelings about the experience. Only a few go through the motions of participating, and there are always one or two who cannot understand why we are not taking public school children on our trips. My response to them is that as soon as they master the outdoor education skills we are teaching, they should, by all means, take their students on a trip. But first they must become skillful themselves.

One of the interesting aspects is the role played by the fantasies that some black and white students have about each other, particularly when the blacks or whites come from different socioeconomic backgrounds. Many black students are surprised to find white students willing to lend them sleeping bags and then also to be willing to sleep in the same tent or alongside them. Also black and white students sometimes have interesting concepts of one another's eating habits, even to the point of expressing some anxieties as to whether they will be able to eat what the other person of a different color eats.

The feelings of most participants are summed up in this excerpt from a student's paper.

> Many obstacles almost prevented me from making the weekend camping trip to Allegany State Park. It is mid-October, the weather has been rainy all week, and the FBI and other local and State law officers were trying to capture an extortionist who had been sighted in the park. As these events began to unfold during the week, I became more discouraged about making the trip. Friday finally arrived; a classmate came to school prepared to make the trip, and his only means of getting there depended on my overcoming my fears. His presence at school—his depending on me—I just couldn't

disappoint him; I realized the distance that he had traveled to meet with me. . . .

The group consisted of people with various ethnic backgrounds, from different parts of the world. This gave the group a nice mix of personalities. . . .

The serenity one captures from being with nature gives a person a sort of reverence; color at this point means nothing here. An individual's inward hostilities towards others seem to disappear. I suppose this can be from the dependence each one has for the other in order to survive with the barest necessities. . . .

I became frightened of a porcupine that had gotten trapped in the bathroom. When I saw it, I screamed and ran, and since it had rained all week, I slipped in the mud trying to get away from it. Although I was muddy and embarrassed it was really a conversation piece for the group. I will always remember it. It cannot be expressed as to the importance of such a trip; for it teaches an individual so many useful things, especially potential teachers who plan to teach in inner city schools. If the potential teacher can capture what living with the other side can project to them they will have defeated one of the biggest obstacles encountered in dealing daily with people of different social-economic backgrounds.[t]

I am now developing a doctoral program in urban education leadership through outdoor education. A requirement for the program will include an adaptive Outward Bound type wilderness camping experience.

My Students Taking Their Students on Outdoor Education Trips

Some of my students go home after class, purchase tents and equipment, and take their families camping. Others take their students on day and weekend outdoor education trips. Still others move their students into the neighborhood surrounding the school or even into the school yard.

This past semester, a number of my graduate students, who are also teachers in the Buffalo public schools, organized outdoor education programs in their schools. At Woodlawn Junior High School, Stephen J. DeGarmo, who earlier had an ecology club, organized The Woodlawn Outdoor Education Club. He and his students have been involved in a number of neighborhood projects such as cleaning up the Tift Farm area, getting rid of abandoned cars, and collecting newspapers. Additionally, they have gone on a number of day trips that included Zoar Valley, a day of horseback riding, and a trip to a friend's farm. The club now has a contest going to design a club patch.

Three graduate students are teachers at Riverside High School in

[t]From a paper "A Learning Experience" by Miss Juanita Brown for class TED 418–Teaching in Inner City School, Fall 1972.

Buffalo. Thor J. Borresen, assisted by Fran Gerace and Carl J. Slone, have gone on a number of weekend trips, one of which was a skiing weekend. Carl has taken out fossil hunting trips. Further plans call for the organization of a bike and outdoor club.

Helen Giroux teaches at P.S. 21 and has taken a number of her students on day trips to Zoar Valley, two of them with the Woodlawn students. Both of the trips were really beautiful. It was two days of hiking, talking, relating, discovering, taking pictures, getting wet (the first time from the creek, the second time from the rain that turned to snow), sitting and eating together, and then falling asleep in the cars going home. There was no yelling or even asking "get in line," "stop talking," or "cut it out." And, of course, there was greater relating and learning back at school.

Kathryn Markochick, an Appalachian Trail hiker from childhood, and a teacher of emotionally disturbed learning adjustment children at P.S. 71, has been taking her class into the school's neighborhood. Meanwhile, they have been conducting cake and cookie sales to raise money for their eventual overnight. They have also devised a program of cooking meals for the school staff to add to their funds.

Throughout all the above experiences, the school curriculum is related to the outdoor experiences; but the big gain is in the affective area of the improvement of teacher-student and peer relationships, and in making school a happy place to be. These are vital considerations when discussing inner city schools.

SOME CONCLUDING COMMENTS

I have made my points about teaching and learning in inner city schools and have given suggestions for improvement. Now, some concluding comments.

Very little has changed in America since the Dutch set up their first school in Fort Amsterdam in March 28, 1638. With some editorial generalizing, the three similarities that existed then are still with us today.

Adam Roelansten, the first schoolmaster in New Amsterdam, was sentenced to be flogged or "scourged with rods (Kilpatrick, 1912, p. 56)."[u] And today the schools and their professionals are still the whipping boys of our society. They are still being blamed and "flogged" for society's ills.

Second, Adam Roelansten was probably "the worst and, shall we say, therefore the most discussed of all the Dutch masters; the one who has most

---

[u]There appears to be some question as to whether schoolmaster Roelansten was actually flogged. Moss (1897, p. 24) reports that "The first instruments of punishment were upon the beach, just outside the walls of the Fort, and there the poor school-teacher received his flogging." However, Kilpatrick (1912, p. 56) reports that "For some reason the sentence was never executed." (Other historians, if interested, possibly could settle this question.)

unjustly been taken as typical of all (Kilpatrick, p. 51)." Similarly, still today, the poor inner city teacher is most often discussed while the majority of dedicated inner city teachers, who work a ten- to twelve-hour day, are for the most part ignored.

Third, is that the Dutch schoolmasters were expected not only to teach but also to make nets, to compose love letters, cut hair, collect taxes, make coffins, cure wounds, mend shoes, ring the church bell, keep the church clean, provide water for baptism and wine for the Holy Supper, lead the singing, give funeral invitations, dig graves, and toll the bell (French, 1936; Kilpatrick, 1912). Today, though the role has changed with time, teachers are still expected, in addition to educating their students, to minister to all of their students' emotional and physical needs.

To overcome this, educators must begin to act more politically. We have foolishly allowed ourselves to be used for the scapegoating of our country's ills. For example, agencies within both the Johnson and Nixon administrations commissioned studies to ascertain why blacks were lagging economically. The studies showed that neither education nor training had that much of an effect on the slow economic progress of blacks. Instead, the studies showed that discrimination was the cause. One study released by The Equal Employment Opportunity Commission concluded:

> The lower educational level of some minority groups is a factor in their lower occupational status, but statistical analyses using two different approaches show that it accounts for only about one-third of the difference in occupational ranking between Negro men and majority group men; the inevitable conclusion is that the other two-thirds must be attributed to discrimination, deliberate or inadvertent (Herbers, 1970, p. 18).

Another study for The Office of Economic Opportunity reflected the same findings.

> Discrimination lowers black incomes, but it is difficult to eliminate. Direct attacks on discrimination generate political protest and pressure. Therefore, we will attempt to circumvent the discrimination problem. We will first use other instruments, such as education and training, to equalize black and white incomes and after this has been accomplished we will worry about discrimination.

The report concluded, however, "Unfortunately all of my research indicates that this strategy will not work (Herbers, 1970, p. 18)."

Actually, both administrations stressed education and training instead of antidiscrimination measures. According to Herbers (1970, p. 18), the government has been stressing education and training instead of antidiscrimination measures "presumably because the policy makers consider discrimination too difficult to combat and education more likely to yield."

Instead of attacking discrimination in industry, the government took the more expedient and what they thought was the easier route by setting up apprenticeship training programs and pushing bussing for school children. The apprenticeship programs appeared, according to Herbert Hill (Herbers, 1970, p. 18) Labor Secretary for the National Association for the Advancement of Colored People, "another device to keep blacks out of journeyman status." Additionally, when the men completed their apprentice training another Government report (Herbers, p. 18) found "for one reason or another, graduates of the training frequently did not find jobs."

A suggestion that may create some jobs and bring about quicker integration in the North without bussing, is for all school boards and local, state, and federal purchasing agencies to write into their contracts with their suppliers that they must be equal opportunity employers. Many large cities already have these clauses written into contracts but the suburban and rural areas usually do not. Hopefully, such an approach would create more jobs for minority workers. Along with the jobs would come a larger black middle class, with its developing political power.

Another debate that we educators have acted foolishly in is that concerning the so-called voucher plan suggested by Christopher Jencks (Jencks, 1970). Basically, the voucher plan calls for parents being given vouchers to cover the cost of educating their children which they can use at a school of their choice. Instead of becoming embroiled in this voucher debate, we should have copied industry and free enterprise by demanding cost plus contracts, which is what Pentagon contracts usually are. In the cost plus contract, we must define what we expect to do in the way of educating children and then the board of education would have to supply the money to complete the job.

What I am saying is that in accepting the types of responsibilities that the schools have, schools have been working at a financial bind that a businessman would never accept. If the schools are supposed to help each child achieve a competency level in reading, for example, then we must have all the human and diagnostic resources and materials and professional help required to achieve the agreed-to level. Where some children may have learning disabilities, or physical or emotional problems, we may have to work with that child on a one-to-one basis. Where the child's emotional problem emanates from the home and this problem prevents him from learning to read, we may have to become involved there too. If we are to truly educate *all* our school children and minister to all the emotional needs as well, it seems that we need some form of open-ended contract to allow for any contingency we may come upon with each child.

The precedent has been with us for a long time for this type of contract. The Pentagon and Congress have been bailing out and rescuing "big businessmen from contracts they entered with their eyes open (Witkin, 1973, p. E3)." We taxpayers have been paying billions of dollars for contract overruns, the products from which have been used to kill people. Remember also that in the summer of 1971, Congress guaranteed a two hundred fifty million dollar loan to save Lockheed from bankruptcy. Instead of firing the management for incompetency, they received raises. How about paying to keep people alive and to educate them!

Another area where we have been singled out is the area of accountability. No one appears to want to be held accountable, but almost everyone wants school teachers to be held accountable. Certainly businessmen are rarely held accountable for their poor products—at least until Ralph Nader came along. Taxpayers just built a new football stadium (Rich Stadium) in Erie County. There was a leak in one of the buildings that cost over one hundred thousand dollars to repair. Neither the architect nor the contractors was accountable, and the taxpayers had to pay the bill. Similarly, Governor Nelson Rockefeller's Albany South Mall project was estimated to cost $250 million in 1962, and is now expected to end up costing $1.6 billion.[v]

I have an accountability for politicians. How about those standing for elective office setting anywhere from five to ten objectives that must be accomplished while in office. In order to stand for reelection, incumbents would have to accomplish, let us say, twenty-five percent of their platform. How many politicians would buy that?

CONCLUSION

In many inner city schools, the youngster with a somewhat street "jones" is moving beyond the game of self-destruction. He is beginning to test his teachers in yet a new way. He is testing his teachers by demanding of them, "Why don't you teach me?"

This book suggests a new model or new approach to the social systems operating in inner city schools which affect teaching and learning. Hopefully, this book will provide educators, lay people, and legislators with new insights into the heretofore unrecognized dilemma of inner city schools, leading to a new and more realistic approach to inner city education.

That black and white relations in America have reached the present state of affairs suggests that as prior out-immigrant groups have, in-immigrant

[v]The original estimate of the Albany South Mall (New York State) project dating back to 1962 was $250 million. As of March 31, 1973, $557.7 million had been expended. Contracts encumbered but not yet expended amount to an additional $200 million. Approximately $4 million has been allocated for expenditure but has not yet been encumbered An additional $30 million is as yet unallocated. Total expenditures, encumbrance and unallocated funds amount to $701.7 million as of August, 1973. New york State Comptroller Arthur Levitt's prognosis, publicly stated a number of times over the past few years, is that the project will reach $1 billion before completion. Indeed, according to Clark (1973, p. 10) the Albany Mall will end up as a "1.6 billion colossus."

blacks have finally reached that historical period where they are experiencing the final stages of their rite of passage into American life.

It is my hope that this book and its arguments will expedite their rites of passage by accelerating their acquisition of those marketable skills required for achieving and sharing in the economic good of American life and guaranteeing the opportunity for upward mobility to present and future generations of inner city black students.

NOTES TO CHAPTER 7

Assault on teachers. *Today's Education*, 61(2): 31-32, 69, 70-71, 1972.

Bigart, H. N.Y.U. clinic stalled in trying to improve school. *New York Times*, November 26, 1967, p. 83.

The Board of Education of the City of New York and Life Camps, Inc. *Extending Education Through Camping*. New York: Life Camps, Inc., 1948.

Brown, C. *Manchild in the Promised Land*. New York: Macmillan, 1965.

Clark, H. Albany Mall $1.6 Billion Colossus. *Buffalo Courier-Express*, December 30, 1973, p. 10.

Davenport, S., Jr. Turn-on for the turn-offs. *New York Times*, December 31, 1973, p. E 5.

Faber, N.G. *Look* 33(7): 39-40, 45, 1969.

Foster, H.L. Scouting in the blackboard jungle. *Scouting Magazine* 49(8): 6-7, 26, 1961.

Foster, H.L. Teaching the disadvantaged child. *Industrial Arts & Vocational Education* 55(1): 47-49, 1966.

Foster, H.L. et al. An analysis of an Outward Bound Experience and its relationship to teacher education. *Research in Education* (July 1972) 7(7): 131. ERIC Index # ED 161 160.

French, W.M. How we began to train teachers in New York. *New York History* 17: 180-191, 1936.

The groomer. *Time*, September 4, 1972, p. 67.

Hannerz, U. *Soulside: Inquiries into Ghetto Culture and Community*. New York: Columbia University Press, 1969.

Herbers, H. Discrimination held main cause of income inequality. *New York Times*, February 25, 1970, p. 18.

Jencks, C. Giving parents money for schooling: education vouchers. *Phi Delta Kappan* 52(1): 49-52, 1970.

Junior Guidance Classes Program. *The Junior Guidance Camp Experience: Outcome of a Grant from The Johanna M. Lindlof Camp Committee*. New York: Junior Guidance Classes Program, December 11, 1964 (mimeo).

Kilpatrick, W.H. *The Dutch schools of New Netherland and Colonial New York*. Washington, D.C.: United States Government Printing Office, 1912.

Long, N.J., Morse, W.C. and Newman, R.G. *Conflict in the Classroom: The Education of Emotionally Disturbed Children.* Belmont, Calif.: Wadsworth, 1965.

Long, N.J. and Newman, R.G. The Teacher's Handling of Children in Conflict. *Bulletin of the School of Education, Indiana University* 37(4): 1-64, 1961.

Moss, F. *The American Metropolis: From Knickerbocker Days to the Present Time: New York City Life in All Its Various Phases* (Vol. 1). New York: Peter Penelon Collier, 1897.

Outward Bound. Greenwich, Conn.: Outward Bound, Inc.

Poussaint, A.F. *Why Blacks Kill Blacks.* New York: Emerson Hall, 1972.

Redl, F. and Wineman, D. *The Aggressive Child.* New York: The Free Press, 1957.

Salisbury, H.E. *The Shook-Up Generation.* New York: Harper & Brothers, 1958.

Sharp, L.B. Introduction. *Outdoor Education for American Youth.* Washington, D.C.: American Association for Health, Physical Education and Recreation, 1957.

UB will prepare teachers to handle core-area pupils. *Buffalo Evening News*, November 13, 1968, p. 17.

Witkin, R. Who pays when the bill goes sky high? *New York Times*, December 17, 1972, p. E 3.

Index

About the Author

Herbert L. Foster is a teacher, researcher, writer and educational consultant. Born in the Bronx, he grew up in Brooklyn, New York, and graduated from the New York School of Printing-A New York City Vocational High School. He received his B.S. and M.A. from New York University, School of Education and his Ed.D. from Columbia University, Teachers College.

He was a teacher and administrator in the New York City Public Schools for 17 years, sixteen of which were in the "600" Schools for socially maladjusted and emotionally disturbed youngsters.

His articles have appeared in *PHI DELTA KAPPEN, Exceptional Children, Urban Education, Encyclopedia of Education, University Review, Industrial Arts and Vocational Education, Scouting Magazine, Recreation, and the New York State Journal of Health Physical Education and Recreation.*

Dr. Foster is now an Associate Professor of Education, Faculty of Educational Studies, State University of New York at Buffalo, and Director of the Woodlawn Teacher Education Center.